SPORTS

THROUGH THE LENS

TERRY AND JAN TODD SERIES ON PHYSICAL CULTURE AND SPORTS

EDITED BY
Sarah K. Fields, Thomas Hunt, Daniel A. Nathan, and Patricia Vertinsky

ALSO IN THE SERIES

Jonathan Silverman, editor, *Astros and Asterisks: Houston's Sign-Stealing Scandal Explained*

Adam Berg, *The Olympics That Never Happened: Denver '76 and the Politics of Growth*

Michella Marino, *Roller Derby: The History of an American Sport*

Ronald A. Smith, *The Myth of the Amateur: A History of College Athletic Scholarships*

Andrew R. M. Smith, *No Way but to Fight: George Foreman and the Business of Boxing*

Jason P. Shurley, Jan Todd, and Terry Todd, *Strength Coaching in America: A History of the Innovation That Transformed Sports*

Kevin Robbins, *Harvey Penick: The Life and Wisdom of the Man Who Wrote the Book on Golf*

John Hoberman, *Dopers in Uniform: The Hidden World of Police on Steroids*

John D. Fair, *Mr. America: The Tragic History of a Bodybuilding Icon*

Thomas Hunt, *Drug Games: The International Olympic Committee and the Politics of Doping, 1960–2008*

SPORTS THROUGH THE LENS

ESSAYS ON 25 ICONIC PHOTOGRAPHS

EDITED BY
MAUREEN M. SMITH,
DANIEL A. NATHAN, AND
SARAH K. FIELDS

UNIVERSITY OF TEXAS PRESS
AUSTIN

Printed in China
First edition, 2024

♾ The paper used in this book meets the minimum requirements of ANSI/NISO Z39.48-1992 (R1997) (Permanence of Paper).

Library of Congress Cataloging-in-Publication Data
Names: Smith, Maureen Margaret, editor. | Nathan, Daniel A., editor. | Fields, Sarah K., editor.
Title: Sports through the lens : essays on 25 iconic photographs / edited by Maureen M. Smith, Daniel A. Nathan, Sarah K. Fields.
Other titles: Terry and Jan Todd series on physical culture and sports.
Description: First edition. | Austin : University of Texas Press, 2024. | Series: Terry and Jan Todd series on physical culture and sports | Includes index.
Identifiers: LCCN 2024003864
ISBN 978-1-4773-3009-8 (hardback)
ISBN 978-1-4773-3070-8 (PDF)
ISBN 978-1-4773- 3071-5 (ePub)
Subjects: LCSH: Photography of sports—United States—20th century. | Sports photographers—United States—20th century. | Professional sports—United States—20th century—Pictorial works. | LCGFT: Essays. | Documentary photographs.
Classification: LCC TR821 .S735 2024 | DDC 778.9/97960973—dc23/eng/20240510
LC record available at https://lccn.loc.gov/2024003864

doi:10.7560/330098

CONTENTS

SPORTS
THROUGH THE LENS

INTRODUCTION

Many of us have mental galleries full of vibrant sporting images. We may have witnessed some of these remarkable feats in person, but more likely we first saw them on television or the internet. Of course, in some cases, what we remember most vividly was photographed. Reggie Jackson of the New York Yankees slugging his third home run in the sixth game of the 1977 World Series against the Los Angeles Dodgers. San Francisco 49ers wide receiver Dwight Clark leaping to catch a touchdown pass in the endzone to beat the Dallas Cowboys in the closing seconds of the 1981 NFC championship game. Basketball superstar Cheryl Miller grabbing a rebound at the 1984 Olympics in Los Angeles. Twenty-one-year-old Tiger Woods pumping his fist at the 1997 Masters. These and countless other images endure, but not because our memories are secure repositories. We know, after all, that memory is notoriously fickle, and that although we rely on it, it is "defective, fragile, impermanent."[1] Rather, many of these images are still with us in large part due to photography, which, almost magically, freezes action, stops time. We recognize that, as historian Alan Trachtenberg puts it, "photographs are not simple depictions but constructions, that the history they show is inseparable from the history they enact."[2] Yes, and sometimes photographs capture something simultaneously beautiful and painful, joyous and disappointing—in any event, meaningful.

That is one of the things that sports photographs do: they craft and convey meaning, today and for posterity. As visual storyteller Bill Frakes asserts, sports photographs are and should be "about motion and emotion, style and scene, and place and purpose," and they sometimes constitute "the intersection of art and athleticism."[3] Yet we are especially interested in sports photographs that capture historical moments that resonate over time, that reveal the richness and complexity of the games we play, follow, and cheer for, and the culture in which they are embedded. We revel in and appreciate sports photographs that make us pause to consider, and then reconsider, what happened at various moments. What do these images mean? How do we make sense of them? In what contexts do they need to be understood? These are some of the questions that undergird the essays anthologized here.

This book examines a wide variety of sports photographs—most of them are famous and iconic; a few of them are relatively obscure—and it carefully considers what they reveal and signify. We are talking about images such as baseball legend Ty Cobb sliding into third base in 1910; the braggadocious Muhammad Ali standing over Sonny Liston during their 1965 rematch in Lewistown, Maine; Tommie Smith and John Carlos's controversial and inspirational Black Power salute at the 1968 Summer Olympics; Secretariat winning the 1973 Belmont Stakes by a remarkable thirty-one lengths; and a joyous Brandi Chastain after her game-winning goal at the 1999 Women's World Cup, among many others. For some people, these images provoke all manner of memories, emotions, and ideas. Frequently reproduced, these photos have also worked their way into our collective consciousness. For these reasons, this book is partly about photography's capacity to narrativize the past, to tell, reveal, and encapsulate meaningful historical stories.

Our project initially asked each contributor to reflect on a specific, iconic sports photograph that has had widespread cultural resonance. We asked our contributors to write about the image's creation, the contexts in which it's best understood, and its sometimes-shifting significance and legacy. Of course, it's no simple matter to define or determine iconicity, and several contributors urged us to consider including some not-so-famous-but-still-interesting photos, which we did.

Editing an anthology is always an exercise in selection. Almost every author (including the editors) wanted to include more than one image, but we limited our authors to one photo per chapter. As a concession, we encouraged authors to put links in their footnotes to photographs that supplemented their original choices where appropriate. There were certainly photos we wish we could have included, such as Nat Fein's famous 1948 photograph of an ailing Babe Ruth (he died less than two months later) at Yankee Stadium, which was the first sports photograph to win a Pulitzer Prize. We would have loved to have included photographs of Venus and Serena Williams at different points in their amazing careers. Wilma Rudolph crossing the finish line at the 1960 Olympic Games, Michael Phelps's fingers touching the pool wall in 2008, a hundredth of a second ahead of Milorad Čavić, and so many other Olympic moments merit consideration. Furthermore, as we talked about this project with friends and colleagues, nearly everyone had a photo in mind that they thought should be included, and many offered to write that chapter. Had we accommodated everyone, this project could easily have been twice as long.

As this book demonstrates, there are many productive ways to think about how a photograph can be a portal to the past and can provide opportunities to ask tough questions about visual representation and historical knowledge. But to be clear, we are not visual theorists or sports photography experts, although we have read many books and articles by people who are, such as Gail Buckland, Jonathan Finn, Mike Huggins, Mike O'Mahony, and Gary Osmond, among others, and practitioners such as photographers Bill Frakes, Walter Iooss Jr., and Neil Leifer.

We are not interested in theorizing about the relationship among sports, photography, and history. Our project is not that lofty or abstract. Nor is this a history of sports photography, which is a fascinating subject. "Since the invention of photography in 1839," notes David E. Little in *The Sports Show: Athletics as Image and Spectacle* (2012), "photographs have shaped the way we imagine and remember sports."[4] How that process has unfolded over time deserves more attention.

Our objective, however, is to produce a multivocal, multifaceted meditation on visual, historical, and cultural meaning using myriad sports photographs.

This book is rooted in several ideas. First, despite the seeming ubiquity of sports photographs, and the privileged place a few of them have in our collective sporting memories, understanding them is not and has never been simple. Like all texts, photographs must be read closely and critically, and doing that well is hard work. Artist and critic Terry Barrett asserts that "all photographs, even straightforward, direct, and realistic-looking ones, need to be interpreted. They are not innocent, free of insinuations and devoid of prejudices, nor are they simple mirror images. They are made, taken, and constructed by skillful artists and deserve to be read, explained, analyzed."[5] We will see his "deserve to" and raise it to "must." That is, a photograph *must* be read, explained, and analyzed. A photograph that no one looks at and reads does no work in the world. It barely exists.

Moreover, as historian Gary Osmond puts it, "An image itself may have clear, direct, and understandable content but in itself has no inherent meaning."[6] For it to have meaning, someone must look at it, engage it, and in the process must confer and *produce* meaning; they must make it signify. Additionally, the cultural critic Susan Sontag correctly declares, "Any photograph has multiple meanings."[7] No photograph means just one thing.

Sports photographs are, of course, historical documents. Fleeting moments frozen in time, disconnected from the continuous flow of events. They provide us with evidence. They have what the critic John Berger describes as "the status of fact."[8] We (usually) trust them. They seem veracious. They often seem indisputable. Seeing is believing, after all. At the same time, Berger proclaims that "photographs are not, as is often assumed, a mechanical record. Every time we look at a photograph, we are aware, however slightly, of the photographer selecting that sight from an infinity of other possible sights."[9] Put differently, sports photographs do not take themselves. They all involve human agency and numerous choices, even if some of those choices are constrained by access, convention, space, time, and technology.

Of course, the photographers whose work appears in this book worked at different historical moments and came from many different backgrounds, although most of them were/are white men. One of this book's referees, veteran sportswriter Alexander Wolff, keenly observes, "I was struck again and again by how frequently the photographer who took the relevant photo was either an immigrant, or very young at the time, or both." We have to admit, we did not notice these patterns while working on this book. Drawing on his decades of journalistic experience and collaboration with talented photographers, Wolff asks several good questions and makes several good points:

> How much of the skill set of the sports photographer comes from the optimism of the immigrant, animated by hope and the belief that the difficult is possible? How much derives from the sweet ignorance of the teenager, who hasn't yet been beaten down by a succession of "nos?" How much owes itself to simple physical endurance, the ability to wait out the action until that moment when everything falls into place? Photojournalism is essentially grunt work. It involves lugging gear, sweet-talking security guards, and coping with a welter of uncertainties and uncontrollable externalities. Salaries in the field have always been modest, thus attracting the young and untried, people willing to bet on themselves. It takes drive, persistence, resourcefulness, and stubbornness to make your mark in photojournalism, as it takes much the same portfolio of virtues to succeed as a newbie, either just off the boat or just off a campus, in many other fields too.

The craftsmanship—and sometimes artistry—found in many of the images anthologized here supports Wolff's observations and ideas.

Maybe it's obvious, but we'll say it anyway: sports photographs must be put in context. Doing so is vital if we want to understand the ways in which they function.[10] But more precisely, sports photographs need to be put in *contexts*, plural, for they exist in many of them. There is, for example, the immediate context in which the image is embedded. In *The Past Within Us* (2005), historian Tessa Morris-Suzuki explains: "The way we identify with and interpret photographs is shaped by the context in which the image is seen: by the pictures and texts which surround it."[11] In many instances, that means the other images and the prose in a specific newspaper, magazine, or book, or perhaps on a website or social media platform. The news story associated with the image can certainly affect the way in which the image is read and understood. The captions matter, too. (So do the comments, if there are any.) There are other contexts as well, such as the specific historical moment being photographed (is it a regular-season game or the World Series?) and the photographer's previous (and perhaps future) body of work.

Sports photography can reflect and shape the worldview of its viewers. Like other forms of photojournalism and art, sports photographs encourage us to see people and events from particular perspectives, experience a range of emotions, and think about subjects from a wide array of vantage points. "What we see," argues historian Robert M. Levine, "reflects to some degree our mind's capacity to filter images and to associate them in ways consonant with our individual perspective."[12] At the same time, sports photographs can provide us with angles, perspectives, and sightlines that are beyond our field of vision, even beyond our imagination. They can reveal things that we would never otherwise see, which is exciting and enriching.

In some cases, sports photographs can become something akin to a "prosthetic memory," to use memory studies scholar Alison Landsberg's evocative term. Prosthetic memory, Landsberg explains, "emerges at the interface between a person and a historical narrative about the past, at an experiential site such as a movie theater or museum. In this moment of contact, an experience occurs through which the person sutures himself or herself into a larger history."[13] The precise suturing process is complicated and idiosyncratic, but Landsberg argues that when it is successful "the person does not simply apprehend a historical narrative but takes on a more personal, deeply felt memory of a past event through which he or she did not live. The resulting prosthetic memory has the ability to shape that person's subjectivity and politics."[14] For some of us, there are sports photographs that are that "experiential site," that "moment of contact," that effectively represent events we could not have experienced or personally remember. There are sports photographs that make us *feel* the past in ways that are hard to articulate.

And yet, in his masterful book *Photography and Sport* (2018), art historian Mike O'Mahony declares that sports photos are

> much more than vehicles of memory for passionate fans. Whether preserved in faded sepia, rich black and white or glorious Kodachrome, whether pinned to a stadium wall, glued into a private album, published in a popular journal or

framed exquisitely for a museum exhibition, the material products of photography's encounter with sport, the stylistic choices made, the acceptance or rejection of visual conventions, even the very ways of looking at sport that these photographs present, have a significant story to tell. More importantly, these images need to be critically analysed in order to understand the crucial role that the medium has played not only in preserving sport's history, but in shaping the very ways that it informs the present day. Photographs of sport, too often disregarded as the ephemeral traces of a cultural activity itself seen as unworthy of historical consideration, simply deserve to be taken more seriously.[15]

This book has taken up that call.

The photos anthologized here cover a great deal of ground, in terms of the historical eras in which they are set and the subjects depicted. Chronologically, which is how they are organized, the images span an almost 130-year period, from 1890 to just a few years ago. Unsurprisingly, most of the photos are from the twentieth century and were taken in the United States. And while it is true that they are mostly action shots, taken by white, male, professional photographers (which tells us something important about their guild), they are also heterogenous. There are photos here of the big four American team sports: baseball, basketball, football, and hockey, as well as soccer, boxing, tennis, horse racing, and different forms of running. There are images of amateurs and professionals, men, women, and children, people of different racial and ethnic identities, and different nationalities. They are mostly, but not exclusively, elite athletes, who have done some remarkable, memorable things.

Collectively, the chapters are also diverse. Our contributors don't all think about or read sports photographs the same way. They don't all share the same presuppositions. They come from different disciplines and backgrounds. Variety is a virtue, and it enhances this anthology. In some cases, the essays brought together here complement one another and in others they enable readers to make some unexpected connections among the photographs.

No fans of hyperbole, we suspect that there is some truth in John Berger's assertion: "All photographs are ambiguous. All photographs have been taken out of a continuity."[16] And when anything is taken out of context, ambiguity ensues, even if it's not immediately obvious. Our job is to reduce that ambiguity, to provide context, to help make meaning. That is what we and our contributors have tried to do in *Sports through the Lens*.

In the end, our hope is that the photographs and essays in this book represent the beginning of what might become an ongoing dialogue, that they trigger memories and critically alert conversations about sport, photography, and history. We recognize, as sportswriter Kostya Kennedy puts it, that "even the most memorable photographs have their borders, limits upon what they might communicate and how they might communicate it. Thus they become Rorschach tests of a kind."[17] They are that and more. They are invitations to reminisce, to locate oneself and others in time, to revel in beauty, and to consider what capturing and revisiting an ephemeral sporting moment might mean.

NOTES

1. Ryszard Kapuściński, *Travels with Herodotus*, trans. Klara Glowczewska (New York: Vintage, [2007] 2008), 75.

2. Alan Trachtenberg, *Reading American Photographs: Images as History, Mathew Brady to Walker Evans* (New York: Hill and Wang, 1989), xvi.

3. Bill Frakes, *Sports Photography: From Snapshots to Great Shots* (Berkeley, CA: Peachpit Press, 2013), ix.

4. David E. Little, *The Sports Show: Athletics as Image and Spectacle* (Minneapolis: Minneapolis Institute of the Arts, 2012), 71.

5. Terry Barrett, *Criticizing Photographs: An Introduction to Understanding Images*, 4th edition (Boston: McGraw-Hill, 2006), 43.

6. Gary Osmond, "Photographs, Materiality and Sport History: Peter Norman and the 1968 Mexico City Black Power Salute," *Journal of Sport History* 37 (Spring 2010): 133.

7. Susan Sontag, *On Photography* (New York: Picador, 1977), 23.

8. John Berger and Jean Mohr, *Another Way of Telling* (New York: Vintage International, [1982] 1995), 98.

9. John Berger, *Ways of Seeing* (London: British Broadcasting Corporation and Penguin Books Ltd, [1972] 1977), 10.

10. Mike Huggins, "The Sporting Gaze: Towards a Visual Turn in Sports History—Documenting Art and Sport," *Journal of Sport History* 35 (Summer 2008): 319.

11. Tessa Morris-Suzuki, *The Past Within Us: Media, Memory, History* (London: Verso, 2005), 99.

12. Robert M. Levine, *Insights into American History: Photographs as Documents* (Upper Saddle River, NJ: Pearson Education, 2004), 9.

13. Alison Landsberg, *Prosthetic Memory: The Transformation of American Remembrance in the Age of Mass Culture* (New York: Columbia University Press, 2004), 2.

14. Landsberg, *Prosthetic Memory*, 2.

15. Mike O'Mahony, *Photography and Sport* (London: Reaktion Books, 2018), 14.

16. Berger and Mohr, *Another Way of Telling*, 91.

17. Kostya Kennedy, *The Story of Baseball in 100 Photographs* (New York: Liberty Street, 2018), 13.

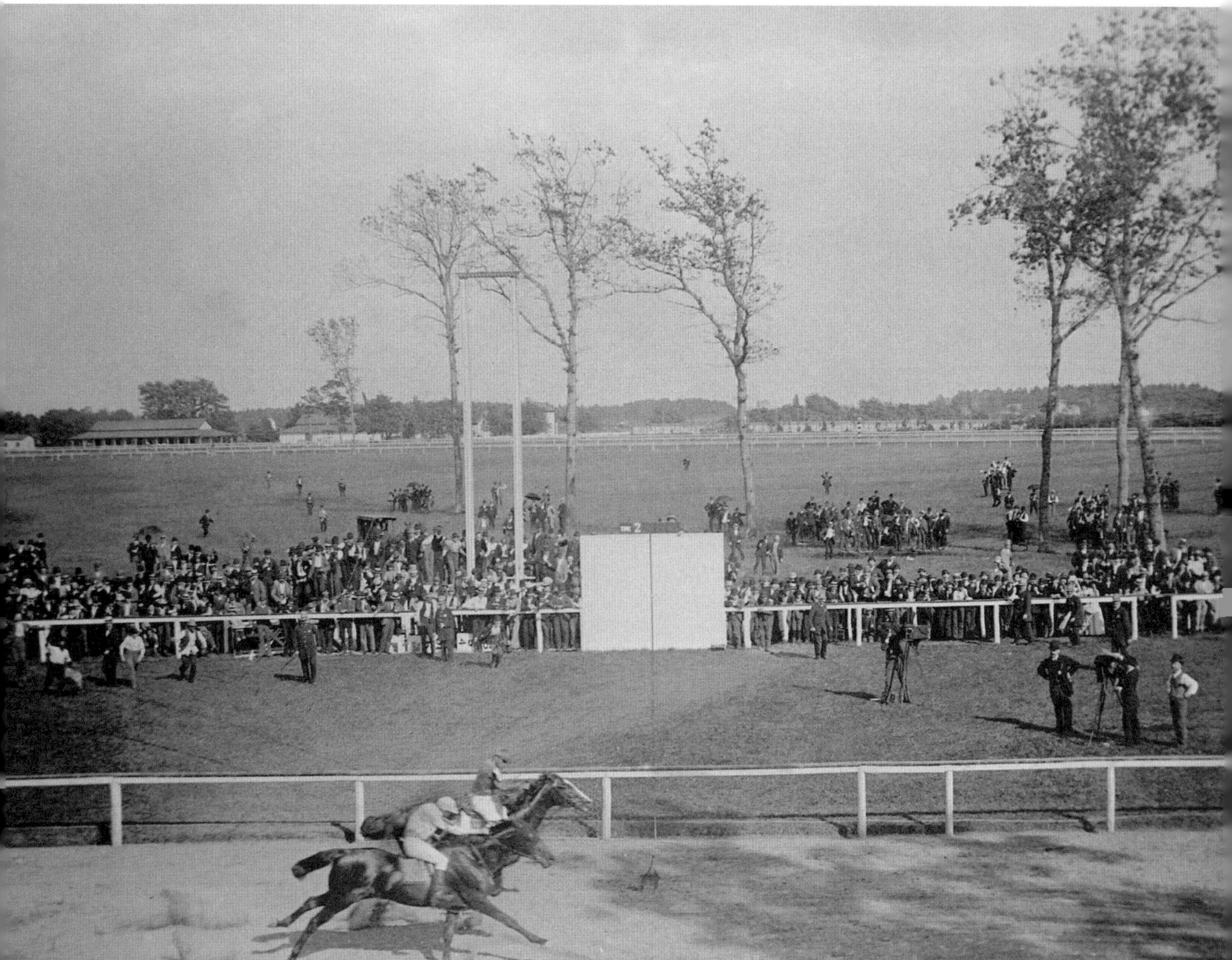

1

THE MAKING OF A NON-ICONIC SPORTS PHOTOGRAPH

John Hemment's *Salvator v. Tenny*

JONATHAN FINN

> "See him come! See him come!" shouted the crowd, as Tenny came up the center of the track. Soon the sound of flying hoofbeats could be heard by the thousands in the grand stands by the finish. Men's faces were blanched white and hard with sympathy or money interest; women sobbed hysterically, and laughed and shouted. Then came a time when people hold their breath, when they live only in the eye and the ear, when the lungs are strained and still, and when the heart ceases its pulsing and hammers the brain with quick, hard blood beats.[1]

The passage above is part of the *Chicago Tribune*'s account of the race captured in the photograph reprinted here: the Salvator v. Tenny match race held at Sheepshead Bay Race Track on June 25, 1890. Salvator was ridden by Isaac Burns Murphy and Tenny by Edward Garrison, with Salvator winning by half a head. The headline of the *Tribune*'s account of the race was "One of the Greatest Ever Witnessed on the American Turf." This was not hyperbole—similar headlines appeared in newspapers across the country. The *San Francisco Examiner* called it "The Greatest Race in Years" and the *Brooklyn Daily Eagle* described it as "The Grandest Race Ever Witnessed in This Country."[2]

Salvator v. Tenny was taken by John C. Hemment, one of the most prolific sports photographers of his era. I first came across Hemment's work when doing research for my book on the history of the photo-finish in sport.[3] Hemment was a, if not *the*, central proponent and practitioner in the late 1800s of the use of the camera to determine placing in sport.[4] He frequently but ultimately erroneously exclaimed that, thanks to the camera, dead-heats and ties in sport would no longer exist. Much of Hemment's work in the 1890s was devoted to this task.[5] He was also a highly accomplished photographer outside the world of sport, publishing images in numerous reputable magazines and journals. Despite this, Hemment is all but completely absent from the history of photography and the history of sport. He is somewhat known within the history of horse racing photography and his work documenting the Spanish-American War periodically appears in reading lists related to military history. But for the most part, Hemment and his images have been ignored by the scholarly community. This being the case, when I was approached to contribute to this project, I asked if I could write about a Hemment photo, even though it is non-iconic. In fact, it was its non-iconicity that was so interesting. Fortunately, the editors agreed.

Within the minimal referencing of Hemment's sports photography, the *Salvator v. Tenny* image is his most recognized. The racing historian Philip von Borries refers to the image as an early example of photo-finish, as does Martin Vanvolsem in his book on strip photography.[6] The accounts of von Borries and Vanvolsem, as well as my own work on the photo-finish notwithstanding, Hemment's image is decidedly non-iconic. It does not belong in the same cultural register as the other images in this collection, nor is it included in other works on famous sports imagery.

What Makes an Icon?

As it is being used in this edited collection—in terms of its secular and non-religious meaning—an iconic photograph is generally one that has achieved broad cultural recognition. Nick Ut's famous image of Kim Phuc and others fleeing a napalmed village in Vietnam; Joe Rosenthal's raising of the American flag at Iwo Jima; and, more recently, Nilufer Demir's images of three-year-old Aylan Kurdi washed up on a Turkish beach are easily understood as iconic images due to their broad, instant recognition. But what makes images such as these iconic? Or, what differentiates these images from the many millions of others that have also received significant public attention yet not risen to the level of icon?

Scholars of art history and visual culture have for centuries been developing language and modes of analysis to describe works of art that stand out as exceptional within the larger field. The influential photographic theorist Roland Barthes uses the terms *studium* and *punctum* in this regard.[7] Barthes described what we might call "good" images with the word studium. Such images are generally clear, balanced, pleasing to the eye, and their message or meaning is similarly unmuddied. By contrast, punctum describes an image that pierces through this more mundane layer to achieve something else. Photographs with punctum incite the viewer to question and think about what they are seeing. Though Barthes did not equate punctum with iconic images, it is a useful distinction here to point to the sometimes-indescribable factor that makes one image more compelling and more memorable than others.

Other scholars offer a more pragmatic approach to understanding photographic icons. In their book *No Caption Needed: Iconic Photographs, Public Culture, and Liberal Democracy* (2007), Robert Hariman and John Louis Lucaites argue that beyond being broadly recognized, iconic images must have a significant impact on society.[8] The authors focus on photojournalistic images and stress that iconic images are those that shift or activate public opinion on a significant scale. Scholars David D. Perlmutter and Gretchen L. Wagner go further to identify a distinct, six-part typology of iconic images: importance of the event depicted; metonymy; celebrity; prominence of display; frequency of use; and primordiality.[9] Like Hariman and Lucaites, Perlmutter and Wagner emphasize that iconic images have impact. They also stress the importance of material factors, including editorial choice, captioning, and placement of the image in news media as central components in how images become iconic.

While it is overly reductive, we can make a useful distinction between these two approaches to addressing iconic images: the approach represented by Barthes looks for iconicity in the image's content—as a feature that the image possesses, largely independent of the material factors surrounding its production, distribution, and consumption. The more pragmatic approach also includes the image's content but places equal if not more attention on the image's context, including where it was used, by whom, and how it was discussed, captioned, and positioned within and by the news media.

Salvator v. Tenny

Like most significant sport matchups, Salvator v. Tenny had a compelling backstory. Nicknamed "the Swayback," Tenny was owned by D. T. Pulsifer and Salvator was owned by James Ben Ali Haggin, both well-established figures in the horse racing industry. During the 1889 racing season the two horses developed a significant rivalry. Then, after a strong opening in 1890, during which Tenny won his first four races, he lost to Salvator at his next race, the Suburban Handicap. Pulsifer was so upset by the loss that he challenged Salvator's owner, Ali Haggin, for the two horses to race head-to-head.

The match race was important for several reasons beyond the rivalry. The $10,000 prize was one of the largest of the era. Drama for the event was heightened by switching the jockeys and their horses. Isaac Burns Murphy typically rode Tenny and Edward Garrison rode Salvator. For the match race at Sheepshead Bay this was reversed, with Murphy on Salvator and Garrison on Tenny. Finally, the race was an important moment in the famed career of Isaac Burns Murphy, an African American jockey who was born into slavery and was the first jockey inducted into the National Museum of Racing and Hall of Fame.[10]

The image itself captures the excitement of race day and is an important historical document. We see a crowd of mostly men watching the result, with several running towards the line in various states of excitement. There are uniformed police officers on hand as well as two other photographers on the infield and in positions considerably closer than Hemment. Hemment is positioned on the finish line but raised up and at a considerable distance.

Hemment outlined his process for race-finish photography in a series of published interviews and written articles.[11] He used a camera with two achromatic lenses so that he could produce two images in rapid succession, and he employed a separate lens mounted to the top of the camera as a finder. The finder allowed him to track the horses as they raced and release the shutter at the precise moment the horses crossed the finish-line. Hemment preferred to be stationed directly perpendicular to the finish with his camera trained on the finish line. To create a strong contrast against the horses' heads, he used a white background with a line representing the finish-line across from his location. He also liked to have a wire running across and above the track that aligned his camera to the finishing line and white backdrop.

The incongruences between Hemment's idealized setup and the *Salvator v. Tenny* image are instructive. There are two key differences. First, Hemment has captured the horses close to but not at the finish line. This is important because it underscores the key challenge to race-finish photography at the time: human reaction time. Hemment and his contemporaries had to train their eyes on the finish line and attempt to release the shutter at precisely the right time—something that photographers were very rarely able to do. Electromagnetic shutter releases, faster film speeds, and better-quality lenses developed over the next decade did much to solve this aspect of the Salvator v. Tenny image. Nonetheless, in the same way that Salvator and Tenny are here captured just before they cross the line, Hemment's photograph is an image slightly before its time.

The second incongruency is the white backdrop. As in other photographic practices of the time, including Muybridge's famous studies of human and animal movement through anthropological and criminological uses, the purpose of the backdrop was the same: to provide a uniform contrast against which the subjects would be more visible. However, as is clear in this particular photo, the backdrop could not fulfill its function, as it floats above and to the right of Hemment's view line. It is, however, highly valuable from a historical perspective because it references the on-again, off-again treatment of race-track photographers. The *Salvator v. Tenny* photo belongs to the nascent stage of race-track photography during which photographers, sports fans, and officials debated its efficacy, including the positioning necessary to create a viable finish-line photograph. Hemment's photographs from the time show that his position varied considerably between tracks and races.

Combined with these two incongruences, the formal features of *Salvator v. Tenny*—what we would call its content including its framing, composition, and focus—make it an interesting historical document. The image is a representation of the late-nineteenth century desire to record race finishes (with all the attendant cultural and financial capital of the practice), as well as the human and technological limitations in doing so. The image is a representation of a particularly heated rivalry in 1890s American horse racing. And the image is a representation of a particular set of race relations in late 1800s America.

However, there is nothing particularly compelling about the image itself. The *Tribune*'s account of the blanched and hard faces of men or the hysterically sobbing women are nowhere to be found. The composition is clear and balanced, and it shows the finish of a reasonably close horse race, but, stripped of the broader sociocultural context, it is an otherwise generic image. There is no *punctum* in Barthes's sense—nothing within the frame that would elevate the image from the ordinary to the extraordinary.

Turning from content to context, Hemment's image could not have reached iconic status in large part due to the limitations of reproducing and disseminating photographs in the 1890s. At the time Hemment was producing his race photography, there was no practical means to publish and circulate photographic images on a mass scale. The half-tone process, which allows photographic-quality images to be produced alongside text, was not widely used until the opening decades of the twentieth century. Instead, illustrations would be made based on photographs.

Newspaper accounts of the Salvator v. Tenny race were therefore almost entirely textual. One notable use of an illustration is found in the *San Francisco Examiner*, the day after the race. The illustration offers the positions of the horses at each quarter of the race centered around profile illustrations of the horses. Interest in visual depictions of the race extended outside news media, as is evidenced in a painting of the race by Henry Stull, an artist noted for depicting scenes of famous races, jockeys, and horses. Currier and Ives also produced a print of the race in 1890, which is available today in miniature form as a fridge magnet from the online retailer Etsy.[12]

Work in communication, media, and photographic histories has noted that the adoption of photographs into news media in the late nineteenth and early twentieth centuries was tied to an increasingly competitive news market.[13] Within such a market, photographic representations and other forms of visual material caught the eyes of prospective readers and could often lead to dramatic increases in circulation. Therefore, it is rational to assume that, had the technology existed for Hemment's photograph to be reprinted and disseminated on a wide scale, it might have attracted significant public attention. Papers across the country described the race as one of the best if not the best race that had ever happened. Surely, Hemment's photograph inserted into such texts would have yielded significant publicity. If the image's content was not enough to elevate it to iconic status, perhaps its positioning alongside stories of the "greatest race ever" would have elevated it to this status.

The technological realities of the 1890s offer a partial rationale for *Salvator v. Tenny*'s non-iconic status. Equally important is Hemment's near total absence within the history of photography. In fact, the *Salvator v. Tenny* image is emblematic of Hemment's entire life and career.

In the same way that the Salvator v. Tenny race benefitted from an enticing backstory, so too did Hemment's career. He was born in England in 1862 and moved to the United States in 1879, taking up photography in the 1880s. He was an accomplished athlete in England, particularly in ice skating, and in the United States he set the 200-yard record in 1895.[14] He was hired as the official photographer for several horse racing tracks in the United States, and his images were published in *Collier's Weekly*, the *Illustrated Sporting News*, *New York Journal*, and *Harper's Weekly*. He became a successful and recognized photographer to the extent that in 1898 he was hired by the U.S. government to photograph the Spanish-American War. This resulted in his 1898 book on the topic, *Cannon and Camera: Sea and Land Battles of the Spanish-American War in Cuba, Camp Life, and the Return of the Soldiers*. Hemment continued his war photography at the beginning of the First World War as the official photographer for the American Red Cross.[15]

In addition to this traditionally reputable work, Hemment also employed the camera in more fringe pursuits. He is cited as a distinguished figure in the field of big-game hunting,[16] and he also worked as an official photographer and motion photographer on expeditions to Africa and the Arctic.[17] In this last capacity he even wrote an article for *Motion Picture Magazine* on his search for the so-called "missing link," a "half-man, half-monkey" that he intended to find and photograph.[18]

As well as having his photographs published in numerous highly reputable outlets, he also received a significant amount of attention by those writing on the topic of sport and photography. His work was championed in *Outing* magazine, the *Photographic Times*, and *The American Annual of Photography*. One journal editor called Hemment "the leading photographer of athletic pictures in this country, if not in the world."[19] And Hemment is cited in an 1892 full-page advertisement for Prosch camera shutters. Prosch was promoting its "athlete" shutter for "athletic and Race-track work" and noted: "The 'king' photographer of sporting events, John C. Hemment, uses it exclusively."[20]

My point here is that Hemment had a long, successful, reputable career and yet he is almost entirely absent within the history of photography. He is not included in the *Oxford Companion to the Photograph* (2005), a nearly eight-hundred-page coffee table book that is a de-facto encyclopedia of photography. He is not included in the many histories of photography that are used to teach the field in colleges and universities. And he is similarly absent from the history of sport, except for work dedicated to nineteenth-century horse racing in America.

To account for this absence, I draw from my own education in art history and visual culture studies and my mid-career turn to the study of sport. In relation to the former, I think that Hemment's absence is a product of the still uneasy relationship between sport and the academic field of visual culture studies (and its cognate areas).[21] Despite the many proclamations from within the field that it is concerned with the visual broadly construed, images of sport are at best of marginal concern. In relation to the latter, Hemment's absence from the history of sport likely reflects the still recent visual turn within sport history, which was partly initiated by historians Mike Huggins and Mike O'Mahony's 2011 call for scholars to take up sport images and visual material as subject matter rather than as mere supplement.[22]

In approaching this topic, my initial goal was to argue that Hemment's photo of Salvator v. Tenny should be considered iconic. Yet this betrays the very notion of iconicity—mainly that an iconic image should be broadly recognized. Hemment's image is not iconic. There is nothing within the frame that elevates it to a level of interest on par with many of the images in this collection. Nor did the image gain broad recognition through its dissemination in the news media. And Hemment's near total absence in the history of photography and the history of sport further ensured the image's non-iconic status. The *Salvator v. Tenny* photo is not iconic, but it is important. By analyzing the non-iconic status of *Salvator v. Tenny*, we can learn a lot about the intersection of sport, photography, and history.

NOTES

1. "Tenny One Head Behind," *Chicago Tribune*, June 26, 1890, 6.

2. "Tenny One Head Behind" and "King of the Turf," *San Francisco Examiner*, June 26, 1890, 1; "A Hot Finish," *Brooklyn Daily Eagle*, June 26, 1890, 1.

3. Jonathan Finn, *Beyond the Finish Line: Images, Evidence, and the History of the Photo-Finish* (Montreal: McGill-Queen's University Press, 2020).

4. For a more thorough discussion of Hemment and his work see the opening chapters of Finn, *Beyond the Finish Line* (2020).

5. The Keeneland Library in Lexington, Kentucky, houses the largest collection of Hemment's horse racing images. See https://www.keeneland.com/keeneland-library.

6. Philip Von Borries, *RaceLens: Vintage Thoroughbred Racing Images* (Gretna, LA: Pelican, 2014); Martin Vanvolsem, *The Art of Strip Photography: Making Still Images with a Moving Camera* (Leuven, Belgium: Leuven University Press, 2011).

7. Roland Barthes, *Camera Lucida: Reflections on Photography*, trans. Richard Howard (New York: Hill and Wang, 1981), 26–27.

8. Robert Hariman and John Louis Lucaites, *No Caption Needed: Iconic Photographs, Public Culture, and Liberal Democracy* (Chicago: University of Chicago Press, 2007).

9. David D. Perlmutter, *Photojournalism and Foreign Policy: Icons of Outrage in International Crises* (Westport, CT: Praeger, 1998); David D. Perlmutter and Gretchen L. Wagner, "The Anatomy of a Photojournalistic Icon: Marginalization of Dissent in

the Selection and Framing of 'A Death in Genoa,'" *Visual Communication* 3, no. 1 (2004): 91–108.

10. The National Museum of Racing and Hall of Fame is a good source for racing history, including photographs, paintings, and sculptures from the racing scene. See https://www.racingmuseum.org/.

11. "Decided by the Camera," *Brooklyn Eagle*, August 2, 1891, 13; "Marginalia: Close Finishes and Other Matters," *Thoroughbred Record*, June 10, 1939, 346.

12. As of July 6, 2022, 703 magnets had been sold. See https://www.etsy.com/listing/242797011/salvator-and-tenny-deco-fridge-magnet.

13. Michael Schudon's work on yellow journalism and the competing models of news as information and news as entertainment is the essential source here. Michael Schudson, *Discovering the News: A Social History of American Newspapers* (New York: Basic Books, 1978).

14. "Skating Records Broken," *New York Times*, January 25, 1895, 7; "Skating," *Sporting Life*, 20.22, February 25, 1893, 15.

15. Lincoln Adams, "Photography and Athletics: First Paper," *Outing*, 19, 1892, 404–408; "Decided by the Camera," 13; "Pershing's Men Well Fed," *New York Times*, October 29, 1917, 6.

16. "About Shooters," *Sporting Life*, 60.23, February 8, 1913, 18; "In Re Shooters," *Sporting Life*, 58.3, September 23, 1911, 28.

17. "Only the Photographer," *Technical World Magazine*, 19.6, 1913, 812–813; "Brooklynite Starts on Troglodyte Hunt," *Brooklyn Eagle*, November 2, 1913, 25; "Jack Hemment Back with Tse-Tse Films," *Brooklyn Eagle*, September 4, 1914, 4; "Great Animal Picture Show in Aid of the Red Cross," *Brooklyn Eagle*, October 29, 1914, 10; "J.C. Hemment Bitten by Tse-Tse Fly, Fears 'Sleeping Sickness,'" *Brooklyn Eagle*, January 21, 1916.

18. John Hemment, "My Search for the Missing Link," *Motion Picture Magazine*, August 1914, 77.

19. Adams, "Photography and Athletics: First Paper," 404.

20. "World Beaters! Satisfaction Givers! Prosch Photographic Shutters. Storage Flash Lamps," *American Annual of Photography and Photographic Times Almanac* 6 (1892): 24.

21. There are too many introductions to visual culture texts to note here. A useful historiography of the field can be found in Margaret Dikovitskaya, *Visual Culture: The Study of the Visual after the Cultural Turn* (Cambridge: MIT Press, 2006).

22. Mike Huggins and Mike O'Mahony, "Prologue: Extending Study of the Visual in the History of Sport," *International Journal of the History of Sport*, 28, no. 8–9 (2011): 1089–1104.

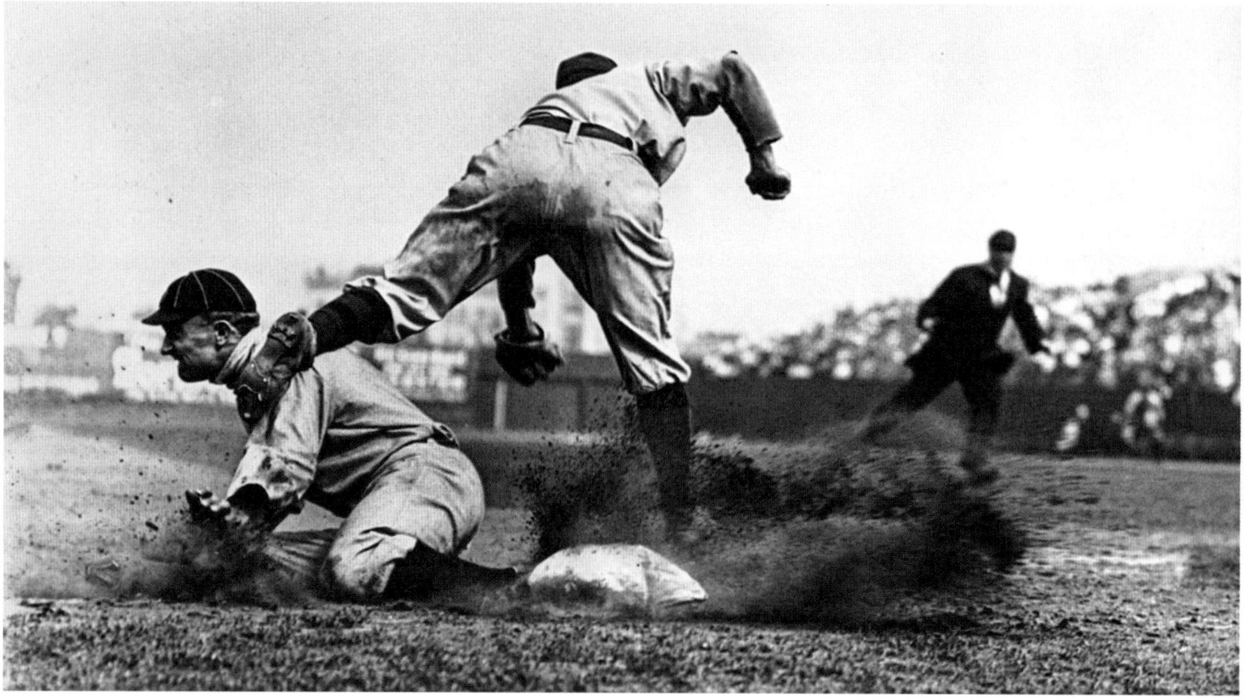

2

THE SLIDE

Ty Cobb Steals Third

NEAL McCABE

In the spring of 1904, thirty-five-year-old Charles M. Conlon was working as a proofreader at the *New York Evening Telegram* when John B. Foster, the editor of the newspaper's sports page, learned that Conlon's hobby was photography. Foster was also the assistant editor of *Spalding's Official Base Ball Guide*, and he made a casual remark that would change Conlon's life: "Charley, they need pictures of ball players for the *Guide* and there is no reason why you can't take pictures of players, as well as landscapes. It will be a good pickup for you, and it will be something for a day off."[1]

Conlon took him up on this modest proposal, and over the next thirty-nine seasons the unassuming yet persistent amateur photographer steadily amassed an astonishing body of work that would make him a legend in his spare time. He never quit his day job, and in 1930 *Telegram* sportswriter Joe Williams was shocked to learn that an elderly proofreader at his newspaper was responsible for "the greatest action picture ever made on the ball field."[2] Conlon loved to talk about his famous photo of Ty Cobb sliding into third base, and he kept the glass negative handy: "Would you like to see the original plate of that picture?" he asked Williams.[3]

In 1937, Conlon told *The Sporting News*: "Some years ago, I found that my plates were running me out of the house in Englewood, New Jersey, so I destroyed hundreds of them. Perhaps it was a mistake, but where would I have put them?"[4] In fact, Conlon destroyed about 80% of the estimated 40,000 negatives he produced. Conlon retired after the 1942 season, and his 8,000 surviving negatives were acquired by *The Sporting News* in St. Louis, where they would languish, largely unappreciated, for the next five decades.

Steve Gietschier, then the archivist at *The Sporting News*, was the first person who truly understood the significance of Conlon's legacy. In 1990, he hired my sister Constance McCabe, an experienced photo conservator, to duplicate the fragile glass and nitrate film negatives in the Conlon Collection. This was just before the digital era, and as my sister toiled in the darkroom day after day she slowly became captivated by the beauty of these images and realized that her brother, a lifelong baseball fan, would share her fascination. She tried to describe these extraordinary photographs to me over the phone, and she assured me that I would be familiar with many of them, but since I had never heard of the photographer, I wasn't the least bit interested. When she finally showed me some of the pictures, however, I was flabbergasted. Why had no one published a book of Conlon photographs? I now desperately wanted to read such a book, but first we would have to write it.

We decided that Conlon's negatives would be the hook of our book, but this meant that his most famous photo would be excluded, since the negative of *The Slide* had gone missing—presumably lost or destroyed. We were naturally disappointed, but we also knew that even without this crucial image, our book would demonstrate conclusively that Conlon deserved to be ranked among the great documentary photographers. Near the end of the editorial process, however, the original 5" × 7" glass negative of *The Slide* was serendipitously discovered in a safe at *The Sporting News*, but our initial euphoria evaporated quickly when my sister saw that it was cracked from corner to corner and held together with adhesive tape. Miraculously, the emulsion had remained intact, and she was able to repair the damage and preserve *The Slide* for posterity.

Conlon gave his earliest version of the circumstances surrounding the photograph in his April 1917 *Baseball Magazine* article entitled "The Greatest Picture I Ever Took":

> Ty Cobb was on second base, restless as always. I took my stand about fifteen feet from third, so that I could get a good view of Cobb should he come tearing into the bag, as he generally does. The infield played in close for the batter.

> [New York Highlanders third baseman Jimmy] Austin moved well in. And then Ty, edging far off second, lowered his head and came tearing down like a gray hound for third base. Austin didn't see him, but he heard the warning cry of some of his teammates. He started backing into the bag. Now Ty never deliberately spikes a player, I believe. But he does insist on his right to the base paths, which is proper. He drove on, spikes first. But Austin, light on his feet as a cat, jumped just in time. Cobb's spikes did tear his shoe, but he was not much hurt, and as he jumped in midair, his own shoe, bristling with spikes, curled around Cobb's neck.
>
> After it was all over, I said to myself, "Well, I have missed a great picture. Why didn't I snap that?" And then the thought came to me: "Did I take it involuntarily?" I couldn't be sure. But I did put the plate to one side. That night I developed it and found that I had indeed "got" that view. It had been pure accident. I had acted without conscious effort, and I had taken it exactly right. It was my masterpiece among pictures.[5]

In 1930, Conlon added that the photo was taken in 1909, and that Cobb was stealing in a one-out sacrifice situation. Such detailed recollections would seem to make the precise date of the slide easy to determine—and sure enough, after eliminating the games where Cobb went hitless or never reached third base, there it was: Cobb stole third on June 10, 1909. But several problems immediately arose: Austin was playing shortstop; it was raining, and the crowd numbered three thousand, while the photo reveals a capacity crowd enjoying shirtsleeve weather. After a painstaking and dispiriting search, it became obvious that the scenario described by Conlon never happened . . . well, at least not in 1909.

It turns out that Conlon was off by one year (not bad for an old man recalling the circumstances of a twenty-year-old photograph) and he had slightly embellished the drama by making it a one-out sacrifice situation as opposed to a straight steal with two outs.

Conlon's famous picture of Wee Willie Keeler in right field at Hilltop Park was taken in 1909. A Morisco Cigarettes sign dominates the background, an E+W Cigars sign is on the left, and a Webster's Cigars sign is on the right. To the far right is a sign painted on the wall in foul territory which appears to read "Broadway Theatre."

In Conlon's 1910 photo of Lou Criger, the Morisco and Webster signs are still there, but the Broadway sign has been completely painted out, and the E+W sign has been replaced. Only a fraction of the new sign can be glimpsed between Criger's wrist and his catcher's mitt, but in Conlon's 1910 photo of

Red Killefer, the entire sign is visible. It is a Paxto Foot Powder sign on the outfield fence, asking baseball fans the timeless question: "FEET ACHE?"

Turning to *The Slide*, note that at Austin's glove, the right-field wall in foul territory is blank. Now look directly to the left of Cobb's eyes. The white spots at the top of the dark rectangle are meaningless until we realize that they are the final clue to the date of the photograph: ". . . HE?"—a fragment of "FEET ACHE?" Further examination of *The Slide* reveals that—in addition to the capacity crowd in the grandstand—fans are seated at the bottom of the Paxto sign.

The presence of the Paxto sign means that the photo was taken in 1910, and we can now determine precisely when Ty Cobb, Jimmy Austin, and a hapless third-string catcher collaborated with Charles M. Conlon to produce a masterpiece.

July 23, 1910, was a beautiful Saturday, the only weekend date the New York Highlanders played against the visiting Detroit Tigers all season. "It was a bright day,"[6] Conlon recalled. The thermometer hit eighty-nine degrees. Sensational rookie pitcher Russell Ford, who would go on to win twenty-six games for New York in 1910, was so popular with the hometown fans that extra security was needed to control the large crowd that turned out for his start. "Thousands of boys and hundreds of girls choked the grandstand long before the game began," reported the *New York American*.[7] By the 3:30 game time, the overflow crowd was lining the outfield fence. This was the only capacity crowd the Tigers attracted to Hilltop Park in 1910.

One cloud appeared on the Highlanders' horizon: first-string catcher Ed Sweeney was disabled by a split finger, and veteran catcher Lou Criger was still recovering from an appendectomy, forcing New York to use a converted pitcher behind the plate. "Fred Mitchell has not had enough work to keep his throwing arm in shape," reported the *New York Evening Mail*, "and if Cobb ever gets on the bases he is apt to play hob with our stocky catcher."[8] This ominous prophecy came true all too soon: in the top of the first inning, with two men out and the bases empty, Ty Cobb "worked a pass and stole second," reported the *New York World*. "The play was close and the fans said so. On the second ball pitched Cobb stole third and tallied on Mitchell's high throw."[9] The phenomenal Ty Cobb had just stolen second and third on consecutive pitches. The *New York American* reported that "Tyrus got a base on balls, and didn't waste any time fussing around the bag. He stole second, he stole third, and came home on Mitchell's bad throw to Austin."[10]

Just before game time, Charles Conlon knelt down beside the third-base coach's box and carefully focused his Graflex camera on the bag in preparation for an action shot. But even the experienced Conlon was startled by Cobb's impetuosity. The uncropped photo shows that the photographer barely caught Cobb in the frame, and an examination of the original glass negative revealed that his camera was tilted downward to the left when Cobb arrived so unexpectedly. Conlon was indeed operating purely on instinct as he juggled his camera and snapped the shutter.

The burly umpire we see in the picture, his coat flapping and his necktie blown over his shoulder as he rushes to make the call, is Big Bill Dinneen; the hand clutching at the right edge of the uncropped photo belongs to the demonstrative Detroit manager and third-base coach, Hughie Jennings. But one person in the uncropped photograph is motionless, unaffected by Cobb's derring-do: New York second baseman Earl Gardner rests with his hands on his knees, observing the play dispassionately. He can do nothing but watch Fred Mitchell's throw sail into left field.

The next day the local papers were aghast at the New York catcher's incompetence: "Mitchell's performance was simply terrible . . . his pegging was so slow and inaccurate that a first-grade schoolboy could have stolen on him."[11] "The weakest spot in the Yankee team was Mitchell behind the bat. He made atrocious pegs to the bases, and was sleepy in chasing pop fouls . . . Ty was very much in the game. He raced the bases like a greyhound. In the first inning he got a pass. Brazenly he stole second and in the same way pilfered third, Mitchell making a miserable toss to catch him. Cobb, of course, came right through on this attack of palsy on the catcher's part."[12] "It was largely due to egregious throwing by Mitchell that the Detroits got their start. And Cobb was one of his greatest beneficiaries. The terrible Tyrus never showed better on the bases than he did yesterday. He was as hard to catch as quicksilver."[13] (Only the *New York Evening Mail* asserted that "Austin muffed the throw.")[14]

The *New York World* tried to put things in perspective: "The fans were inclined to be severe on Mitchell, overlooking the fact that Cobb pulls off his base stealing stunts against every team in the league."[15] After his execrable performance, Mitchell was benched in favor of the barely ambulatory Criger, but he remained optimistic: "I know that I have been catching the worst ball that I have caught, but I will be working along in good shape, as I know I can catch. I went kind of bad and was anxious to get that ball away quick and was using the sidearm throw to get base runners. But there are better times coming."[16] Better times came for Fred Mitchell when he managed the Chicago Cubs to a pennant in 1918, but his playing career ended with barely a whimper.

Despite his ignominious role in Conlon's masterpiece, Jimmy Austin spoke proudly of the photograph to Lawrence S. Ritter in *The Glory of Their Times* (1966): "See that picture? It's a famous picture. It's Cobb sliding into third, and the other guy is me, being knocked sprawling. He took my left foot with his shoulder as he came in, and down I went."[17] Fred Mitchell's role went unmentioned, and no doubt unremembered, but without his rotten sidearm throw, Austin would never have assumed the awkward yet balletic pose that assures his immortality, and Cobb would never have followed the flight of the ball into left field with the demonic, lip-biting grimace that has haunted baseball fans for more than a century.

"The picture was not printed the next day," Conlon noted in 1937. "It did not appear until the *Spalding Guide* came out the following spring."[18] In fact, Conlon set the photo aside for a year and a half before it was published in the 1912 *Spalding Guide*. That same spring *The Slide* made its first appearance on a baseball card, the gorgeous Hassan Triple Folder, and before long the image was omnipresent in newspapers, magazines, and books. Conlon boasted in 1937 that the picture "has been reproduced hundreds of times, and still is being bought from me."[19] One might assume from this statement that original Conlon prints of his masterpiece would be plentiful today, but, incredibly, nearly every one of those photos ended up in the trash, and as of 2024, only two examples were known to exist. In 2015, a torn and battered print sold at auction for $77,098; in 2020, a mediocre print earned an astronomical $390,000.[20] The auction catalog compared this exceptionally rare and highly sought-after photo to the *Mona Lisa* and a Stradivarius violin, which may be stretching things just a bit, but there can be no doubt that any collector who manages to find a pristine vintage print of *The Slide* can look forward to a comfortable retirement.

Conlon's posthumous reputation is remarkably similar to that of his exact contemporary Scott Joplin, the "King of Ragtime." The composer of the *Maple Leaf Rag* enjoyed fleeting fame early in the twentieth century, but despite his ambitious artistic aims his music was never taken seriously, and soon after his death in 1917 Joplin sank into obscurity, relegated to the ranks of one-hit wonders. Outside of a few jazz musicians and a handful of dogged researchers, his stunning body of work was ignored for more than five decades until musicologist Joshua Rifkin recorded *Scott Joplin: Piano Rags*, a million-selling 1970 album that inspired a ragtime revival. The next year the New York Public Library published the *Collected Works of Scott Joplin*, and he is now universally regarded as a great American composer.

Conlon never achieved fame in his lifetime, and he didn't even rise to the level of one-hit wonder after his death in 1945, since nobody really knew or cared who had taken that iconic Ty Cobb photo, which—as far as baseball fans were concerned—seemed to have existed forever. *The Slide* was in some ways a lucky fluke, but the thousands of classic player portraits Conlon produced over the next three decades demonstrate that there was a lot more than luck involved in his success. In 1984, a Conlon exhibition opened at the National Portrait Gallery in Washington, DC, but the pictures on display were poorly chosen and attracted scant attention. More impressive was the beautiful baseball card series issued in 1991 by Megacards and *The Sporting News*, which reproduced images my sister had printed from the original negatives in the Conlon Collection.

When *Baseball's Golden Age: The Photographs of Charles M. Conlon* was published in 1993, the reviews were raves, and the very first fan letter we received was from Lawrence Ritter: "The Conlon book is without doubt the most beautiful baseball book I have ever seen," he wrote. "Both of you did a wonderful once-in-a-lifetime job."[21] We were honored and flattered by such praise, but we were most gratified by the fact that Conlon was finally receiving the critical acclaim he had so coveted during his lifetime.

In 1913, Conlon entered The *Photographic Times* Print Contest, sponsored by a magazine aimed at serious amateur photographers. The theme of the competition was "Vacation Memories." Conlon did not win first prize. He didn't even earn an honorable mention. The editors did their best to console the losers: "Other pictures, not good enough in the estimation of the judges to receive Honorable Mention or High Commendation, nevertheless received their hearty approval as excellent examples of pictorial photography."[22] Near the end of a long list of also-rans, we find this brief description of a failed entry: "A series of excellent bear pictures, by Charles M. Conlon, of New York City."[23]

Conlon's raw, in-your-face aesthetic, as exemplified by *The Slide*, had absolutely nothing in common with pictorial photography, the prevailing soft-focus style of the early twentieth century. If only poor Charley had known that his baseball pictures would earn him the ultimate accolade early in the twenty-first century, when hundreds of Conlon photographs entered the permanent collection of the Metropolitan Museum of Art.

Not too shabby for a newspaper proofreader.

NOTES

1. *The Sporting News*, May 27, 1937, 4.
2. *The Sporting News*, October 30, 1930, 5.
3. *The Sporting News*, October 30, 1930, 5.
4. *The Sporting News*, May 27, 1937, 4.
5. "The Greatest Picture I Ever Took," *Baseball Magazine*, April 1917, 165.
6. *The Sporting News*, October 30, 1930, 5.
7. *New York American*, July 24, 1910.
8. *New York Evening Mail*, July 23, 1910.
9. *New York World*, July 24, 1910.
10. *New York American*, July 24, 1910.
11. *New York Evening Journal*, July 24, 1910.
12. *New York Times*, July 24, 1910.
13. *New York Herald*, July 24, 1910.
14. *New York Evening Mail*, July 24, 1910.
15. *New York World*, July 24, 1910.
16. *New York Globe*, July 26, 1910.
17. Lawrence S. Ritter, *The Glory of Their Times: The Story of the Early Days of Baseball Told by the Men Who Played It* (New York: William Morrow and Company, Inc., [1966] 1984), 89.
18. *The Sporting News*, May 27, 1937, 4.
19. *The Sporting News*, May 27, 1937, 4.
20. Rich Mueller, "Famous Charles Conlon Ty Cobb Photo Sells for $77,098," December 6, 2015, www.sportscollectorsdaily.com/famous-charles-conlon-ty-cobb-photo-hits-auction-block/; "Conlon photo of Ty Cobb stealing third sells for $390K," December 11, 2020, https://www.liveauctioneers.com/news/top-news/collectiblesandpopculture/conlon-photo-of-ty-cobb-stealing-third-sells-for-390k/.
21. Letter from Lawrence S. Ritter, October 28, 1993, author's collection.
22. *Photographic Times*, February 1914, 52.
23. *Photographic Times*, February 1914, 53.

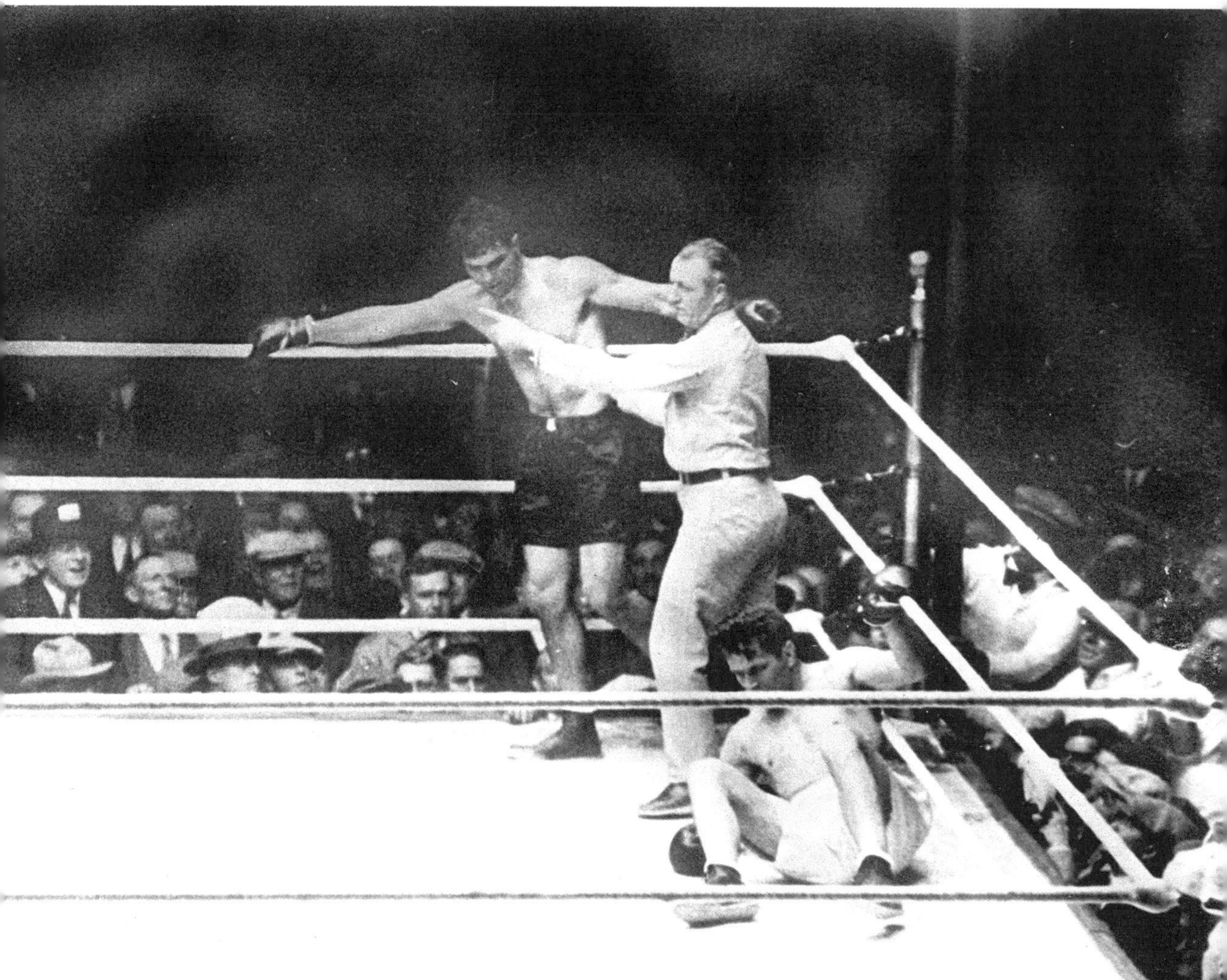

3

THE LONG COUNT

Dempsey and Tunney

ELLIOTT J. GORN

"If either man falls through weakness or otherwise, he must get up unassisted, the boxer has ten seconds to allow him to do so, *the other man meanwhile to return to his corner* . . ."[1] So stated the rules governing prizefighting in the 1920s. The referee was not supposed to begin counting over a fallen man until his opponent had moved away. The rule was not new, but it was also not always enforced.

And so in the unattributed photo seen here, one fighter lies crumpled on the canvas, knocked down by the man who stands nearby, ready to keep punching. Enforcing the rules, the referee signals for the upright boxer to move away. A technicality, some said, but on this detail hung the outcome of a legendary championship match. The setting was Chicago. The year was 1927. The fighters were heavyweights Jack Dempsey and Gene Tunney.

The photo was one of a sequence widely seen in newspapers across the country. In the picture reprinted here, the referee (Dave Barry) delays the count and addresses not the fallen man, but the one resisting his command to retire to a neutral corner. Follow the sequence and the man in black trunks finally walks away from his opponent until he is standing as far off as he can, with the turnbuckle to his back and each of his gloved hands resting on the top ropes. Now the referee begins counting. The boxer in white stays down, but finally rises, having received precious extra seconds to recover. Many photographers were at ringside that night, and there are multiple versions of these moments, each slightly different, but all telling the same dramatic story—one fighter has gone down, the referee enforces the rules, thereby giving him a few extra seconds. Will the downed man rise before the count of ten?

Jack Dempsey and Gene Tunney fought each other for the heavyweight title twice, once on September 23, 1926, in Philadelphia, and once on September 22, 1927, in Chicago. Each fight drew roughly a hundred thousand fans to a football-size outdoor arena.

Prizefighting had mostly been illegal in America throughout the nineteenth century, yet by the twenties the old stigma was gone. The rich and famous attended the first battle. Movie stars like William S. Hart, Tom Mix, and Norma Talmadge sat in the audience along with sports heroes such as Babe Ruth and John McGraw, and even famous businessmen like William Randolph Hearst, Andrew Mellon, Charles Schwab, and Vincent Astor. Newspapers across America gave the fights frontpage coverage, and half the population listened to the second bout on the radio, a new consumer product that had just entered American households.[2]

The 1920s was a relatively prosperous decade, a peak era of American consumer culture. A world of goods was more available to the growing middle class than ever before. They filled new suburban homes with phonographs and washing machines and, out at the curb, automobiles. It was also an age of mass entertainment. More than ever, sports heroes, movie stars, singers, and comedians became American icons. Knowledge of popular culture, of who was hot and who was not, was a hallmark of the 1920s.

One of the most famous sports heroes of that or any era was Heavyweight Champion William Harrison "Jack" Dempsey. He was widely considered one of the grittiest, hardest-punching boxers of all time. In the twenties age of heroes—Charles Lindbergh, Amelia Earhart, Clara Bow, Jim Thorpe, Charlie Chaplain, and the rest—Dempsey stood out. He won his title in 1919 and held it still when he met Gene Tunney for the first time seven years later in Philadelphia. Along the way, he fought a series of spectacular matches.

Like so many prizefighters, Dempsey came out of poverty and obscurity. He traced his ancestry to the Scotch Irish of West Virginia, but his family moved to the Rocky Mountains late in the nineteenth century. His ring name, "The Manassa Mauler," evoked his rough background. He was one of thirteen Dempsey children born in Manassa, Colorado. His father was a miner. Labor radicalism and violent struggles to organize workers had long been associated with mining, especially with militant unions like the Industrial Workers of the World and the Western Federation of Miners. Dempsey's early life resonated with images of poverty, labor violence, and economic exploitation—he won his title just a few years after the infamous Ludlow Massacre, when a private security force hired by the mining company to put down the strike murdered two dozen people, half of them women and children.

Young Dempsey left home in his teens, hopping boxcars, drifting around Colorado and Utah, and working in copper mines. The violent male world of labor camps and company towns taught him to defend himself, and his fighting talent quickly became apparent. Dempsey's older brother helped him train and taught him to strengthen his jaw by chewing pine tar, and to toughen his skin by pickling it in brine. Steadily, the young fighter earned a reputation and a modest living fighting bullies and roughnecks in saloons and mining camps throughout the West. He would bet on himself, and also, when he won, collect a small percentage of the winnings of those at ringside. Dempsey ratified his decision to become a professional fighter by adopting the name "Jack" after the great nineteenth century lightweight, Nonpareil Jack Dempsey.

His career was good but not spectacular, yet on July 4, 1919, in Toledo, Ohio, he was matched against six-foot six-inch, 250-pound Jess Willard, the Heavyweight Champion, conqueror of the infamous Jack Johnson. Overmatched by half a foot and sixty pounds, Dempsey was given little chance. But reporters noticed his look—thick stubble on his face, his body bronzed and lean, and pure rage in his eyes. Dempsey knocked Willard down seven times in the first round. His jaw broken, cheekbone shattered, and ribs cracked, the champion failed to come out of his corner for the fourth round. Rumors circulated that something besides mere fists filled Dempsey's gloves. From then on, fans thought of Dempsey as the consummate brawler—reporters called him a "jungle fighter," a "mauler," a "killer"—dangerous, out of control, someone to marvel at, but not necessarily admire.[3]

Over the next eight years, Dempsey became the single greatest drawing card in the history of American sports, repeatedly pulling down million-dollar gates, and a total of $9 million dollars for his five biggest fights. Not until the 1960s did boxing surpass such figures. But Dempsey was not exactly a popular champion, not in the conventional sense anyway. In *Dempsey: The Autobiography of Jack Dempsey*, he recalled his 1921 fight against French

Champion Georges Carpentier: "The crowd was pulling hysterically for Georges. They wanted me to lose, even to a foreigner."[4] Carpentier was a war hero, an aviator and winner of the Croix de Guerre, whereas Dempsey failed to fight in the Great War and was accused of draft evasion. He claimed to be the sole support for his mother, father, and wife. He raised thousands of dollars for the Red Cross. But the "slacker" charge held on. Why were weaker men dying while this ring warrior fled from battle? It didn't help that a publicity photo of him "working" in a shipyard revealed pinstriped slacks and patent leather boots under his overalls. Dempsey beat Carpentier, but many fans remained ambivalent about him.

Two years later, in 1923, Dempsey fought the Argentine boxer Luis Ángel Firpo, the "Wild Bull of the Pampas." In a scene painted by the great American artist George Bellows, Firpo stands at the edge of the ropes, following through on a blow that sends Dempsey out of the ring and into the seats. That actually happened. *Ring Magazine* editor Nat Fleischer considered this the most exciting fight he ever witnessed. As soon as the first bell rang, Firpo sprang from his corner, met Dempsey mid-ring, and immediately dropped him to his knees with a right uppercut. Dempsey rose, charged the Wild Bull, sent him to the canvas with a left to the jaw. Dempsey stood over him—against the rules—and each time Firpo tried to rise, Dempsey punched him down again. There were seven total knockdowns by the end of the first round. *Then,* in the second round, Firpo charged and punched Dempsey out of the ropes, into the arms of reporters. He scrambled back into the ring and, one minute into the second round, Dempsey knocked Firpo out for good.

Despite the unparalleled excitement of his fights, Dempsey still failed to become a fan favorite. In an age of hyper-patriotism, the "slacker" charge held firm. But more, Dempsey violated the era's expectations of sporting heroes as cultural exemplars, clean of mind and body. Once he became champion, he hung out with a loose-moraled, thrill-hungry, big-spending crowd. Gamblers, hucksters, and minor hoodlums lurked around his training camps. Divorce was rare in the 1920s, yet Dempsey left his first wife to marry the movie star Estelle Taylor. In addition, some of his unpopularity came from the ring itself. On the one hand, Dempsey was seen as filled with rage, out of control, dangerous; in a violent sport, the Manassa Mauler stood out. On the other hand, after the Firpo fight, he avoided the ring and failed to defend his title for three years.

All of this contrasted with James Joseph "Gene" Tunney, whose life both in the ring and out was bland next to Dempsey's. Tunney was born in New York City to respectable working-class Irish-American parents. He was handsome, clean-cut, and blond, with none of the facial scars or cauliflower ears associated with boxers. Tunney avoided the gamblers and racketeers so common around the ring. He exuded poise and confidence, trained hard, shunned tobacco, alcohol, and profanity. The press depicted him as a model American man. He surprised journalists with his intellectual qualities; rather than monosyllables and grunts, they reported, he spoke of literature and philosophy. Above all, he embodied patriotism. His ring name, "The Fighting Marine," evoked his service overseas in the Great War, as did his boxing title: Light-Heavyweight Champion of the American Expeditionary Force.

It is in the contrast of the two fighters that we understand how their battles galvanized the nation. Even the metaphors journalists used to describe them give us a sense of how fans saw the fight. Tunney was a "synthetic fighter," a practitioner of "ring science," a "ring-general." He was disciplined and self-controlled; he approached boxing as a "mechanical business undertaking"; he applied a "mathematical method of fighting." He was a "boxer," his opponent a "bruiser," a "jungle fighter," a "killer," a man of "concentrated cruelty."[5] *Time* magazine evoked this primitive quality of Dempsey in the ring: ". . . his body, muscled like a panther cat's, seems to ignite with malice, to burn and flash; then his fists reach out, savagely, lethally, to destroy the weaving shape in front of him and get revenge for something that he has just remembered, a wrong done, a score that must be evened, something that happened to him long ago."[6] Science, modernity, and rationality versus all that was primal, atavistic, and savage.

This metaphorical battle expressed deep underlying tensions in early-twentieth century America. New technologies, progress, material advancement—the culture of the 1920s extolled these as hallmarks of American civilization. The cluster of values Tunney embodied were the very core of patriotism; he was the avatar of bourgeois respectability, of hard work and steady habits. Dempsey seemed the opposite. Dempsey embodied rage, blind passion, nihilistic violence. Reporters described him with metaphors of destruction, of nature wreaking havoc, of id impulses smashing through the constraints of modern industrial life. Though a son of America's white working class, the metaphors used to describe Dempsey were the very ones usually reserved for despised minorities, especially Native American and African American men. The juxtaposition of the two sets of images helps explain the unprecedented outpouring of interest in their fight.

Challenger Tunney was given very little chance to win their first fight. Reporters and boxing mavens felt that his cool defense would break down as

Dempsey bore in. But it didn't happen that way. In the first ten-rounder, Tunney managed to elude the champion's rushes, never sustaining much punishment while continually counter-punching, piling up points, and finally winning a clear decision. Now champion himself, Tunney agreed to a rematch, which took place almost exactly a year later. Through six rounds, their second battle resembled the first, Dempsey charging in, bobbing and weaving, trying to land a few cleanly, Tunney cagey and cool, keeping him at bay. Then suddenly in the seventh round, the Manassa Mauler tagged the Fighting Marine with a left hook to the jaw. Tunney went down hard. Dempsey stood nearby, ready to rush in as he did against Willard and Firpo. But this time the referee enforced the rules, insisting Dempsey retire to a neutral corner before beginning the count, giving Tunney precious extra seconds to clear his head. Tunney rose to his feet, and ended the round peddling backward, out of harm's way. "Enough running. Come on and fight," Dempsey blurted, according to ringside reporters.[7] But Tunney kept counterpunching in the late rounds and won their second fight by decision.

Let's go back to the photograph. In sports, rules and rule-keepers should be as unobtrusive as possible—ideally, fair play and the regulations that enforce it are internalized by the athletes themselves. We all know that umpires and referees are fallible; that is part of the game, any game. But fans are there to watch athletic contests, not the officiating. In the second Dempsey-Tunney fight, however, the "third man in the ring" was crucial to the outcome. He enforced a rule that was central to boxing's long evolution. You can't tell the story of the second Dempsey-Tunney fight without the "long count." So this is an iconic photograph of an iconic moment in sport. Referee Dave Barry, right in the middle of the action, signaling for Dempsey to move away from his fallen opponent was the highlight of the fight, the turning point captured in the photograph.

For decades, boxing fans debated the long count. Was the referee right or wrong? Did the few extra seconds make the difference in the outcome? Which man was really the better fighter: the cool scientific boxer or the wild raging panther? The battle crystalized the tension that makes prizefighting so compelling, the knife-edged balance of mayhem and control, aggression and discipline. The long count brought that tension into sharp focus. More, the photograph of the long count made visible something fundamental to sports and life, something usually hiding in plain sight: rules, hopefully applied fairly and equally, which we follow, bend, ignore, and strain against.

NOTES

1. For more on the Marquess of Queensberry rules, see Elliott J. Gorn, *The Manly Art: Bare-Knuckle Prize Fighting in America* (Ithaca: Cornell University Press, 1986), 202–206.

2. For more on this fight, see Elliott J. Gorn, "The Manassa Mauler and the Fighting Marine: An Interpretation of the Dempsey-Tunney Fights," *Journal of American Studies* 19 (April 1985): 27–47; Bruce J. Evensen, *When Dempsey Fought Tunney: Heroes, Hokum, and Storytelling in the Jazz Age* (Knoxville: University of Tennessee Press, 1996).

3. See Gorn, "The Manassa Mauler and the Fighting Marine," 42.

4. Jack Dempsey with Barbara Piatelli Dempsey, *Dempsey: The Autobiography of Jack Dempsey* (London: W. H. Allen, 1977), 143.

5. See Gorn, "The Manassa Mauler and the Fighting Marine," 34, 41.

6. *Time*, August 30, 1926, 24–25.

7. Randy Roberts, *Jack Dempsey, The Manassa Mauler* (Baton Rouge: Louisiana State Press, [1979] 1984), 261.

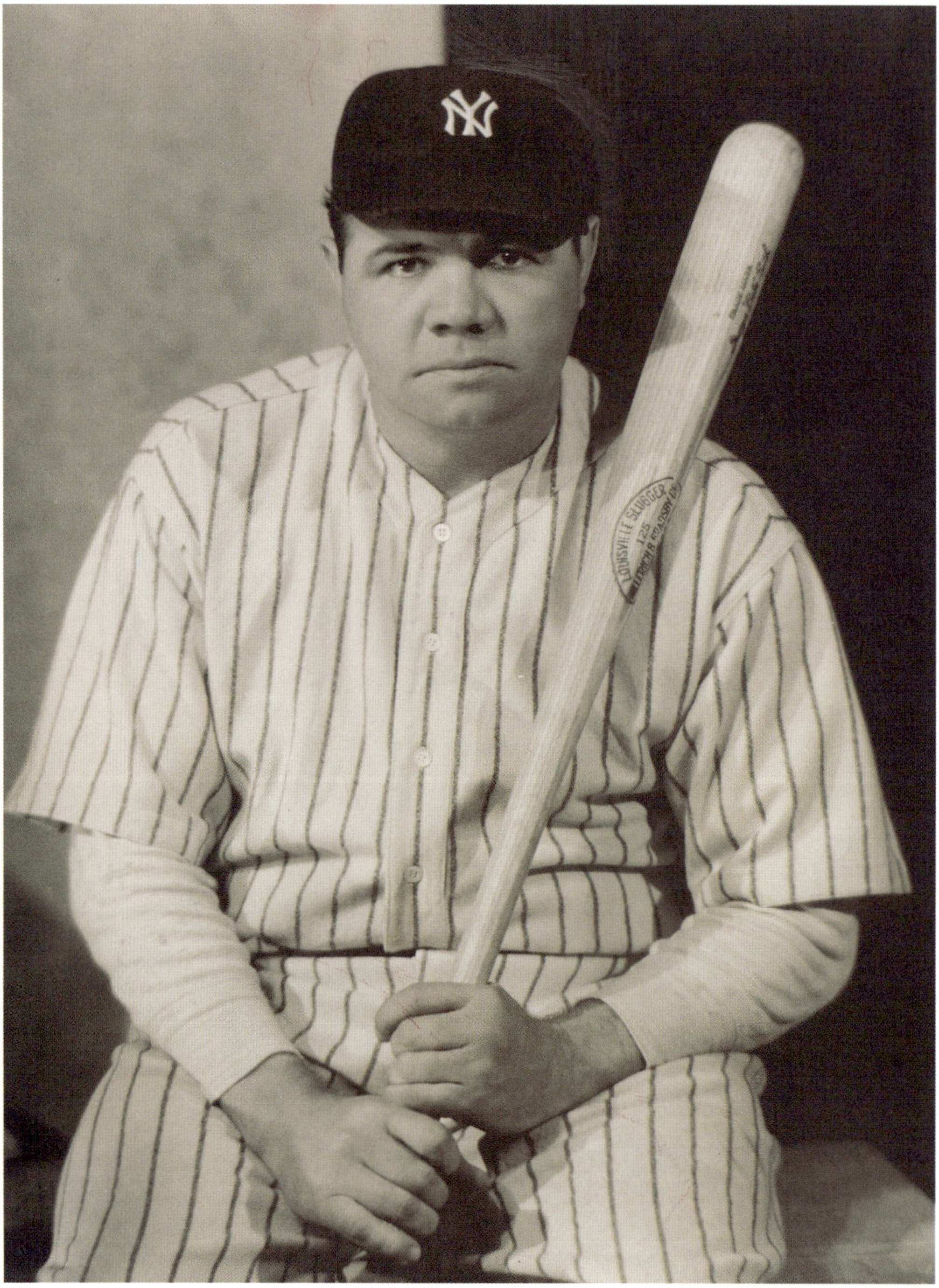
NY
LOUISVILLE SLUGGER
125

4

"SOME ARE EASY AND SOME ARE TOUGH—THAT'S ALL THERE IS TO IT"

Nickolas Muray's Portrait of Babe Ruth

EDMUND F. WEHRLE

In the late 1920s, Babe Ruth sat atop the sports world. He also sat for a session with famed portrait photographer Nickolas Muray. For Ruth, the sitting offered a rare opportunity to redefine his public image. Despite his meteoric rise to sports heroism, personal and public tumult had marked his baseball career and private life. Yet by the time of his session with Muray, the Yankee slugger seemed to have wrestled order out of his previously chaotic baseball life. A new commitment to conditioning and personal discipline brought him a sense of stability that had long seemed elusive. While sportswriters had generally treated the Babe as a fun-loving, licentious man-child, Ruth pined to be taken seriously—to bring his public image in line with the man he had become. Muray's portrait spoke to those longings: Ruth appears stone-faced and serious with eyes fixed intensely forward, his huge hands wrapped around the bat leaning on his shoulder. On display is power, skill, and determination—a far cry from the cartoonish image so often associated with Ruth. In Muray, Ruth found a sympathetic student of character. Both rose from humble beginnings. Both were athletes and devoted themselves to honing the skills and discipline that would earn them fame.

As is well known, Ruth had much to overcome in his early life. Legend has him an orphan rescued by kindly Xaverian Brothers who were also, conveniently, baseball fanatics and great coaches. Much of the story, in fact, is true. The more traumatic side of the legend, however, is usually glossed over. From an early age, young George Ruth was essentially abandoned to the dangerous streets of Baltimore. Poverty and violence, undoubtedly, were seared into his young mind. The only responsibility his parents seem to have taken was to place the boy at St. Mary's Industrial School. This new existence was an improvement only by contrast to his earlier semi-abandonment. At St. Mary's, Ruth led a starkly regimented life, something akin to a prisoner, but he was fed and housed. On the baseball diamonds which surrounded the school, Ruth found his first sense of self-worth.[1] Throughout his life, Ruth truly relished the game, and his ability and instincts were second to none.

His obvious talents catapulted the teenage Ruth into professional baseball. Soon the hometown hero played for the minor league Baltimore Orioles, where he became an emerging star. But Ruth was ill prepared for life outside the walls of St. Mary's. When he rose to the majors with the Boston Red Sox, Ruth earned his first taste of fame and fortune.[2] Yet personal and professional peace eluded him. His temper, while always fleeting, could be alarming. In 1917, Ruth punched an umpire during a dispute. Police had to be called to restrain him. The next year, due to a quarrel over playing time, he absconded mid-season to join the Delaware River Shipbuilders League, where many major leaguers had found refuge from the threat of the World War I draft. Ruth returned quickly to the Red Sox, but he refused to sign his contract the next season, holding out for more money in the early weeks of 1919 spring training. The young star was earning quite a reputation.[3] He caroused late into the night with friends—many of which were fair-weather, hanger-on types. Ruth understood he needed structure in his life: in 1914, at the age of nineteen, he married a sixteen-year-old waitress to whom he had taken a shine. He hoped to create the family life he'd never had. But he knew little of such things, and he was on the road too much. The marriage grew strained.[4]

In January 1920, news arrived of "the most stupendous deal in the history of the national game."[5] Ruth had been sold to the New York Yankees for $100,000. In New York, Ruth soared to national, even international, stardom during the 1920 season. Moving from the pitching mound to become a daily hitter, he walloped home runs around the league, and drew fans in record numbers wherever he played. Everywhere mobs ambushed the superstar, and sportswriters wore out typewriters describing his feats. He kept turnstiles clicking and profits piling up for the first time in many years.[6] At 6'2" and usually weighing over two hundred pounds, Ruth, with his broad round face, was a favorite of photographers. His image seemed ubiquitous in the 1920s, although he had never before received the sort of artistic attention that came with the Muray photographs.

Baseball needed and appreciated its rainmaker, but anxieties brewed as well. Ruth remained an outspoken rebel. He made little secret that he believed most baseball players were underpaid—including himself. He deserved, he thought, a bigger chunk of the revenue from the crowds he drew to ballparks. An even greater threat existed: Major League Baseball had just fended off a challenge from an upstart rival, the Federal League. During his off-seasons, Ruth joined in barnstorming tours that drew colossal crowds and revenue. These popular traveling shows, some feared, might be the basis for a new challenge—this one led by baseball's biggest star.

The effort to rein in Ruth began at the end of the 1921 season. Following his first World Series appearance as a Yankee, the slugger prepared for his annual fall barnstorming extravaganza. But the new commissioner of baseball, Judge Kenesaw Mountain Landis, had other plans. Citing a long-ignored rule that participants in that year's World Series could not play in exhibition games, Landis banned the tour. With schedules set, and fans and promoters expecting him, Ruth decided to defy the commissioner. He quickly found, however, the entire baseball establishment lined up against him. In December 1921, the commissioner suspended Ruth for thirty-nine days starting on opening day of the next season. Landis brazenly branded the tour "a mutinous defiance."[7] The suspension was followed by a miserable season marked by fights with umpires and bad press.[8]

His 1922 season was a bust. Seeing the powers of baseball aligned against him, the star decided to further capitulate. At the end of the season, he vowed to reform. Able to go through his normal spring training routine in 1923, Ruth returned to form, hitting a home run on the opening day of the new Yankee Stadium. Sportswriters described Ruth as rising "like a phoenix."[9]

Ruth's roller-coaster ride, however, was hardly over. The slugger began spring training in 1925 overweight and in a raw mood. He disparaged his Yankee manager and suggested himself as a potential replacement. Then Ruth took ill, likely with a case of influenza. Still, he continued to play in exhibition games and make the rounds with buddies afterwards. On April 7, as the Yankees were traveling north, Ruth collapsed after an exhibition game in Asheville, North Carolina. He was raced back to New York and hospitalized, where he slowly recovered. Meanwhile, rumors circulated that overeating, insobriety, and/or sexual promiscuity were the real cause of his illness. Again, a troubled season followed. Suspensions and clashes with Yankee management persisted throughout 1925. Spurred by the Yankee front office, sportswriters also reported the collapse of Ruth's marriage and unmasked his live-in lover, Claire Hodgson, a widow with whom he had fallen in love. The 1925 season understandably left Ruth exhausted and resentful.[10]

At that point, Ruth moved aggressively to order the chaos that had long ruled his life. He had a strong advocate now in his corner: Hodgson. Smart, beautiful, and outspoken, Hodgson took up Ruth's cause. Together they found a trainer to help Ruth shed pounds and prepare for a comeback. Ruth made peace with Yankee management, set aside the nightlife, and set up a home with Hodgson, who had a young daughter.[11]

The 1926 season was a marked contrast from 1925. It culminated with a World Series appearance, where Ruth blasted his famous home runs promised to a gravely ill boy.[12] When the 1927 season arrived, Ruth was backed by one of the strongest teams ever assembled in baseball history. It included first baseman Lou Gehrig, among others. The Yankees dominated, and Ruth set a single-season home run record that lasted thirty-four years. The next year, Ruth and the Yankees made a third straight World Series appearance, and the team won its second consecutive World Series. It was this Yankee superstar, at the pinnacle of his powers, who arrived at Muray's studio at 38 East 50th Street in Manhattan.

Ruth's image had permeated America by the late 1920s. His broad visage, usually smiling, seemed everywhere. During darker periods, such as his 1925 "stomachache heard around the world" episode, Ruth would appear melodramatically drawn and forlorn. Muray's Ruth portrait was altogether different. An athlete himself from humble roots, Muray seemed to understand Ruth's quest to be taken seriously. Despite his general good humor, Ruth, according to a *Collier's* magazine profile, "has long smarted under the imputations of light-worded sportswriters that he is not as bright as he might be."[13] Too often the media, encouraged by Yankee management eager to keep Ruth in his place, turned the star into a clownish figure in good times and into a delinquent when he made demands on his team. Having achieved some level of stability, Ruth now sought to project his true self.

Whether Ruth realized it or not, Muray shared a parallel rags-to-riches rise with him. Born into a working-class family in Hungary three years before Ruth's birth, Muray felt the sting of limited economic means and frequent anti-Semitic barbs and taunts growing up. As Ruth found refuge in baseball, Muray became enamored with fencing and photography, which he quickly mastered. He eventually became a journeyman engraver, doing lithographic reproductions. As his interest and skill in photography grew, so too did his ambitions. At seventeen, he moved to Munich to study photography production, and then he moved to Berlin. Next, like so many people at the time, he left for America. In 1913, he arrived at Ellis Island, knowing only a handful of English words and with only twenty-five dollars to his name.[14]

After working in Brooklyn in engraving and color selection, Muray briefly moved to Chicago. In 1920, the year of Ruth's celebrated sale to the Yankees, Muray also arrived in Manhattan and took up residence in a two-room apartment in Greenwich Village, which served for a time both as home and studio. Things were tight at first. To save money, Muray kept his lights out unless a client was visiting. While Muray never achieved Ruth's level of fame (few ever did), his rise to renown in the photography world came quickly. Soon, prominent publications such as *Harper's Bazaar* and the *New York Tribune* began publishing Muray's work. A veritable who's who of 1920s literary and cultural figures sat for him: O'Neill, Graham, Robeson, Coolidge, Garbo, and others. Muray hadn't given up fencing either. In fact, he became national saber champion, destined to represent his adopted country in two Olympics.[15]

By the late 1920s, the two celebrity athletes reached the apex of their careers. At that point, their fates briefly converged at Muray's Studios, which had moved from Greenwich Village to a midtown Manhattan location. The plan was to produce a series of action shots to be published in the *American Magazine*. Muray recalled that Ruth's mere presence sparked a "mob scene," and the building's lobby was "jammed" with gaping fans. In the studio, Muray prepared for a complex shoot that involved attaching a "small vector lamp" to the end of Ruth's bat.[16] In darkness except for the lamp, Ruth swung his bat, as Muray used a slow shutter speed to create light lines, then a sudden flash revealed Ruth. Attired in his Yankee uniform, with his bat and glove handy, Ruth looked ready to play. To loosen up his subject, the photographer made small talk.

"What kind of pitch do you hit best—high, low, outside, or close in?" asked Muray.

"It doesn't matter. Some are easy and some are tough—that's all there is to it," Ruth replied.[17]

Most likely, Ruth sat for his famous portrait during the *American Magazine* session. It is possible as well that Muray shot the portraits at an earlier sitting, although his archives refer only to the *American Magazine* session in which Ruth appeared attired in the same uniform as in the portrait shot. If the action photographs and Muray's famed portrait were shot together, the sitting probably came later than 1927, perhaps closer to 1930, when the *American Magazine* published its illustrated piece on Ruth.[18]

For the portrait, Muray seated Ruth on a bench looking straight ahead into the camera. One thinks immediately of a focused batter ready to go to plate in a crucial game. Editor Marianne Fulton Margolis later linked the expressionless Ruth holding his tool of the trade to "daguerrean portraits of 1840s and 1850s tradesmen with their tools."[19] Certainly, Ruth viewed himself as a particularly skilled craftsman, "with the confident quietness of a man certain of his identity."[20] Ruth, a union member earlier in his career (when a players' union briefly existed), later described himself as among the "crusaders for the rights of ball players."[21]

The uncharacteristic seriousness of the portrait also suggests the equilibrium Ruth had found in his life by the late 1920s. This was no playboy or cartoon character. This was a determined adult, confident of his talents and ability. At the same time, Muray selected a striking but simple background for the photograph, dark on one side, light on the other. This allowed Ruth's bat to stand out against a dark background, but the choice may have also alluded to the struggles and temptations his subject had faced almost from birth.

Magazine publisher Frank Crowninshield described Muray as a photographer with "an inspired devotion to composition, balance, arrangement, lighting and an honest desire to abide by the truth that inheres in his subject."[22] Those attributes are all manifest in Muray's Ruth portrait. His treatment stands out from the thousands of Ruth photographs that cluttered newspaper sports sections, magazine profiles, and cereal boxes during the 1920s and 30s. At Muray's studio, an athlete captured the fortitude and focus of another athlete.

Interestingly, however, the Muray portrait was rarely seen for decades. Instead, fans continued to see in newspapers and magazines a familiar revolving gallery of images with captions such as "Babe Ruth Bags a Gator," "The Babe Visits a Hospital," "Bambino and wife in Florida," and so on.[23] The *American Magazine* did not include the photograph in its "The Babe Shows How" pictorial in 1930. Nor does it show up in any of the photographic retrospectives published when Ruth died in 1948. The first real publication of the now-famous portrait came in 1967 in a compilation of Muray's work with commentary by sportswriter Paul Gallico.[24] After Muray's death, his family donated either negatives or the portrait photograph to the George Eastman House and the Museum of Modern Art. Images from the Muray shoot also found their way to the Smithsonian's National Portrait Gallery, likely when his daughter donated the photographer's papers to the Smithsonian Archives of American Art. Available more readily to the public, the portrait slowly gained currency. Historian Marshall Smelser used it as cover art for his 1974 biography *The Life That Ruth Built*—a work which sought to recognize the man behind the myth. Later in the 1970s, it appeared as back-page art for a 1978 compilation of Muray's celebrity photographs.

Today, alongside the painful Nat Fein Pulitzer-Prize winning image of a cancer-ridden Ruth in uniform at Yankee Stadium in 1948, Muray's portrait is perhaps the most famous photo of Ruth. It serves—as Ruth might have wanted—as a counterbalance to the commercialized Babe of legend and tall tales. When it came to Ruth, Muray, who did much to create the glamorized and idealized legends of the time, managed to cut through the excesses and get to the man.

NOTES

1. George Herman Ruth, *Babe Ruth's Own Book of Baseball* (Lincoln: University of Nebraska Press, [1928] 1992), 3–4; Leigh Montville, *The Big Bam: The Life and Times of Babe Ruth* (New York: Doubleday, 2006), 19–31; Robert Creamer, *Babe: The Legend Comes to Life* (New York: Penguin, 1974), 28–40.

2. Edmund Wehrle, *Breaking Babe Ruth: Baseball's Campaign Against Its Greatest Star* (Columbia: University of Missouri Press, 2018), 14–15; Montville, *The Big Bam*, 33–41; Creamer, *Babe*, 41–83.

3. Wehrle, *Breaking Babe Ruth*, 24–29.

4. Montville, *The Big Bam*, 45–46, 52–55; Creamer, *Babe*, 131–204.

5. Damon Runyon, "The Mornin's Mornin," *New York American*, January 7, 1920.

6. Wehrle, *Breaking Babe Ruth*, 55–63.

7. Wehrle, *Breaking Babe Ruth*, 71–84; Montville, *The Big Bam*, 142–149; Creamer, *Babe*, 244–252.

8. Wehrle, *Breaking Babe Ruth*, 84–93; Montville, *The Big Bam*, 149–156; Creamer, *Babe*, 253–270.

9. Wehrle, *Breaking Babe Ruth*, 95–112; Montville, *The Big Bam*, 153–158, 172–177; Creamer, *Babe*, 271–280.

10. Wehrle, *Breaking Babe Ruth*, 115–132; Montville, *The Big Bam*, 198–216; Creamer, *Babe*, 281–301.

11. Creamer, *Babe*, 302–314.

12. Montville, *The Big Bam*, 216–239; Wehrle, *Breaking Babe Ruth*, 141–184.

13. John B. Kennedy, "Innocents Abroad," *Collier's*, April 14, 1928.

14. Salomon Grimbey, *I Will Never Forget You: Frida Kahlo to Nikolas Muray, Unpublished Photos and Letters* (Munich: Schirmerl and Mosel, 2004), 9–11; "Nickolas Muray, Fencer, 73, Dies," *New York Times*, November 3, 1965, 39.

15. Grimbey, *I Will Never Forget You*, 10–12; "Nickolas Muray, Fencer, 73, Dies," 39.

16. "Notes Celebrity Sittings, 1920–1960," Nickolas Muray Papers, Smithsonian Archives of American Art, https://edan.si.edu/slideshow/viewer/?damspath=/CollectionsOnline/muranick/Box_0001/Folder_021.

17. "The Babe Shows How," *American Magazine*, September 1930, 107–110.

18. Images from the Ruth sitting including the portrait and action shots with light lines can be viewed at the Eastman Museum's website: https://collections.eastman.org/search/babe%20ruth.

19. Marianne Fulton Margolis, "Introduction," in Nickolas Muray, *Celebrity Portraits of the Twenties and Thirties*, ed. Marianne Fulton Margolis (New York: Dover, 1978), np.

20. Margolis, "Introduction," np.

21. Wehrle, *Breaking Babe Ruth*, 75.

22. Frank Crowninshield, "A World About 'Artistic Photography,'" in "Muray Studios," nd, Nickolas Muray Papers, Smithsonian Archives of American Art, https://edan.si.edu/slideshow/viewer/?damspath=/CollectionsOnline/muranick/Box_0002/Folder_005.

23. "Babe Ruth Bags a Gator," *The Sunday Star, Washington*, March 3, 1932; "Bambino and Wife in Florida," *The Bismarck Tribune*, January 25, 1930; "Babe Ruth Visits Hospital," *The Evening Star, Washington*, June 26, 1923.

24. Nickolas Muray and Paul Gallico, *The Revealing Eye: Personalities of the 1920s* (New York: Atheneum, 1967), 250–251.

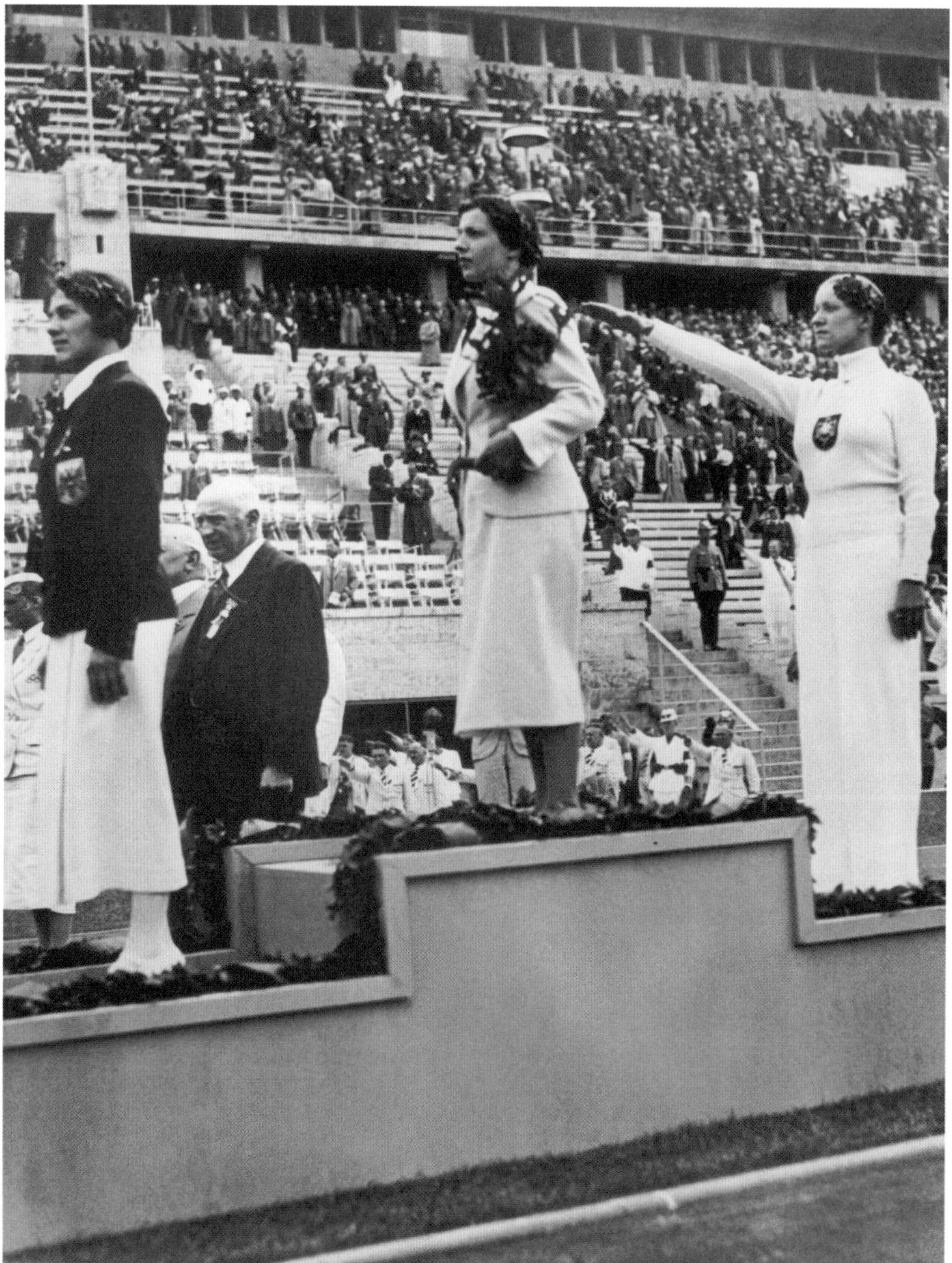

5

WOMAN IN WHITE WITH AN OUTSTRETCHED ARM

Helene Mayer, 1936

ALLEN GUTTMANN

What do we see in the uncaptioned image? Three women photographed during what looks to be some sort of victory ceremony. The background seems to be a sports stadium, with the stands half filled. The women wear long skirts, the cut of which suggests that the ceremony probably took place between 1920 and 1940. The women are dressed differently, which indicates that they were competitors rather than teammates. The woman in the middle is slightly elevated above the ones to her right and her left, which suggests that she is the victor. That she carries some sort of potted plant indicates, to those familiar with sports history, that the photograph captures a moment from the Berlin Olympics of 1936, where victors received small potted oak plants. (The others had to be content with their bronze and silver medals.) Close inspection of the image reveals that the woman on the right is wearing the uniform of the German Olympic team, which surely explains why she has her arm raised in a Nazi salute.

Those knowledgeable about German sports history might very well assume, as I once did, that the image is a still from Leni Riefenstahl's grand two-part documentary film *Olympia* (1938), which is an unsurpassed aesthetic achievement and an unfortunate glorification of Adolf Hitler. (The film was released, with much fanfare, on the Führer's forty-ninth birthday.) My assumption was wrong. The famous image appeared in a two-volume book of photographs published by the German tobacco company Reemtsma, which purchased rights to the image from the photographic firm Presse Bild Zentrale Berlin. (The photographer's identity is unknown.) Smokers who purchased Reemtsma cigarettes were given photographs to paste into the two-volume book with which the firm celebrated the 1936 games. (That Philipp F. Reemtsma, who headed the firm, had good relations with Hermann Göring may explain why Reemtsma rather than some more prestigious firm received permission to publish the Olympic book.)

The text and photograph identify the fencers. The winner was Ilona Elek (Hungary); the silver medalist was Helene Mayer (Germany); the bronze went to Ellen Preis (Austria). So far so good, but what did it signify that Mayer has her hand raised in the *Hitler salute*? It's a long story.

Mayer was born in Offenbach am Main, December 20, 1910, the daughter of a German Jewish physician, Ludwig Karl Mayer, and a Lutheran mother, whose maiden name was Anna Bertha Becker. Although her birth certificate listed her as an *Israelite*, there was, as historian Gertrud Pfister notes, "no evidence that she considered [Jewishness] an important aspect of her identity."[1]

There is, however, an abundance of evidence about Mayer's identity as an athlete. She was a fencer. At the age of fourteen she placed second in the national fencing championship. From 1925 to 1930, she was national champion in foils. At the 1928 Olympics in Amsterdam, she won gold. Tall, blue-eyed, blond, she became an iconic figure of the German sports world, quite literally a poster child for modern German womanhood. For admirers who wanted more than a poster, there were statuettes designed by the sculptor Lilli Wislicenus-Finzelberg.

Hoping for a career in the diplomatic corps, Mayer studied in Frankfurt, Paris, and then, with a stipend from the German Academic Exchange Service, in California. While still abroad, she participated as a member of the German team in the 1932 Los Angeles Olympics. The journalist Les Carpenter has explained her disappointing fifth-place finish by the fact that she "found out two hours before her final matches that her boyfriend back in Germany had died in a military training mission."[2]

After the 1932 games she decided to remain in the United States to study at Scripps College and then at the University of California, Berkeley. After graduation, she taught German at Mills College and then at San Francisco City College. And she fenced. Between 1934 and 1942 she won the American championship eight times.[3]

In 1935, acting on the basis of the anti-Semitic Nuremberg laws, the Nazi regime stripped her of her German citizenship and cancelled her stipend. How did it happen that, one year later, she was a member of the German Olympic team? It came about, paradoxically, because there was great concern in the International Olympic Committee (IOC) that German Jews should not be barred from the national team, which would, of course, have been blatantly contrary to the Olympic Charter. As early as June 7, 1933, three years before the games, when the IOC met in Vienna for its annual session, the IOC's president, the Belgian aristocrat Henri de Baillet-Latour, expressed his personal concern about the blatant contradiction. Two of the IOC's three American members, Charles H. Sherrill and William May Garland, aggressively questioned two of their German colleagues, Theodor Lewald and Karl Ritter von Halt, about the eligibility of German Jews for their national Olympic team. Lewald and von Halt were, in some respects, an unlikely pair. Lewald was the son of a Jew who had converted to Christianity. Von Halt, although troubled by Hitler's rabid anti-Semitism, had joined the National Socialist (i.e., Nazi) party, on May 1, less than six weeks before the Vienna meeting. Lewald and von Halt consulted the Reich Ministry for Public Enlightenment and Propaganda by telephone and were able to procure a written guarantee that German Jews would, in principle, be allowed to compete for the team.[4]

Sherrill and Garland were delighted by their success, but there were many skeptics within and beyond the IOC who doubted the honesty of Nazi promises. Skepticism increased when individual German Jews were expelled from all nondenominational sports clubs. The Offenbach Fencing Club, which had for years basked in the reflected glory of its most successful fencer, expelled her in April 1933, two months before the IOC's Vienna meeting. Skepticism increased even more when all Jewish clubs were expelled from the nation's sports federations. Skepticism about the Reich Ministry honoring its pledge became out-and-out undisguised disbelief when all of Germany's individual sports federations, even those that had enthusiastically welcomed Hitler's seizure of power, were themselves dissolved and replaced with a single Nazi-controlled sports federation under the leadership of *Reichssportführer* Hans von Tschammer und Osten.[5]

One of the most outspoken skeptics was Gustavus Towne Kirby, an influential member of the American Olympic Committee (AOC). As early as the organization's November 1933 convention, Kirby offered a resolution that threatened a U.S. boycott of the games unless German Jews were allowed in fact as well as theory to "train, prepare for, and participate in the Olympic Games of 1936." Despite the fierce opposition of Avery Brundage, who had followed General Douglas MacArthur as president of the AOC, an amended, somewhat milder version of the resolution passed.[6]

It did nothing to dissuade the Nazi government from its determination to field an entirely Aryan team. As evidence that the German government was acting in bad faith became indisputable, an international boycott movement, which was especially strong in the United States, arose. Von Tschammer und Osten attempted to disarm the boycotters with a statement that Jews were not barred from German sports clubs by any official *governmental* decree, but the obvious sophistry of this distinction was too much even for Brundage. He wrote to Baillet-Latour, "The German authorities have displayed a singular lack of astuteness . . . Every news dispatch from Germany seems to indicate that the Hitlerites do not intend to live up to the pledges given the IOC at Vienna."[7]

When the IOC met in Athens on May 15, 1934, Garland once again pressed the German members for assurances that Jews really would be allowed to try out for the team. Lewald and von Halt reiterated the pledge given a year earlier: "Non-Aryan" athletes would, indeed, be allowed to compete for Germany if they were qualified.[8]

The IOC was satisfied, but the AOC was not. Meeting on June 14, 1934, the organization voted to postpone acceptance of the official German invitation until Brundage returned from a fact-finding European tour. Brundage sailed to Germany and questioned Jewish sports officials—in the presence of Nazi officials—and consulted with his close friend Carl Diem, who was then acting as the organizing committee's secretary. Citing the Jewish officials' obviously coerced testimony and on his friend's word of honor, Brundage found what he very much wanted to find. He returned to the United States and reported to the AOC that the Nazi government was, indeed, faithfully fulfilling its pledge, which, of course, it was not. The committee, naively accepting Brundage's report, voted unanimously to accept the invitation.[9]

This was by no means the end of the controversy. The international boycott movement, citing the mounting evidence of Nazi duplicity, intensified its pressure. In November 1935, the boycotters won the support of Ernest Lee Jahncke, the third American member of the IOC. In an open letter to Baillet-Latour, he pointed out, quite correctly, that the Nazis had been "lavish with their promises" but "stingy" when it came to fulfillment of them. Jahncke had an impolitic request: that Baillet-Latour take his place in the history of the Olympics at the side of the games' founder, Pierre de Coubertin, "instead of Hitler."[10] Baillet-Latour's response was to ask for Jahncke's resignation and, when Jahncke refused, to expel him from the IOC. (At the IOC's July 1936 meeting, the day before the opening of the Berlin games, Brundage was elected to the committee explicitly as "en replacement de M. Lee Jahncke.")[11]

Jahncke's public appeal was in vain. In the United States, the debate raged until December 1935, when the bitterly divided AOC met in New York and voted by fifty-eight and a quarter to fifty-five and a quarter to send an American team to Berlin.[12]

The American team, which included a number of Jews, competed in the games and was almost as successful as the German team—which had no Jews other than Mayer. Gretel Bergmann, one of Germany's best high jumpers, had been invited by Von Tschammer und Osten to train for the Olympics. In June 1936, she tied the national record, clearing the bar at 1.6 meters, four centimeters better than her Aryan rival Elfriede Kaun. Bergmann was nonetheless dropped from the team. Von Tsammer and Osten gave two weak if not laughable reasons for his action. Bergmann's sports club, Stuttgarter Schild, was not a member of the national track-and-field federation (from which it had been barred by Nazi fiat) and her performance was "inadequate" (which it obviously was not).

This totally unpersuasive bad faith explanation was met, quite properly, with utter disbelief. The undeniable revelation of the Nazi regime's dishonesty was an embarrassment. How could Berlin claim to have honored the regime's repeated pledges if there were no Jews on the team? The German response was to proclaim that Helene Mayer was, after all, a Jew. There is some evidence that she had taken the initiative and offered herself as proof that Germany was following IOC rules. It was reported, by a not very reliable source, that she "yearned for her rebirth as an authentic German."[13] We do know that, after the passage of the infamous Nuremberg Laws of September 1935, which stripped German Jews of their citizenship, Mayer had questioned Von Tsammer und Osten about her status under German law and that he had replied, in December 1935, that nothing stood in the way of her participation. Did Von Tschammer und Osten go beyond this statement to request that she return to Germany and compete at the games? Did he threaten her or her family if she were to refuse to give him this much-needed opportunity to claim that Germany had, despite appearances, lived up to its pledge? We are not privy to his thoughts, nor to hers. When questioned by the *New York Times* in February 1936, she replied merely that she had received a personal invitation from Von Tschammer und Osten. Was that an apology or a boast? There is no way of knowing, but there she is, in the photograph, her arm stretched in the Nazi salute, standing next to Ilona Elek and Ellen Preis, both of whom, like Mayer, had one parent who was a Jew and another who was not. What she thought at that moment, what she felt at that moment, will never be known.

Helene Mayer remained in the United States for the remainder of the years of Nazi rule, and even became a United States citizen, but she returned to Germany in 1952 and married Baron Erwin Falkner von Sonnenburg, who was, to the best of my knowledge, not Jewish. She died October 10, 1953, at the age of forty-three.[14]

NOTES

1. Gertrud Pfister, "Mayer, Helene," in *International Encyclopedia of Women and Sports*, Vol. 2, ed. Karen Christensen, Allen Guttmann, and Gertrud Pfister (New York: Macmillan Reference USA, 2001), 710–711.

2. Les Carpenter, "Nazi Germany's Jewish Champion: The Mystery of Helene Mayer Endures," *Guardian*, July 28, 2016, https://www.theguardian.com/sport/2016/jul/28/helene-mayer-nazi-germanys-jewish-champion-fencer.

3. "Helene Mayer, 43, Fencing Star, Dies," *New York Times*, October 16, 1953, 27.

4. Allen Guttmann, *The Games Must Go On: Avery Brundage and the Olympic Movement* (New York: Columbia University Press, 1984), 66.

5. For reliable information on Von Tshammer und Osten, see Dieter Steinhöfer, *Hans von Tschammer und Osten* (Berlin: Bartels & Wernitz, 1973).

6. Avery Brundage Collection, 1908–82, University of Illinois Archives, box 28. Although not directly relevant to the photograph, it is worth noting that Brundage, who became president of the IOC in 1952, proclaimed at the 1972 Munich games, during which Palestinian terrorists murdered eleven Israeli athletes, that "the games must go on."

7. Avery Brundage to Henri de Baillet-Latour, December 28, 1933, Avery Brundage Collection, box 42.

8. Guttmann, *The Games Must Go On*, 68.

9. Guttmann, *The Games Must Go On*, 68–70.

10. "Jahncke Asks Ban of Olympic Games," *New York Times*, November 27, 1935, 2.

11. International Olympic Committee, *Procès-Verbale de la 35ième Session du Comité International Olympique*, 2 (IOC archives).

12. Guttmann, *The Games Must Go On*, 74.

13. Milly Mogulof, *Foiled, Hitler's Jewish Olympian: The Helene Mayer Story* (Oakland: RDR Books, 2002), 159.

14. "Helene Mayer, 43, Fencing Star, Dies."

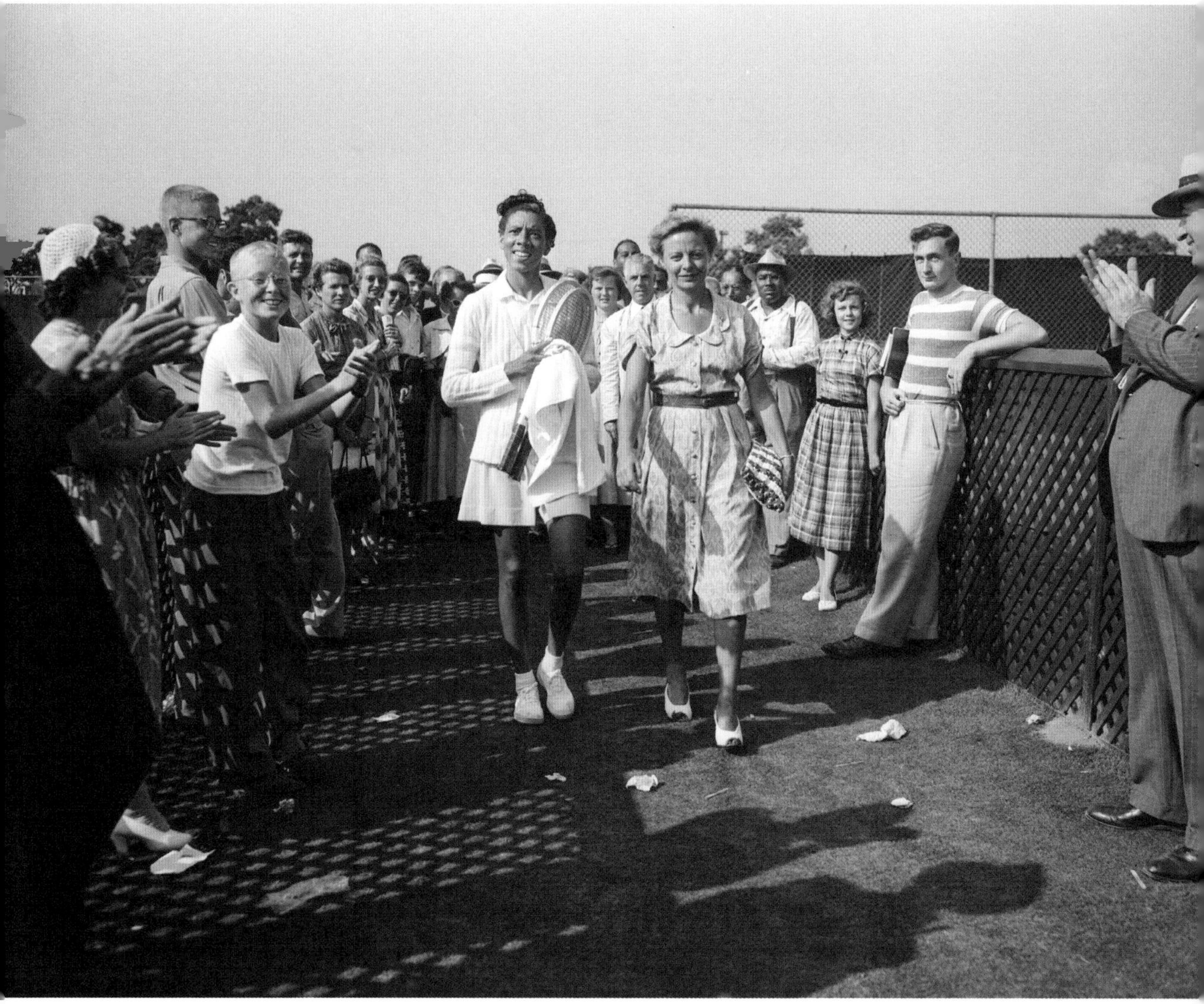

6

THE ODD COUPLE

Althea Gibson and Alice Marble, Forest Hills, 1950

ASHLEY BROWN

On Monday, August 28, 1950, Curt Gunther, a photographer for Manhattan's Keystone Pictures, packed his camera and headed to the West Side Tennis Club, an American sports shrine, in Forest Hills, New York, searching for a riveting moment. In a career that would span five decades, Gunther, a German émigré, photographed some of the most influential people in American popular culture—Marilyn Monroe, Elvis Presley, Frank Sinatra, and, most famously, the Beatles. He was the photographer the band chose to document its first North American tour in 1964. But that was still years away. This was opening day of the most prestigious tennis tournament in America, the National Championships of the United States Lawn Tennis Association (USLTA), the sport's governing body. But it was no ordinary opening day at Forest Hills, the tournament's byname. At 1 P.M. Althea Gibson, a twenty-three-year-old sophomore at Florida Agricultural and Mechanical College, was to make her tournament debut. Gibson was the four-time winner (1947–1950) of the National Women's Singles Championship of the American Tennis Association (ATA), the USLTA's Black counterpart. Since the first U.S. Nationals in 1881, the USLTA had not permitted Black players to compete for America's outdoor tennis title.[1]

The tournament committee designated court no. 14, a playing ground as nondescript as Barbara Knapp, Gibson's overmatched opponent, for the event. The court was "far out in the 'country,'" wrote Al Laney of the *New York Herald Tribune*, and its seating capacity was unsuited for sportive business sixty-nine years in the making. Focused on the match, not its location, Gibson defeated Knapp, 6–2, 6–2, despite the distractions of photographers who occupied the tennis court for the first two games and curiosity seekers who, unable to get seats, peered over the surrounding fence.[2]

Alice Marble did get a seat. Marble, four-time winner of the women's singles title at Forest Hills between 1936 and 1940 and the Wimbledon champion of 1939, had gone to bat for Gibson weeks earlier, and caused a racket. In March, Gibson had finished second in the National Indoor Tennis Championships. *Life* magazine wrote: "Her performance posed a question for tennis moguls: would she be the first Negro to play in the outdoor championship at Forest Hills next August?"[3] Played on grass, Forest Hills was, in the words of the USLTA executive secretary, "our real championship."[4] Focused on results, not race, some tennis experts believed that Gibson should play there. USLTA leaders—all of whom were white—disagreed.[5] ATA leaders negotiated with USLTA heads to little avail. Believing that racism was thwarting Gibson, Marble, a columnist for *American Lawn Tennis*, decided to publicize the injustice.

Published on July 1, "A Vital Issue" made Gibson's longshot bid a cause célèbre and was covered in newspapers and magazines nationwide. The USLTA soon invited Gibson to compete at Forest Hills. Marble had closed her stirring editorial with a pledge worthy of Tom Joad from *The Grapes of Wrath*: "I will be glad to help Althea Gibson in any way I can . . . If I can give her an iota more of confidence by rooting my heart out from the gallery, she can take my word for it: I'll be there."[6] When the day came, Marble was indeed there and, pleased by Gibson's victory, she moved to congratulate her.[7]

Seeing his shot, Gunther moved too. Camera poised, he clicked away as Gibson and Marble left the tennis court trailed by a throng that included Gibson supporters. Gunther had found his riveting, historic shot: a rich and rare image of women—Black and white—as leaders, allies, and accomplices in the male-dominated saga of American sports integration, showing the erosion of the color barrier in an elite sport.[8]

The figures seen in the most famous images of interracial sports photography during the first half of the twentieth century belong to men in popular sports. The history of sports as training and proving grounds for masculinity and as symbolic sites where equality and superiority are demonstrated is apparent in a sample montage. Remember Jack Johnson lying on the canvas and shielding his eyes from the bright, hot Havana sun in 1915 as Jess Willard, a Great White Hope, stalks over him, satisfied that he has won the world heavyweight boxing championship, thereby regaining a symbolic mantle of white supremacy that Johnson had held since 1908. Consider Joe Louis and Max Schmeling together in and out of the boxing ring in 1936 and again in 1938 as World War II loomed. Think of Larry Doby and Steve Gromek embracing after Cleveland's victory in the 1948 World Series. Recall any picture of Jackie Robinson and Branch Rickey, player and president, respectively, of the Brooklyn Dodgers, and catalysts for African Americans' entry into Major League Baseball in 1947 and, eventually, all other sports leagues.

Gibson credited Robinson with advancing her tennis career. "If he hadn't paved the way, I probably never would have got my chance," she wrote in her autobiography, *I Always Wanted to Be Somebody* (1958). In 1949, Gibson was the first Black woman to enter the National Indoor Tennis Championships, a year after the admittance of Reginald Weir, a Black man. To Gibson, Major League Baseball's racial integration signaled that "a great social change was in the making in this country."[9]

Yet social change was slow in amateur tennis. Unlike professional sports, amateur athletics were based on the concepts of honor and social equality. A contest between Black and white amateurs implied that the competitors were equals, an idea rejected by segregationists.[10]

Gunther's photograph shows an integrated crowd, but this was not the norm in tennis. Usually, racially mixed galleries and brackets were seen only when African Americans were in charge or in some tournaments played on public tennis courts outside the South. Unlike the USLTA, the ATA had a reputation for welcoming players and spectators regardless of race. Anyone could join ATA clubs and enter the association's tournaments. Gibson won her first tournament, a junior event, in 1942, by defeating a white opponent, Nina Irwin, at New York's Cosmopolitan Tennis Club, a Black sports sanctum that had white members and hosted white professionals for exhibition matches on its courts. In 1944, Marble and Mary Hardwick, a popular English player, played at the Cosmopolitan as Gibson, sixteen, watched.[11]

Nationwide, white-operated country, golf, and tennis clubs, including the West Side Tennis Club, barred African Americans. The faulty white supremacist logic that Black people were innately gauche and unsuited for high-toned places guided the clubs' and the USLTA's practices.[12] The conservatively attired, feminine-presenting Gibson seen in Gunther's picture was the product of ten years' worth of efforts by middle- and upper-class

Black mentors to teach her to fit the standards of ladylikeness expected of women tennis players. Some of these guides are visible in other pictures taken that day. Fred Johnson, the Cosmopolitan's teaching professional, walked a few paces behind Gibson, the tomboyish oldest daughter of a Harlem garage worker, Daniel, and his wife, Annie. The family had migrated from rural South Carolina early in the Great Depression. Believing that she showed athletic promise, a group of Cosmopolitan members paid Gibson's membership dues and for her tennis lessons. Johnson "tried to help me improve my personal ways," including "my arrogant attitude," Gibson remembered.[13] Rhoda Smith, a socialite, stood behind Johnson. Smith bought tennis apparel for Gibson and instructed her in tennis etiquette, a strange concept to Gibson, who got into fistfights on Harlem's streets and loved basketball, football, and boxing.[14]

The two men most responsible for Gibson's presence at Forest Hills are absent from Gunther's picture, though they had watched the match from the stands. Beginning in 1946—the year the National Football League reintegrated and Robinson played his first season with a Dodgers' farm team—Hubert A. Eaton of Wilmington, North Carolina, and Robert Walter Johnson of Lynchburg, Virginia, began their years-long sponsorship of Gibson. Eaton and Johnson, doctors, tennis enthusiasts, and believers in social justice, thought that with gender-based modifications, Gibson could blaze trails for other Black tennis players. Her preference for pants and disinterest in traditional feminine norms, her occasionally combative personality, especially after losing, and a willingness to fight when offended risked perpetuating stereotypes of Black women. The doctors' challenge was to mold Gibson into an embodiment of middle-class ladyhood that could counter white supremacist ideas about African Americans.[15]

Dr. Eaton and Dr. Johnson coached Gibson on their respective backyard tennis courts and oversaw her aesthetic transformation. "She didn't know how to dress or anything," Dr. Johnson said later. "We tried to show her that."[16] He hid Gibson's pants, forcing her to wear only skirts and dresses when she visited his home in the summer. Dr. Eaton endeavored "to show Althea how to be a lady on the court," emphasizing the placidity, regardless of victory or defeat, expected in tennis.[17] His wife, Celeste, bought dresses for Gibson, taught her to apply makeup, and brought her to a local salon to have her hair straightened. Gibson "was a fine player, but she had too many rough edges to go into those tennis clubs," Dr. Eaton recalled.[18]

Edges softened, Gibson debuted at Forest Hills and earned praise in the Black press for clearing the braided barriers of race, class, and gender that guarded the tennis bastion. Gibson "struck a blow for democracy" in the "snooty precincts of country clubs and exclusive sports associations throughout the land," wrote the *Chicago Defender*.[19] *Ebony* cheered her for "proving that Negro women today deserve a place in the sports spotlight right alongside Jackie Robinson and Joe Louis."[20]

Gibson stood there alone. Neither her parents nor any other members of her family saw her compete that August day. Buddy Walker was there, walking several steps behind Marble after the tennis match. Walker had given Gibson her first tennis rackets and his social connections helped her get the Cosmopolitan membership. Walker had encouraged the streetwise Gibson to play tennis to "meet a better class of people."[21] Gibson's family seemed not to make the cut.

In the picture, Gibson and Marble stride shoulder to shoulder like soldiers leaving a battle victorious. "Have courage. You're just like the rest of us," Marble told Gibson.[22] Few things in American culture vouched for that. Hollywood depicted Black women as white women's maids, tending to the standards of beauty and leisure denied women of African descent. In wartime, white women plant workers had refused to share spaces, including restrooms, with Black women. Weeks after Gibson won Wimbledon and Forest Hills in 1957 (she successfully defended both titles in 1958, and she had won the French national title in 1956), a photographer in Arkansas captured a defining image of the Civil Rights Movement: Elizabeth Eckford, a member of the Little Rock Nine, walking toward Central High School as Hazel Bryan, her face contorted by hate, yells at her. Bryan, white, did not see Eckford, Black, as her equal. Bryan's animus resonated with writer Angelina Weld Grimke's assertion that white women were "about the worst enemies with which the colored race has to contend."[23]

Gunther's picture has two white allies. Marble is foremost. She applied her reputation as one of the most respected women in America, earned through her five Grand Slams and her voluntarism during World War II, to advocate for Gibson. And, unlike Branch Rickey and other white executives who profited from sports integration, Marble had nothing material to gain by standing up for what was right. Mary Hardwick is the other ally. Wearing sunglasses and an argyle-printed dress, she stands on the left. Hardwick played in several ATA exhibitions, including one with Gibson in 1947. She believed that African Americans should be permitted to play in the four majors before Germany and Japan reentered the Davis Cup after the war. With her husband, Charles Hare, she worked behind the scenes in 1950 to get Gibson an invitation to the National Clay Courts Championship in

Chicago, a qualifier for Forest Hills. Later, Hardwick coached a promising Black junior, Lorraine Williams.[24]

Gunther's picture, a visual artifact of the middle twentieth century, draws our attention to the discourse of social justice in the twenty-first. Marble and Hardwick were white allies with white privilege. Both women benefited from Jim Crow, their white skins the first requisite for entering tennis tournaments and clubs. Some in the Black press hailed Marble as a "discrimination fighter" after she supported Gibson.[25] Yet to Lester Granger, a leader of the National Urban League, Marble's salvo was "about fifteen years late."[26] As a teenager and young adult from a working-class family, Marble had played tennis with men and boys of Chinese, Japanese, and Filipino descent at San Francisco's public Golden Gate Park, but she had not challenged segregation during her amateur career. Granger, rightly, warned against seeing Marble as a white savior.[27]

Still, Marble counts as a white accomplice. Accomplices share in the price paid for challenging discrimination. After "A Vital Issue" appeared, Marble faced ostracism. "People who had called me 'Champ' since 1938 suddenly remembered that I was 'Miss Marble,'" she wrote. "People who had taken ostentatious advantage of our kissing acquaintance gave me a chilly handshake or failed to notice my acquaintance, or glared."[28] Some players that Marble had coached "turn[ed] their backs" on her.[29] Marble kept the "reactions" in perspective: "I was never so sorry that I brought up the issue" and, while "it was rather a rough time for me . . . [it was] nothing compared to that for Althea Gibson," who endured racism and sexism throughout her tennis and, later, her golf career.[30]

The 2020s have generated a montage that might be called "White Women Behaving Badly," with so-called Karens being recorded treating African Americans with hostility and malice. For decades, writers have interrogated relations between Black and white women. Sports history is hard-pressed for stories of progressive female pairs like Gibson and Marble, who remained acquainted until the latter's death. Gunther's photograph and our contemporary moment beg for more.

NOTES

1. Althea Gibson, *I Always Wanted to Be Somebody*, ed. Ed Fitzgerald (New York: Harper and Row, Publishers, 1958), 70.

2. Al Laney, "McNeil Upsets McGregor in National Tennis; Louise Brough, Althea Gibson Gain," *New York Herald Tribune*, August 29, 1950, 24; Ted Poston,

"The Story of Althea Gibson: Article V," *New York Post Daily Magazine*, August 30, 1957, M2.

3. "New Tennis Threat," *Life*, April 3, 1950, 32.

4. Harold Rosenthal, "National Tennis Accepts Entry of First Negro in Its History," *New York Herald Tribune*, March 9, 1948, 27.

5. Alice Marble, "A Vital Issue," *American Lawn Tennis*, July 1, 1950, 14; Al Laney, "Don McNeil, Miss Chaffee Win Net Titles," *New York Herald Tribune*, March 26, 1950, B1; "Althea Gibson: Tomboyish Coed Startles Tennis World with Natural Ability on Court," *Ebony*, November 1950, 99.

6. Marble, "A Vital Issue," 14.

7. Alice Marble, "As I See It: Open Letter to Althea Gibson," *American Lawn Tennis*, November 1950, 19.

8. Curt Gunther for Keystone Pictures, "Championed by a Champion," *Pittsburgh Courier*, September 2, 1950, 16.

9. Fred Hawthorne, "Gonzales Beats Schnaar in Net Match, 6–3, 6–2," *New York Herald Tribune*, March 20, 1949, B3; Gibson, *I Always Wanted to Be Somebody*, 158, 54.

10. Furman Bisher, "What about the Negro Athlete in the South?" *Sport*, May 1956, 88.

11. Al Laney, "Views of Sport: Negroes Revive Title Tennis Next Week," *New York Herald Tribune*, August 12, 1944, 13A; Bertram L. Baker, Letter to the Editor, *American Lawn Tennis*, November 1950, 3; Gibson, *I Always Wanted to Be Somebody*, 32, 31; "American TA Championships," *American Lawn Tennis*, November 1944, 28–29.

12. Kate Masur, "Color Was a Bar to the Entrance: African American Activism and the Question of Social Equality in Lincoln's White House," *American Quarterly* 69, no. 3 (March 2017): 2; Philip Benjamin, "Stark Acts to Force Forest Hills to Drop Bias or Cup Matches," *New York Times*, July 11, 1959, 1.

13. Gibson, *I Always Wanted to Be Somebody*, 1–28.

14. Gibson, *I Always Wanted to Be Somebody*, 30–31, 11–14; Ted Poston, "The Althea Gibson Story: Article I," *New York Post Daily Magazine*, August 26, 1957, M2.

15. For more on Gibson and reactions to her gender performativity, see Ashley Brown, "'Uncomplimentary Things': Tennis Player Althea Gibson, Sexism, Homophobia, and Anti-Queerness in the Black Media," *Journal of African American History* 106, no. 2 (Spring 2021): 249–277.

16. Halsey Melone, "Physician Aids Negro Net Growth, Takes Young Players into His Home," *Miami Herald*, April 13, 1969, 5-F.

17. Serrell Hillman, "That Gibson Girl," *Time*, August 26, 1957, 46.

18. Crispin Y. Campbell, "Althea Gibson Legend Lives On," *Biloxi Sun Herald* (Biloxi, Mississippi), May 1, 1988, D3.

19. Editorial, "All Honors for Althea," *Chicago Defender*, September 16, 1950, 6.

20. "Althea Gibson: Tomboyish Coed Startles Tennis World with Natural Ability on Court," 96.

21. Gibson, *I Always Wanted to Be Somebody*, 27.

22. *This Is Your* Life, Tribute to Alice Marble, episode 75, February 3, 1954, Revised Television Script, Container 11, Folder 4, Ralph Edwards Productions Radio and Television Scripts, Manuscript Division, Library of Congress, Washington, DC.

23. Quoted in Kathy A. Perkins and Judith L. Stephens, eds., *Strange Fruit: Plays on Lynching by American Women* (Bloomington: Indiana University Press, 1998), 23.

24. Ashley Brown, "Swinging for the State Department: American Women Tennis Players in Diplomatic Goodwill Tours, 1941–1959," *Journal of Sport History* 42 (Fall 2015): 292–295; Fay Young, "Through the Years," *Chicago Defender,* August 30, 1947, 11; "Bouncing Around," *American Lawn Tennis,* August 1, 1949, 24; "The New Gibson Girl," *Sports Illustrated,* July 2, 1956, 60; "Girl Tennis Star," *Ebony,* June 1952, 41.

25. Alvin Moses, "Beating the Gun: Salute to Alice Marble," *Philadelphia Tribune,* September 5, 1950, 11.

26. Lester B. Granger, "Althea Gibson Leads the Way," *New York Amsterdam News,* August 5, 1950, 6.

27. Alice Marble, *The Road to Wimbledon* (London: W. H. Allen, 1946), 47.

28. Marble, "An Open Letter to Althea Gibson," 19.

29. Alice Marble, "The Net Set: Althea Gibson Paved the Way," *Palm Desert Post,* September 21, 1972, 7.

30. Marble, "The Net Set: Althea Gibson Paved the Way."

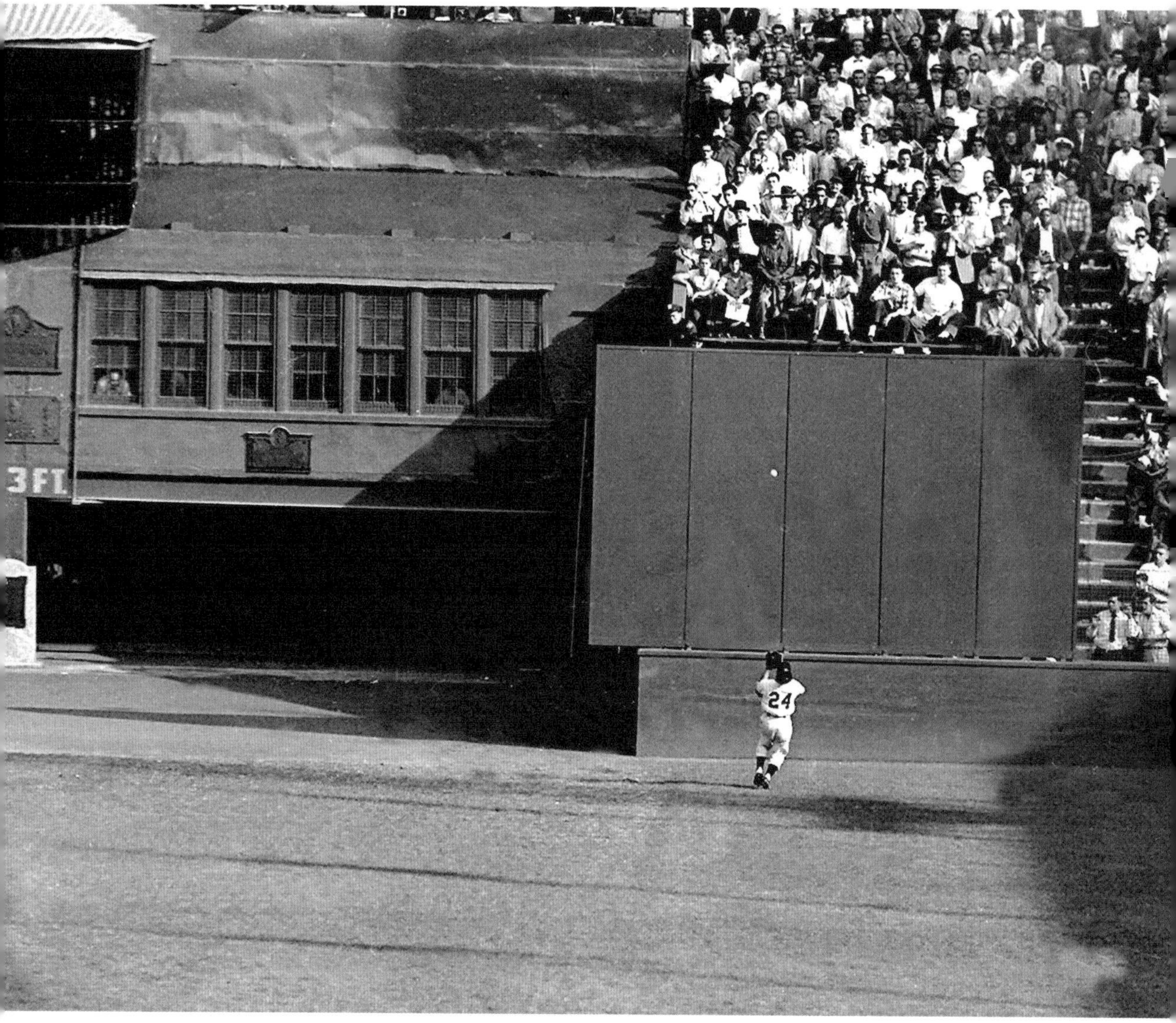
3 FT.
24

7

WILLIE MAYS AND THE CATCH HEARD 'ROUND THE WORLD

GEORGE GMELCH AND HOWARD J. DE NIKE

In the eighth inning of the first game of the 1954 World Series between the Cleveland Indians and the New York Giants, the score tied 2–2, NBC broadcaster Jack Brickhouse described the action: "There's a long drive, way back in centerfield . . . way back, back! . . . It is . . . oh, what a catch by Mays! . . . Willie Mays just brought this crowd to its feet with a catch which must have been an optical illusion to a lot of people. Boy! I didn't think he had a chance to catch it when it was hit."[1]

The image of Mays making the over-the-shoulder catch, preserved by *New York Daily News* photographer Frank Hurley, is still familiar to many baseball fans nearly seven decades later.[2] Its longevity can be attributed to Mays's spectacular catch, followed by an equally spectacular throw, and to his remarkable career. Other circumstances contributed to the image's endurance in the consciousness of so many people: the game was played in the ancient Polo Grounds, which was known for the extraordinary dimensions of its outfield, and the closely fought game was won in extra innings by the underdog Giants, beginning their sweep of the powerful Indians.

Unlike many of the images examined in this book, we have an in-depth eyewitness account of the setting, the people, and the action behind the play from writer, journalist, and longtime baseball fan and bleacherite Arnold Hano. In his acclaimed book, *A Day in the Bleachers* (1955), Hano describes his early morning arrival at the ballpark, his interactions with people in the crowd, the teams' batting and infield practice, and then the game with its inning-by-inning strategies and heroics, and, above all, the most talked about catch in baseball history. Other writers, including Willie Mays's biographers, have provided their own stories about the game and the significance and lasting impact of the catch.

The Stage

In the 1950s, World Series games were played during the day. Hano traveled to the ballpark by subway, arriving with scores of other early morning fans. Some fans had even arrived the evening before, waiting through the night to be sure of entry when the bleacher gates opened at 9 A.M. The dilapidated and usually ill-maintained Polo Grounds was on this day, "swept, scrubbed and decked in bunting, a dowager in finery."[3]

By game time, the crowd had reached capacity with 52,751 people. Among them were Hollywood stars Jackie Gleason, Danny Kaye, and Lorraine Day, who was accompanied by Spencer Tracy. Men wore sports coats and ties; women wore dresses and pearls. "The Polo Grounds was a place to see and to be seen and call friendly greetings," reported the *New York Herald Tribune*.[4] We learn from Hano that a popular band performed in centerfield during practice, featuring Latin rhythms and a "shimmying female vocalist."[5]

The unique ballpark—that great green horseshoe of a stadium called the Polo Grounds—is an important part of this story. Shaped like a bathtub and hosting football and soccer games as well as baseball, the Polo Grounds was noted for its very short distances to left and right fields and its mammoth distance to centerfield. The right field fence at the foul line was only 257 feet from home plate, the shortest distance in either league, while the centerfield wall was 483 feet from home, by far the longest of any baseball park. These dimensions yielded pop fly home runs and tape measure outs. Only four players ever managed to hit a home run over the centerfield barrier after the park's reconstruction in 1923.[6] In the photograph of Mays's catch, a runway leading to the clubhouse is visible to the left of the bleachers; further to the left is the 483-foot marker. The clubhouse windows, with a man looking out, is also visible to the right of the marker. The wacky ground rules of the Polo Grounds stipulated that if a ball went through an open window in the clubhouse, it was a ground rule double, rather than a home run. The rule was never tested since no ball ever landed there.

The Polo Grounds was the scene of other notable moments in baseball history before Mays's famous catch. Best known is Bobby Thomson's walk-off home run, popularly known as "The Shot Heard 'Round the World," that decided the 1951 National League pennant playoff series between the Giants and their crosstown rival Brooklyn Dodgers. The Polo Grounds was also the tragic setting of the only fatal injury incurred by a player during a Major League Baseball game; on August 16, 1920, Indians shortstop Ray Chapman was hit in the head by a pitch thrown by the Yankees' Carl Mays. It was also the place of arguably the game's biggest gaffe when Fred Merkle failed to touch second base in a premature celebration that cost the Giants the 1908 pennant.[7]

The Crowd

According to Hano, the crowd that day was "quiet, well-behaved," with Giants fans demonstrating no enmity towards the Indians or their fans. "They did not hate them, for instance, the way they hated the Dodgers or the Yankees."[8] Giants fans, observed Hano, were "intelligent, polite, yet loyal spectators. Perhaps because they love baseball even more than they do the Giants."[9] Hano also attributed the quietness of the crowd, which some reporters puzzled over in the following day's papers, to the game's tight pitchers' duel.

The Contestants

The talented Cleveland Indians came to the Series with a season record of 111–43, which was then the all-time single-season record for winning percentage (.721) by an American League team. Twice that season they had eleven-game winning streaks. The bookmaking odds heavily favored the Indians at seventeen to ten. The betting was brisk with big bidders putting their money on the Indians, while small bettors—mostly Giants fans—wagered on the Giants.[10] Two of the star pitchers for the Indians were Bob Feller and Bob Lemon, names still known to some fans. The Indians' star hitter was the brawny Vic Wertz, who had started the season with the Baltimore Orioles. He was hitting just .202 for the Orioles before he was traded to Cleveland. But as the Indians starting first baseman, Wertz found his stroke, hitting .275 and slugging .478 during the season while anchoring the middle of the Indians batting order. He hit .500 in the World Series.

The underdog Giants, notes Hano, "had fantastic luck" all season.[11] Lucky or not, the Giants had stars of their own in Mays, Monte Irvin, Dusty Rhodes, Alvin Dark, Hank Thompson, and Don Mueller. Mays led the National League, batting .345. Hano describes him as "the finest ballplayer [in] the National League . . . [with] astonishing ability to get rid of the ball quickly, he seems a better centerfielder than Joe DiMaggio, who threw on a lower trajectory but who did not possess the speed of foot or hand that are Mays'."[12]

Twenty-three years old in 1954, Mays had grown up in Alabama. Both his parents were gifted athletes: his mother was a champion sprinter and his father played on all-Black, semi-pro teams in the segregated South. Willie broke into professional baseball at age sixteen, playing for the Birmingham Black Barons in the Negro Southern League. The day he graduated from high school, he was signed by the New York Giants, and over the next two years he quickly advanced through its minor league system. He was just twenty years old when he was called up to join the big-league Giants in 1951. Within a few years, some sportswriters proclaimed Mays the greatest centerfielder in baseball.[13]

The Catch

By the seventh inning, the game had already lasted nearly two hours, which was long for an era when fewer pitching changes made games much shorter than they are today. The sun hovered over the grandstand behind first base, casting shadows past the right-field foul line as the Indians went down in order, and the Giants failed to score as well. Going into the eighth inning the score remained knotted at 2–2; Cleveland had been shut out since the first inning. It seemed likely that the next team to score would win the game.

In the top of the eighth inning, Giants' starting pitcher Sal Maglie walked the Indians leadoff hitter Larry Doby. Then third baseman Al Rosen singled, putting runners on first and second. The Giants manager Leo Durocher summoned left-handed relief pitcher Don Liddle to pitch to Vic Wertz, who already had three hits in the game. Wertz worked the count to two and one before driving the ball to deep center field. Hano, sitting in the right-field bleachers, wrote that the ball was hit "about as hard as I have ever seen a ball hit, on a high line to dead center field."[14] Almost immediately, "Mays was turned full around, head down, running as hard as he could, straight toward the runway between the two bleachers sections."[15] Wertz later said in an interview, "I don't think I ever hit a ball better or harder than that one."[16]

This is how Mays described the play to his biographer James S. Hirsch:

> I'm playing a shallow centerfield. It's the eighth inning, score is tied, and I don't want Larry Doby scoring from second base. One run could be the ball game. The ball game could be the Series. You never know.
>
> Wertz hits it. A solid sound. I learn a lot from the sound of the ball on the bat. Always did. I could tell from the sound whether to come in or go back. This time I'm going back, a long way back, but there is never any doubt in my mind. I am going to catch this ball. I turn and run for the bleachers. But I got it. Maybe you didn't know that, but I knew I'd catch this ball.
>
> But that wasn't the problem. The problem was Larry Doby on second base. On a deep fly to center field at the Polo Grounds, a runner could score all the way from second. I've done that myself and more than once. So if I make the catch, which I will, and Larry scores from second, they still get the run that puts them ahead.
>
> All the time I'm running back, I'm thinking, "Willie, you've got to get this ball back to the infield."
>
> I run 50 or 75 yards—right to the warning track—and I take the ball a little over my left shoulder.[17]

In most retellings of the play, what Mays does after the catch is as extraordinary as the catch itself. As Hano describes it, Mays "whirled and threw, like some golden statue of a Greek javelin hurler, his head twisted away to the left as his right arm swept out and around."[18] Hano continues, "This was the throw of a giant, the throw of a howitzer made human, arriving at second base . . . just as Doby was pulling into third and as Rosen was scampering back to first."[19]

When asked about the catch, Mays was usually self-effacing, often saying he was prouder of the throw.[20] In Mays's words, "I was young and cocky enough to know that I could catch any ball in the ballpark. But the important thing was for the runners to stay on the bases. Doby got only one base and Rosen went back to first."[21] Mays was bothered when some people said that he threw the ball by "instinct," a statement that trivialized the multiple skills and artistry involved in the play, from judging the distance and direction of the flight of the ball from its sound off the bat to the coordination and strength required in making the powerful throw to second base.[22]

Some of the major newspaper coverage at the time, like the Hano book, showed the play in a progression of four images—not just the catch but also the throw. See, for instance, the *New York Times* the day after the game.[23] Over the decades, the play has often been reduced to a single image, the one shown here of Mays about to catch the ball. Consequently, most fans today know little or nothing about Mays's spectacular throw—the aspect of the play which Mays himself thought was the most significant. The exception to this might be those who have seen the grainy film footage of the play in Ken Burns's documentary *Baseball* (1994) or on YouTube.[24]

The folklore around the catch often includes a humorous remark made by the Giants' pitcher Don Liddle to manager Leo Durocher, upon being taken out of the game following Wertz's mammoth drive. On his way off the mound, Liddle is reported to have boasted, or more likely joked, "I got my man."[25]

The Aftermath

Mays's catch prevented the Indians from taking the lead. In the tenth inning the Giants' Dusty Rhodes came off the bench and hit a short fly ball that barely cleared the right-field wall next to the foul pole—a mere 257 feet from home plate, about 200 fewer feet than Wertz's mammoth clout that Mays had hauled in. Rhodes's home run won the game for the Giants, beginning a four-game sweep of the heavily favored Indians. Some pundits say the Giants' championship was one of the greatest upsets in World Series history.[26] While two of the Indians' best players, Larry Doby and Al Rosen, were hampered by injuries that may have contributed to Cleveland's demise, Indians' manager Al Lopez also credited the catch: "Willie Mays made that great catch on Wertz's drive, and after that we never were the same."[27] In Hirsch's words, Mays's catch "crushed the spirit of the mighty Indians."[28]

Thanks to the 1954 World Series, the fading Polo Grounds reclaimed some glory. Horace Stoneham, after eighteen years as the Giants' owner, finally won a World Series. Nonetheless, just three years later he moved his team to San Francisco. The expansion New York Mets would play at the Polo Grounds in their inaugural 1962 and 1963 seasons, before moving to

Shea Stadium. The Polo Grounds was demolished in 1964 and public housing was built on the site. The Giants would not win another World Series until 2010.

Today, Vic Wertz is mostly remembered for his long out in the 1954 World Series. Two decades after Mays's catch, Wertz told *The Sporting News*: "Even now, wherever I go, I'd say 90 percent of the people who recognize me ask me about the catch. It really has given me a name. Heck, if the ball had gone over Willie's head, I might have gotten an inside-the-park home run, and it would have given me 5-for-5 in a World Series game. But who'd have remembered?"[29]

As for Mays, he played twenty-four seasons in the Major Leagues, winning two Most Valuable Player awards, amassing over 3,000 hits and 660 home runs, and earning twelve Gold Gloves. He was voted to twenty-four All-Star games. *The Catch* helped create Mays's legacy as one of the best ballplayers of all time. When *The Sporting News* compiled a book titled *Baseball's 25 Greatest Moments* to mark the end of the twentieth century, the only fielding play among them was Mays's catch.[30]

The Photo

It wasn't just Frank Hurley's photograph that became iconic. The World Series was televised nationally, allowing the baseball world not only to see the game but to hear NBC announcer Jack Brickhouse's excited narration. The grainy black-and-white film footage of Mays's play is still seen on ESPN and other sports channels and internet sites. *The Catch* is likely today's generation of fans' most tangible connection to Willie Mays.

Given Mays's extraordinary athleticism, it seems appropriate that a film clip and an image, not a statistic, would define him. Unlike other great baseball players who are associated with numbers—56, .406, 61, 714, 755, 762—Mays holds no single record with historical resonance. His brilliance was in how he played the game, and *The Catch* evokes the awe and wonder of his skills. Even though Mays often downplayed his catch, virtually all who saw it recognized its greatness. As broadcaster Bob Costas said with only some hyperbole, "It was more than just a great catch. It was a catch no one had ever seen before . . . When the ball left Vic Wertz's bat in the massive Polo Grounds, where it was headed, where Mays was standing, there was only one possibility. Could he get to it before it was an inside-the-park home run? . . . Catching it was out of the question."[31]

The 1954 World Series was photographed by many photographers, making the identity of the individual who captured the now iconic image relatively unimportant. Frank Hurley is not part of the image's story in the way that, say, Dorothea Lange is to the well-known Depression-era image *Migrant Mother* (1936) in which, through composition, lighting, and choice of subject, the anguish of a seasonal crop-picker and mother is poignantly depicted. Nor can *The Catch* be likened to combat photographer Joe Rosenthal's famous image of the American flag being raised on Iwo Jima at the end of World War II, which raised the spirit of a nation. Although that image was staged, it similarly relies on the photographer's skill (as well as its symbolism) for its power. No, *The Catch* is an ordinary sports photograph shot by a talented lens-man on the job. An unnamed Associated Press photographer, and most likely others as well, recorded a nearly identical image of the catch.[32] What makes the image iconic is that in a tight World Series opening game it captured a virtually impossible play made by one of baseball's most extraordinary players.

NOTES

1. To hear Brickhouse's call, see https://www.youtube.com/watch?v=1vrsg_-dV7Q.

2. Frank Hurley, who took the iconic picture of Willie Mays's over-the-shoulder World Series catch, had a forty-five-year career at the *Daily News*. Hurley is also known for taking memorable photos of the Muhammad Ali-Joe Frazier fights and the White House years of President John F. Kennedy. One of his most famous photos is of Brooklyn Dodger Jackie Robinson's disputed steal of home in the 1955 World Series. Hurley was on the paper's photo staff that won the Pulitzer for "consistently excellent" work in 1955.

3. James S. Hirsch, *Willie Mays: The Life, The Legend* (New York: Scribner, 2010), 191.

4. Quoted in Hirsch, *Willie Mays*, 192.

5. Arnold Hano, *A Day in the Bleachers* (Cambridge, MA: Da Capo Press, [1955] 1995), 48.

6. See https://thisgreatgame.com/ballparks-polo-grounds/.

7. See https://thisgreatgame.com/ballparks-polo-grounds/.

8. Hano, *A Day in the Bleachers*, 33.

9. Hano, *A Day in the Bleachers*, 37.

10. Hano, *A Day in the Bleachers*, 16

11. Hano, *A Day in the Bleachers*, 39.

12. Hano, *A Day in the Bleachers*, 45.

13. John Thorn quoted in John N. McMurray, "Even Today, Willie Mays Remains a Giant in Baseball History," *Smithsonian Magazine*, June 5, 2018, https://www.smithsonianmag.com/smithsonian-institution/event-today-willie-mays-remains-giant-baseball-history-180969229/.

14. Hano, *A Day in the Bleachers*, 116.

15. Hano, *A Day in the Bleachers*, 118.

16. Wertz added, "I've put balls on the roof at Briggs Stadium [later renamed Tiger Stadium] at Detroit and hit some other real smashes, but this drive, which just ended up as a big out, was tagged as well or better than any of them. I never thought Mays had a chance to get the ball, but he did." Quoted in Tracy Ingolsby, "62 Years Ago, Mays Made a Catch That Still Dazzles," September 19, 2016, https://www.mlb.com/news/62-years-ago-willie-mays-made-the-catch-c204108488.

17. Hirsch, *Willie Mays*, 200–201.

18. Hano, *A Day in the Bleachers*, 123.

19. Hano, *A Day in the Bleachers*, 124.

20. See https://www.youtube.com/watch?v=4gKSgHsekaM.

21. Willie Mays and John Shea, *24: Life Stories and Lessons from the Say Hey Kid* (New York: St. Martin's Press, 2020), 83.

22. While working on this essay, George Gmelch remembered, while playing in the Detroit Tiger minor leagues in the 1960s, stories told about Mays by one of his coaches, George Spencer, who had been on the pitching staff of the 1954 Giants. The garrulous Spencer had enjoyed sharing his stories of the 1951 and '54 Giants with Gmelch and his teammates, often told in hotel lobbies at night after games on road trips. Gmelch can recall Spencer's description of Mays's powerful and accurate arm.

23. *New York Times*, September 30, 1954, 40.

24. See https://www.youtube.com/watch?v=1vrsg_-dV7Q.

25. Hirsch, *Willie Mays*, 196.

26. Hirsch, *Willie Mays*, 203.

27. Quoted in Hirsch, *Willie Mays*, 203.

28. Hirsch, *Willie Mays*, 203.

29. Quoted in Hirsch, *Willie Mays*, 204.

30. Ron Smith, *Baseball's 25 Greatest Moments* (St. Louis, MO: Sporting News Pub. Co., 1999).

31. Quoted in Joe Garner, *And the Fans Roared: The Sports Broadcasts That Kept Us on the Edge of Our Seats* (Naperville, IL: Sourcebooks, 2000).

32. See the *New York Times*, September 29, 1954, 40.

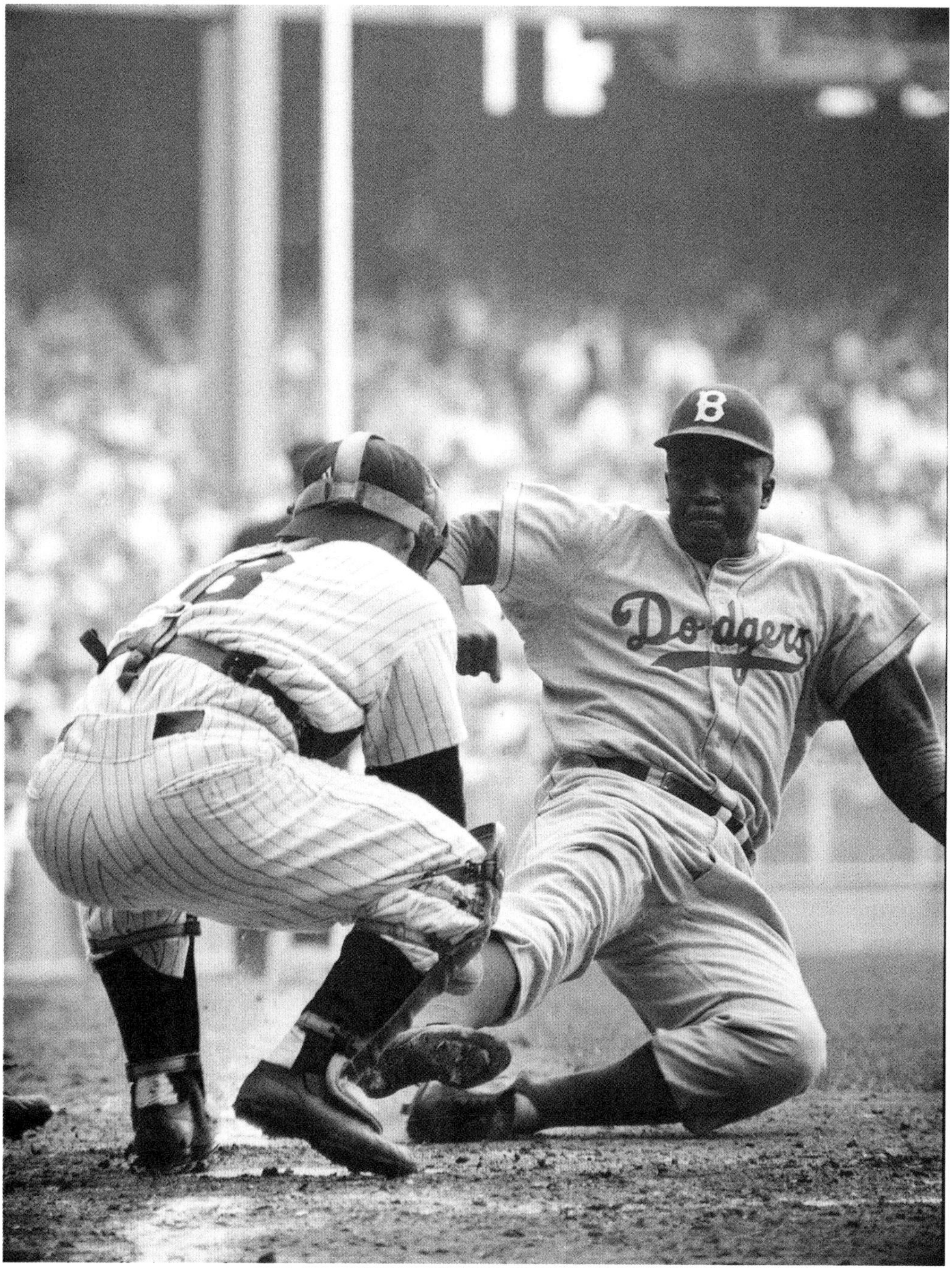
Dodgers

8

JACKIE ROBINSON

Safe at Home

MAUREEN M. SMITH

Readers of the *New York Times* on the morning of September 29, 1955, were greeted with front-page news of the New York Yankees' World Series Game One win over the visiting Brooklyn Dodgers. The headline proclaimed: "Yanks Win First; Collins' 2 Homers Beat Dodgers, 6–5." A subhead read: "Robinson Steals Home, His Feat Thrills 63,869." Robinson's "electrifying steal" was captured most notably by photographer Mark Kauffman, who was working for *Sports Illustrated*.[1]

Kauffman was the magazine's founding photo editor, largely due to his innovative use of technology, such as motorized cameras and telephoto lenses at ground level, to bring sports photography closer to sport fans and readers. Kauffman got his start with *Life* magazine at age seventeen, when he became the youngest photographer to have his work on the prestigious weekly's cover, with his image of Eleanor Roosevelt.[2] His photo of third baseman Eddie Matthews of the Milwaukee Braves appears on the inaugural cover of *Sports Illustrated* on August 16, 1954.[3]

The first game of the 1955 World Series at Yankee Stadium was between the crosstown rivals, who had most recently met in the 1952 and 1953 World Series, with the Yankees winning both. During the top of the eighth inning,

Whitey Ford was pitching for the Yankees. A Gil McDougald error on a hard hit by Jackie Robinson put Carl Furillo on third and Robinson on second. Don Zimmer's sacrifice fly scored Furillo, making the score 6–4, with the Yankees ahead. "A moment later," wrote John Drebinger of the *New York Times*, "Robinson stunned the American Leaguers with a daring steal of home while Ford was delivering a pitch. Yogi Berra, the Yankee catcher, protested vehemently that he had made the tag in time."[4] Only two innings earlier, the Yankees second baseman Billy Martin had failed in his attempt to steal home. Robinson's steal of home was the first in a World Series game since Monte Irvin's in 1951, also against the Yankees, and only the ninth steal of home in World Series history.[5] Considered one of the most iconic moments and photographs in baseball history, Robinson's steal of home marks the last time home plate was stolen in the World Series.[6] Kauffman's image did not appear in newspapers the next day, appearing solely in *Sports Illustrated*. Instead, the *New York Times* printed a variation of the home plate fracas, with Robinson still at least ten feet from home plate.[7]

Kauffman's image of this iconic moment, captured from behind Berra, almost in the position of an umpire, seems as if had he been anticipating a steal of home, as the shutter snapped "a millisecond or two before Berra tagged Robinson—or, as history records, Robinson's foot safely touched the plate."[8] Robinson's left leg is tucked underneath, and his right leg is extended, several inches above home plate. Robinson's eyes are cast downward at home plate, almost like he is looking himself and wondering "Am I safe?" His mouth is closed, pursed, full of breath like he is playing a trumpet. In 1955, batting helmets had no ear coverings, so both ears are visible. His uniform is big on him, and the fabric appears as if it is blowing across and downward. His right arm is bent at the elbow like he could punch Berra. Berra has his left foot planted lightly on the ground, and his right foot makes contact with the ground through his toes. The top half of his body leans forward, but the bottom half seems like he could be knocked over. Berra's glove is obscured by his right knee, but you can see Robinson's foot is beneath Berra's glove. The ball is not visible. Umpire Bill Summers and pitch hitter Frank Kellert are not in the photo, but we know they are outside the frame, with Summers calling Robinson safe.

Over a week later, in the October 10 issue of *Sports Illustrated*, the magazine declared "Robinson was safe." The sporting weekly led off its summary of the Series, won by the Dodgers, by calling Robinson "that vivid competitor" and credited his steal of home as getting the Series off to a "steaming start" and "instantly provoking a rhubarb." Was Robinson "really safe as

Umpire Bill Summers called him—or out, as Yankee Catcher Yogi Berra burningly insisted?" Citing newspaper photographs, "several taken from distorting angles," as evidence of Berra's claim, *Sports Illustrated* included two Associated Press photos to support Summers's call.[9] The article concluded with a celebration of Robinson, "self-described as 'old, fat, and gray,'" for his Series performance, which was "one of the best he has ever played."[10]

Robinson's steal, considered the most iconic steal in baseball history, was certainly the most dramatic of his twenty career steals of home.[11] Stealing home has become synonymous with Robinson, with the phrase used for at least five books about the Dodger great.[12] Considered Robinson's "most famous steal of home," the steal is also one of baseball's "most memorable and replayed moments in the game's history."[13] Baseball photographer Brad Mangin ranks Kauffman's image among the top ten in baseball history. Mangin explains that when one thinks about this "historic Series . . . you think of Dodgers base runner Jackie Robinson showing his daring skills by stealing home plate in a controversial call that is still challenged to this day by Yankees catcher Yogi Berra." Noting that he has "seen the video replay over and over and it is still hard to see if Jackie was safe or out," Mangin continues, "The only thing I definitely know about this play is it made a great picture that was captured so beautifully by Mark Kauffman of *Sports Illustrated*. One thing that makes this image so special to me is the fact that it is one of the first great telephoto pictures made with a long lens from the field level." Prior to this photo, most baseball shots were taken with "long lenses . . . from overhead baskets with Big Bertha cameras." Mangin's bottom line was the "great peak action and expression on Jackie's face, combined with the unique (for the time) low to the ground angle," resulting in this special photograph.[14]

Kauffman's photograph continues to provide fodder for the classic debate about a moment in baseball well before instant replay was created. Retired MLB umpire Randy Marsh considers the photograph to be evidence of his trade, telling one reporter, "I look at that photo all the time and, you know, there it is, stopped in time forever, and I still can't tell you if he's safe or out. . . . I show people that photo and tell them: There, *that's* being an umpire."[15] Kauffman's skill and artistry as a photographer looms large for Mangin and Marsh, among others, as they remember the moment and rely on the image as a piece of their memory.

Artist Graig Kreindler represents the iconic moment with his own oil on linen painting, *A Photo Finish* (2014), one of several he has painted of Robinson. Kreindler waxes poetic:

> There are few moments in Jackie Robinson's career that are more iconic than this one. Heck, there are few moments in baseball history that are more iconic than this one. You've seen photos of it. You've seen prose about it. You've seen the grainy kinescope footage. It still never ceases to amaze me how a call from almost sixty-five years ago can still be debated with as much fury and vitriol as whatever might have transpired the night before.[16]

Unlike Kauffman's photo, Kreindler's painting is resplendent in color. Of his painting, Kreindler comments:

> What was most important to me in this painting was getting Jackie's uniform right. Not in its style, as there's nothing too complicated about the Brooklyn togs from that era, but more so how it undulated through space. With Jackie in midair after a sprint, that baggy uniform was going to be completely at the mercy of that momentum. But as it fluttered in the wind, it also had to reveal the shape of Jackie's body. I can't take much credit for making that happen, as Mark Kauffman (the original photographer) was responsible for that. But through texture, edge and chroma control on the painting, the illusion is pulled off that much more (in my opinion).[17]

Washington Post photography columnist and photographer Frank van Riper had a similar romantic recollection of Robinson's famous steal. He recalls:

> In a flurry of legs, dust and spikes, Jackie, having sensed exactly when to make his move, barreled toward the plate from third just as the pitcher began his windup. Barely avoiding the tag, Robinson did it again. He stole home. To see such a display, especially in real time, is to have it stamped in your consciousness—one of those happy events that you then can recall at will in an endless loop of memory.[18]

Kauffman's image played a prominent role in van Riper's memory of the event, a moment he considers "one of the most dramatic steals" of Robinson's twenty career thefts. He comments, "photographer Mark Kauffman's great image shows Robinson feet first in mid-air, flying toward the solid squat form of Yankee catcher Yogi Berra. Yogi would insist for years that he made the tag, but the ump saw it differently."[19]

Berra's own recollections of Robinson's steal is certainly central to the continued dialogue around the photograph. In real time, Berra protested

Summers's call, visibly objecting, even bumping the umpire, his own theatrics captured in photos.[20] According to Berra's account, he had warned pitcher Whitey Ford of the threat of Robinson on third: "I reminded him Brooklyn was two runs behind and I said I didn't think Robinson would try to steal home. . . . Sure, we were surprised. It was a dumb play with his team two runs behind, but it worked and so it was a good one."[21] Berra biographer Jon Pessah recalled Berra's version of the events: "The ball arrived a split second before Robinson slid into home late, and Berra is sure—no, he's absolutely positive—he put the tag on Robinson for the out." Berra knew "for certain . . . Summers was far behind the plate and in no position to make the call." When the subject came up, as it often did, Berra would shout, "He was out, he was out, he was out," delighting crowds.[22] Until his death in 2015, Berra maintained a "dogged defense of his reputation" that Robinson was out.[23]

After hearing President Barack Obama refer to the famous scene at home plate, Berra gifted Obama an autographed copy of the photo. He autographed it, "Dear Mr. President, he was out!" in blue ink. Five years later, in the days following Berra's death, sportswriter Dave Brown recalled the contentious play, noting that Berra had never "got over that play at the plate." Brown relies on video footage of the play at home, suggesting it would be "inelegant for modern video review to have been used for one of the most iconic moments" in the game's history, in part because the delay of such a review at the time would have "ruined the aesthetic of what we see."[24]

Robinson, of course, viewed the play at home differently than his opponent. In one account, he explained, "It's easier to get one run than two and when they give me the run, I'm certainly going to take it. The only ridiculous thing about that play was the Yankees' squawking about me being called safe. There wasn't any question about it. I was over the plate before Berra got the ball on me."[25] In another account, the Dodger assuredly claimed, "I was safe." Robinson added, "No doubt in my mind at all. I could see the plate when I slid in. Yogi was back of the plate. I suppose Yogi figured he had me or he wouldn't have raised such a fuss. In my opinion it wasn't close. Probably in Yogi's it was."[26]

Robinson, nearing the end of his baseball career, had cemented his place in American history for his role in re-integrating Major League baseball. Robinson, as captured by Kauffman, and as etched into the consciousness of a nation, left an enduring legacy. Stealing home during a World Series contest was simply one play of his notable career, but it stands as an iconic moment frozen in time in an iconic photograph. North Philadelphia residents are treated to a building-size mural version of Kauffman's photo—a black, white, and gray mural depicting Robinson's most famous steal of home, which represents something far greater to the neighborhood's residents.[27] For artist Graig Kreindler, the significance of Robinson as a barrier breaker in American society was part of the larger context in which he viewed the World Series steal of home, and subsequently his artwork depicting the ballplayer. Kreindler explains, "No matter what I tried to do in the painting, what Kauffman captured, or what we argue about regarding the play, what's most important is Jackie Robinson himself. The profundity of his person can never be overstated."[28] Jackie Robinson's stealing home cannot be overstated.

So synonymous with stealing home was Robinson that the imagery was central to his eulogy, which was delivered in 1972 by Reverend Jesse Jackson. Jackson shared with mourners, "The Lord's arms of protection enabled him to go through dangers seen and unseen, and he had the capacity to wear glory with grace. . . . The mercy of God . . . permitted him to steal away home, where referees are out of place, and only the supreme judge of the universe speaks."[29] For Jackson, Robinson's death was his last "steal away home," reminding mourners of the ball player's metaphorical, and literal, efforts to find safety and peace. In another example of Robinson's renown for stealing home, the Los Angeles Dodgers erected a statue of Robinson stealing home (albeit not from the 1955 World Series), a lasting image of a Brooklyn player who never played in Chavez Ravine, but who looms large in Dodger history.

Decades after Robinson's death, President Obama made a speech at the Edmund Pettus Bridge in Selma, Alabama, to commemorate the fiftieth anniversary of the Selma to Montgomery civil rights marches. He told the audience, "We are Jackie Robinson, enduring scorn and spiked cleats and pitches coming straight to his head, and stealing home in the World Series anyway."[30] A White Sox fan, Obama was born six years after Robinson's steal of home in the 1955 World Series, and yet the moment and the image had been communicated to him and resonated with his audience. Some of that sense of history is no doubt due to Kauffman's photo, which is a powerful image of Jackie Robinson safe at home.

NOTES

1. John Drebinger, "Yanks Win First; Collins' 2 Homers Beat Dodgers, 6–5," *New York Times*, September 29, 1955, 1, 40. The editors of *Sports Illustrated* used the phrase "electrifying steal" in their October 10, 1955, Table of Contents, page 3.

2. Mark Kauffman won the Photographer of the Year Award from Encyclopedia Britannica and the White House News Photographer Grand Award in 1952. He worked for *LIFE* for thirty years, with twenty covers. He also served as director of photography for *Playboy*. See https://www.life.com/photographer/mark-kauffman/; https://www.latimes.com/archives/la-xpm-1994-08-09-mn-25054-story.html; https://vault.si.com/vault/1994/08/16/to-our-readers; https://www.nytimescom/1994/08/11/obituaries/mark-kauffman-photographer-71.html.

3. For more on Kauffman's craftsmanship, see John Zimmerman, Mark Kauffman, and Neil Leifer, *Photographing Sports: Capturing the Excitement of People in Action* (New York: Morgan Morgan, 1975).

4. Drebinger, "Yanks Win First," 1, 40.

5. Drebinger, "Yanks Win First," 40.

6. Matt Kelly, "A Rare Feat: The History of WS Steals of Home," MLB.com, November 4, 2021, https://www.mlb.com/news/world-series-steal-of-home-history.

7. Drebinger, "Yanks Win First," 40. The caption reads: "A Steal That Succeeded: Jackie Robinson of the Dodgers races home in the eighth inning. Catcher Yogi Berra moves up in hope of getting the ball in time. Frank Kellert was the Brooklyn batter." Also included is a photo of Billy Martin failing to steal home, along with a third photo of Berra protesting Summers's call.

8. Zev Borow, "Law & Order," ESPN.com, August 14, 2006, https://www.espn.com/espnmag/story?id=3661613.

9. "Robinson Was Safe," *Sports Illustrated*, October 10, 1955, 14.

10. "Robinson Was Safe," 17.

11. Robinson stole home twenty times in his career. For a listing of each attempt, see Bill Nowlin, "Jackie Robinson's Steals of Home," Society for American Baseball Research (SABR), https://sabr.org/journal/article/jackie-robinsons-steals-of-home/#calibre_link-1438. Ty Cobb stole home more times than Robinson. See Warren W. Mouch, "Ty Cobb Steals Home!" SABR, http://research.sabr.org/journals/ty-cobb; Cobb holds the record for the most steals of home with 54.

12. The phrase "Stealing Home" has been used for several Robinson-related books, including for young readers. See Robert Burleigh, *Stealing Home: Jackie Robinson against the Odds* (New York: Simon & Schuster, 2007); Barry Denenberg, *Stealing Home: The Story of Jackie Robinson* (New York: Scholastic Paperbacks, 1990); Sharon Robinson, *Stealing Home: Intimate Family Portrait by the Daughter of Jackie Robinson* (New York: Harper, 1996); and Ellen Schwartz, *Stealing Home* (Toronto: Tundra Books, 2006). Brandon Terrell's graphic novel does not use the phrase in its title, but it focuses almost entirely on the event. "Stealing Home" is used for the title of his third chapter. See Brandon Terrell, *Dodger Dreams: The Courage of Jackie Robinson* (Minneapolis: Stone Arch Books, 2010).

13. Cliff Corcoran, "The 10 Most Significant Steals of Home in Baseball History," *Sports Illustrated*, June 29, 2009, https://www.si.com/mlb/2009/06/29/stealing-home-0; Will Brown, "Jacob Ellsbury and the 9 Most Amazing Straight Steals of Home in

MLB History," BleacherReport.com, August 10, 2011, https://bleacherreport.com/articles/800685-jacoby-ellsbury-and-the-9-most-amazing-straight-steals-of-home-in-mlb-history.

14. Grover Sanschagrin, "The 10 Greatest World Series Photos of All Time," October 26, 2010, *PhotoShelter*, https://blog.photoshelter.com/2010/10/the-10-greatest-world-series-photos-of-all-time/.

15. Borow, "Law & Order."

16. Quoted in Phil Hecken, "Remembering Jackie Robinson Day," Uni-Watch, April 15, 2018, https://uni-watch.com/2018/04/15/remembering-jackie-robinson-day/.

17. Quoted in Hecken, "Remembering Jackie Robinson Day."

18. Frank van Riper, "Of Diamonds and Dugouts and Polaroid Fantasy," *Washington Post*, April 4, 2008, https://www.washingtonpost.com/wp-srv/photo/essays/vanRiper/040408.htm.

19. van Riper, "Of Diamonds and Dugouts and Polaroid Fantasy."

20. For example, in a photo of Berra's protest accompanying the article, the caption reads, "Indian War Dance?: No, Berra is merely objecting to Umpire Summers' safe call on Robinson's steal in eighth." Also see Nowlin, "Jackie Robinson's Steals of Home."

21. "Berra Takes Blame for Steal," *Boston Globe*, September 9, 1955: 14.

22. Jon Pessah, *Yogi: A Life behind the Mask* (New York: Little, Brown and Company, 2020), 225, 475. In an earlier autobiography, Berra did not mention the disputed steal of home, only telling the reader that he would warn pitchers about Robinson when the Dodger was on third. See, for example, Yogi Berra and Ed Fitzgerald, *Yogi: The Autobiography of a Professional Baseball Player* (New York: Doubleday & Company, 1961), 194–195.

23. Dave Brown, "Remember Jackie Robinson Stealing Home with Yogi Berra Catching," CBSSports.com, September 23, 2015, https://www.cbssports.com/mlb/news/remember-jackie-robinson-stealing-home-with-yogi-berra-catching/.

24. Stan Silliman, "Obama, Yogi, and the Magnet: The Strange Story of a Presidential Present," August 23, 2010, Bleacher Report, https://bleacherreport.com/articles/441573-yogi-to-obama-latest-mission-for-celebrity-magnet; Kiki Ryan, "President Obama Gets a Gift from Yogi Berra," *Politico*, August 26, 2010, https://www.politico.com/click/stories/1008/potus_gets_gift_from_berra.html; Brown, "Remember Jackie Robinson Stealing Home with Yogi Berra Catching."

25. Roscoe McGowen, "Brooks Disappointed, Not Discouraged by Defeat and Showing of Newcombe," *New York Times*, September 29, 1955, 40.

26. "Berra Takes Blame for Steal," 14.

27. For more on the Robinson mural in Philadelphia, see https://www.muralarts.org/artworks/jackie-robinson/.

28. Hecken, "Remembering Jackie Robinson Day."

29. Reverend Jesse Jackson, "Jackie Robinson Eulogy," *Baseball Almanac*, https://www.baseball-almanac.com/players/p_robij5.shtml.

30. Maya Rhodan, March 7, 2015, "Transcript: Read Full Text of Barack Obama's Speech in Selma," *Time*, https://time.com/3736357/barack-obama-selma-speech-transcript/.

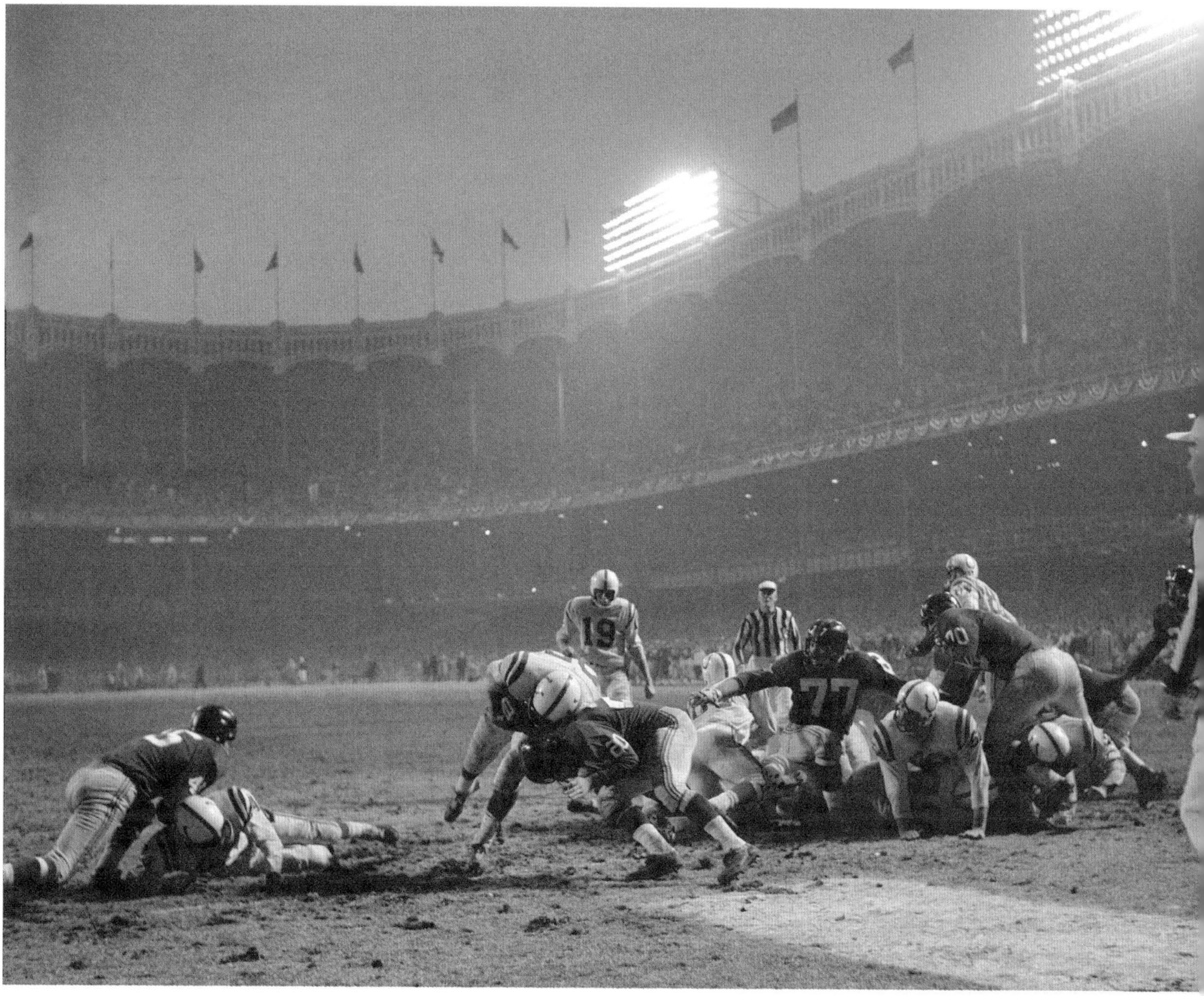

9

ALAN AMECHE FROM THE ONE

The 1958 NFL Championship Game

DANIEL A. NATHAN

It looks like a misty late afternoon or early evening.

A football game in dingy twilight is being played.

There are bright banks of flood lights, bunting and flags.

The turf is churned (which might suggest that it is late in the game).

I see twelve football players and two referees.

They are men at play, men at work.

Old, antiquated, or perhaps retro uniforms and equipment.

A huge hole in the line for the running back.

A collision in (what seems like) the end zone.

Many people interested in professional football history probably know that this is a photograph of the touchdown that concluded the famous 1958 NFL championship game between the Baltimore Colts and New York Giants played in Yankee Stadium. The Colts won the game, in sudden-death overtime, 23–17, on a one-yard touchdown run by fullback Alan Ameche, which is pictured here.

It was December 28, and when the game started the late afternoon sky was bright and, for a time, the weather was unseasonably mild. Later, as darkness fell, it turned freezing cold. Undaunted, Neil Leifer took this photograph with a Yashica-Mat camera. A Giants fan who grew up in a housing project on the Lower East Side of Manhattan, Leifer turned sixteen years old that very day.[1] At the time, Leifer considered photography a hobby.[2] He was a member of the Henry Street Settlement House's camera club.[3] Talented and ambitious, he would become one of the most successful sports photographers of the twentieth century.[4] His photos have appeared on more than two hundred *Sports Illustrated, Time,* and *People* magazine covers, and he has published sixteen books.[5] We will return to how the uncredentialed teenage Leifer happened to be at the right place and the right time to shoot Ameche scoring from the one-yard line.

First, though, to appreciate and understand the photograph, it is important to know something about the game itself and why it is often (portentously) called "The Greatest Game Ever Played."[6]

On that memorable Sunday, the Colts were "a young team of castoffs from a small city that had never participated in a national championship in any sport," writes Mark Bowden in *The Best Game Ever: Giants vs. Colts, 1958, and the Birth of the Modern NFL* (2008).[7] The Giants were led by linebacker Sam Huff and the top-ranked defense in football. The Colts were led by quarterback John Unitas and the league's best offense. Seven weeks earlier in the Bronx, the Giants beat the Colts in the regular season, 24–21.[8] But on December 28, with over 64,000 people in attendance and an estimated 45 million more watching on television (a device on the verge of becoming ubiquitous and increasingly influential), the Colts capitalized on three Giants fumbles and took a 14–3 halftime lead.[9]

Over the years, this game has taken on mythic dimensions. It is often hailed for catapulting the NFL into the national consciousness and for signifying, as sportswriter Michael MacCambridge puts it, that "pro football had arrived as a viable alternative to baseball, not merely as the most popular sport, but the one that best defined America."[10]

In truth, except for two extraordinary Unitas-led scoring drives late in the contest, it was generally a sloppy, if unusually dramatic game. "It had structure and pace that the best novelists would envy," critic Jonathan Yardley remarks.[11] Still, both teams made costly turnovers (seven, in all) and the poor field conditions adversely affected play. Then again, the game is best remembered and historically important for what happened late in the fourth quarter and in overtime.

In a surprising reversal, New York dominated most of the second half. The Giants defense stiffened, most famously stopping the Colts from scoring late in the third quarter from the three-yard line, with first down and goal to go. The Giants then scored two touchdowns to take a 17–14 lead, which they held for most of the fourth quarter. With 1:56 left in the game, Baltimore took over on its own 14-yard line. In a masterful display of time management, play selection, and execution, Unitas calmly led the Colts downfield. With seven seconds left on the clock, Steve Myhra, an erratic placekicker who played linebacker for much of the day, booted a twenty-yard field goal to send the game into sudden-death overtime. It was the first such game in NFL history. Several of the players thought the game was over, having ended in a tie. Instead, Tex Maule of *Sports Illustrated* reported: "The teams rested for three minutes, flipped a coin to see which would kick and which receive, and the Giants won and took the kickoff."[12] Unable to move the ball, New York punted. The Colts took over on their own 20-yard line. With time no longer an issue, Unitas, Maule wrote, "mixing runs and passes carefully and throwing the ball wonderfully true under this pressure, moved them downfield surely."[13] On the drive's thirteenth play, the powerful Ameche plunged into the end zone, head down, from the one-yard line to give the Colts the victory. Bedlam ensued, as thousands of delirious Colts fans rushed the field, tore down the goalpost, and carried Ameche off the field on their shoulders.

Over the years, Neil Leifer has explained many times how he was in position to take his celebrated photo of Ameche's game-winning touchdown. The most fulsome version is in his book *Relentless: The Stories behind the Photographs* (2016). From a working-class Jewish family, Leifer was a clever teenager, something of a hustler. He shined shoes, scalped New York Yankees tickets, and was a delivery boy for the Stage Deli.[14] He loved the Giants but could not afford tickets to the team's games. No matter. Leifer saw an opportunity. "He had learned that before every game," Bowden writes, "busloads of disabled veterans arrived at the loading ramps outside Yankee Stadium's outfield walls. There was no place for men in wheelchairs up in the stands, but the Giants allowed them to watch from their chairs against the outfield wall behind the end zone."[15] Leifer was one of the volunteers who pushed the vets into the stadium. Once inside, he would stay on the field. Hoping to ingratiate himself with the security guards, he would fetch them coffee. "In time," Leifer reminisces, "they'd look the other way when I stole over to take pictures of the players huddled on the bench—or crept in for a close-up of the action."[16] This did not endear Leifer to the professional photographers working the game.

On his sixteenth birthday, Leifer was especially fortunate. He was lucky that he was standing in the right end zone when the game went into overtime.

He was lucky that on second down and goal, after catching a pass from Unitas, the Colts tight end Jim Mutscheller was unable to score because he lost his footing and slid out of bounds, thus setting up Ameche's one-yard run on the next play. In ESPN's documentary *The Greatest Game Ever Played* (2008), Leifer, in a conversation with the Baltimore-born filmmaker Barry Levinson, says: "Well, thank God it [Mutscheller's reception] didn't go for a touchdown. That might have been the end of a career that hadn't begun."[17]

It was "not purely by accident," he recalls in *Relentless,* writing in the present tense, but Leifer was also lucky that he was "standing ten yards behind the goal line, directly in front of Ameche and, with the stadium darkening and fog swirling across the field, I snap one shot and capture Ameche cradling the ball as he tumbles into the end zone."[18]

Initiative and good fortune, talent and serendipity. Whatever it was, the gods smiled on Neil Leifer that evening.[19] In *Relentless,* he muses: "Little could I have imagined that blustery day that this black-and-white photo would become one of the iconic sports pictures of the twentieth century."[20]

For many years, I thought the photograph of Ameche scoring from the one-yard line that appeared on the front pages of the *New York Times* and the *Baltimore Sun* was Leifer's shot. It's not, but if you put them side by side, you can see why I thought so. The image in these and many other newspapers around the country is an uncredited Associated Press photo. Clearly, the two photographs are similar. The composition and angle are similar: field level and straight on. They both feature Ameche running with his head down. They both feature halfback Lenny Moore making an excellent block on the Giants' defensive back Emlen Tunnell.[21] They both feature John Unitas in the background, watching the play unfold. There are other similarities.

At the same time, their differences are notable and important. The AP photo is tighter, narrower, and was obviously taken a split second before Leifer's. We know this because in the AP photo, Ameche has not yet made contact with the Giants' safety Jim Patton. In Leifer's photo, Ameche is plowing into (and subsequently through) the relatively undersized Patton.[22] Leifer's photograph is more panoramic, wider than the AP image. It shows the grandeur of Yankee Stadium, and the lights suggest something about when the game was being played. Because the shot is wider, we also see more of the players involved in the play, the wild tangle of humanity that allowed Ameche to score so easily.

Part of the reason Leifer's photo is different is due to the camera he used. The Yashica Mat was a basic, easy-to-use camera. It had a fixed rather than a telephoto lens, which has a longer focal length than standard and provides a narrow field of view and a magnified image.[23] This "meant that his picture would be not just of Ameche hurtling toward" Leifer and the other fans in the endzone, "but of a broad panorama," Bowden writes, "the long empty, illuminated field behind him, the encircling stands, the dark sky. Leifer didn't consider it in that moment, but his picture told the bigger story, of a team that had just driven the length of the field, of a game that had stretched from early afternoon into night. It would be the first picture he ever sold, and would become the most famous photo of the game."[24]

That took time, however. After *Sports Illustrated* rejected it the day after the game, Leifer's photograph was purchased by *Dell Sports Magazine*, which first published it in November 1959, as part of its pro football preview issue.[25] In a 2016 interview, Leifer explained, "It took a long time before the picture got any recognition. You have to understand, a lot of pictures aren't appreciated when they're first taken and they get a life of their own."[26] Today, Leifer's photograph is widely respected and celebrated.

And yet a photograph never means just one thing. This one meant and means something different, say, to the men who played in the game (only a few of whom are still with us, such as Lenny Moore and Raymond Berry) and to Colts fans and Giants fans, then and now.

Reflecting on the 1958 NFL championship game, Baltimore journalist Michael Olesker asserts that "its impact on professional football, and on the American sporting culture, was breathtaking. And its emotional impact on Baltimore lingers half a century later, when aging men [and women] still choke up when they hear the playing of the Colts fight song or see that picture of Ameche with his head down. It's not only a touchdown he's scoring; it's the birth of a generation finally feeling terrific about itself."[27] He is of course referring to Baltimoreans.

Most New York football fans did not and do not have warm, nostalgic memories or sentiments about the 1958 NFL championship game and certainly do not associate Leifer's photo with a moment of glory. For them, as seemed to be the case with former Giants halfback Frank Gifford in the ESPN documentary about the game, Ameche's game-winning touchdown was (and may still be) a powerful moment of disappointment.

Furthermore, it is worth mentioning what one of Leifer's principal competitors thinks about Leifer's 1958 photo of Ameche. Walter Iooss, Jr., a tremendously successful sports photographer, once said:

> If there was one Neil [Leifer] picture I wish I had shot, it would have been the Ameche photo, hands down. It was one of the most defining moments in the

history of sport. What's so amazing is it showed what he had at such a young age. I think so many of the great pictures he took as a teenager and in his early twenties, with his perception of the bigger scene—what I never could even have imagined—are remarkable. It shows this magic moment in one of the great events in the history of sport, the single greatest event in football history.[28]

This is high praise, even if, as historian Richard C. Crepeau correctly notes, "the game did not take place in a social and historical vacuum. There was considerable context here, many decisions, developments, and personalities, both within and outside the league, that converged to make the NFL the new national pastime over the next decade."[29]

In the end, Leifer's photograph of Ameche's touchdown, viewed on its own, without any previous knowledge, without context, without analysis, is probably close to meaningless, indecipherable to most people. As a result, it drives home the idea that photographs must be interpreted and put in context, that photos, alone, at least in terms of their explanatory capacity, are in a sense inadequate and suggest something about the limits of visual representation. "Images appear mute: we as historians have to provide the words," writes historian Mike Huggins. "They depend on conventions of signification and thus can be 'read,' but the meanings derived from such readings are not intrinsic but contingent and subject to alternative interpretations."[30] Does the Leifer photograph convey joy? Victory? A sense of accomplishment? Yes, it does, but only from certain perspectives. From others, it signifies something other than the thrill of victory a long time ago.

For some Baltimoreans, perhaps especially working- and middle-class baby boomers, the photo exemplifies a romantic vision of the past—back when the Colts belonged to Baltimore, when the city was seemingly more cohesive and less troubled, before the team packed up and moved to Indianapolis on a dark and stormy night. At the same time, for some New Yorkers the image conjures memories of a missed opportunity, a stinging loss, something akin to the agony of defeat. After the game, Frank Gifford was "left [with] an unbelievably empty feeling. You'd done the best you could—we all had—and it hadn't been good enough. There was nothing more to be said. It was time to move on."[31] Many Giants fans felt the same way.

NOTES

1. Gail Buckland, *Who Shot Sports: A Photographic History, 1843 to the Present* (New York: Alfred A. Knopf, 2016), 172.

2. *The Greatest Game Ever Played: The Baltimore Colts vs. New York Giants*, DVD, produced by Marc Kinderman (New York: ESPN Films in association with NFL Films, 2008).

3. Neil Leifer, with Diane K. Shah, *Relentless: The Stories behind the Photographs* (Austin: University of Texas Press, 2016), 9.

4. Curator Gail Buckland writes: "Celebrity is relative, but in the world of sports photographers, Leifer is royalty and probably the world's best known sports photographer." Buckland, *Who Shot Sports*, 172.

5. See https://neilleifer.com/biography/.

6. Some of my account of the game is drawn from Daniel A. Nathan, "The Baltimore Blues: The Colts and Civic Identity," in *Rooting for the Home Team: Sport, Community, and Identity*, ed. Daniel A. Nathan (Urbana: University of Illinois Press, 2013), 110–113.

7. Mark Bowden, *The Best Game Ever: Giants vs. Colts, 1958, and the Birth of the Modern NFL* (New York: Atlantic Monthly Press, 2008), 8. Also see Dave Klein, *The Game of Their Lives: The 1958 NFL Championship* (Lanham, MD: Taylor Trade, [1976] 2008); John F. Steadman, *The Greatest Football Game Ever Played: When the Baltimore Colts and New York Giants Faced Sudden Death* (Baltimore: Press Box, Inc., 1988); Lou Sahadi, *One Sunday in December: The 1958 NFL Championship Game and How It Changed Professional Football* (Guilford, CT: Lyons Press, 2008); and Frank Gifford, with Peter Richmond, *The Glory Game: How the 1958 NFL Championship Changed Football Forever* (New York: Harper, 2008).

8. Both teams finished the regular season 9–3.

9. Bowden, *The Best Game Ever*, 2, 8.

10. Michael MacCambridge, *America's Game: The Epic Story of How Pro Football Captured a Nation* (New York: Random House, 2004), 112, 113.

11. Jonathan Yardley, "A Truly Communal, Live, National Event—and One to Remember," *Washington Post*, June 8, 2008, BW15.

12. Tex Maule, "The Best Football Game Ever Played," *Sports Illustrated*, January 5, 1959, 60.

13. Maule, "The Best Football Game Ever Played," 60.

14. Leifer, *Relentless*, 8–10.

15. Bowden, *The Best Game Ever*, 4.

16. Leifer, *Relentless*, 2.

17. *The Greatest Game Ever Played*.

18. Leifer, *Relentless*, 3.

19. In a 2016 interview, Neil Leifer said: "Luck in sports photography is everything and what separates the really top sports photographer from the ordinary is that when he or she gets lucky, they don't miss. That is the key. But you have to be lucky." Quoted in David Katz, "Neil Leifer Recalls Shooting Iconic Muhammad Ali Photos," June 4, 2016, ThePostGame, http://www.thepostgame.com/muhammad-ali-famous-photos-neil-leifer.

20. Leifer, *Relentless*, 3.

21. Tunnell was the first African American to play for the Giants and the first to be inducted into the Pro Football Hall of Fame.

22. Ameche outweighed Patton by more than thirty pounds.

23. Leifer, *Relentless*, 2.

24. Bowden, *The Best Game Ever*, 208.

25. Leifer, *Relentless*, 16-17.

26. Quoted in Katz, "Neil Leifer Recalls Shooting Iconic Muhammad Ali Photos."

27. Michael Olesker, *The Colts' Baltimore: A City and Its Love Affair in the 1950s* (Baltimore: Johns Hopkins University Press, 2008), 198.

28. Quoted in Leifer, *Relentless*, 7.

29. Richard C. Crepeau, "The Greatest Game Ever?" in *Replays, Rivalries, and Rumbles: The Most Iconic Moments in American Sports*, ed. Steven Gietschier (Urbana: University of Illinois Press, 2017), 98.

30. Mike Huggins, "The Sporting Gaze: Towards a Visual Turn in Sports History—Documenting Art and Sport," *Journal of Sport History* 35 (Summer 2008): 325.

31. Gifford, *The Glory Game*, 229.

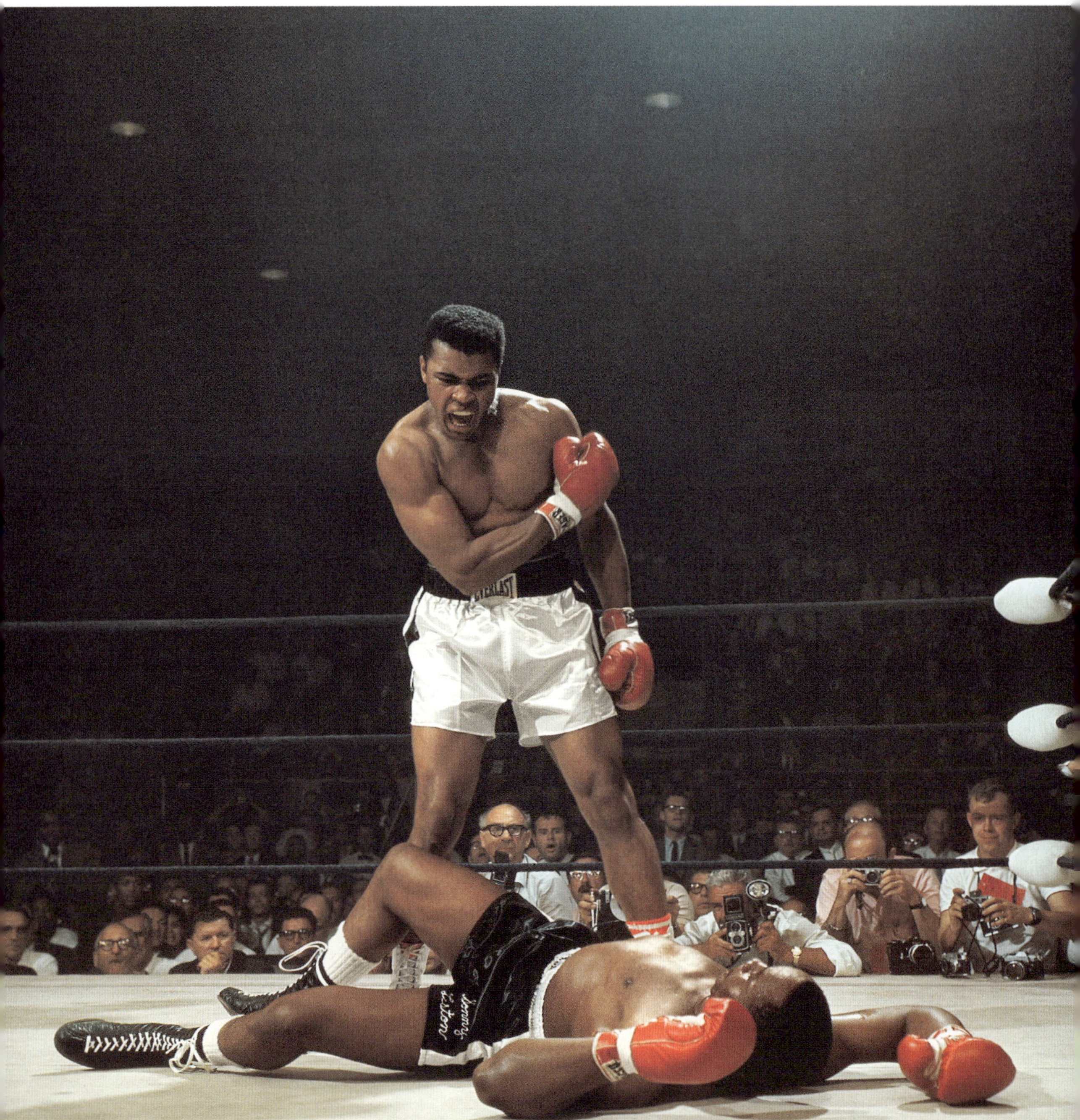

10

THE MOMENT OF TRUTH

Ali-Liston II

CARLO ROTELLA

Ali is vertical and Liston is horizontal, which is generally understood to be the point of the picture. Ali's mouth is open, his face filled with strong feeling that looks like an impassioned blend of pride and anger, and he's making a get-up-and-fight gesture with his bent right arm pulled tightly across his chest, the ridged muscular tension of his body radiating dynamic potency. In contrast to Ali's dominance display, Liston lies supine, slack-bodied, hands thrown back over his head to expose belly and throat, abjectly defenseless. A great mass of blackness suggesting a cavernous arena forms a backdrop for the brightly lit brown of the fighters' skins, the red of their gloves, and innumerable white highlights: the strip of canvas at the bottom of the frame, three turnbuckle pads on the ropes, Ali's shorts and mouthpiece and bared lower teeth, Liston's laces and the stripe and waistband on his shorts, both men's socks, the tape on their gloves, shirts on the ringsiders behind the fighters and on fans well back in the gloom behind the ringsiders, here and there a glint of light reflecting on the lenses of eyeglasses. Photographers are bellied up to the ring, one with his elbow on the canvas, to shoot pictures; those without cameras crane to see around them. The *Sports Illustrated* photographer Herbie Scharfman, who ended up facing Ali's back when Liston went down and was therefore not in position to get the iconic shot taken by his colleague Neil Leifer, is visible in the inverted V between Ali's tensed legs. So is Larry Merchant, at that point only thirty-four and still a newspaperman, not yet the crusty TV talking head he would become. Merchant's mouth, like Ali's, is open.

Often hailed as The Greatest Sports Picture of All Time, or One of the Greatest, or whatever, Leifer's picture is generally taken to be about victory and defeat, the highs and lows of competition, pride and humiliation in the aftermath of the moment of truth. To the limited extent that it's also associated with Ali's reputation as a then-controversial political figure, I suspect that this image has become semiotically cross-contaminated with the identity drama of Ali's thrashing of Ernie Terrell two years later—during which Ali repeatedly asked Terrell "What's my name?" to taunt him for referring to Ali as Cassius Clay in the build-up to the bout. But it's mostly as a money shot of triumph that the figure of Ali standing over Liston has become canonical dorm-room and gym-wall poster material in the class of the airborne Bobby Orr or Brandi Chastain with ripped-off jersey in raised fist. Ali's pose resembles—and may well have inspired—those of countless goal- and touchdown-scorers and three-point-shot-makers who have followed in his wake, and it's also a cousin of the pumping-fist stance conventionally assumed by golfers who have sunk a putt and salesmen who have closed a deal.

But the image is better understood, I think, as a picture of a decisive spasm of action having freshly happened and the meaning-making getting underway in response to it. And what has very probably just happened in the picture is that one guy said, "Fuck it, if I'm going to lose, I might as well get it over with right now in the first round and not spend all night chasing this lightning-fast showoff and getting jabbed in the face," and the other guy has suddenly realized that he wasted a whole lot of effort in training and now better think very fast of some plausible explanation for a second fishy victory in a row—much fishier than the first one, even—over the same opponent. Persistent rumors of a fix or other such interference by organized crime had been one of the main reasons that the promoters moved the rematch from Boston to Lewiston, Maine, way out in the sticks. With an announced crowd of just 2,434, Ali-Liston II, contested on May 25, 1965, has to be the heavyweight title fight with the highest proportion of fight-world insiders to civilians in attendance. The picture falsely implies a larger scale of crowd and arena, but, while the ghostly forms of some ticket-holders can be made out far back in the dark, what we mostly see are the insiders, massed at ringside just behind the fighters, beginning to react to the first-round stoppage. Like the two Black men in the foreground, who know that their brief and inconclusive encounter will oblige them to do some explaining, the white men at ringside are beginning to formulate hot takes on what just happened, a first draft of history. So the heroic spectacle here is not just Ali's rampant triumph and Liston's languishing on the canvas but also the frenzy of recording and representing and narrating and spin doctoring and analytical glossing to which their encounter gave rise. In that sense, this picture is the *Las Meninas* of classic boxing shots, a painting about painting.

Yelling at an opponent to get up and fight is a bush-league move, no matter what the situation. If Ali felt that he had genuinely dropped Liston, then he was taunting a fallen foe, which would make him an asshole. It was also wildly premature, since Liston had just gone down and had not been counted out yet. If the picture captures the moment when Ali realized that Liston was taking a dive, his righteously calling attention to it—*Good heavens, this unsporting fellow is proving to be less than a gentleman!*—was a Boy Scout move that only hurt his own chances to get credit for a legitimate win. Ringsiders remember Ali saying, "Get up and fight, sucker" (which could mean he said "motherfucker," for which "sucker" sometimes stood in) and "Nobody's gonna believe this," both of which would make sense if Liston's tank job had come as a nasty surprise to him.[1] That's the norm in a worked fight: you don't warn the designated winner in advance, since you want him to compete in earnest, which makes the whole thing look better. If that's what was going on, Ali, who always did recover well, swiftly got over any initial surprise—which would have been strongly inflected with frustrated anger, since he believed he could beat Liston or anyone else in an honest match—and got to work figuring out something plausible and entertainingly on-brand to say to the press about the fight. He came up with a stretchily beguiling tale about an "anchor punch" he learned from the comic actor Stepin Fetchit, who learned it from Jack Johnson. Ali thereby succeeded in shrouding in esoteric mystery a blow that even if it did land cleanly, and even if it just might conceivably have caused a flash knockdown, could not possibly have finished Liston in the first round.

Ali had come straight across the ring to Liston at the opening bell and thrown a couple of right hands, then settled into circling and changing directions, flicking occasional punches. When midway through the first round he clipped Liston with a chopping little counter right over Liston's jab,

Liston plunged to the canvas as if zapped by a slaughterhouse cattle-stunner. He rose to one knee before collapsing and rolling onto his back again. Meanwhile the referee, the former heavyweight champion Jersey Joe Walcott, had to shoo away the shouting and gesticulating Ali and was late picking up the count. Liston was down for seventeen seconds, but he eventually got up and the fighters briefly started boxing again before Walcott finally stepped between them to declare that Liston had been counted out after all and the fight was over. It was a mess.

Some ringside observers, including Merchant, the *Sports Illustrated* writer Tex Maule, and the former champions Floyd Patterson, James J. Braddock, and Rocky Marciano (who reversed from his initial skepticism after he reviewed the film, and perhaps heard from some of his mob associates), argued that Ali's chopping right really had finished Liston. But plenty of others dismissed the result as an outright sham, including the veteran ring announcer Don Dunphy, the heavyweight tough guy George Chuvalo, and the sportswriter Jimmy Cannon, who said, "I saw that punch, and it couldn't have crushed a grape."[2] Many in the tiny crowd booed and shouted "Fix!" and "Fake!"[3] Liston, whose career was a wholly owned subsidiary of the criminal enterprise operated by the Philadelphia mobster Frankie Carbo and his crew, had been favored going into this rematch because a lot of people regarded his first loss to Ali as a fluke or a fix, so there was still good money to be made betting against him. Both Liston and Ali said immediately after the fight that the punch had been the real thing, but in later years Liston told writers and friends that he hadn't been hurt by it, and that he had chosen to go down or been confused by Walcott's confusion, and even the absurdly self-confident Ali expressed doubt that the punch had hurt Liston so badly that he couldn't have gotten up.

Ali was a big strong guy, and he would mature into a very effective grappler with a knack for wearing out opponents in the clinches, but he never had classic one-shot knockout power. He preferred to use his speed to move in and out and flick and flare his blows and accrue damage incrementally, rather than sitting down on his punches to generate decisive broadside power in the traditional heavyweight style. And Liston was an enormously strong heavyweight with a titanium chin. Even if he had been surprised by Ali's mystic anchor punch, even if it had landed flush enough to genuinely upset his balance for a moment, even if Liston (who was probably years older than his stated age) had crested the hill and started on the sort of sudden steep decline that can happen to fighters—though Liston's solid post-prime career, in which his chin mostly held up, suggests no such precipitous falloff—it seems ridiculous that he could be seriously hurt in the first round by a snap punch that Ali threw mostly with his arm, with much of his weight on his back foot and without the full torque of a classic right cross behind it.

It's possible that Liston was not badly hurt but rather confused by the botched count and believed that he could take a bit longer on the canvas before getting up, which is the explanation he eventually gave to several writers, but it's more likely that he just wasn't very good at losing a boxing match on purpose and declined to continue the charade. Liston's inability to convincingly throw a fight may well have ended up getting him killed by his handlers five years later, in 1970: not long after beating up the hopelessly outclassed Chuck Wepner in a bout Liston was apparently supposed to lose, he suffered a dubious heroin overdose that looked a great deal like murder-by-hotshot.[4]

The tension between two very different possibilities—shabby flop or decisive punch so swiftly and shrewdly delivered that most of those in the arena missed it entirely—makes Leifer's picture a confluence of the sporting epic and the noir tale. These are the two main kinds of stories we tell to impose meaning on the mute naked fact of violence at the core of boxing. Put a sporting epic frame around the picture and we're looking at the immediate aftermath of Ali's brilliance. Unbelievably fast, a genius-level ring general and psychologist, inspired to extraordinary athletic feats by his passionate commitment to justice and freedom, he has just added another big win to his heroic record by yet again undoing Liston, whose fearsome strength and power and boxing acumen aren't nearly enough to cope with the Ali-ness of Ali. The sporting epic endows the Phantom Punch, as Ali's right-hand shot came to be known, with an otherworldly aura of space-and-time-altering potency.

Put a noir frame around the picture and we're looking at a fix, a fake, another instance of the smart money getting what it wants and the gullible buying the cover story. Now the Phantom Punch becomes just another scam, another thing that's supposed to have happened that didn't really happen. The noir tale turns the sporting epic into sentimental smoke and mirrors, a soothing bedtime story that the naive tell themselves while players in the know work the inside angles for profit. Follow the money, the noir tale reminds us, and stop telling yourself fairy tales about the thrill of victory and the agony of defeat. Of course, the noir tale can curdle into its own kind of sentimental fairy tale, as even a cursory glance at the sort of doomy mumbo jumbo written about Liston makes clear: "Born with a dead man's eyes, he had passed from the darkness of those scars on his back to the darkness of the criminal underworld, to a darkness beyond, a darkness whose final form was the last thing his eyes ever saw," and so on.[5] When noir tale and sporting epic get liquored up on sentiment, they stumble home in a dead heat for last.

The deathbed confession phase is behind us, and everybody who can tell us with authority what happened in the two Ali-Liston fights is gone: Liston and Ali; Carbo and his crew, including his trusted Liston-minder Al Braverman; Ali's trainer, Angelo Dundee, and his mobbed-up brother Chris; inner-circle Nation of Islam figures who might have known something. Even most of those who might have heard anything useful secondhand from these principals are also gone. So just what happened in Leifer's picture will have to remain one of history's many gray areas. But it's fair to say with some confidence that the case against Ali-Liston II being a fix has to make its way uphill against the rank implausibility of the so-called anchor punch finishing Liston.

There's also an argument to be made that Ali's first-round KO of Liston in Lewiston was the second worked fight in their series, not the first. If Liston tanked in the first fight too, Leifer's picture shows us the denouement of a two-phase fix that took two fights and fifteen months to play out. The case for a fix in Ali-Liston I, held in Miami on February 25, 1964, has to make its way uphill against the received understanding of that bout as the moment when the world-historical figure of Ali definitively emerged from the chrysalis of the young heavyweight Cassius Clay and commenced his ascent to godlike status by overwhelming the previously terrifying Liston. This is the account of Ali-Liston I that most people, including most experts, believe comes closest to the truth: the young Ali was too fast, too brilliantly determined, too theatrically astute, already too *Ali* for Liston, wearing him down physically and psychologically until he quit on his stool before Ali could knock him out. That's the Ali in Leifer's picture—beautiful, untouchable, impassioned, fairly electric with pugilistic genius and cultural significance.

But to what extent is that a fairy tale? The two boxing experts whose clear-eyed and entirely unsentimental opinions I value most in this matter are divided. Mike Ezra—the most penetrating of Ali historians, and particularly astute about the behind-the-scenes business dealings that enabled the creation of Ali the icon—argues that the result of Ali-Liston I was most likely what it looked like. "There's a chance that both fights were fixed, but I believe that the first was not," he told me. "Mostly likely, they"—meaning

Liston's mafia handlers, bossed from federal prison by Carbo—"ran into a guy they underestimated, and Liston was probably years older than the record indicated. Haven't we seen it a million times in boxing? Younger fighter is much better than we expected, older champion who has all the respect in the world suddenly declines. Foreman-Frazier, Hatton-Tszyu, Jones-Tarver II—in case after case, it's like you blink and they're suddenly post-prime."

Charles Farrell, who knows boxing from the inside as a former manager, argues for a fix. He starts with the business situation faced by Carbo and company. "They have the heavyweight champ, which is a major coup, and Liston would have been champ forever, but it turns out there are no takers, no plausible opponents for anybody to get excited about," he told me. Farrell got this version directly from Al Braverman, who did the day-to-day minding of Liston for Carbo and in later years went on to become Don King's long-serving director of boxing operations. Farrell reports that Braverman, who died in 1997, told him that both Ali-Liston fights were fixed. "The thing Braverman emphasized was Carbo's strong, reasoned conviction that they weren't going to make any money with Liston as the heavyweight champion," says Farrell. "One fight per year, 90 percent chopped off in income tax, low ticket sales, horrible betting odds, etc. It just made business sense to make all the money and more in one fell swoop. So they get 8–1 odds to bet against their guy and they clean up." Liston's murky, non-decisive loss to Ali in their first bout—he retired after the sixth round claiming a shoulder injury, the classic un-disprovable excuse of choice for boxers, and not at all the same as being knocked out or decisively outpointed—set up a rematch that would allow them to milk the same play for a second killing. Farrell says, "Then they promote the rematch themselves, get another 6–5 to 8–5, depending on who you believe, and score again."

Farrell told me, "The strongest evidence I have is definitely Braverman out and out telling me the first fight was fixed. Braverman was bedrock. But Johnny Tocco"—a long-time gym owner in Las Vegas—"told me the same thing, and Tocco was not only Liston's best friend but also a deep insider in the business. Hank Kaplan told me the same thing, and nobody knew as much boxing as Kaplan, who lived in Miami Beach. Sonny's friends Adolph Pruitt and Charles Hamm in St. Louis told me Liston told them the fights were fixed." In Farrell's account, the mafia-connected promoter Chris Dundee, who had fixed fights with Carbo before, was the mob's point man for the first fix, in Miami. Ali trained at Dundee's gym in Miami; Dundee promoted the bout; and his younger brother, Angelo, was in Ali's corner, keeping an eye on things. When Ali was temporarily blinded during the bout by an astringent substance—probably liniment—that accidentally got onto Liston's gloves (a genuine screw-up in Liston's corner, not some sort of nefarious ploy), Ali wanted to stop the fight and asked his cornermen to cut off his gloves, but Angelo, the only one in Ali's corner who knew that the fix was in, stayed the course and told his fighter to get out there and run from Liston until his eyes cleared. "Absent having been in on the fixes directly, I've never been so sure that two fights were fixed," says Farrell. "People want a smoking gun here, but these are pros who really don't leave smoking guns. So the biggest arguments for whether specific fights are fixed is if there's a clear-cut business decision to fix them—what are the odds, what strategic freight would the fix carry—and whether fixing fights was a staple among the people involved."

Farrell, author of the finest piece of writing about the backstage business of boxing ever published, an essay titled "Why I Fixed Fights" that defends the practice of fight-fixing on both business and humanitarian grounds, regards a Carbo fix of both Ali-Liston bouts as "a great moment in boxing history, a beautiful move—the ambiguous loss and rematch, the betting coup." In a case of noir tale impinging on the purview of sporting epic, writing off both Ali-Liston fights as fixes also reshapes the all-time heavyweight rankings. If you throw out both of Liston's losses to Ali, it suddenly becomes easy to put Liston up there with or even above Ali at the top of those rankings. Indeed, Farrell believes that Ali might not have been quite ready to take Liston in a straight-up contest the first time. He says, "Ali would have been champ eventually, because there's no doubt that he was a great fighter, but he would have had to work up to it, grind it out, and he wouldn't have become the Ali we know—untouchable, pretty, perfect. And the Nation of Islam would have dumped him if he lost to Liston," an assessment with which Ezra, an expert on Ali's NOI-related affairs, concurs. "Without Carbo, there's no Ali," concludes Farrell. Playing a brief but decisive role in shaping Ali's early trajectory would mean that the mafia had a hand in shaping everything that followed: Ali the countercultural political hero of the canonical Sixties, Ali the global icon, Ali the god.

A purveyor of sporting epic from way back, Neil Leifer specializes in taking pictures of the big moment when the big star wins the big fight, the big game, the gold medal. Like Ken Burns, he gravitates to the middle of the middle of the road, staking out as his cultural work the photographic equivalent of carving the standard take, the conventional version, into the face of Mount Rushmore. "In boxing it all comes down to one moment: when one of the fighters is on the canvas," Leifer has written. "The knockout. It's the only picture the editor of the magazine is going to be looking for."[6] Actually, editors are just as partial to another visual cliché that strikes me as much more expressive of what makes boxing boxing: the near-simultaneous exchange of blows, preferably early in a round after the two fighters have been splashed with water in their corners, so that the droplets flying from the combatants make it look as if they're entering hyperspace.

Leifer's insistence on the primacy of the knockout seems to miss the point of his own picture. Ali is vertical and Liston is horizontal, but certainty ends there. All we have are stronger and weaker arguments for what we're looking at, dive or KO or some of both at once, and there's nothing but open mouths and interpretive turtles all the way down. That uncertainty, and the felt need by everyone—fighters, ringsiders, fans, people who weren't even born yet when the fight took place—to make arguments to fill the void it creates, forms the subject of the picture. It shows us the suspended interval between the violently opaque, ambiguous moment of truth and the endless process of arguing for this or that version of the meaning, the significance, the truth of what just happened.

NOTES

My thanks to Mike Ezra and Charles Farrell for generously sharing their deep expertise.

1. Tex Maule, "A Quick, Hard Right and a Needless Storm of Protest," *Sports Illustrated*, June 7, 1965, 22; David Remnick, *King of the World: Muhammad Ali and the Rise of an American Hero* (New York: Random House, 1998), 258.

2. Quoted in Mark Ribowsky, *Howard Cosell: The Man, the Myth, and the Transformation of American Sports* (New York: W. W. Norton, 2012), 147.

3. Rob Sneddon, *The Phantom Punch: The Story behind Boxing's Most Controversial Bout* (Camden, ME: Down East Books, 2015), 200–201.

4. On Liston's suspicious death, see Gareth Evans, "The Mysterious Death That Haunts Boxing," BBC Sport, July 15, 2019, https://www.bbc.com/sport/boxing/48974341.

5. Nick Tosches, *Night Train: The Sonny Liston Story* (New York: Penguin, 2001), 3.

6. Neil Leifer, *Relentless: The Story behind the Photographs* (Austin: University of Texas Press, 2016), 77.

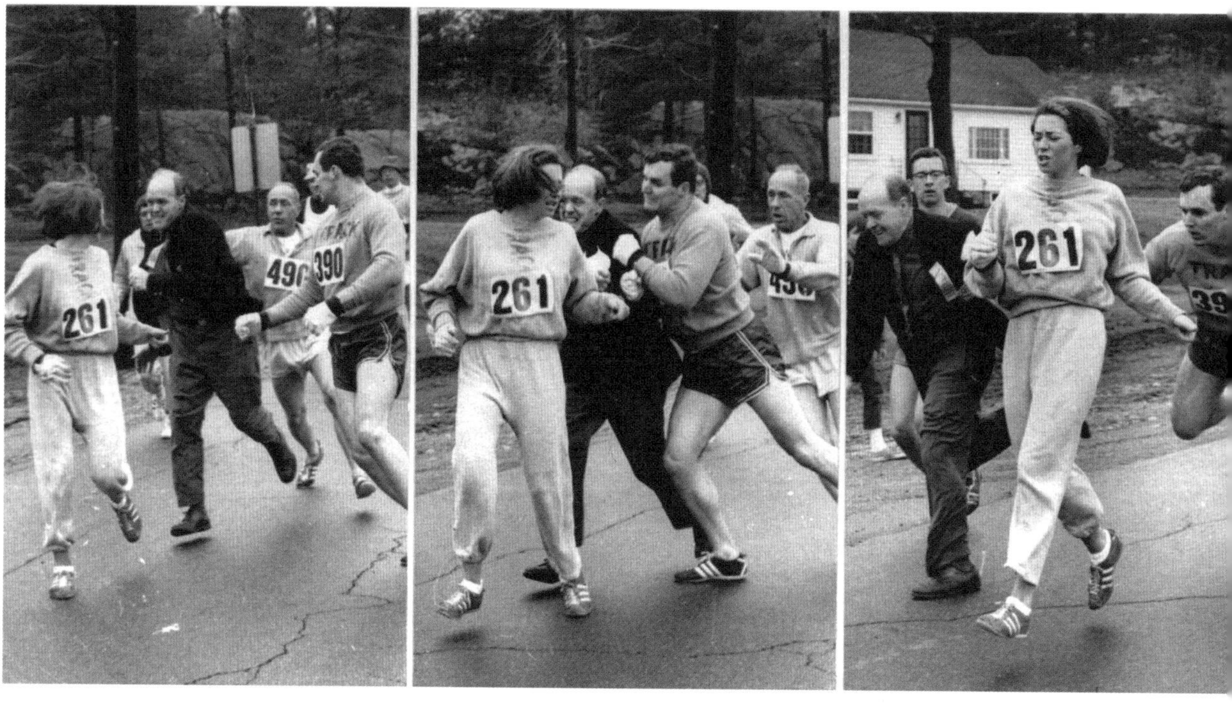
261
490
390
261
261

11

WHEN PUSH CAME TO SHOVE

Kathrine Switzer, Jock Semple, and the Boston Marathon

SUSAN WARE

The photograph of Jock Semple forcibly trying to eject Kathrine Switzer from the Boston Marathon on April 19, 1967, is often credited as being the spark that started the boom in women's distance running, if not the whole women's sports revolution. That's a bit of hyperbole: women's distance running still would have taken off; a women's marathon eventually would have been added to the Olympics; companies would have started creating athletic gear for women runners. Still, the incident was a wake-up call that huge changes in women's sports were on the horizon. Demands for equal rights are often abstract and fuzzy, but there was nothing abstract about a photograph which powerfully captured women's struggle to compete on an equal basis with men and the lengths that some men would go to prevent that.

The three-part photo, shot in rapid succession by *Boston Traveler* photographer Harry Trask around mile four of the marathon, captures the rawness of the moment. This is literally a physical confrontation—Switzer later compared it to being man-handled by Jock Semple, a former marathoner who served as the race codirector. Semple is grimacing with rage as he comes up behind her. This is his race, his face says, and this girl has no place in it. In the first frame you see her turning sideways to face her attacker, while her running buddies try to protect her, especially her coach Arnie Briggs (#490), who tries to talk Semple down. Very quickly it becomes clear that isn't going to work, and in frame two boyfriend Tom Miller (#390), a hammer-thrower who is much heftier than the typical marathoner, decides to take action by tackling Semple. In the third frame, as Semple falls toward the ground, Switzer resumes her stride, her blank expression suggesting that she has not yet begun to process what just happened. The original Associated Press caption read "Who says chivalry is dead?" but an alternate header could just as easily have been "Patriarchy, thy name is Jock Semple."[1]

That is the bare bones version. Here is a fuller rendition of the events leading up to the iconic image and its aftermath. The Boston Marathon, then a fairly small event attracting a die-hard core of runners, was sanctioned by the American Athletic Union (AAU). According to the extremely restrictive AAU rules at the time, women were not allowed to compete in events longer than one and a half miles, which made the marathon an all-male affair. The rationale was that women were physically incapable of long-distance running and risked collapse or serious bodily harm if they tried.

Claiming that she was unaware of this rule, Kathrine Switzer, a twenty-year-old Syracuse University student who had taken up distance running, decided to enter the race, submitting her application as "K. V. Switzer" and declaring herself a member of the Syracuse Harriers, which also included her coach, Arnie Briggs, and her boyfriend at the time, Tom Miller. She received an official bib, #261. When the team showed up at the start in Hopkinton, the weather was cold and sleeting and she wore a hooded sweatshirt over her number. She wasn't expecting problems because of her gender, but having the hood gave her some protection just in case. Several miles into the race she discarded the sweatshirt, which made her gender more apparent. The male runners she encountered were uniformly supportive; the Boston Marathon officials were anything but.

Word got out that a "girl" was running with an official number, which infuriated Jock Semple, who, along with race codirector Will Cloney, had worked tirelessly to stage the marathon with limited resources. Well known not just for his Scottish brogue but his terrible temper, Semple could not stand that a woman would tarnish the reputation of his race with what he saw as a prank. Around mile four the race officials decided to take action. After telling the press bus to slow down, Will Cloney hopped off and planted himself in the middle of the road, shaking his finger at Switzer and grabbing one of her gloves as she passed. She continued on.

Then came the moment that the photographer Harry Trask captured on camera. Semple had also gotten off the bus and made a beeline for Switzer, screaming "Get the hell out of my race and give me those numbers." Switzer was overcome with embarrassment and fear, as this hysterical man "with the most vicious face I'd ever seen . . . a big man, a huge man, with bared teeth" pounced on her and clutched at her shirt. This was the point when Switzer's boyfriend, Tom Miller, dressed in an orange Syracuse sweatshirt, came from the side to throw a decisive block to Semple, sending him airborne before he thudded to the ground. "Run like hell," shouted her coach and the three of them took off down the course. Switzer was scared out of her mind—what if they had done serious bodily harm to the official?—and briefly considered dropping out of the race but quickly reconsidered. "I knew if I quit, nobody would ever believe that women had the capability to run the marathon distance." Even worse, "If I quit, Jock Semple and all those like him would win." She pulled herself together and went on to finish the race in approximately four hours and twenty minutes.[2]

It was on the drive back to Syracuse that night that she first saw the pictures that would literally change her life. Around midnight the runners stopped at a rest area on the New York State Thruway, where they saw the sequence of photos plastered on the front and back pages of an evening newspaper. This was not just some local news story. Switzer soon learned that photos of her altercation with Jock Semple were being flashed around the world by the wire services. Would the story have had legs without the photographic documentation to back it up? Almost certainly not, given the general lack of media interest in anything having to do with women's sports at that time. A series of pictures which captured a dramatic confrontation, however, was another story.

If there is any question about the power of photographs to shape our view of history, look at the fate of Roberta "Bobbi" Gibb, who also ran the 1967 marathon, albeit without a number, and finished an hour ahead of Switzer with a time of 3:27. The year before, then known as Roberta Bingay, she had been the first woman to run the course, finishing ahead of 290 of that year's 415 finishers. Her feat received a small amount of press coverage, including a mention in *Sports Illustrated*, where race director Will Cloney was forced to engage in these verbal gymnastics to defend the sanctity of his supposedly all-male race: "She merely covered the same route as the official race while it was in progress. No girl has ever run in the Boston Marathon."[3] Gibb recognized this as a classic double bind: "How can I prove I can do something I'm not allowed to do?"[4]

Coverage of Gibb's 1967 race was totally overshadowed by the Switzer incident: "2 Girls in Marathon Don't Have a Lovely Leg to Stand On," headlined the *New York Times* in the casual sexism of the time.[5] Gibb ran Boston again in 1968, but with little publicity, certainly nothing on par with the year before. After the Trask photos went viral (they were later chosen for Time-Life's *100 Photos That Changed the World*), far too many people mistakenly believed that Kathrine Switzer had been the first woman to run the Boston Marathon. Only in 1996 was Gibb retroactively awarded medals for her victories in 1966, 1967, and 1968 and her name inscribed alongside the male finishers on the Boston Marathon Winners Memorial in Copley Square.[6]

Back in April of 1967, while the press was relegating Gibb to footnote status, Kathrine Switzer found herself an overnight celebrity, even appearing on the *Tonight Show* with Johnny Carson. Press coverage mainly focused on the anomaly of "girls" running the marathon, as if they were exotic creatures from another planet. Switzer was especially disappointed that the initial news reports did not include the fact that she completed the race. Officials stopped tallying results after four hours and she didn't finish for another twenty minutes.

Two days after the race, Switzer personally contacted Frank Litsky of the *New York Times* to set the record straight. The resulting piece reflected the challenges women athletes faced in being taken seriously by the media. The story was titled "Lady with Desire to Run Crashed Marathon" and illustrated by a glam shot of Switzer in an evening dress alongside one of the frames from the AP series. The writer peppered the story with multiple references to her appearance and demeanor—describing her as a former beauty contestant with "soft brown hair and [a] winsome look" who spoke "in a high-pitched voice filled with girlish enthusiasm." She called the rules limiting women to short races "archaic" and pointed out, "A lot of people said women couldn't run a marathon. But I'm glad I ran—you know, equal rights and all that kind of business." That sounds like a rather tepid endorsement of feminism, but Switzer was dead serious about challenging stereotypes of women's supposed physical inferiority. When interviewed by the reporter, race director Will Cloney refused to budge: "Women can't run in the marathon because the rules forbid it. Unless we have rules, society will be in chaos. . . . If that girl were my daughter, I would spank her." The article concluded condescendingly, "Not if you gazed into those big, brown eyes, you wouldn't."[7]

Switzer countered such male intransigence with various strategies. While she was committed to demonstrating beyond a doubt that women were capable of running long distances, she wanted to make sure that "this wasn't a woman-trying-to-beat-a-man thing; it was all of us running as hard as we could."[8] She was also determined to show that women could look nice while doing so. As she said to the *New York Times*, "Women can run, and they can still be women and look like women."[9] To that end, Switzer took great care with her appearance, choosing flattering outfits and hairstyles and even wearing lipstick when she raced. As part of her effort to get more women to take up running, she wanted to show them that they could still look attractive while they competed, a not-so-subtle dig at the fear that athleticism would turn women into heavily muscled creatures with moustaches. "I always felt beautiful when I ran," she recalled years later, and she wanted other women to feel that way too.[10]

Vanity aside, the question of what to wear was a serious one for early women athletes, when all athletic gear, running and otherwise, was made for men. Returning again to the photo sequence, we see that Switzer is dressed in comfortable sweats, appropriate for a damp and chilly day, although it appears in the third frame she may have cut the legs for length. Eventually she discarded the bottoms, revealing a pair of cast-off men's shorts she had found in her coach's trunk that actually fit her (most men's shorts were not suited for women's rounder hips and fleshier thighs, which could cause serious chafing), which she had carefully dyed burgundy to match the top she chose to wear. This top was never revealed, since she kept the sweatshirt with her bib number on during the entire race.

Choosing an outfit remained as much a part of Switzer's pre-race preparations as mileage for the rest of her career. For the 1972 Boston Marathon, she wore a leotard top covered by a white tunic over black tights, which didn't chafe and had the additional advantage of hiding menstrual blood if she got her period during a race. She described this look as "a combination of my two heroines, Atalanta and Margot Fonteyn,"[11] and was so tickled by a photograph of her in it fixing her hair that she used it as the frontispiece of her 2007 autobiography, *Marathon Woman*. But tights were no good in hot weather, and in the 1974 New York City marathon she competed in a sleeveless white tennis dress. Jock Semple wasn't the only obstacle women runners had to overcome.

Stepping back to place Switzer's historic race in the context of sports history and the history of feminism, one thing that jumps out is how ahead of her time she was. In 1967, the National Organization for Women was only a year old. Women couldn't get credit cards in their own names and the Equal Rights Amendment had languished in Congress for decades. Colleges and universities maintained arbitrary quotas limiting women's enrollment, especially in graduate fields such as medicine and law. Women's sports programs in schools were practically nonexistent. Title IX, the law which did the most to address discrimination on campus, wasn't passed until 1972. The famous "Battle of the Sexes" between Billie Jean King and Bobby Riggs didn't take place until 1973.

And yet something was definitely percolating in the 1960s, for women's sports and feminism in general. Social movements do not suddenly emerge out of nowhere—they have roots and forerunners. Ditto with women's sports. Moments like Kathrine Switzer's decision to run Boston showed that women were already challenging the old stereotypes—and were none the worse for it. Women who had been individually following their athletic muses suddenly realized that they were not freaks, that other women felt the same way. Soon women marathoners like Nina Kuscsik, Sara Mae Berman, and Michiko (Miki) Gorman began entering and winning races, further demonstrating that the old shibboleths about women being physically unable to run long distances were totally outdated and wrong. All this was happening in the 1960s, before second-wave feminism really took root.

And then in the 1970s everything exploded, in women's running and beyond. In 1970, there were perhaps twenty women around the world who ran marathons; the next year, a hundred women in the United States alone completed the course; from 1975 to 1978 the number of sub-four-hour women marathoners increased from 237 to 2,082. In 1971 the American Athletic Union (which had suspended Switzer after her Boston race for, among other things, running more than "the longest distance allowable for women" and doing so without a chaperone!) removed the previous limit of 1.5 miles, which opened the door for women to run Boston in 1972—as long as they met the men's qualifying time of 3:30. New names emerged in the field, such as Grete Waitz, Lorraine Moller, and Jacqueline Hansen, and their times dropped dramatically, with the three-hour barrier quickly falling and Waitz running an incredible 2:32:30 in the New York City Marathon in 1978. The decade of the 1970s saw the founding of women-led, women-oriented clothing lines like Title Nine, Moving Comfort, and Jogbra, with companies like Nike and Adidas also hopping on the women's sports bandwagon, meaning that women athletes finally had comfortable clothing that enhanced, rather than impeded, their ability to run. All this was happening as part of the general running boom of the 1970s, when running rivaled tennis as one of the decade's fastest-growing sports.

Kathrine Switzer was right in the middle of all these sweeping changes. Her experience in Boston in 1967 opened opportunities she could never have previously imagined. Determined to show that the 1967 race was not a fluke, she continued to train, bringing her times down steadily to a personal best of 2:51:37 in Boston in 1975, which made her the sixth-ranking woman marathoner in the world. Combining her background in journalism with her passion for running, she worked with various companies to expand opportunities and sponsorships for women's races. Most significant was her work on the Avon International Women's Running Circuit, which staged the Avon International Marathon through the streets of London in 1980. The success of that event, and the growing depth of the marathon field, in turn convinced the International Olympic Committee (a bastion of patriarchy, if there ever was one) to introduce a women's marathon in Los Angeles in 1984, which was won by Joan Benoit Samuelson. Kathrine Switzer is rightly credited with being one of the most persistent and effective lobbyists behind that Olympic breakthrough.

After their tussle on the course in 1967, Switzer and Jock Semple initially kept each other at a wary distance. When Semple presented Switzer with her third-place trophy for the inaugural women's race in 1972, he sputtered, "I've been mad at you for five years and you deserve a broken trophy."[12] (The trophy was indeed broken.) But faced with incontrovertible evidence that women runners were real athletes and not just using Boston as a feminist publicity stunt, he changed his tune. The next year Semple and Switzer mugged it up for the cameras at the starting line: "C'mon, lass, let's get a wee bit o' notoriety," he said, as he planted a kiss on her cheek.[13] Echoing Bobby Riggs's statement that he had done more for women's tennis than anyone by challenging Billie Jean King to the Battle of the Sexes, Kathrine Switzer introduced Jock Semple at a press conference as "the man who, in spite of himself, has probably done more for women's marathon running than anyone else in the world."[14] That endorsement was in large part testimony to the enduring power of the photographic record.

Kathrine Switzer always believed that running would change women's lives in positive and inspirational ways. It certainly changed hers, and those of a lot of the rest of us. To mark the fiftieth anniversary of her historic 1967 race, in 2017, the seventy-year-old Switzer ran Boston one more time, finishing in a respectable 4:44 and having the honor of her number 261 retired, only the second retired Boston Marathon number in history. This time no race official tried to shove her off the course.

NOTES

1. The sequence and the original caption are reproduced in the photo insert of Kathrine Switzer, *Marathon Woman: Running the Race to Revolutionize Women's Sports* (New York: Carroll & Graf, 2007).

2. Switzer, *Marathon Woman*, 91–93.

3. Gwilym S. Brown, "A Game Girl in a Man's Game," *Sports Illustrated*, May 2, 1966, quoted in Oren Renick and Lea Robin Velez, "Racing into the Storm: Roberta Gibb, Kathrine Switzer, and Women's Marathoning," in *A Locker Room of Her Own: Celebrity, Sexuality, and Female Athletes*, ed. David C. Ogden and Joel Nathan Rosen (Jackson: University Press of Mississippi, 2013), 167.

4. Bobbi Gibb, *Wind in the Fire: A Personal Journey* (Cambridge, MA: Institute of Natural Systems Press, 2011), 373.

5. "2 Girls in Marathon Don't Have Lovely Leg to Stand On," *New York Times*, April 20, 1967, 55.

6. Gibb, *Wind in the Fire*, 392.

7. "Lady with Desire to Run Crashed Marathon," *New York Times*, April 23, 1967, 199. Litsky did not receive a byline.

8. Switzer, *Marathon Woman*, 288.

9. Quoted in "Lady with Desire to Run Crashed Marathon."

10. Switzer, *Marathon Woman*, 170.

11. Switzer, *Marathon Woman*, 170.

12. Switzer, *Marathon Woman*, 173.

13. Switzer, *Marathon Woman*, 217.

14. Switzer, *Marathon Woman*, 343.

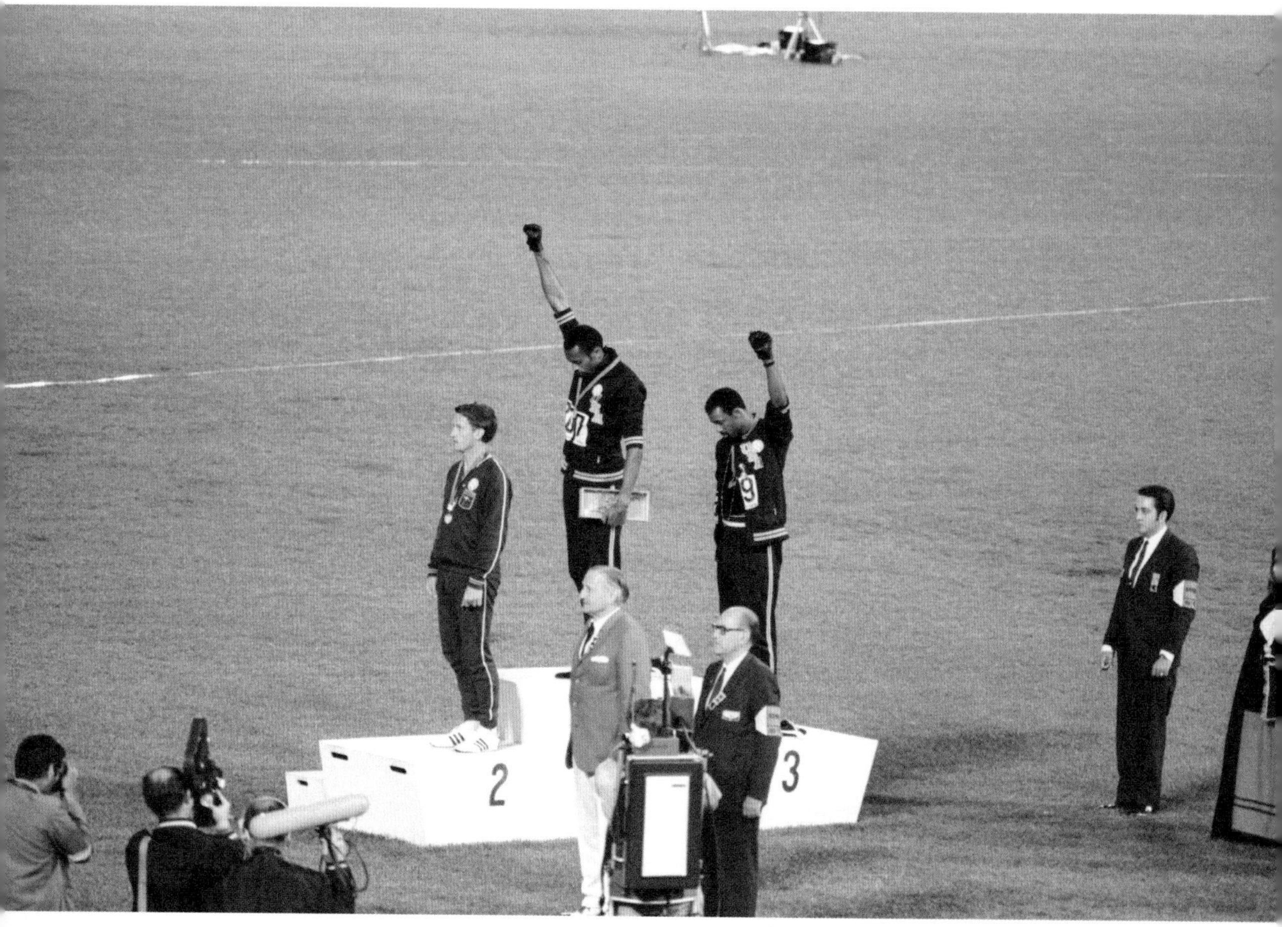
2
3

12

PERCHED VALOR

The Black Power Photograph That Exposed Injustice and Transformed Generations

TERRY ANNE SCOTT

When John Dominis, an American photojournalist, captured an image of Tommie Smith and John Carlos perched atop the men's track and field 200-meter award podium during the 1968 Mexico City Olympic Games, he immortalized more than a gesture. Smith and Carlos's choice to use the corporeal show of Black Power extended beyond a quiet, somatic display of discontent. In that moment, the Olympic athletes unmistakably aligned themselves with the racially oppressed, the downtrodden, the Black masses whose persecution and steadfast resistance had captured the attention of the world during the decades that preceded their remonstration. Their actions bespoke a rejection of a white supremacy that would, ironically, define their punishment in the days and years following their October 16, 1968, protest. Retribution was swift and enduring, which demonstrated how challenging systemic racism functioned as an intolerable threat to the extant racial hierarchy—in large measure due to the lasting testimony to resistance encapsulated in a single photograph. Known widely now as *The Black Power Salute*, Dominis's photograph, first published in *Life* magazine and then circulated in periodicals and newspapers around the world, has become one of the most reproduced and iconic displays of resistance, dignity, and courage in American history.[1]

By the time of the 1968 Olympics, Dominis had long established himself as a preeminent sports photographer. A former athlete who played football at the University of Southern California, Dominis and his photographic sensibility were informed by varied experiences. Years later, he confessed that he had dismissed the image he captured of Smith, Carlos, and Australian sprinter Peter Norman as "not much of a photograph."[2] Whether he was being self-deprecating or sincere, Dominis's assertion falls palpably short of how his photograph captured and popularized the powerfully disquieting moment. Sociologist Douglas Hartmann contends that Dominis's image occupies a position of "prominence and power as an object of meaning and collective memory."[3] Over the last half century, the image has adorned everything from T-shirts and buttons to postcards and murals. *Life* recognized it, in 2003, as among the hundred most important photographs ever taken. In 2018, to commemorate *The Black Power Salute*, the athletic clothing and shoe company Puma ran its #REFORM campaign, which encouraged people to post images of themselves on social media platforms with their fists raised in the air. It is a singular image that, even bereft of accompanying commentary and context, projects a message that has reverberated throughout the world for decades.

The lasting visibility and significance of the photograph were shaped immeasurably by the historical moment in which the image was captured. John Carlos and Tommie Smith raised their fists in courageous protest during an era defined by structural inequity and racialized violence—an era in which racial capitalism continued to extract the labor of Black people to enrich financial systems while simultaneously barring them from wealth accumulation through redlining, employment discrimination, and other forms of structural inequity. It was a time when federal legislation designed to dismantle a Jim Crow regime did little to address nationwide systemic racism. Moreover, extreme racialized police brutality and the seemingly constant assassination of civil rights activists and Black leaders functioned as a menacing backdrop to Carlos and Smith's formative years. National Association for the Advancement of Colored People leader Medgar Evers was murdered on June 12, 1963, in Jackson, Mississippi. Assassins opened fired on El-Hajj Malik El-Shabazz (Malcom X) as he delivered a speech at the Audubon Ballroom in New York City on February 21, 1965. Dr. Martin Luther King Jr. was murdered in Memphis, Tennessee, on April 4, 1968, while visiting the city to help striking sanitation workers. Countless other

Black men and women also violently lost their lives during the era at the hands of white people who were opposed to their struggle for racial equality. Additionally, upwards of a hundred racial uprisings defined the social landscapes of cities across the nation during the months leading to the Mexico City Olympics. The era required Black athletes to reconcile the complexity of identities that rendered them both the receivers of racism and lauded public figures.

Historically, there has not been a monolithic expression of discontent or activism among high-profile athletes, as evidenced by the diversity of responses to racial injustice from people such as Muhammad Ali, Wilma Rudolph, and Lenny Wilkens. And while multiple athletes, regardless of their racial identity, have engaged in a range of actions to protest racism, Black athletes have occupied a particularly visible space in the struggle for equality. Blackness has functioned as a complex historical determinant of racial interaction, domination, and racial disparities in the interpretations of crime and the applications of "justice."[4] Certain phenomena and historical processes (e.g., minstrel shows, convict leasing, Jim Crow practices, and more) have defined African Americans as objects of entertainment and persecution and have placed an alternate value on their lives. Black athletes are not exempt from such realities, particularly those who worked to reconcile the complexity of their identities during the civil rights and Black Power movements. They were burdened, and frequently driven, by what I refer to as a *triple-consciousness*, a concept of multiple identities used here to nuance Dr. W. E. B. Du Bois's brilliant theory of *double-consciousness*.[5]

Du Bois, a famed intellectual, writer, and activist, first became aware of his perceived status as a racialized *other* through the taunting and disparaging actions of his white classmate in a Massachusetts schoolhouse late in the nineteenth century. The only Black child among his classmates, Du Bois was refused a playing card by a white classmate due to the color of his skin. This instance of acute racial awareness became the topic first of an 1897 article in the *Atlantic* and then his 1903 essay "Of Our Spiritual Strivings."[6] The encounter resulted, Du Bois suggested, in two paths that presented themselves to him. He knew that he could either relax into a nihilistic existence in which a debased racialized status was internalized, only to become sullen and unproductive—a stereotype of sorts pandering to racist notions of Blackness—or he could emerge as a victor in all things. He chose the latter. But this required the reconciling of two identities, a "double consciousness," being at once American and Black. As an American, he should be provided all the protections and respect inherent in being a citizen of a democratic country. Yet as a Black person, he was continuously subject to racial discrimination and terror. Du Bois, much like the Black athletes protesting racial injustice, would thereby work to lift his Blackness beyond the reach of oppressive systems while ensuring that he was afforded all the liberties due an American citizen.

A third consciousness complicated and enhanced the identity of many Black athletes during the mid-twentieth century. Highly visible athletic success typically affords one a certain lionized existence that often allows the sports star to be treated as a celebrity. Nevertheless, the social mores of a particular period are often reflected in the interplay between race and daily life. Therefore, even celebrity status was not strong enough to buffer Black athletes from the perils of racism and allow them to overcome the debased status of Blackness. How could such an existence be addressed, and perhaps reconciled? Harry Edwards provided a solution.

Born in East St. Louis, Illinois, in 1942, Edwards was a star high school athlete and an exceptional student. After graduating from San Jose State University (SJSU) in 1964, he did his graduate work at Cornell University. Now recognized as a pioneer in the sociology of sport, Edwards was subject to abject scrutiny and racist reproach while a doctoral student. He recalls:

> I . . . lived every day as one of those Negro students on campus who was shut out, isolated, and alienated . . . who was starkly aware of the paucity of Black faculty, of no Black coaches, no Black administrators, and of the dearth of non-athlete Black students; who was the target of "nigger" and "coon" epithets shouted from the upper-floor windows of "fraternity row" student housing . . . who was sometimes only within "earshot," sometimes the intended audience of "Sambo" and "jungle bunny" jokes by white teammates and classmates . . .[7]

His experience was hardly unique among African Americans in higher education and was a stark reminder that achieving an elevated educational and class status would do little to assuage the racism that defined America. Even Edwards's research was subject to racialized suspicion and contemptuous review. His dissertation, which focused on the intersection of race and activism among Black athletes, was dismissed, questioned, even disdained by certain faculty members. As a result, they required him to write more than 1,200 pages in a clear attempt to either dissuade him from completing it or render it nearly impossible to do so.[8]

When Edwards published his first monograph in 1969, it became one of the only studies on sport written by a social scientist. *The Revolt of the Black*

Athlete (1969), which connects the activism of Black athletes to the broader protest movements of Black citizens nationwide, helped advance his career and national visibility while further solidifying the ire of federal agents. Edwards's writings, together with his activism while a professor at SJSU and later the University of California, Berkeley, where he began teaching in 1970, afforded him the dubious status of having an extensive Federal Bureau of Investigation (FBI) file. By 1967, Edwards had been added to the FBI's ADEX list, a compilation of people FBI director J. Edgar Hoover deemed anti-American and a domestic threat. Thus, by the time Edwards met John Carlos and Tommie Smith, he was already a target of Hoover's revulsion.[9]

Born and raised in Harlem, New York, in 1945, John Carlos experienced a world defined by racial disparities in education and housing and plagued by drug dealing and abuse, as well as racialized police brutality. When East Texas State University recruited him to run track, it seemed like an opportunity to escape, to perhaps start anew. The racism he experienced at the institution was so grave and overwhelming, however, that he transferred to SJSU after his first year. Tommie Smith had just started classes at the institution.[10]

A Texas native, Smith was well aware of the racism that defined the social landscape Carlos had fled. Born in Clarksville in 1945, Smith and his family left Texas in search of better educational opportunities when he was a child. They relocated to California, where Smith quickly realized that while his new environment did not bear "whites only" signs like those found across the South, racism was nonetheless present. "One day my mother gave me a nickel," Smith recalled, "and I bought an ice-cream cone. And this white kid, Wesley, knocked it out of my hand and said, 'Niggers don't eat ice cream.' I didn't know what to do. I went home and pondered it in my heart."[11] The encounter, reminiscent of Du Bois's experience with his white classmate, informed Smith's later activism.

During the fall of 1967, what Edwards described as "a revolt of Black students and athletes" at SJSU further catalyzed Smith and Carlos and led in part to the inception of the Olympic Project for Human Rights (OPHR). Smith and Carlos were SJSU students at the time and Edwards had just started teaching sociology at the institution. Seventy-two Black students protested racism in campus housing. They also called attention to the continued mistreatment of Black athletes. Smith once overheard his SJSU coach, for instance, make a bet with the coach from an opposing team: "My niggers could outrun your niggers."[12] When administrators failed to adequately address their concerns, Edwards and others threatened to hold a protest at the SJSU football game against the University of Texas at El Paso, a school that the previous year had made history by playing five Black starting players during the NCAA men's basketball championship game against the University of Kentucky. The administration relented by cancelling the game. Continual racial injustice across the nation during the preceding summer, together with the limited success they experienced at SJSU, led Edwards and the students to broaden their efforts. The upcoming Olympic Games, they reasoned, could provide a platform to call attention to issues that plagued Black America, a way to reconcile a triple-consciousness. Their concerns and efforts coalesced in the OPHR.[13]

The organization's demands were ostensibly simple, if ambitious. They included the removal of Avery Brundage, a white supremacist and anti-Semite known widely as "slavery Avery," from his post as the head of the International Olympic Committee (IOC); the restoration of Muhammad Ali's heavyweight championship boxing title, which had been stripped from him for his refusal to enter the Vietnam War draft; the exclusion of South Africa and Indonesia from the Olympic Games due to their continued human rights violations; and the hiring of more Black coaches on United States Olympic teams. In addition to drafting this list of grievances, members of the organization, including Smith and Carlos, discussed potentially boycotting the 1968 Olympic Games to protest racial inequality and racialized violence in the United States. In the end, Smith and Carlos decided to participate in the Olympics. "I wasn't there for the race or to win the gold medal as a typical Olympian would be," Carlos insisted. Instead, he viewed his participation in the games as a profound act that would "prove something to the world" and protest the treatment of their brethren in the United States.[14] Minutes before the 200-meter race, Carlos and Smith collaborated in the stadium's dressing room on a strategy to bring visibility to their cause. "We knew that what we were going to do was far greater than any athletic feat," Carlos recalled.[15]

When Smith situated himself in the blocks that sat firmly on the third lane of the track, he had already set eleven world records. He was a superstar in the world of track and field, a phenomenon whose athletic dexterity and equally adamant social consciousness would soon compete, or perhaps collaborate, for metamorphic visibility. Carlos occupied lane four. The Australian runner Peter Norman readied himself in lane six. One need not struggle to imagine the setting: On your mark, get set . . . (the blast of the flare gun). In 19.83 seconds, Smith crossed the finish line with a new world record. Norman followed, with Carlos in third place.[16]

Several photographers awaited the medal ceremony from twenty feet away in the media pen. John Dominis was among them. He later noted that he was "expecting a normal ceremony."[17] Each of the men's 200-meter medal recipients donned an OPHR patch on the lapel of their warm-up jacket, a seemingly innocuous act that would work to define and, in many respects, destroy Peter Norman in his home country. There was no escaping Norman's clear allyship with his Black competitors—the evidence would soon be captured by a camera. Each Olympian accepted his respective medal. Smith also received a box that contained an olive tree sapling, a symbol of peace. The American national anthem began to play throughout the stadium. Then, as upwards of 80,000 spectators gazed upon the podium, Smith and Carlos lowered their heads and lifted their gloved fists (Smith's right and Carlos's left) powerfully, proudly in the air to acknowledge and mitigate the anguish of their brethren, to help destroy the disease of racism. They lifted generations on their arms and spoke for a nation filled with the voices of the downtrodden. "Oh shit," 400-meter sprinter and OPHR member Lee Evans slowly exclaimed.[18] He understood the grandeur of the demonstration, and the inevitable repercussions. "Click, click, click!" "I hardly noticed what was happening when I was shooting," Dominis remembered in 2008.[19] He had unknowingly captured one of the most iconic images in American history. Two Black men stood as victors at the helm of Olympic greatness while broadening the visibility of a movement for civil rights, human rights, and Black Power. Their protest was the dawn of something different, something burgeoning, yet something instructed by the courage and success of the activists who came before them.

Many of the people who filled the stadium seemed mystified. Some applauded in a clear show of acceptance, if not respect. Others let out resounding boos, while still others began to scream the national anthem in what Carlos perceived as a rabid demonstration of opposition and fury. They were "Homo sapiens with hate in [their] face[s]," he would later recall. "I threw up my arm again and said, 'Please, God, get me out of here.'"[20]

Their gloved hands, as well as other carefully constructed aspects of their aesthetic, epitomized the cumulative, persistent struggle and resilience of a people. In an interview that occurred shortly after the Olympic ceremony, Smith explained the symbolism of the protest: "the right glove that I wore on my right hand signified the power within Black America."[21] Smith and Carlos stood without shoes, wearing black socks, with a single shoe perched next to each of them to represent the impoverished living conditions that plagued Black America. The beads Carlos draped around his neck symbolized the lynching of Black men. Each judiciously created aspect of their ensembles was seized by a single click of a camera. Smith and Carlos had determined how to reconcile their triple-consciousness, how to express pride in their Blackness while demanding to be brought into the fold of American democracy atop a literal and figurative athletic platform.[22]

The two men were given twenty-four hours to leave the Olympic Village by the IOC, but eviction from the village was only the beginning of their challenges. The IOC and many in the press were relentless in admonishing Smith and Carlos, and even attempted to erase any evidence of the occurrence. Historian Allen Guttmann notes that Brundage "did succeed in eliminating pictures of the Black Power protests from the lavishly illustrated official report published by the USOC," but such actions ostensibly did little to quell the visibility and impact of the image.[23] Months later, Brundage drafted a letter charging, "The action . . . was an insult to the Mexican hosts and a disgrace to the United States."[24] During an interview, a BBC reporter flippantly remarked to Carlos: "You might say you've got it all. You've got publicity, you've got medals, you've got martyrdom as well."[25] Carlos replied: "I can't eat that. And the kids around my block, that grew up with me, they can't eat that. And the kids that grew up after them, they can't eat it. They can't eat gold medals. Like Tommie Smith said, 'All we're asking for is an equal chance.'"[26] Despite the disheartening and frightening repercussions (they received death threats and hate mail for months, and their families were subject to admonishment years later) neither Smith nor Carlos regretted their actions.

Dominis lent an enduring legacy to the display of Black Power exhibited on the podium that extraordinary day in 1968 through a single compelling image that rendered a particular moment eternally impactful. The image helped court the wrath of those who sought to quiet and destroy any suggestion of discontent with the status quo. It has also served as an inimitable display of courage and resounding resilience, one that continues to inform the resolve of countless others who work to dismantle racial injustice in all forms and use history as a primer in their efforts. The image has thus become one of the most iconic displays of resistance, dignity, and valor in American history. Those athletes who, like Smith and Carlos, have chosen to use their platforms and to stand together with so many others in the long movement for social change—who risked much for the cause of liberty, of justice, to force a nation to confront its wicked reality and to make the words written in the nation's founding documents apply to all—demonstrate that *nothing is impossible*. Today, a statue of Tommie Smith and John Carlos is on the SJSU campus to memorialize their courageous actions. It was cast using the details preserved and disseminated in a single photograph.

NOTES

1. DeNeen L. Brown, "'A Cry for Freedom': The Black Power Salute That Rocked the World 50 Years Ago," *Washington Post*, October 16, 2018, https://www.washington post.com/history/2018/10/16/a-cry-freedom-black-power-salute-that-rocked-world -years-ago/.

2. Quoted in Paul Vitello, "John Dominis, Photographer, Dies at 92," *New York Times*, December 31, 2013, B14.

3. Gary Osmond, "Photographs, Materiality and Sport History: Peter Norman and the 1968 Mexico City Black Power Salute," *Journal of Sport History* 37 (Spring 2010): 119–137.

4. See Terry Anne Scott, *Lynching and Leisure: Race and the Transformation of Mob Violence in Texas* (Fayetteville: University of Arkansas Press, 2022).

5. Thomas C. Holt, *The Movement: The African American Struggle for Civil Rights* (Oxford: Oxford University Press, 2021), 113; Edward M. Kennedy, *True Compass: A Memoir* (New York: Twelve, 2009), 217; W. E. B. Du Bois (edited and introduction by David W. Blight and Robert Gooding-Williams), *The Souls of Black Folk* (Boston: Bedford Books, [1903] 1997), 38; Minrose Gwin, *Remembering Medgar Evers: Writing the Long Civil Rights Movement* (Athens: The University of Georgia Press, 2013), 63.

6. Du Bois, *The Souls of Black Folk*, 38.

7. Harry Edwards, *The Revolt of the Black Athlete*, 50th anniversary edition (Urbana: University of Illinois Press, 2009), xxiv.

8. Years later, one of Edwards's advisors apologized for his role in the situation. Personal communication with Harry Edwards, April 2016; David K. Wiggins, *More than a Game: A History of the African American Experience in Sport* (Lanham, MD: Rowman & Littlefield, 2018), 138–139.

9. Personal communication with Harry Edwards, December 18, 2023; Jai Lennard, "Harry Edwards Is Not Who You Think He Is," *Victory Journal*, https://victory journal.com/stories/harry-edwards/; Earl Smith, ed., *Sociology of Sport and Social Theory* (Champaign, IL: Human Kinetics, 2010), xii.

10. John Carlos, oral interview with David P. Cline, New York, August 18, 2013, Library of Congress, https://www.loc.gov/item/2015669202/.

11. Quoted in Kenny Moore, "A Courageous Stand," *Sports Illustrated*, August 5, 1991, 63.

12. Quoted in Christopher Hrynkow, "Players or Pawns? Protest, Participation, and Principled Nonviolence at the 1968 Summer Olympics," in *Conflict Transformation, Peacebuilding, and Storytelling*, ed. Laura E. Reimer, Katerina Standish, and Chuck Theissen (Lanham, MD: Lexington Books, 2018), 199.

13. Wiggins, *More than a Game*, 139–141.

14. Quoted in Danielle Smith-Leira, *Black Power Salute: How a Photograph Captured a Political Protest* (North Mankato, MN: Compass Point Books, 2017), 6.

15. Quoted in "A Silent Salute That Roared around the World," *Amsterdam News*, October 22, 2012, https://amsterdamnews.com/news/2012/10/22/a-silent-salute-that-roared-around-the-world/.

16. Smith-Leira, *Black Power Salute*, 5.

17. Quoted in Vitello, "John Dominis, Photographer, Dies at 92," B14.

18. Quoted in *The Journey of the African American Athlete*, VHS, produced by Leslie D. Farrell, Paul H. Hutchinson, and Kendall Reid (New York: HBO Sports, 1996).

19. Quoted in Vitello, "John Dominis, Photographer, Dies at 92," B14.

20. Quoted in Moore, "A Courageous Stand," 62.

21. Quoted in *The Journey of the African American Athlete*.

22. Tim Layden, "Fists of Fury," *Sports Illustrated*, October 8, 2018, 76.

23. Allen Guttmann, *The Olympics: A History of the Modern Games* (Urbana: University of Illinois Press, 1992), 132.

24. Amy Bass, "Whose Broad Stripes and Bright Stars? Race, Nation, and Power at the 1968 Mexico City Olympics," in *Sports Matters: Race, Recreation, and Culture*, ed. John Bloom and Michael Nevin Willard (New York: New York University Press, 2002), 199.

25. Quoted in Layden, "Fists of Fury," 81; for additional information on the Olympic Project for Human Rights, see Amy Bass, *Not the Triumph but the Struggle: The 1968 Olympics and the Making of the Black Athlete* (Minneapolis: University of Minnesota Press, 2002); Kevin B. Witherspoon, *Before the Eyes of the World: Mexico and the 1968 Olympic Games* (DeKalb: Northern Illinois University Press, 2008); Richard Hoffer, *Something in the Air: American Passion and Defiance in the 1968 Mexico City Olympics* (New York: Free Press, 2009).

26. Quoted in Layden, "Fists of Fury," 81.

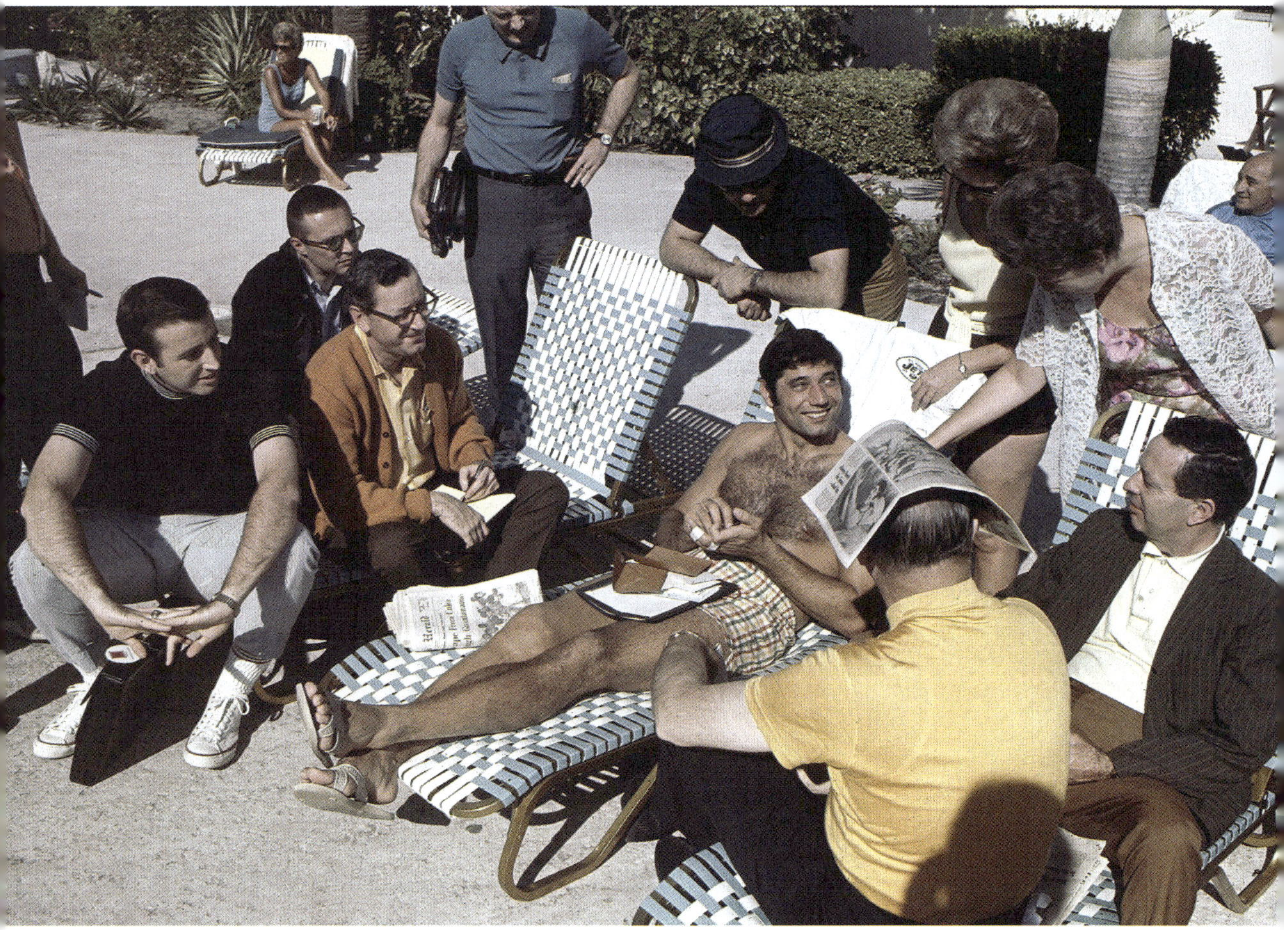

13

THE UNBEARABLE LIGHTNESS OF BEING BROADWAY JOE

Joe Namath in Fort Lauderdale, 1969

TRAVIS VOGAN

New York Jets quarterback Joe Willie Namath was infamous before he even played a down in the American Football League. In 1965, the Jets signed the rookie to a record $427,000 contract after a bidding war with the rival National Football League. The leagues merged the following year in part to avoid the escalating salaries their competition created. The historic payday made Namath an immediate target among traditionalists, who questioned whether the quarterback—or any player—was worth so much.

But Jets co-owner Sonny Werblin knew he was getting far more than a signal caller when he convinced his partners to sign Namath. The Jets had to find a way to thrive in a city with another professional football team, the NFL's Giants, and a plentitude of leisure options. Werblin, who was an executive at the Music Corporation of America before entering the football business, approached this obstacle by treating his sports franchise like any other entertainment property. He knew that no attraction could be successful without a recognizable name to put on the marquee. "I believe in the star system," he said. "It's the only thing that sells tickets. It's what you put on the stage or playing field that draws people."[1]

Broadway Joe was the Jets' leading man. "Namath has the presence of a star," Werblin remarked. "You know how a real star lights up a room when he comes in. Joe has that quality."[2] Namath lived in an Upper East Side apartment which was decorated by Frank Sinatra's interior designer and featured a white llama rug, Italian marble bar, and an oversized oval bed beneath a ceiling-mounted mirror. He frequented Manhattan nightclubs wearing five-hundred-dollar suits, and, when it was chilly, bundled up in an ankle-length mink coat. The quarterback unapologetically bragged about his looks, money, and sexual exploits. "I believe in letting a guy live the way he wants to if he doesn't hurt anyone," he told sportswriter Dan Jenkins.[3]

But many sportswriters viewed Namath as little more than a gimmick—a rakish grin with brittle knees wrapped in expensive threads. The quarterback began proving the naysayers wrong by leading the Jets to the 1968 AFL title. As a result, Namath's Jets were set to face the Baltimore Colts in the AFL-NFL Championship on January 12, 1969, at Miami's Orange Bowl. It was the third AFL-NFL title game since the merger and the first to be dubbed the Super Bowl—an effort to stress the contest's spectacular status. But few thought Namath's team stood a chance. *Sports Illustrated*'s Tex Maule picked the Colts to shut the Jets out 43–0 and *Detroit Free Press* columnist Joe Falls joked that "it could finish Colts 270, Jets 0."[4]

The underdog status did not muzzle Namath. He held court daily with reporters at the Galt Ocean Mile Hotel in Fort Lauderdale, where the Jets stayed while preparing for the Super Bowl. Namath, as the *New York Post*'s Larry Merchant put it, "began a week-long assault on all the time-honored traditions of pregame conduct."[5] He called the Colts overrated and bragged about the women who were keeping him company in Florida. The comments at once gave the press colorful copy and irked those who expected football heroes to exhibit greater focus and humility. By Wednesday, January 8, Namath was peeved by the many critical reports circulating in the daily papers. He announced that he would no longer give audience to journalists he did not know "because there's been too much crap written about me already."[6] The Jets, however, intervened. The organization reiterated to Namath the importance of press coverage—positive or negative—and persuaded Broadway Joe to rescind his hasty ban. One of the temporarily stonewalled scribes was *Dayton Daily News* sports editor Si Burick, who closed his daily report by mentioning Namath's unexpected and ultimately short-lived blackout. "I don't want to be rude, but I don't have anything to say," the exasperated quarterback told Burick when the journalist requested an interview. Shortly thereafter, Burick received a call from Jets Public Relations director Frank Ramos. "Joe Namath asked me to call you," Ramos explained to Burick. "He said he's sorry he was short with you and would like to talk with you at poolside at 10 A.M. on Thursday."[7]

Burick joined a pack of reporters on Thursday morning for Namath's media availability—a brief window sandwiched between his team practice, film study in the hotel's Imperial Room, and treatment on his fragile knees. One member of the poolside press corps was the twenty-five-year-old *Sports Illustrated* photographer Walter Iooss. The precocious photographer, who started publishing in *Sports Illustrated* at seventeen, was disappointed that his editors assigned him to cover the Jets instead of the Colts, his favorite team. Iooss's similarly prodigious colleague Neil Leifer received the Colts assignment. But Iooss—who faced some resentment among industry colleagues because of his age—identified with Namath's youthful irreverence and sought to capture the quarterback's polarizing but undeniably charming style. And Namath would not have to worry about critical depictions coming from Iooss's camera. "I won't do negative stories on athletes I know," Iooss later explained. "I want to make athletes look strong and heroic, like comic-book superheroes. Sometimes I'm the opposite of a writer, who tries to humanize them."[8] At the time, Iooss was also working for Atlantic Records, which had him shoot the likes of James Brown, Buddy Guy, Janis Joplin, and the Rolling Stones. Broadway Joe proved a perfect fit for the heroic and glamorous template Iooss employed to capture athletes and rock stars. The quarterback—as Iooss rendered him—would compose a new crossbreed of celebrity that blended these previously distinct pop cultural categories.

With a 50 mm lens on his Nikon F camera, Iooss caught Namath sprawling shirtless in checkered swimming trunks on a white and blue woven lounger surrounded by journalists. The reporters, reprieved from the previous day's temporary media embargo, were working to wring more quotes out of the quarterback for their daily dispatches. Iooss shot the scrum from multiple angles.[9] But the photograph that became a canonical image of Broadway Joe was taken from a slightly elevated poolside ledge just beyond the quarterback's feet and to his left. It provides a low-angle view of Namath at enough of a distance to capture the scene orbiting around the magnetic athlete.

Namath, of course, occupies the middle of the photograph and composes its focal point. Burick sits on the lounger to Namath's left wearing a short-sleeved velour shirt, on which Iooss's shadow is visible. Burick has a copy of the *New York Daily News*—New York's salacious picture newspaper—

draped over his head to protect his bald pate from the inhospitable Florida sun. Appropriately, the makeshift shade features a photograph of Namath alongside Jets coach Weeb Ewbank with a caption that jabs at the quarterback's increasingly prickly relationship with the press: "Joe, who's practically always all business, missed a press conference yesterday because, he said, 'There's been too much baloney written already.'"[10] It is ironic that a report on Namath's tension with the media is being used to guard a sensitive reporter against sunburn. Journalists like Burick, quite simply, needed Namath as much as, and probably more than, the quarterback needed them. Broadway Joe was the key narrative resource at their disposal leading to the Super Bowl and they aimed to harvest him for all they could get.

Next to Burick, wearing a striped jacket and brown slacks, sits Chuck Heaton of the *Cleveland Plain Dealer*. A young Brent Musburger, who had recently joined the Chicago CBS affiliate WBBM TV2, sits on the opposite side at Namath's feet wearing white Converse low-tops and fidgeting with his hands. To Musburger's left—sporting a rust-colored cardigan over a yellow shirt with pens protruding from the breast pocket—is Ray Sons of the *Chicago Daily News*. Jerry Green of the *Detroit News* sits behind Sons, and WCBS New York's Ed Ingles, whose head is cut out of the frame, stands to Green's left with a tape recorder resting at his hip. A handful of other notable reporters—including Larry Merchant—are present beyond the frame Iooss shares in this shot. As Burick's improvised paper hat indicates, the northern reporters seem uncomfortable in the southern heat and are not dressed for the weather. Namath had also traveled from cooler climes, but he looks as if he is in his native habitat. His skin, already naturally olive, is bronzed but not burned. The shadows in the photo suggest the sun is shining right in Broadway Joe's face, but the quarterback does not so much as squint. The press surrounding him—all pale, soft-bodied, and slightly disheveled in their inexpensive clothes—only amplify Namath's fitness, looks, and confidence. The frustration that caused Namath to suspend his media availability the previous day is completely absent. With his legs crossed at the ankle, the quarterback appears far more comfortable and relaxed than the reporters scrunched together and concentrating to take in whatever morsels he decides to serve up for their notepads, tape recorders, and cameras.

The other shots Iooss took during this short session show Namath's face expressionless and even tense. But the quarterback smiles—with his mouth and his eyes—in this famous photo. "His eyes are just so powerful," Iooss said while reflecting on the shot and his other encounters with Namath over the years.[11] Namath's smile is directed at two middle-aged women wearing bouffant hairdos who rush to his chair to say hello. One of them reaches over to give Namath an encouraging pat on the shoulder, a gesture he welcomes. Her neck cranes toward the superstar and her face is tightened around the eyes to suggest the excitement driving her actions. The women were not casual passersby, but two super fans from Tuscaloosa, Alabama, who attended all of Namath's college games, and, according to Iooss, would bring him sandwiches to make sure he was not playing on an empty stomach. The intrusion of these old friends gave Namath a momentary respite from the journalists he did not really want to be around. He seems genuinely happy to see the women (although the truly charismatic have a way of making everyone they encounter feel welcome and valued) and pleased that they made the twelve-hour drive to see him play the biggest game of his career. Moreover, Namath was disappointed that his mother, who feared that her plane might be hijacked to Cuba, decided not to make the trip from Beaver Falls, Pennsylvania, to Miami for the Super Bowl.[12] The presence of these familiar and maternal figures provided a comfort.

A pile of mail sits on Namath's lap and a folded copy of the day's *Miami Herald* lies next to him. The *Miami Herald*'s front page reported eighty Cubans escaping the country through the Guantanamo Bay naval base in hopes of accessing the boundless economic opportunity Americans like Namath embodied. The edition also included two sports articles that continued the press's generally dismissive attitude toward Namath and his Super Bowl prospects. Sports editor Edwin Pope called the quarterback a "man-child" and Bob Elliot poked fun at Namath's publicly stated belief that his team could beat the mighty Colts.[13] While he might have carted the *Miami Herald* poolside looking for some distraction, he would have found more of what he considered to be "crap" and "baloney" when he started leafing through its pages.

Namath was also in considerable physical pain—a constant throughout his career. His left middle and ring fingers are taped together in two places. His right leg features a long scar just beneath the kneecap—a grisly relic of the days before arthroscopic surgery—and is shaved so his knee can be easily taped and re-taped before practices and games. Earlier in the week, Jets doctor James Nicholas removed two ounces of fluid from his right knee. Namath would get another treatment shortly after this shot was taken. Dr. Nicholas injected each of his knees with 25 milligrams of the anti-inflammatory Prednisone. The doctor also wanted to inject Namath's right thumb, but the quarterback refused the shot out of concern that it might impact his feel for the ball on Sunday.[14] He would rather endure the pain than compromise his ability to throw the passes that helped land the Jets in the Super Bowl.

This is all to say that Namath had a lot going on despite the languid pose, easy grin, and bedroom eyes Iooss captures. Namath was irritated by the press but constrained to indulge them, dealing with enough physical pain to warrant injections in both knees, and preparing for the biggest game of his career. He also missed his mom. But Iooss depicts a man who seems completely at ease and untroubled. The image captures the coolness that became Namath's stylistic calling card.

After finishing the poolside appearance, Namath spent most of the day studying film and receiving treatments on his knees. That evening he was scheduled to attend a dinner at the Miami Touchdown Club, which had chosen him as professional football's player of the year. Namath did not want to go. But it was the first time an AFL player had won the award and Jets management made it clear that the quarterback's attendance was not optional. Namath continued his characteristic jawing while giving a short acceptance speech, during which he offhandedly said, "We'll win on Sunday. I guarantee it."[15] The statement generated some coverage, but it was mostly disregarded as the latest quip from the showboating quarterback.

"If the Jets had lost, I would have had to throw it in the garbage bin," Iooss recalls of his famous photograph.[16] Namath's guarantee likely also would have been forgotten. But the Jets won. The victory reframed Iooss's photo and Namath's guarantee as testaments to the ability that the confident quarterback knew he had all along and harbingers of the new era in sports that he ushered in.

Tex Maule's report on Super Bowl III for *Sports Illustrated* opened with an acknowledgment of Namath's arrival and cultural import. "Broadway Joe Namath is the folk hero of the new generation" whose style "spells insouciant youth in the Jet Age."[17] Iooss's photograph accompanied Maule's story. *Sports Illustrated* arranged the photo vertically atop another Iooss shot of the quarterback in action during the big game. The top photo has Namath reclining poolside in Fort Lauderdale; the bottom image shows him in the pocket about to throw a pass in Miami. The eyes that so captivated Iooss are peering in the same direction in both images—toward his female admirers on top and at his receiver on the bottom. The juxtaposition articulates a connection between Namath's charismatic off-field persona and dazzling on-field ability. Whether swarmed by journalists or defensive linemen, Namath looks good, keeps calm, and wins. His style was substance.

NFL Films, the National Football League's film production company and official chronicler, similarly installed Iooss's photo into professional football lore by including it in the Super Bowl III highlight film released shortly after the game. NFL Films documentaries typically use only the footage its cinematographers shoot in 16 mm. But the company saw fit to license Iooss's photo for this documentary to explain Namath's ascendance as a mold-breaking football idol. "A relaxed and confident Joe Namath made it clear that in his mind there was no doubt that the Jets would win," NFL Films' baritone narrator John Facenda intones as the documentary displays Iooss's photo during its early moments. The rest of the film builds on the photograph to make the case that Namath represents a new epoch in pro football in which athletes can at once be fashionable stars and battle-scarred warriors.

Namath capitalized heartily on the carefree and fetching image Iooss's photo helped to solidify. Shortly after Super Bowl III, he published the tongue-in-cheek memoir *I Can't Wait until Tomorrow . . . 'Cause I Get Better Looking Every Day* with the sportswriter Dick Schaap. Later that year, he and Schaap teamed up to co-host *The Joe Namath Show*, an interview-driven syndicated television program that lasted only thirteen episodes and aired alongside the Jets' 1969 season. In 1970, Broadway Joe realized what was perhaps the logical conclusion of his meteoric celebrity trajectory by starring in two Hollywood films—*Norwood* (dir. Jack Haley Jr.) and C. C. *and Company* (dir. Seymour Robbie). As Iooss's poolside photograph implied, Namath's stardom was not limited to—and refused to be contained by—the gridiron. Namath's marketable charisma stretched football's cultural boundaries in unprecedented directions that complemented the entertainment-friendly aspirations informing the nascent Super Bowl and its increasing reliance on commercial television.

Broadway Joe was not the first sports star to achieve celebrity outside of his primary occupation—or even the first to be featured in major motion pictures. Notable athletes had entertained on the vaudeville stage since the late nineteenth century, and Babe Ruth, Jack Dempsey, and Joe Louis all starred in films. But Namath was arguably the first to do so in a way that so explicitly shopped his masculine sexuality. This is partly a function of white privilege. Muhammad Ali had been bragging about his good looks for years. The boxer's Blackness, politics, and religion, however, made it impossible for him to enjoy the sort of opportunities that seemed to fall into Namath's lap. This is not to say that being Broadway Joe was easy. The quarterback faced enormous pressure, endured excruciating pain, and worked very hard. But it's a lot more fun to imagine that being Joe Namath was effortless—that success followed him like just another reporter or autograph hound. Iooss's iconic photograph captures the unbearable lightness of being Broadway Joe.

Iooss went on to become one of the world's most decorated sports photographers. But he is best known for his work on *Sports Illustrated*'s annual swimsuit issue, to which the photographer has contributed since 1972. Iooss's poolside shot of Joe Namath composes a precursor to his depictions of bikini-clad models posing in far flung tropical locales. It also marks a turning point in the sexual economy of popular sports media in which male athletes could, under certain cultural circumstances, occasionally be elevated as objects of a desiring gaze.

NOTES

1. Quoted in Robert H. Boyle, "Show-Biz Sonny and His Quest for Stars," *Sports Illustrated*, July 19, 1965, 66.

2. Quoted in Boyle, "Show-Biz Sonny and His Quest for Stars," 68–69.

3. Quoted in Dan Jenkins, "The Sweet Life of Swinging Joe," *Sports Illustrated*, October 17, 1966, 44.

4. Joe Falls, "It Could Finish Colts 270, Jets 0," *Detroit Free Press*, December 30, 1968, 1D.

5. Larry Merchant, . . . *And Every Day You Take Another Bite* (Garden City, NY: Doubleday, 1971), 123.

6. Quoted in Dave Anderson, *Countdown to the Super Bowl* (New York: Random House, 1969), 148.

7. Quoted in Si Burick, *Dayton Daily News*, January 9, 1969, 12.

8. "The Education of Walter Iooss," *Sports Illustrated*, December 12, 2011, 131.

9. Other angles from Iooss's photo session that day can be accessed via Getty Images.

10. *New York Daily News*, January 9, 1969, 92.

11. Walter Iooss, interview with author, December 10, 2021.

12. Anderson, *Countdown to the Super Bowl*, 140.

13. Edwin Pope, "Weeb and His Boys," *Miami Herald*, January 9, 1964, 1C; Bob Elliott, "Talk Is Cheap," *Miami Herald*, January 9, 1969, 4C.

14. Mark Kreigel, *Namath: A Biography* (New York: Penguin, 2005), 267; Anderson, *Countdown to the Super Bowl*, 157–158.

15. Kreigel, *Namath*, 268–269.

16. Iooss, interview.

17. Tex Maule, "Say It's So, Joe," *Sports Illustrated*, January 20, 1969, 10.

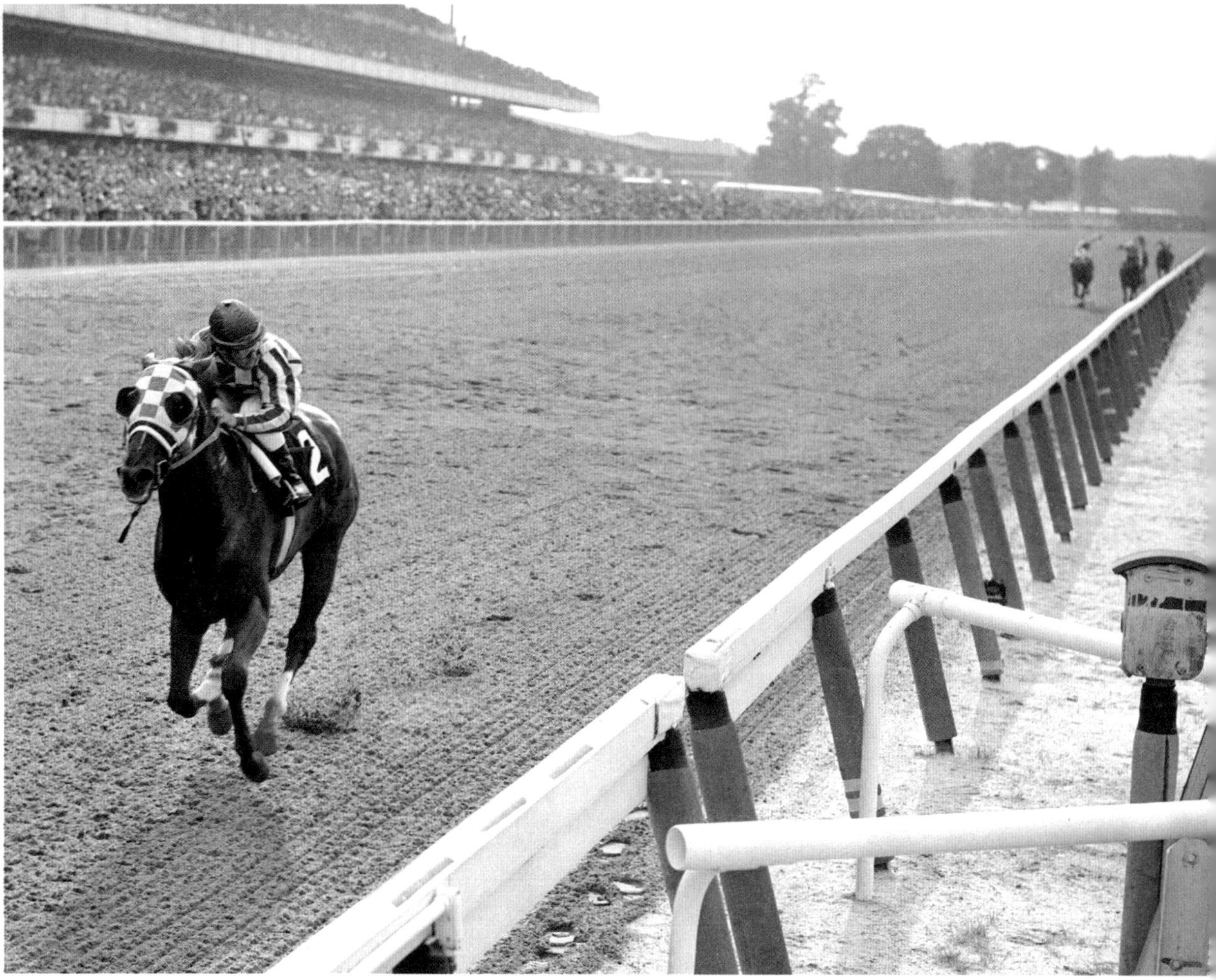
2

14

SECRETARIAT AT THE BELMONT

Jonathan Silverman

The black-and-white photo captures a horse in motion, all four legs in the air. The jockey is firmly on the horse, glancing back over his shoulder. The viewer follows the jockey's eyes to the trailing horses, so far behind they are blurry. Our eyes move to a grandstand that seems full but is also blurry. The rail on the left looks industrial and even a little forbidding; it takes little imagination to think about the horse bumping into it.

The horse is wearing a uniform, number 2. Racing fans know the 2 corresponds to the post position, the place where the horse leaves the starting gate, which is randomly assigned. Numbers are on horses because they are used by bettors. You cannot go up to a betting window and say, "I want the big beautiful fast horse to win." The horse needs a number.

There are hoofprints in the dirt. Some of them come from this horse, but other horses have also been on this dirt, this track. There is a whip to the side of the horse. The jockey is not using it. Many jockeys still use whips, but this horse does not need whipping.[1]

There is much we do not know about this photo. Before we know its context, we are short on details. We do not know the race, the track, the name of the horse, the jockey, or the other horses. The photo is in black and white, so we are not sure of the weather, the time of day it was taken, or the year when it was taken. Is the horse big or small? The viewer might find it hard to tell because the other horses are so far away. Is the horse fast? We can imagine this is true—this horse is so far away from the other horses, but could there be another horse ahead of this one? Are the other horses just slow?

In his essay "Observation as Photography: A Metaphor," scholar Hervé Laroche suggests that, when assessing crime scene photos, "photography is conceived as a tool that will retain relevant clues until they are sifted out from irrelevant details."[2] That is the purpose of this essay—to think about what the photo tells us.

Is this an iconic photo, and if it is, what elevates it to that status? Without context to understand and frame the photo, the horse is on its edge (of course photos can be manipulated, but editing a photo might not make it less great). That the main horse is in focus while the others are not adds to its intrigue. The mix of the industrial and the pastoral, the animals and humans, compels one's attention. An argument for the photo's greatness comes perhaps from the contrast between the way the horse is looking forward while the jockey is looking backward. The horse is all business, while the jockey cannot help but try to situate himself and the horse.

The photo itself is wonderful and captivating, and the composition is artistic. But the context determines its meaning and iconicity. The context is Secretariat's history-making performance in the third leg of the Triple Crown in 1973, the Belmont Stakes. The image shows the dominance of Secretariat's performance at Belmont and perhaps the entire Triple Crown run. Studying it reveals more about Secretariat, about photography at the racetrack and, more generally, about technology and its relationship to time. It facilitates the necessary understanding of Secretariat that makes this image among the greatest sports photographs of all time.

"That's a picture that tells so many stories. I mean, it's well made, of course," said Henry Horenstein, photographer and co-author of the horse racing book *Racing Days* (1995). "The photographer knew what to look for, and he stood at the finish line and made his picture with the Speed Graphic . . . but it tells a story of a horse that was so superior. You know that he was able to beat the best horses in the country by [thirty-one] lengths. And he was in here, and he wasn't even being whipped or pressed."[3] Horenstein claims a photographer could make their reputation on that one photo. "I would live and die on that photo. It is one of the great photos, and I'm sure I'm not the only one that thinks this is one of the great photos in the history of sport."

The Horse and the Race

Secretariat was a foal of Bold Ruler and Somethingroyal. Bold Ruler won the Preakness Stakes in 1957, and while Somethingroyal only raced once, her father (Secretariat's grandfather), Princequillo, set a track record at Saratoga Race Course at 1.75 miles in 1943. Secretariat was bred at Meadow Stable in Virginia, overseen by Helen "Penny" Chenery (Tweedy), and named by her father's former secretary, because of her prior connection to the secretariat at the League of Nations.[4]

On June 9, 1973, Secretariat raced in the Belmont Stakes, the last race of horse racing's Triple Crown, consisting of three of horse racing's most storied races: the Kentucky Derby, the Preakness, and the Belmont Stakes. The Triple Crown is an extremely challenging stretch of races; all three races have different lengths, with the Belmont the longest at 1 ½ miles. Secretariat won all but one race before the Kentucky Derby, which he ran under two minutes for the mile-and-a-quarter race, the first to break the two-minute mark. He was similarly fast in the Preakness, winning that race too.

The Belmont has a long and storied history. As journalist Melissa Hoppert notes, "The Belmont, first run in 1867 at Jerome Park in the Bronx and won by a filly named Ruthless, is the oldest of the three Triple Crown races, predating the Preakness by six years and the Derby by eight."[5] Belmont Park, opened in Elmont, New York, in 1905, is enormous, and the track is too, fully 1 ½ miles, whereas most tracks are a mile long.

For the Belmont, Secretariat was a one-to-five favorite, which means you would win a dollar twenty on a one-dollar bet. Five horses competed in the Belmont race, making it a "short field," which is typically fewer than eight horses in a race.[6] Secretariat got away well, and battled with Sham, who had finished close behind him in the Preakness and Kentucky Derby, almost matching Secretariat's record time in both. Ron Turcotte, Secretariat's jockey, recalled, "My plan was to sit behind Sham in the early going. That changed when I felt the power beneath me and Secretariat broke sharply. I let him get his feet under him and picked his head up entering the first turn."[7]

The head-to-head battle between Secretariat and Sham lasted for a good half mile. In battles this early, one or both horses often suffer. When handicapping, in fact, if you know two horses like speed, or as they say, "like the front," it often opens up the race for a slower horse with greater endurance to win. This is particularly true with the Belmont, as speed duels often lead to late charges. That did not happen, Turcotte said, because Secretariat was running so well. "Sham and jockey Laffit Pincay decided to try to stay with us early, but I knew there was no way Sham could stay with Secretariat, whose tremendous stride allowed him to cover a great amount of ground," Turcotte said. "I never felt such strength under me as I did that day. We were flying along. We covered the opening half-mile in 46 $^{1}/_{5}$ seconds, three-quarters in 1:09 $^{4}/_{5}$ and the mile in 1:34 $^{4}/_{5}$."[8]

Turcotte said he knew Secretariat was running well enough to keep their current pace, explaining, "Lucien [Laurin, Secretariat's trainer] and others in the stands thought I was crazy. But I am the one on the horse. I knew he was well within himself. He was doing everything easily. His stride was beautiful. His breathing was good. Everything was going to my liking."[9] On the backstretch Sham retreated, and Secretariat gradually drew off, winning the race by thirty-one lengths.[10]

Back to the photo and Turcotte's famous turn of his head. Turcotte cited different reasons for turning. One explanation was to see what the time was: "When I peeked that last time, it was not to see where the other horses were. I was looking for the time."[11] In another explanation, Turcotte was curious as to where his opponents were. He recalled, "I kept hearing Chic Anderson. I finally had to turn to see where the other horses were. I know this sounds crazy, but the horse did it by himself. I was along for the ride."[12] Turcotte's turn seemed instinctual, as if to sneak a peek at immortality.

Secretariat's Triple Crown triumph was the first since Citation in 1948 and just the ninth horse in history to pull off the feat; four more have done it since 1973. Secretariat is considered one of the best horses of all time, and there is a case to be made that he was the best because of his Triple Crown performance, including his dominant performance in the Belmont.[13]

Audax Minor of the *New Yorker* certainly thought the performance was the best he had seen: "Predictably, and magnificently, the Meadow Stable's Secretariat galloped away with the Belmont Stakes by thirty-one lengths at Belmont Park last Saturday afternoon. Nothing I've ever seen in this race, which is called the Test of the Champion (and, if you must know, I go back to Man o' War), was more comprehensive and no triumph more thorough."[14]

The Photo

The photo was taken by Bob Coglianese, the track photographer for the New York Racing Association (NYRA); he died in 2022 at age 88. Its first purpose is documentary and journalistic; Coglianese was a NYRA track photographer trying to capture the finish of a race to convey it to the world. Not surprisingly, it was his favorite shot. In an interview, Coglianese described the photo: "Secretariat winning the Belmont Stakes by thirty-one lengths, which *Sports Illustrated* called the greatest racing photo of the twentieth century. It was a big race, it was the Belmont Stakes, and there was a photo stand over there and I was on it, shooting the race and it just so happened I got that shot."[15]

One of a photograph's basic purposes is to capture what is happening at the moment. There is art in intention, witnessed by the precision of the equipment used, the precise location of the stand, which is designed for a track photographer to get a great shot. Experience matters, too, and experience put Coglianese on the track in a position to take the great shot. And it was just one shot. Coglianese explains, "When I took Secretariat, I took it with one shot, that's all I had. That was when it was difficult, but today with digital and motorized, it's a lot easier."[16]

A lot had to go right to get the shot. Secretariat had to defeat his opponents in a decisive manner, which is rare in the Triple Crown races. Most races are relatively close, and even with dominant horses, the average winning distance is in the single digits, nowhere near thirty-one lengths. Coglianese had to be in a specific location to catch the image, relying on his experience and status as the track photographer. Coglianese's camera had to function in such a way that focused on the immediate subject, making the other horses appear blurry, adding to the image of Secretariat's dominance. The lighting had to be good. The timing caught the turn of the jockey's head and Secretariat in the air. Such timing was fortunate and leads us to think about the relationship between animal and machine. In real time, the naked eye would not see that Secretariat was airborne, as in this image.

In other words, the shot is fortunate in its construction, but it would be odd to call it lucky, especially since many of the conditions identified were true for most of the races Bob Coglianese shot. Adam Coglianese, Bob's son, who has taken over his role as NYRA photographer, explained that the mechanics of his father's shot were much different than the way photography works today. "Years ago, you only had one shot. You didn't have a motorized camera. So the image, forty, almost fifty years later, still, is fresh in people's minds because there's no other image of that race like that. That's composed the way it is. It's one of those shots that can't be reproduced."[17] He said the photo was taken with a Speed Graphic camera, which was "used by most photographers, and that's how images were captured" in the era in which the camera was dominant.

The Speed Graphic was a legendary camera, and according to John Durniak, the late executive editor of *Popular Photography* magazine, it "ruled newspaper photography in the United States."[18] Introduced in 1899 by W. F. Folmer, the Speed Graphic "became the most popular camera in photojournalism," and is credited with "some of the greatest news pictures of the last few decades." Durniak cites a number of famous photos captured with the Speed Graphic, such as Joe Rosenthal's photo of the raising of the American flag on Iwo Jima in 1945. Its versatility was its appeal. It "could do almost anything, anywhere," claimed Durniak, "as a hand-held camera for news, a sports camera that froze action at an incredible 1/1000 second."

Adam Coglianese said the Speed Graphic is designed to take one shot at a time: "You focus the camera by pulling the lens in and out. And you put the film in the back of the camera, and you have one shot to get what you're aiming for." He acknowledges that with the way cameras are today, his father's shot might not have been the only one like it. "In today's world if that race ran today, every photographer would have had the same picture because we all have a motorized camera." In this way, technology contributed to his father's unique image. "When my father didn't have a motorized camera, he pushed the button at the right time. He composed it the way it's supposed to be composed," Coglianese notes. According to the younger Coglianese, the reason the shot is in focus is the length of the lens. He explains there is "no such thing as a real long lens" on the Speed Graphic. "It doesn't have a lot of depth of field. So most everything would be in focus." In contrast, when contemporary photographers use long lenses at sporting events, "most everything is out of focus except the player."

Adam Coglianese identified the location of his father's shot as the multi-level photographer's stand set up just past the finish line on the inside of the track, which is "intended for photographers to stand on so they would capture the images of the races." That photographer's stand remains at Belmont, and as the NYRA photographer, Adam Coglianese, says, he's "a firm believer in a very standard product. It's very hard to reinvent the wheel." Adam suggests his father probably did not shoot Secretariat straight on, which is reflected in the shot itself. "A little more frontal view of the horse that makes him look better than shooting straight." Adam Coglianese's view is confirmed by looking at other versions of the race finish. These photos are wonderful in ways that are different from Coglianese's photo.

The Other Photos

Meyer Liebowitz, a veteran horse racing photographer, snapped a photo that appeared in the *New York Times* and looks very similar to the Coglianese photo. Liebowitz's photo is a bit more head-on than the Coglianese picture; you can still see the horses in the distance, and Turcotte's turning is captured. Liebowitz seems to be a little more distant from the horse than Bob Coglianese. Bill Meurer, whose image appeared in the *Daily News*, shot his photo below horse level. His image also looks very similar to Coglianese's, though Secretariat looks precarious, balanced on one leg. We see one horse, Twice a Prince, in second at the time of the shot, and the angle is a little more head-on than the Coglianese photo and less so than the Liebowitz photo. An AP wirephoto, shot almost straight on, does not have the same depth of perception to show how far behind the other horses are, but does provide a good view of Secretariat from the front.

When I showed the Coglianese photo and the others to a gathering of people, they all noted the photo's superiority was due to the sharp focus of Secretariat and the way the horse almost seems to run off the photo, as well as the angle of the photograph that allows the camera to catch Secretariat in focus and the distant horses blurred. Overall, the shot came about from a mix of professional preparation, good fortune, and a rare performance from an even rarer horse.

"A Tremendous Machine": A Photo Finished

One of the interesting things about the photo is that it likely did not appear in public until well after the Belmont race. Adam Coglianese said the track would send the photos to the AP and UPI, but in an admittedly small sample of twenty-five Virginia papers the next day, June 10, 1973, and in the week after, there was no evidence of the photo. The AP used another similar, arguably great shot. The UPI used a few other shots from the day, but not that one. Searches on Getty Images, which own the UPI archive, did not reveal any of those shots, nor did the UPI's own site, nor did any of the other UPI archives. The Coglianese shot abounds online, but they do not seem to be from a periodical printed at the time of the race. Adam Coglianese said he and his father found the shot while looking through the NYRA archive.

The photo process reminds us of the complicated relationship between horses and machines, one that undergirds horse racing, which is echoed in the CBS call of the race by Chic Anderson. The broadcaster seemed almost stunned by Secretariat's performance, saying "Secretariat is moving like a tremendous machine," which is a telling simile.[19] The connection of horses to machines is obvious. For much of human history, horses aided humans in doing all sorts of work. They were the preferred method of travel until the combustion engine was invented. Horses have regressed in importance as a form of transportation but that has led to their ascendance as a means of performance and spectacle. The photo captures this performance, this machine-like horse, existing as an airborne creation of nature, while establishing itself as dominant on the man-made track. The camera participates in this process, documenting and elevating the photograph past simile into metaphor.

It also reminds us of the famous experiments by Eadweard Muybridge in the nineteenth century. Muybridge demonstrated that horses did run in a way where all four hooves were off the ground at the same time. When Muybridge did that, it was shocking. "He showed the world what could be guessed but never seen—every stage of a horse's gallop when it sped across a track," journalist Haleema Shah writes. "In the nineteenth century, it seemed as though Muybridge had used photography to stop time. When the Industrial Revolution was underway, and scholars were obsessed with identifying, cataloging and potentially mechanizing nature, Muybridge's photo sequence of a moving horse was a milestone."[20]

Secretariat's four hoofs in the air took place at a different time. In 1973, we were at the advent of the video age in sports, one that in many ways left horse racing, once the most popular sport in the country, behind. The Belmont was shown on television, and the video of the Belmont available on YouTube is much worse in quality than the Coglianese photo. When watching the video, the narrative is different. You see Sham fight for half the race, then withdraw, exhausted. There is no other horse coming; Secretariat has left them all behind. The narrative tension of the race is released at the top of the stretch, when it is clear no one will catch Secretariat; the only thing left to decide is the extent to which the race will immortalize him.

The photo captures something that the video cannot. "The breakthrough is that the camera can see things that the human eye can't see, and that we can use photography to access our world beyond what we know it to be," says Shannon Perich, the Smithsonian's curator of photography at the National Museum of American History.[21]

The photo captures the culmination of the race, which in a traditional sense was without narrative tension; races are more exciting when they are close. But the photo resets the race for eternity. It shows us the distance between Secretariat and the other horses, which now becomes permanent. In the photo, Ron Turcotte is punctuating the distance, glancing behind him to confirm visually what he sensed physically: Secretariat had made the race immortal.

We see the moment at the culmination of greatness. The photo reveals Turcotte's turn. It reveals the distance in a new way, from the front/side, rather than the version viewers saw on television. It shows Secretariat flying. It shows the value of photography.

What we are left with is a wonderful snapshot of history, when arguably one of the greatest horses showed the power, beauty, and maybe even vulnerability of a moment. Horse racing photos sometimes seem like miracles in the way they capture an animal so fast and majestic. Coglianese's photo may be the most miraculous horse racing photo of all time.

NOTES

1. If you watch the 1973 Belmont Stakes on YouTube, you can verify that the jockey never uses the whip on this horse. He handrides him, which means the jockey grabs the horse's bridle and urges him that way.

2. Hervé Laroche, "Observation as Photography: A Metaphor," *M@n@gement* 23, no. 3 (2020): 81.

3. Conversation with Henry Horenstein, March 31, 2022.

4. "Ask Penny," Secretariat.com, https://www.secretariat.com/ask-penny/.

5. Melissa Hoppert, "The Longest Ride: Historical Images from Belmont Park, the Challenging Track Where Horse Racing Legends Are Made—or Not," *New York Times*, June 4, 2021, https://www.nytimes.com/2021/06/04/sports/horse-racing/belmont-stakes-triple-crown.html.

6. Gamblers hate short fields, while owners love them because the odds tend to be short, which is good for owners and bad for gamblers.

7. Tom Pedulla, "In Their Own Words: Secretariat Moves 'Like a Tremendous Machine' in Epic Belmont," June 6, 2018, New York Racing Association, NYRA.com .https://www.belmontstakes.com/news/in-their-own-words-secretariat-moves-like-a-tremendous-machine-in-epic-belmont.

8. Pedulla, "In Their Own Words."

9. Pedulla, "In Their Own Words."

10. Steve Cady, "Pvt. Smiles Fits Profile of Belmont Spoiler," *New York Times*, June 8, 1973, 30.

11. Pedulla, "In Their Own Words."

12. Ron Flatter, "Secretariat Remains No. 1 Name in Racing," https://www.espn.com/sportscentury/features/00016464.html. The video about him aired on May 21, 1999. Anderson called the CBS broadcast. Turcotte would have heard Dave Johnson, who called the race at Belmont.

13. For an example of a "best of" list, see "10 Best Racehorses of All Time," *Guardian*, May 23, 2000, https://www.theguardian.com/observer/osm/story/0,,255383,00.html. Secretariat was third on this list. Most lists include him somewhere in the top ten, and many American-only lists have him at number one.

14. Audax Minor, "The Race Track: Thirty-One Lengths," *New Yorker*, June 16, 1973, 105.

15. Heather Pettinger, "Saratoga Q&A with Bob Coglianese," New York Racing Association, August 18, 2018, https://www.nyra.com/saratoga/news/saratoga-q-and-a-with-bob-coglianese.

16. Pettinger, "Saratoga Q&A with Bob Coglianese."

17. In conversation with Adam Coglianese, February 28, 2022. The rest of the quotes from Adam Coglianese are from this interview.

18. John Durniak, "Camera: The Speed Graphic Is Alive and Kicking," *New York Times*, June 15, 1986, 55.

19. "SECRETARIAT—1973 Belmont Stakes—Part 4 (CBS)," Vintage North American Horse Racing, https://www.youtube.com/watch?v=kZ6XuoSFqHo.

20. Haleema Shah, "How a 19th-Century Photographer Made the First 'GIF' of a Galloping Horse," *Smithsonian*, December 13, 2018, https://www.smithsonianmag.com/smithsonian-institution/how-19th-century-photographer-first-gif-galloping-horse-180970990/.

21. Quoted in Shah, "How a 19th-Century Photographer Made the First 'GIF.'"

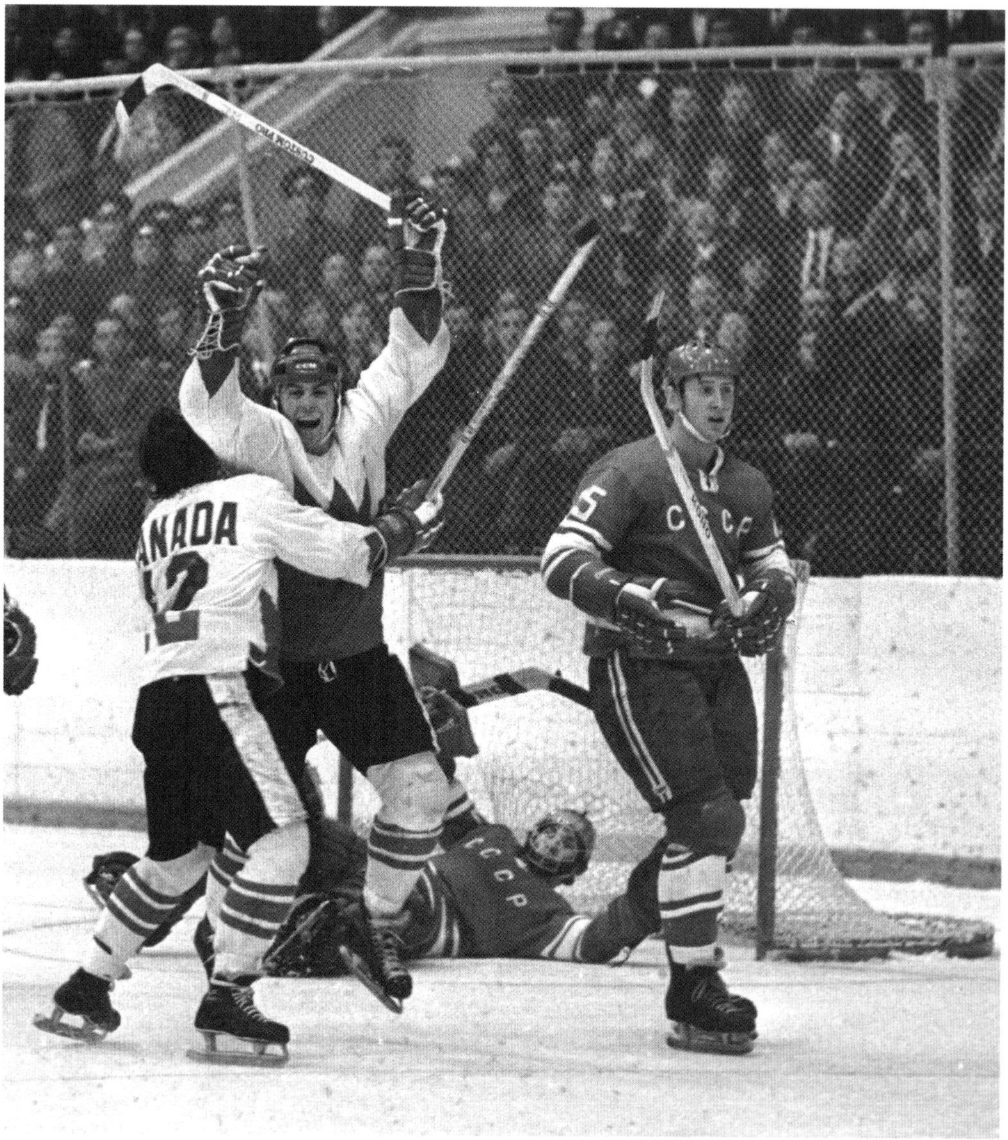
ANADA
12
CCCP
CCCP

15

"HENDERSON HAS SCORED FOR CANADA"

Photographing Canadian Nationalism

RUSSELL FIELD

It's the most famous image in Canadian sport history, freezing in time the immediate aftermath of the most famous moment in Canadian sport history. With thirty-four seconds left in the final and deciding game of a hotly contested hockey series, Paul Henderson of Canada scored the tie-breaking and series-clinching goal versus the Soviet national team. He jumped into a teammate's embrace as the then record-setting television audience across Canada exhaled a palpable sigh of relief and camera shutters clicked throughout Moscow's Luzhniki Ice Palace.

The best known of the many photos that celebrate this signature moment are in fact two photos. Taken by two well-known Canadian sport photographers who were sitting next to each other, the images have regularly been mistaken for each other in the ensuing half century, essentially fusing into a single image in the public imagination.[1] More importantly, their collective representation of Canada's ultimate hockey triumph has come to overshadow all other images that captured a moment suffused with nationalist overtones and a Cold War subtext. In their multiple subsequent reproductions, these two often-confused images have stood as representations of national pride and been used to evoke a very particular affective response—one that celebrates a multicultural Canadian nationalism yet allows for only a narrow set of responses to the image of Henderson scoring for Canada.

The Summit Series

The Summit Series consisted of eight games played in September 1972 between the Soviet Union's national ice hockey team and what was fashioned as Team Canada, which included only Canadian-born National Hockey League (NHL) players.[2] Motivated in part by the increasing dominance of Soviet teams over Canadian amateurs in international play—which, along with assertions by Canadian officials that state-funded Soviet amateur players were thinly veiled professionals, while Canada's professionals were unable to participate, had led Canada to withdraw from international ice hockey in 1970—the "exhibition" games were intended to pit the two countries' best players against each other. Taking place before the NHL season began, the series consisted of four games in Canada—in Montreal, Toronto, Winnipeg, and Vancouver—followed by four games in Moscow.

Despite the best-vs.-best format, the Canadian team was heavily favored. Two early goals by Canada in game one confirmed this presumption, before the unheralded and (to most Canadian observers) unknown Soviet team stormed back to win, 7–3. A Canadian victory in game two was followed by a draw in game three and a dominant Soviet performance in game four. When the series resumed in Moscow, a late Soviet comeback in game five left the Canadian team needing to win the final three games to capture the series. With less than a minute left in the eighth game, which was tied 5–5, the Canadians were a goal away from pulling off just such a comeback for a series win that, only weeks earlier, had seemed a foregone conclusion. This set the stage for Henderson's heroics and the two photographers who would immortalize the moment.

Photographing Canadian Sport History

The Summit Series has been the focus of considerable attention, particularly by Canadian scholars exploring the intersections of hockey, nationalism, and politics, often focusing on the series' Cold War context and the fractured Canadian political scene of the early 1970s. More recent scholarship has added to how the series is understood.[3] Considerations of representations of the series have focused primarily on Canadian national television coverage.[4] Yet little has been written about the photographers' images. Despite this, photography has received increasing attention as an element of the visual turn in sport studies.[5] This has included explorations of sport and modernity or examinations of heretofore unrecognized moments in the history of, for example, women's sport.[6]

Nevertheless, one of Canada's most celebrated sport photographs captures neither a hidden moment nor a women's sporting achievement. Rather, it can be best understood, as Mike O'Mahony argues, as one of many "photographs taken during key sporting events that are assumed, to a significant extent, to derive their value and meaning from an awareness of the event rather than the intrinsic values of the image itself."[7] In Canadian sport, specifically hockey, photography capturing game action at ice level—as distinct from team photos and the portraiture typical of trading cards—is most commonly associated with the brothers Lou and Nat Turofsky and their Alexandra Studios in Toronto in the first half of the twentieth century.[8] Their images, published in daily newspapers and elsewhere, brought viewers into the arena and made visual events that were, except for ticket holders, only available over the radio. By 1972, television was well established on the sport media landscape and a large Canadian audience was watching game eight of the Summit Series from Moscow. Three thousand Canadians—famously chanting "da, da, Kanada; nyet, nyet, Soviet"—attended the game, including two of the country's most accomplished sport photographers.

Frank Lennon started his forty-seven-year career at the *Toronto Star* in 1944 as a messenger in the newsroom. His stints as a darkroom technician and wire photo receiver led to his interest in photography. He soon became one of the *Star*'s first staff photographers, remaining in that position until 1990. With an interest in sport, particularly hockey, he soon became a fixture at Toronto's Maple Leaf Gardens.[9] Denis Brodeur picked up photography after a career as an amateur goalie, which included a bronze medal as part of the Canadian hockey team at the 1956 Olympics. Freelance work with the now-defunct newspaper *Montréal-Matin* and other outlets also led Brodeur to become a regular attendee at NHL games, shooting photographs at the Montreal Forum.[10]

Lennon was in Moscow working for the *Toronto Star*. He spent much of game eight situated high above the rink capturing the action from that vantage point. Late in the game, with the score tied, he decided to move closer to ice level and found himself next to Brodeur. The latter, unlike Lennon, was freelancing in Moscow, shooting for *Montréal-Matin* and a prospective book project. As game eight unfolded, Brodeur was already ensconced in what had become his preferred location in the arena—"I got friendly with an usher, gave him some chocolate and he gave me good spots to shoot"—before Lennon migrated to the position next to him.[11] Both equipped with Nikon F cameras and 135 mm lenses, they were on the verge of capturing a defining moment in Canadian sport history.

The Photograph(s)

Late in game eight, Paul Henderson righted himself after sliding behind the Soviet goal while stabbing at a loose puck, circled the net, and fired the rebound of a Phil Esposito shot past sprawling Soviet goalkeeper Vladislav Tretiak. Having broken a 5–5 tie, with the clock showing only thirty-four seconds remaining in the game, Henderson jumped into the arms of teammate Yvan Cournoyer. Both Lennon and Brodeur captured this embrace—in nearly indistinguishable photos. Although their collective representation of this moment has become a nearly ubiquitous image in Canadian popular culture, it was not widely circulated at the time.

Lennon's only-now-iconic photograph appeared on the cover of the *Toronto Star* on September 29, 1972, the day after the last game of the series. However, newspapers across Canada opted for other cover images.[12] The *Montreal Gazette* and the national *Globe and Mail* featured the same Associated Press wire photo, which did not capture Henderson, Cournoyer, or Esposito in the frame. This photo also appeared on the covers of the *Albertan* (Calgary), *Kingston Whig-Standard*, and *Sault Daily Star*, as well as *Le Droit* (Ottawa) and *Le Devoir* (Montreal). Other French-language newspapers ran different photos, including a wire photo from the Soviet news agency, TASS (*La Presse* [Montreal] and *Le Nouvelliste* [Trois-Rivières]), while *Le Soleil* (Quebec City) ran a Canadian Press photo. Other newspapers opted for images of local residents celebrating Team Canada's victory, rather than a shot from the game (e.g., *Victoria Times-Colonist*, *Regina Leader-Post*, *Brantford Expositor*). The *Vancouver Sun*, *Calgary Herald*, and *Ottawa Citizen* used different photos.

Brodeur's near-identical photograph was the thirty-seventh or thirty-eighth frame of a thirty-six-shot roll, and one of over three thousand photos he took while in the Soviet Union, many of which were developed in the darkroom of the Soviet newspaper *Izvestia*.[13] Remarkably, the image for which Brodeur is best known did not appear in *Montréal-Matin*. The front page on

September 29 featured Henderson's posed team portrait, although the game coverage included some of Brodeur's photos, but not the Henderson-Cournoyer celebration. That sequence—the goal and its aftermath—comprises seventeen photographs, another of which was featured in Gilles Terroux's *Face-Off of the Century*.[14] That Henderson-Cournoyer photo—not the subsequently famous one—only appears on page seventy-three, one of more than a hundred Brodeur photos included in the book.

Brodeur-Lennon's representations of what was being framed as a nationally significant moment would soon gain popularity. Lennon's photo was rewarded at the end of 1972 with a National Newspaper Award and celebrated as the Canadian Press Picture of the Year. The photo has been reproduced regularly since 1972, often with a fluid provenance: the *New York Times* credited the photograph to AP while the CBC published the photo online unattributed.[15] Brodeur recalls, "The picture has been [used] many times without my authorization."[16] Even when Lennon is credited, as by Wikimedia Commons, he is wrongly associated with CP rather than the *Toronto Star*.[17]

The elision of the two images speaks to the enduring popularity of this specific vantage point of the series-winning goal. But the published photograph seen by Canadian viewers was a very particular one. Both images were shot in the horizontal 3:2 aspect ratio typical of 35 mm negatives. The original photograph(s) captures not only Henderson and Cournoyer, but also a prone Tretiak having failed to prevent the winning goal as well as the dejected faces of three of his nearby teammates. Of these Soviet players, only Tretiak appears in the Lennon photo that was cropped for the cover of the *Toronto Star*; Brodeur's image in Terroux's book includes two of the Soviet skaters, while Tretiak is obscured behind the two celebrating Canadian players. In the background, the stunned expressions of the hundreds of Muscovites—largely absent in the best-known, cropped version—heighten the contrast with the joy visible in Henderson's face. The live audience is seen behind the wire fencing that separated the crowd from the playing surface. As modern North American rinks had switched to Plexiglass to protect fans, the photograph also contributes to narratives of cultural difference, which were inflected by notions of modernity and freedom, distinguishing Canada from the Soviet Union (the mysterious "other" behind the Iron Curtain) that circulated throughout the series.

The editorial placement of the images and their accompanying captions influence understandings of the photograph(s). In its wider, uncropped format, the image conveys painful defeat as much as it does ecstatic victory.

Brodeur and Terroux acknowledged this, captioning the photograph they selected for inclusion in their volume, in English: "The Russians can't believe their eyes."[18] The Lennon shot appeared on the cover of one of Canada's largest daily circulation newspapers, above the fold. There, the cropped image, in a portrait orientation, captures only Henderson's joyful expression, arms raised and wrapped in Cournoyer's embrace, with "Canada" visible on the back of the latter's jersey, as the prone Tretiak embodies a defeated foe. The image was, as the caption noted for all who did not know, "an ecstatic Paul Henderson."

A Photograph Becomes The Photograph

Such usage and what it signified fit within prevailing narratives. In an era when the Canadian federal state faced challenges to its authority from separatists in Quebec and unrest elsewhere, diversity within Canada was celebrated for the ways it contributed to pan-Canadian unity. Pierre Trudeau was elected prime minister in 1968, a year after the nationalist outpouring that accompanied Expo '67, the World's Fair celebrating Canada's centennial. His view of the federal state would see bilingualism (English and French as official national languages) and multiculturalism (integrating diverse cultural groups into Canadian society) become government policies, the latter of which was critiqued for being primarily a symbolic effort "to modestly contribute to good community relations in Canada."[19]

The federal government's support—financial and bureaucratic—of high-performance sport would reflect similar pan-Canadian values. Beginning in the 1970s, it "recruited athletes from every national and regional group for teams that would march behind a single Canadian flag, compete in identical red-and-white uniforms and glorify teamwork and discipline."[20] The Summit Series was contested in—and its representations reflected—this context. The series-winning goal captured multicultural Canada: An Anglo-Canadian (Henderson) scored on the rebound of a shot taken by the son of Italian-Canadian immigrants (Esposito) before jumping into the arms of a French-Canadian (Cournoyer).[21]

The power of this narrative is revealed in the subsequent uses of the Brodeur-Lennon photo(s), most of which correspond with notable anniversaries.[22] In 1997, the Royal Canadian Mint issued a commemorative silver one-dollar coin for the twenty-fifth anniversary of the Summit Series.[23]

Interestingly, the image on the reverse of the coin adds Esposito to the Henderson-Cournoyer post-goal tableau. He did quickly join the celebration, but he was not captured in the famous image on which the coin is based, and his inclusion broadens the nationalist reading. The Brodeur-Lennon photograph has also been featured on commemorative postage stamps issued by Canada Post in 1997 and 2017, the latter as part of a series of memorable moments in Canadian history on the Confederation's sesquicentennial.[24] The photo, or stylized representations of it, has also been featured on the covers of DVD collections of the series' broadcasts and commemorative documentary films, as well as on art prints and collectible trading cards and as illustrations in a number of books celebrating the series.[25]

The image has evolved from one of many photographs of the series, and one of a number that captured the winning goal, to the defining image of what is positioned as a (if not *the*) seminal moment in Canadian sport history. It has become the dominant representation of the Summit Series in Canadian popular culture, overshadowing thousands of other images.

Affective Nationalism and the Challenge of Singular Representations

The photo—and its legacy established by these multiple reproductions—has perpetuated the idea of a shared national moment, even for those not in attendance (and, in more recent uses, for those not even born at the time of the Summit Series). But, as these varied objects suggest, the Brodeur-Lennon image long ago ceased to be just a photograph. It has a material existence through which it operates as a representational signifier of a particular, mainstream variant of Canadian nationalism, and its increasing ubiquity has narrowed the potential meanings that can be read into the event's representations.

Photographs of everyday life have been read through Michael Billig's notion of "banal nationalism." An interdisciplinary social scientist, Billig argues that everyday objects such as postage stamps, coins, magazines—and the Brodeur-Lennon photo—are implicated in the "continual 'flagging', or reminding of nationhood."[26] Such objects reflect "the performative enrolment of a great many things in the staging of the nation."[27] In this way, photographs contribute to "crafting a unified vision of national life" through the seeming ordinariness of their subjects.[28]

The Brodeur-Lennon photo, however, anticipates a different response, both in its subject matter and how it has been mobilized. The photo does not just capture a moment. From its original publication on the cover of the *Toronto Star*, where it was associated with ecstasy, to all its subsequent uses, the image has intentionally provoked an affective, emotional response. The ways in which this image in its varied forms elicits this affective response is what links the physical and the symbolic. Emotions can be "formed in relation to objects, but they can also influence the shape of objects," argues art historian Sarah Bassnett, and "are transmitted through objects."[29]

One media account suggested that Brodeur and Lennon, along with Henderson and his Canadian teammates, "share the same sliver of time" and "that sliver some say helped define the nation," while a recent oral history project was titled *The Goal That United Canada*.[30] In the same spirit, a national history magazine included Lennon's photo among its list of "10 photos that changed Canada."[31] So, while photographs may operate as "contested sites of encounter and cultural exchange," the prominence of the Brodeur-Lennon photo—and the particular affective response its use has been intended to elicit: joy and unquestioned pride in the nation—operates to limit alternate readings of or engagement with the image.[32] Such an affective nationalism "might resonate with the progressive idea of a plural, inclusive nation," suggest scholars Marco Antonsich and Michael Skey, but this risks "lumping affected and affecting bodies together into a single mass, undifferentiated in terms of race, gender, sexuality, age, class, dis-ability, and personal stories."[33] This is particularly significant for an image meant to invoke pride in the nation, while representing white, male, able-bodied professional athletes playing a sport long associated with heteronormative hyper-masculinity.[34]

While some "mediated visual representations" of sport have "responded to and challenged the meanings conventionally associated with sport," the affective impact of the Brodeur-Lennon photo makes it seemingly "impermeable to any issues of power and exclusion."[35] But, interrogated on these terms, the Henderson-Cournoyer image—in its material existence—reveals the "shallow nationalism" undergirding hockey as an affective signpost of Canadian-ness.[36] The "Canada" signaled by this photo does not necessarily suggest an increasingly diverse population, encourage women's participation in hockey, or reveal the ways in which the game was one of the tools of cultural genocide used against Indigenous peoples, for "rarely is hockey challenged as part of a broader colonial project and history."[37] The photograph's ultimate impact is its role in perpetuating the myth that a goal scored late one night in Moscow remains a cultural touchstone of pan-Canadian unity.

The enduring and affective impact of the Brodeur-Lennon photograph has contributed to its continued popularity. Its increasing use as *the* representation of the Canadian team's victory in Moscow is intended to provoke a nationalist response. The image represents success in a sport celebrated in popular culture as central to "Canadian" identity. The ways in which the photo has been mobilized—not only in its materiality and the products with which it has been associated, but also in the physical manipulation of the image to focus the viewer's attention solely on the Henderson-Cournoyer celebration at the expense of the wider context, including Soviet players—has emphasized its use as a signifier for expressions of pan-Canadian unity.

NOTES

1. While separate photographs, the Brodeur and Lennon images are referred to here in the singular (i.e., the Brodeur-Lennon photo) due to their visual similarity, the fact that they are often mistaken for one another, and because they, in combination, have become the singular ubiquitous image of the series in Canadian popular culture.

2. These parameters intentionally precluded the participation of any players who had signed contracts with the NHL's upstart rival, the World Hockey Association. This meant that Canadian-born WHA stars, most prominently Bobby Hull, were excluded from Team Canada. Star defenseman Bobby Orr also missed the series due to an injury.

3. Brian Kennedy, ed., *Coming Down from the Mountain: Rethinking the 1972 Summit Series* (Hamilton, ON: Wolsak & Wynn, 2014); Taylor McKee, ed., *Reaching the Summit: Reimagining the Summit Series in the Canadian Cultural Memory* (St. Catharines, ON: JESS Press, 2022).

4. See, for example, Neil Earle, "Hockey as Canadian Popular Culture: Team Canada 1972, Television and the Canadian Identity," *Journal of Canadian Studies* 30 (Summer 1995): 107–123; Russell Field, "'How We Think about Hockey, and Ourselves': Television, the 1972 Summit Series, and the Construction of a Pan-Canadian Identity," *Canadian Issues/Thèmes canadiens* (Winter 2012): 40–45.

5. See Mike Huggins, "The Sporting Gaze: Towards a Visual Turn in Sports History—Documenting Art and Sport," *Journal of Sport History* 35 (Summer 2008): 311–329; Mike O'Mahony, *Photography and Sport* (London: Reaktion Books, 2018); Murray G. Phillips, Mark E. O'Neill, and Gary Osmond, "Broadening Horizons in Sport History: Films, Photographs, and Monuments," *Journal of Sport History* 34 (Summer 2007): 271–291.

6. There is a growing scholarship exploring sport history using photography that highlights these issues. An excellent starting point is the special issue on "Sport and the Visual" in the *International Journal for the History of Sport* 28, no. 8/9 (2011).

7. O'Mahony, *Photography and Sport*, 11.

8. Kevin Plummer, "Historicist: The Brothers Turofsky," *Torontoist*, June 6, 2009, https://torontoist.com/2009/06/historicist_the_brothers_turofsky/.

9. "Photographer Who Captured Henderson's Winning Goal Dead at 80," CBC Arts, August 22, 2006, https://alt.obituaries.narkive.com/KBL3VnCg/frank-lennon-photographer-who-captured-the-most-joyous-moment-in-the-1972-canada-soviet-hockey.

10. Dave Stubbs, "Denis Brodeur Was a Photography Legend," *Montreal Gazette*, September 25, 2013, https://montrealgazette.com/sports/denis-brodeur-was-a-photography-legend. Beyond photography, Brodeur was also well known for being the father of Hall of Fame goalie Martin Brodeur. Brodeur *père* passed away in 2013. Lennon died in 2006.

11. Brodeur quoted in Steve Russell, "A Moment in History, Frank Lennon, Denis Brodeur and Paul Henderson," *Toronto Star*, November 15, 2010, https://www.thestar.com/photos/toronto_star_photo_blog/2010/11/a-moment-in-history-frank-lennon-denis-brodeur-and-paul-henderson.html.

12. Lennon was in Moscow shooting exclusively for the *Toronto Star*, rather than a wire service.

13. Russell, "A Moment in History."

14. Gilles Terroux, *Face-Off of the Century, the New Era: Canada-U.S.S.R.* (Toronto: Collier-Macmillan, 1972). The book was also published as *Le match du siècle: Canada-U.R.S.S.* (Montreal: Les Éditions de l'Homme, 1972).

15. Jeff Z. Klein, "In 1972, Hockey's Cold War Boiled Over," *New York Times*, September 1, 2012, SP15; "Where Were You for the Epic '72 Summit Series? 3 Canadians Remember," CBC, September 28, 2017, https://www.cbc.ca/2017/where-were-you-for-the-epic-72-summit-series-3-canadians-remember-1.4287441.

16. Brodeur quoted in Russell, "A Moment in History."

17. https://en.wikipedia.org/wiki/Paul_Henderson#/media/File:Paul_Henderson_1972.jpg.

18. Terroux, *Face-Off of the Century*, 73.

19. Sarah V. Wayland, "Immigration, Multiculturalism and National Identity in Canada," *International Journal on Minority and Group Rights* 5 (January 1997): 47; see also Peter S. Li, "The Multiculturalism Debate," in *Race and Ethnic Relations in Canada*, 2nd edition, ed. Peter S. Li (Don Mills, ON: Oxford University Press, 1999).

20. Bruce Kidd, "The Philosophy of Excellence: Olympic Performances, Class Power and the Canadian State," *Sport in Society* 16, no. 4 (2013): 377.

21. Indigenous peoples are often absent from discussions of multiculturalism. Some critics have argued that multiculturalism in Canada was an attempt "to resolve long-standing tensions between French and English Canada" and only later became "a master narrative with which to address . . . the status of Aboriginal Peoples." In this view, "multiculturalism is itself a politics of settlement." May Chazan, Lisa Helps, Anna Stanley, and Sonali Thakkar, "Introduction: Labours, lands, bodies," in *Home and Native Land: Unsettling Multiculturalism in Canada*, ed. May Chazan, Lisa Helps, Anna Stanley, and Sonali Thakkar (Toronto: Between the Lines, 2011), 2, 1.

22. The year 2022 marks the 50th anniversary of the Summit Series, and a new round of celebratory books—e.g., Scott Morrison, *1972: The Series That Changed Hockey Forever* (Toronto: Simon & Schuster, 2022)—and products are expected, including a commemorative $2 coin from the Royal Canadian Mint. See Lance Hornby,

"Team Canada '72 Gets a 50-Year Party," *Toronto Sun*, February 8, 2022, https://torontosun.com/sports/hockey/team-canada-72-gets-a-50-year-party.

23. "$1—Sterling Silver Coin, 1972 Canada/Russia Hockey Series (1997)," Royal Canadian Mint, https://www.mint.ca/en/shop/coins/pre-2010/$1—-sterling-silver-coin-1972-canadarussia-hockey-series-1997.

24. Rather than directly selecting images for new stamps, Canada Post's Advisory Committee Board reviews submitted designs. There are no publicly accessible archives of these deliberations. The 2017 sesquicentennial collection was designed by Subplot Design Inc., https://www.subplot.com/portfolio/canada_post_canada150_collection/2/. For the 1997 stamp, see https://postagestampguide.com/stamps/17006/paul-henderson-and-yvan-cournoyer-1997-canada-postage-stamp-the-series-of-the-century-1972.

25. DVD collections to feature this image on their cover include "Canada's Team of the Century: 1972 Canada vs USSR" (2002) and "Team Canada '72: The Ultimate Collector's Edition of the 1972 Summit Series" (2012). Stylized artworks based upon this photo include work by Danial Parry, which has been reproduced in both portrait ("Goal of the Century") and landscape ("Series Winner: Henderson Scores for Canada") orientations, and "The Goal" (2008) by Murray Henderson. Trading cards featuring the image include #81: The Moment in the 1991-92 Future Trends Canada '72 set (where the image also appears on the package wrapping); #105: The Goal in the 1992 Future Trend Experience set; and a collectible audio card, "Goal of the Century" (which focuses on Henderson by removing Cournoyer from the image). Books that reprint the photo include Mike Leonetti, *Titans of '72: Team Canada's Summit Series Heroes* (Toronto: Dundurn Press: 2012) and Brian McFarlane, *Team Canada 1972: Where Are They Now?* (Toronto: Winding Stair Press, 2001).

26. Michael Billig, *Banal Nationalism* (London: Sage, 1995), 8.

27. Peter Merriman and Rhys Jones, "Nations, Materialities and Affects," *Progress in Human Geography* 41 (October 2017): 601–602.

28. Jacqueline McIsaac, "Review of *The Official Picture: The National Film Board of Canada's Still Photography Division and the Image of Canada, 1941–1971* by Carol Payne," *History of Photography* 38, no. 3 (2014): 324.

29. Sarah Bassnett, *Picturing Toronto: Photography and the Making of a Modern City* (Montreal and Kingston: McGill-Queen's University Press, 2016), 14.

30. Russell, "A Moment in History." Sean Mitton and Jim Prime, *The Goal That United Canada* (The '72 Project, 2012).

31. Chris Webb, "Henderson's Goal," *The Beaver*, August-September 2008: 20–21, https://www.canadashistoryarchive.ca/canadas-history/the-beaver-aug-sep-2008/flipbook/20/.

32. Elizabeth Edwards and Christopher Morton, "Introduction," in *Photography, Anthropology and History: Expanding the Frame*, ed. Christopher Morton and Elizabeth Edwards (London: Routledge, 2016), 4.

33. Marco Antonsich and Michael Skey, "Affective Nationalism: Issues of Power, Agency and Method," *Progress in Human Geography* 41 (December 2017): 843. For an application of the concept of affective nationalism to a sporting context, see Angharad Closs Stephens, "The Affective Atmospheres of Nationalism," *Cultural Geographies* 23 (April 2016): 181–198.

34. See, for example, Mary Louise Adams, "The Game of Whose Lives? Gender, Race, and Entitlements in Canada's 'National' Games," and Robert Pitter, "Racializa-

tion and Hockey in Canada: From Personal Troubles to a Canadian Challenge," in *Artificial Ice: Hockey, Culture, and Commerce*, ed. David Whitson and Richard Gruneau (Peterborough: Broadview Press, 2006).

35. O'Mahony, *Photography and Sport*, 11; Antonsich and Skey, "Affective Nationalism," 843.

36. Courtney Szto, *Changing on the Fly: Hockey through the Voices of South Asian Canadians* (New Brunswick, NJ: Rutgers University Press, 2021), 25. Szto asserts that "shallow nationalism" within hockey in Canada reflects "the celebration of culture and difference [yet] simultaneously protects the white privilege that takes place on the ice." On the impact of the Summit Series on women's hockey in Canada, see Julie Stevens and Anna H. Lathrop, "Boom or Bust? The Impact of the 1972 Summit Series on the Development of Women's Hockey in Canada," in Kennedy, *Coming Down from the Mountain*. There is an important body of literature on the complicated legacy of hockey within Canadian Indian Residential schools: e.g., Taylor McKee and Janice Forsyth, "Witnessing Painful Pasts: Understanding Images of Sports at Canadian Indian Residential Schools," *Journal of Sport History* 46 (Summer 2019): 175–188; Andrew Narraway, "Settler Colonial Power and Indigenous Survival: Hockey Programs at Three Indian Residential Schools in Northwestern Ontario and Manitoba, 1929–1969," unpublished master's thesis, Carleton University, 2018; Braden Te Hiwi and Janice Forsyth, "'A Rink at This School Is Almost as Essential as a Classroom': Hockey and Discipline at Pelican Lake Indian Residential School, 1945–1951," *Canadian Journal of History* 52 (Spring–Summer 2017): 80–108.

37. Szto, *Changing on the Fly*, 27.

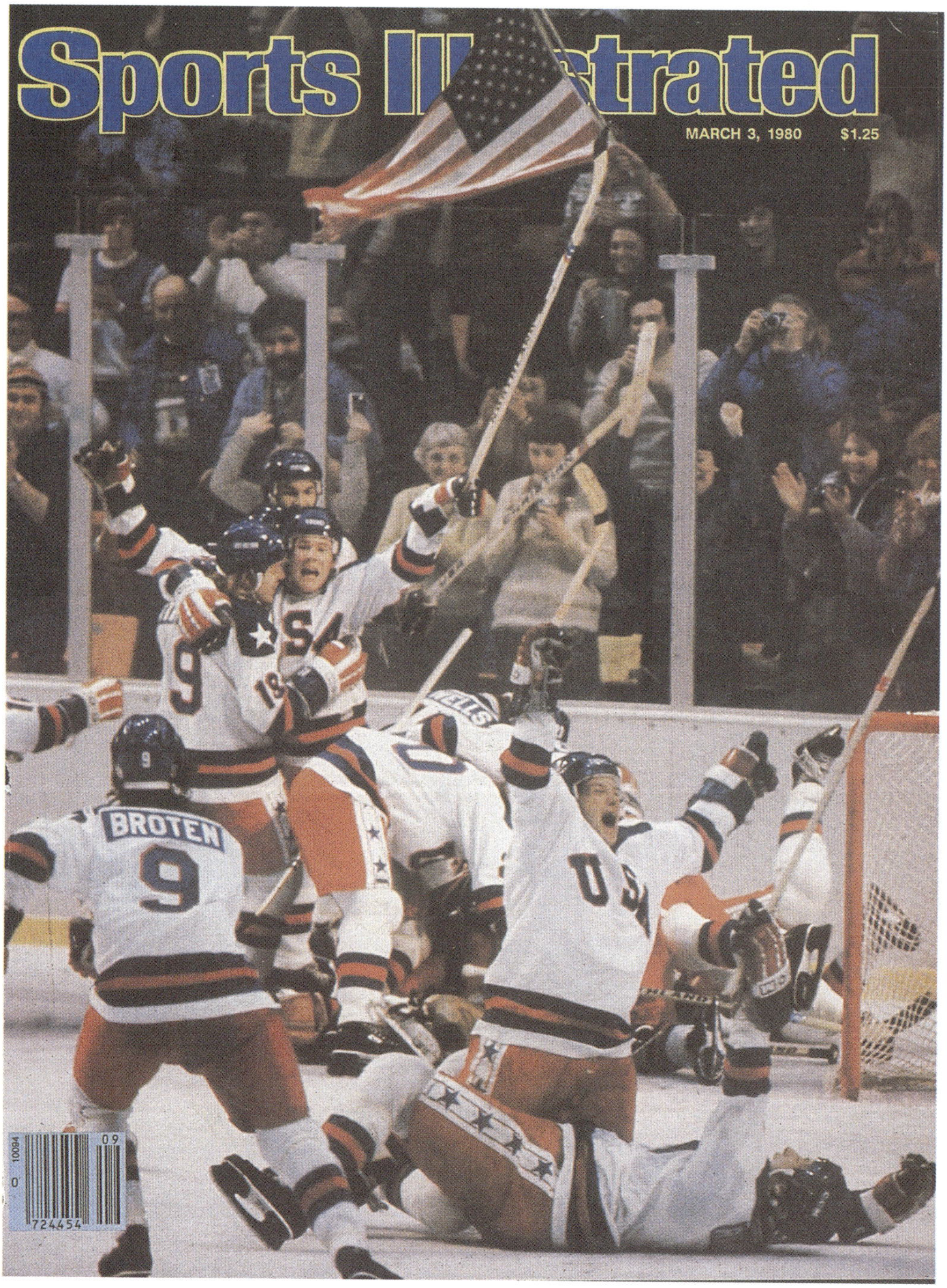
Sports Illustrated
MARCH 3, 1980
$1.25
USA
BROTEN
9
USA

16

U.S. VS. THEM

American Nationalism and *Sports Illustrated*'s Famous Cover Image of the Miracle on Ice

CHRIS ELZEY

For Americans, the photo that graced the cover of the March 3, 1980, issue of *Sports Illustrated* is one of the most indelible images—sporting or otherwise—of the 1980s. Snapped by *Sports Illustrated* photographer Heinz Kluetmeier, the picture shows ecstatic United States hockey players celebrating their unlikely triumph over the Soviet Union at the 1980 Lake Placid Olympics, famously known as the "Miracle on Ice." In the years since it was first published, the picture has become synonymous with the game. It has been reproduced at least eleven times in *Sports Illustrated* and has appeared in *Life*, *Reader's Digest*, books, and documentaries.[1] The USA Hockey and the International Ice Hockey Federation websites also contain the shot, as does Wikipedia.[2]

Initially, however, not everyone recognized the artistry of Kluetmeier's photo. The shot was not included in *Life*'s annual *The Year in Pictures* issue.[3] Time-Life Books' 1983 edition of *Photojournalism* did not run the picture either.[4] Kluetmeier's image even failed to win an award at the National Press Photographers Association and University of Missouri School of Journalism's 1981 Pictures of the Year contest. The photo, though, did catch the eye of the judges. "When so many Americans go red-white [*sic*], and blue crazy over the winnings of the U.S. Hockey Team that defeated the Soviets and Finland for a Gold Medal," the catalog for the contest explained, "it is difficult to evaluate the pictures and not the euphoria we remember experiencing that cold February night."[5]

The catalog got it wrong. It is precisely because of the patriotism and euphoria Kluetmeier captured that the photo is so remarkable. All the elements are there: the jubilant, postgame pile-on of players; fists celebratorily flung skyward; faces evincing joyous disbelief; smiling, exuberant fans; USA written across the top of a player's uniform; and an American flag suspended high above the scene, held in place by the outstretched arm of a smiling spectator. The composition of the picture draws our gaze from the foreground, where two players—one, kneeling, straddles the other, who is supine on the ice—are raucously celebrating, to the tangle of bodies behind, and finally to the American flag, which appears to be attached to the end of a player's hockey stick, raised in a kind of triumphal, victory salute. The point of the picture is clear: history has just been made, and the beneficiary is not only the U.S. team but America too.

Maybe that is why the image has endured. It reminds us how emotionally powerful that moment was. In 1980, Cold War feelings were running high, fanned white-hot by the Soviet invasion of Afghanistan in late December 1979 and the ensuing threat of a U.S. boycott of the 1980 Moscow Olympics. Americans were also bedeviled by surging inflation, high unemployment, gas shortages, and the Iranian hostage crisis. The victory realized by baby-faced undergrads over arguably the then-preeminent hockey squad on the planet was a source of inspiration to many—so much so, it helped spawn a wave of patriotism that washed over the country during the early 1980s. Kluetmeier's photograph is iconic not only because it reflects this patriotic zeal, but also because it foretells a new era of American nationalism. Viewed this way, the image can be seen as pictorial shorthand for the end of one decade, fraught with disappointment and cynicism, and the start of another, which seemed to promise better times.

Heinz Kluetmeier understood what made a photo special. He had been honing his picture-taking skills ever since he was a boy. A German émigré who arrived in America in the early 1950s as a nine-year-old, Kluetmeier grew up in Milwaukee. As a youngster, he developed an interest in photography. Soon, the budding cameraman had sharpened his ability enough to sell some of his shots to the Associated Press (AP)—an arrangement that continued throughout his college days at Dartmouth. Upon completing his degree, Kluetmeier accepted a job in engineering. But photography was his calling. Eager to pursue his true métier, he began working as a photographer in 1969 at Time Inc., a media giant whose publications included *Sports Illustrated* and *Life*. Four years later, he was hired by *Sports Illustrated*. By the end of 1979, fifty-two of his images had made the magazine's cover.[6]

Kluetmeier became known for his innovative techniques. At the 2008 Beijing Games, for example, he had a camera deployed at the bottom of the Olympic pool. Several of the resulting photos confirmed that American swimmer Michael Phelps had eked out the scantest of victories in the 100-meter butterfly. *The Miracle on Ice* image, by contrast, was taken the old-fashioned way—no photographic gimmickry, no visual manipulation. Just aim, focus, and shoot. The only adjustment Kluetmeier made was to change his location during the third period of the game, moving from a spot in the stands to an ABC-TV stage closer to the rink. There, he trained his camera on the frenzied, end-of-game celebration unfolding near the Americans' net and started taking pictures. Among the six dozen photos he took was the renowned *Sports Illustrated* cover image.

One emotion expressed in the picture is sheer joy. It is easily detectable on the face of defenseman Jack O'Callahan, the player kneeling over his teammate, nineteen-year-old Mike Ramsey, in the photo's foreground. Both have their arms raised, but O'Callahan is more noticeable, in part because we can see his face. Also in the foreground, twenty-year-old Neal Broten is seen skating toward the jumble of bodies beside the net as if he were a first grader late for recess. The tilt of his body alone suggests childlike exuberance. In the background, behind the on-ice rejoicing, spectators watch from the stands, beaming. The euphoria is palpable.

The volcanic eruption of glee indicates just how improbable the American victory was. No one gave the U.S. a chance. The Soviets seemed unbeatable. History certainly was on their side. Of the six previous Olympic hockey competitions, the U.S.S.R. had won five. The Soviet squad in Lake Placid was prodigiously talented, comprised of wily quasi-professionals who had competed in multiple Olympics and World Championships. The Americans, by contrast, were young—average age, just twenty-two. Moreover, they had played together for only six months. *Time* later described them as a "pond-hockey pickup crew of collegians."[7]

Age and experience won first. In an exhibition contest at Madison Square Garden four days before the official start of the Lake Placid Games, the U.S.S.R. demolished the U.S., 10–3. Confident, the Soviets rode the victory into Olympic group play, winning all five of their games by a combined tally of 51–11. Meanwhile, the Americans amassed a record of 4–0–1, but they had looked less dominant. When the two superpowers finally met in the medal round, predictions of a Soviet victory seemed like they would hold true. But with less than eleven and a half minutes to go in the third period and the U.S. trailing, 3–2, American center Mark Johnson scored. A minute, twenty-one seconds later, Mike Eruzione, the U.S. captain, smashed another shot into the U.S.S.R. net. The crowd erupted. Thunderous cheers of "USA! USA! USA!" rocked the arena. In the stands, U.S. flags fluttered. For the rest of the period, the Soviets tried desperately to even the score, but could not. The game ended. Pandemonium was unloosed. Incredibly, remarkably, miraculously—somehow, the U.S. had won.

Kluetmeier's photo captures that sense of astonishment. The look on the face of right winger John Harrington expresses it perfectly. The viewer sees Harrington embrace teammate Eric Strobel, who is turned sideways. Harrington looks exhausted yet overjoyed. He is also the only one in the photo who stares back at us. His eyes seem to ask what ABC sportscaster Al Michaels famously exclaimed during the waning seconds of the game: "Do you believe in miracles? Yes!" Harrington has his right arm around Strobel, while his left hand, raised high, thrusts his hockey stick upward. In the picture, the curved head of the stick overlaps the bottom corner of an American flag being waved by a spectator, creating the illusion that Harrington, not the fan, is the one waving it. Behind Harrington and Strobel is a teammate, barely detectable, except for the crown of his helmet and what appears to be his right arm, which is raised above his head. The visual effect here tricks us into thinking that Harrington is doing three things at once: raising his arms, hugging Strobel, and waving a U.S. flag. The Escher-like scene merges victory with patriotism. Players and spectators rejoice.

It is difficult to argue that patriotism is not one of the most prominent themes of the image. The colors and design of the uniform worn by American players denote it. "USA" is plainly visible on O'Callahan's jersey. The U.S. flag seen on the *Sports Illustrated* cover is conspicuously situated so that it conceals the "us" in "Illustrated."[8] The fan taking a photo in the picture seems to be pointing his camera at the flag, suggesting we view the victory through a patriotic lens. The composite tableau of the photograph—Harrington appearing to raise the American flag, his teammates rushing to his side, the triangular mass of bodies, the focus on the U.S. banner—evokes one of the best-known images of patriotism in American photographic history: *Raising the Flag on Iwo Jima* (1945) by AP cameraman Joe Rosenthal.

(In obvious reference to Rosenthal's photo, a two-page ad for All-State Insurance in *Sports Illustrated* in 2002 showed the hands of five players from the 1980 team hoisting a hockey stick painted like an American flag.)[9]

As in the picture, so too in life. News of the upset in Lake Placid was greeted with patriotic exuberance nationwide. People sang "The Star-Spangled Banner" and "God Bless America." Others yelled "USA! USA! USA!" Some hugged each other. Still others wept. Countless American flags were waved. A Roper poll taken just after the Lake Placid Olympics found that 75 percent of respondents believed the Games had "made [them] feel more proud of [America]," rather than "less proud," or neither "one way [n]or the other."[10]

So incredible was the victory that the U.S. team became a national symbol. It seemed as if the whole country had defeated the Soviets. The Olympic squad was called "Team America!" "America's Team," and "the red, white, and blue kids."[11] The *Buffalo Evening News*, making use of some clever wordplay, headlined: "We Did It; U.S. 4, Soviets 3."[12] Similarly, a day after the U.S. won the gold medal by defeating Finland, a *New York Daily News* headline asked: "Who's No. 1? It's US!" Next to the headline, the *News* ran a near length-of-the page photo of goalie Jim Craig grasping his hockey stick, which is partially wrapped in an American flag, clearly associating the team with patriotism.[13] Just before the famous AP picture was taken, the flag had draped Craig's shoulders. To Leigh Montville of the *Boston Globe*, the U.S. goalie "looked like the Statue of Liberty on skates."[14] Lauding the U.S. team's gold-medal-winning performance two days after the Lake Placid Games, Minnesota Senator David Durenberger stated: "For one moment, the nation is a family. This moment is ours."[15]

What is not seen in *The Miracle on Ice* photo conveys meaning too. Consider the U.S.S.R. team. Nowhere in the picture does it appear. We see no CCCP sewn across red jerseys, no hammer and sickle insignia. The *Sports Illustrated* cover does not even include a caption, so well-known was news of the upset. Indeed, nothing in the image indicates that the two Cold War archrivals have just played a hockey game. The photo is utterly devoid of any reference to the Soviets.

And yet we feel their presence. The Soviets are there, of course, just beyond the border of the picture, making their way to the blue line to await the traditional postgame handshake. Paradoxically, their absence only draws attention to their non-presence, which, in turn, heightens our awareness of their exclusion. The logic is counterintuitive. The more we cannot see them, the more we see them. The less they are there, the more they are. For

Americans, the omnipresence of an unseen red menace was a familiar trope for much of the Cold War.

East-West rancor lingers just below the surface in Kluetmeier's photograph. The viewer senses it in the riotous celebration and flag-waving in the image. The animosity becomes more pronounced once we consider that the contest was played amid growing anti-Soviet sentiment caused by the U.S.S.R. invasion of Afghanistan in late 1979. That the Kremlin ignored an American ultimatum demanding Soviet troops begin their withdrawal from the central Asian country by February 20—two days before the game—or face a U.S. boycott of the 1980 Moscow Olympics that summer enflamed passions even more. Consequently, the hockey matchup was cast as a do-or-die battle between *us* and *them*, between good and evil. "Beat those commie bastards," a telegram to the U.S. team implored.[16] A day after the Americans' victory, a *Chicago Tribune* headline announced, "Good guys triumph in the ultimate showdown."[17] *Newsweek* termed the game "a morality play on ice."[18] Kluetmeier's photograph unequivocally showed Americans that the forces of goodness had prevailed.

The elation seen in the photo also hints at a desire for national renewal. The problems of the late 1970s and early 1980s had left many people questioning the validity of American exceptionalism. Unemployment rates were climbing, reaching almost 8 percent by July 1980.[19] Alongside its page-one coverage of the U.S. triumph over the U.S.S.R. in hockey, the *New York Times* delivered less cheerful news: yearly adjusted inflation stood at an eye-popping 18.2 percent, the prime rate had surged to 16.5 percent, and the cost of gas had jumped 7.4 percent.[20] The specter of a deep recession loomed.

Economic woes were not the only worry. In February 1980 the Iran hostage crisis seemed no closer to resolution than it had at the outset, nearly four months earlier. "Has America Lost Its Clout?" a *Newsweek* cover queried in late November 1979.[21] A Roper poll taken in February 1980 found that 70 percent of those surveyed thought "things [in America had] seriously gotten off on the wrong track."[22] Seven months earlier, President Jimmy Carter had delivered his infamous "malaise" speech.

The Miracle on Ice photo communicates a different story. It shows that even in the face of overwhelming odds, success is possible. To a dispirited nation that had grown accustomed to second-guessing itself, the U.S. triumph in hockey was a much-needed salve. Two days after the Lake Placid Olympics, Illinois Congressman John Edward Porter declared, "[The] spirit of 'can do' brought glory upon [the team] and to [America] and rekindled in all of us a renewed belief in ourselves and what we and our nation stand for."[23] The defeat of the Soviet team prompted a columnist for the *Minneapolis Star* to write: "America works. America's team proved that."[24] *Sports Illustrated* named the U.S. team the 1980 "Sportsmen of the Year." The accompanying article was titled "A Reminder of What We Can Be."[25] (Paraphrasing "The Star-Spangled Banner," the tagline of a *Sports Illustrated* ad for the Sportsmen of the Year issue read, "Whom so proudly we hailed." Kluetmeier's *Miracle on Ice* cover photo was included in the ad.)[26]

The symbolic "we" in Kluetmeier's photograph—the crowd—occupies more than half the space of the *Sports Illustrated* cover, and roughly two-thirds in the uncropped version.[27] No doubt Kluetmeier consciously framed the photo this way. In 1999 he told *Sports Illustrated*'s Richard Hoffer: "Keep in mind how charmed we are by old-time pictures. It's not the action, it's the people in the stands."[28]

The Miracle on Ice shot shows a mix of people: men, women, adults, teenagers. There appears to be a Black man, applauding, in the top left corner of the image, but the "P" in "Sports Illustrated" covers much of his face. All other fans are white. The whiteness of the crowd and the concealment of the Black spectator remind us of the racial disparities that existed, and still exist, in hockey. Compositionally, the contrast between the semi-darkened background of the stands and the lighter-colored clothing worn by spectators draws our attention to their behavior. Most smile. Some cheer. Others clap. Two women in the first row raise their arms in exultation. A silver-haired, grandmotherly-looking woman gazes ahead approvingly, lending an air of wholesomeness to the on-ice revelry just in front of her. The gleeful outpouring in the stands mirrors the rejoicing by U.S. team members. In the split second it took the aperture of Kluetmeier's camera to open and close, spectators and players became one.

The patriotic ardor uniting players and fans in the photograph presaged a tsunami-like surge in American patriotism during the early 1980s. Public celebrations on patriotic holidays were regularly thronged. Purchases of U.S. flags rose. In 1982, President Ronald Reagan signed Proclamation 4898, which "designate[d] the week beginning February 15, 1982, as National Patriotism Week."[29] A 1983 *New York Times* poll revealed that 53 percent of respondents were "very patriotic," while another 37 percent were "somewhat patriotic."[30]

Nineteen eighty-four, particularly, witnessed a torrent of patriotic emotion. The economy seemed to be improving, brightening the country's mood. National pride was exhibited at ceremonies commemorating the fortieth anniversary of D-Day. The Republican and Democratic National

Conventions that summer saw an abundance of flag-waving. The 1984 Los Angeles Olympics especially yielded impassioned displays of patriotism. The torch relay, for instance, which attracted an estimated 30 million viewers, featured a surfeit of U.S. flags and pro-American cheers. With the U.S.S.R. boycotting the Games, U.S. athletes won a record eighty-three gold medals, giving the nation plenty to cheer about (critics labeled the gushy celebration chauvinistic). Afterward, the U.S. team was fêted with a ticker-tape parade in New York. Approximately two million people attended. "The *zeitgeist* has turned zesty," quipped *Time* in September 1984, adding, "Americans are feeling more sanguine and comfortable about their country than they have felt in two decades."[31] That optimism was expressed in a TV commercial for President Reagan's 1984 reelection campaign. "It's morning again in America," the popular spot began.[32] Some four years earlier, Kluetmeier's *Miracle on Ice* photograph had communicated a similar message.

In the days immediately following the Miracle on Ice, newspapers and magazines published a variety of photographs documenting the U.S. team's euphoric celebration. None, however, resonate like Kluetmeier's. The pictures either encompass too broad a field of vision or fail to show the crowd's response. One image shot by a United Press International (UPI) photojournalist comes close to resembling Kluetmeier's photograph, but the composition is slightly different—it was taken just after Kluetmeier took his—and it focuses almost entirely on the joy-filled mayhem occurring on the ice.[32] Rather than amplifying the cultural meaning and Cold War undertones of the game, it merely dramatizes the unpredictability of sport.

The genius of Kluetmeier's photograph is that it does all three. The viewer readily grasps just how incredible the upset was, while discerning the reasons it meant so much to Americans. The visual markers in the image—smiling, jubilant fans; the U.S. flag; the incredulity expressed by winger John Harrington; the spectator-photographer in the stands; the joy etched on defenseman Jack O'Callahan's face; and the conspicuous absence of Soviet players—guide us to a deeper conclusion: the Miracle on Ice was more than simply an upset of gargantuan proportions. It was a monumental event that carried profound significance for a nation wracked with self-doubt and engaged in what appeared to be an existential struggle with its archnemesis. Kluetmeier's image of perhaps the most famous game-ending moment in the history of sport foreshadowed the rush of national pride that enthralled much of the country in the years after the Lake Placid Olympics.

Instantly recognizable, the photo will remain forever connected to the Miracle on Ice. Both are part of the story we tell ourselves about the reemergence of American optimism in the 1980s.

NOTES

1. *Sports Illustrated*, December 22–29, 1980; September 21, 1987, 47; November 15, 1989, 160; December 13, 1993, special advertising section; February 21, 1994, 37; November 14, 1994, 178; August 10, 1998, 54; July 26, 1999, 96; February 4, 2002, 106; February 9, 2004, 70; and July 11–18, 2005, 155. See for example, *Life Special Issue: The 1980s*, 1989, 181; *Reader's Digest*, August 1980, 7; William Oscar Johnson, *The Olympics: A History of the Games* (New York: Bishop Books, [1992] 1993; 1996), 166–167; *Greatest Pictures: Memorable Images from Sport History* (New York: Bishop Books, 1998), 34; *Pride and Prosperity: The 80s* (Alexandria, VA: Time-Life Books, 1999), 98–99; Steven Hoffman, *Slide Show* (New York: Time Inc. Home Entertainment, 2009), 32–33; *The Eighties* (NBC News, 1989); *Do You Believe in Miracles? The Story of the 1980 U.S. Hockey Team* (HBO Sports, 2001); and *Miracle on Ice—40th Anniversary Special* (NBCSN, 2020).

2. See https://www.ushockeyhalloffame.com/page/show/831562-the-1980-u-s-olympic-team; https://webarchive.iihf.com/channels/iihf-world-championship/top-story-of-the-century/; and https://en.wikipedia.org/wiki/Miracle_on_Ice.

3. *Life*, January 1981.

4. *Photojournalism*, revised ed. (Alexandria, VA: Time-Life Books, 1983).

5. *The Best of Photojournalism/6*, 209.

6. *Sports Illustrated, Special Issue: 35 Years of Covers*, March 28, 1990, 190. For more on Kluetmeier and how he took the *Miracle on Ice* photo, see David Davis, "Two of the Most Famous Olympic Photos Were All About Location and Dumb Luck," Deadspin, August 17, 2017, https://deadspin.com/two-of-the-most-famous-olympic-photos-were-all-about-lo-1797645015.

7. *Time*, March 3, 1980, 30.

8. See Davis, "Two of the Most Famous Olympic Photos."

9. https://vault.si.com/vault/2002/02/04/702842#&gid=ci0258c0bc901426ef&pid=702842—-004—-image, and https://vault.si.com/vault/2002/02/04/702842#&gid=ci0258c0bc901426ef&pid=702842—-005—-image.

10. See Nicholas Evan Sarantakes, *Dropping the Torch: Jimmy Carter, The Olympic Boycott, and the Cold War* (New York: Cambridge University Press, 2011), 133.

11. *Reader's Digest*, August 1980, 7, and *New York Post*, February 23, 1980, 44.

12. *Buffalo Evening News*, February 23, 1980, front page of "The News Sports Magazine."

13. *New York Daily News*, February 25, 1980, 72.

14. *Boston Globe*, February 25, 1980, 1.

15. *Congressional Record*, February 26, 1980, 3762.

16. Quoted in *Do You Believe in Miracles? The Story of the 1980 U.S. Hockey Team.*

17. *Chicago Tribune*, February 23, 1980, sec. 2, 1.

18. *Newsweek*, March 3, 1980, 81.

19. Susan Ockert, ed., *Business Statistics of the United States: Patterns of Economic Change*, 21st edition (Lanham, MD: Bernan Press, 2016), 342.

20. *New York Times*, February 23, 1980, 1.

21. *Newsweek*, November 26, 1979, cover.

22. The Roper Organization, Roper Reports poll #1980-03: Foreign Affairs/Consumerism, Question 16, USROPER.80-3.R04, The Roper Organization (Ithaca, NY: Roper Center for Public Opinion Research, 1980).

23. *Congressional Record—Extension of Remarks*, February 26, 1980, 3916.

24. *Minneapolis Star*, February 23, 1980, 1.

25. *Sports Illustrated*, December 22–29, 1980, 30.

26. For ad, see *Detroit Free Press*, December 18, 1980, 8E; *Los Angeles Times*, December 18, 1980, 5, sec. IV; and *Boston Globe*, December 18, 1980, 84.

27. For the uncropped picture, see Hoffman, *Slide Show*, 32.

28. https://vault.si.com/vault/1999/07/26/703898#&gid=ci0258c0a3900126ef&pid=703898—-044—-image.

29. https://www.presidency.ucsb.edu/documents/proclamation-4898-national-patriotism-week-1982.

30. NYT Poll: Second Patriotism Survey, NYT (Ithaca, NY: Roper Center for Public Opinion Research, 1983).

31. *Time*, September 24, 1984, 10.

32. For commercial, see Lou Canon, *President Reagan: The Role of a Lifetime* (New York: Public Affairs, [1991] 2000), 451–452.

33. For example, see *Baltimore Sun*, February 23, 1980, B5; *Denver Post*, February 23, 1980, 41; *Miami Herald*, February 23, 1980, 1; *New York Post*, February 23, 1980, 1; and *Washington Post*, February 23, 1980, D1.

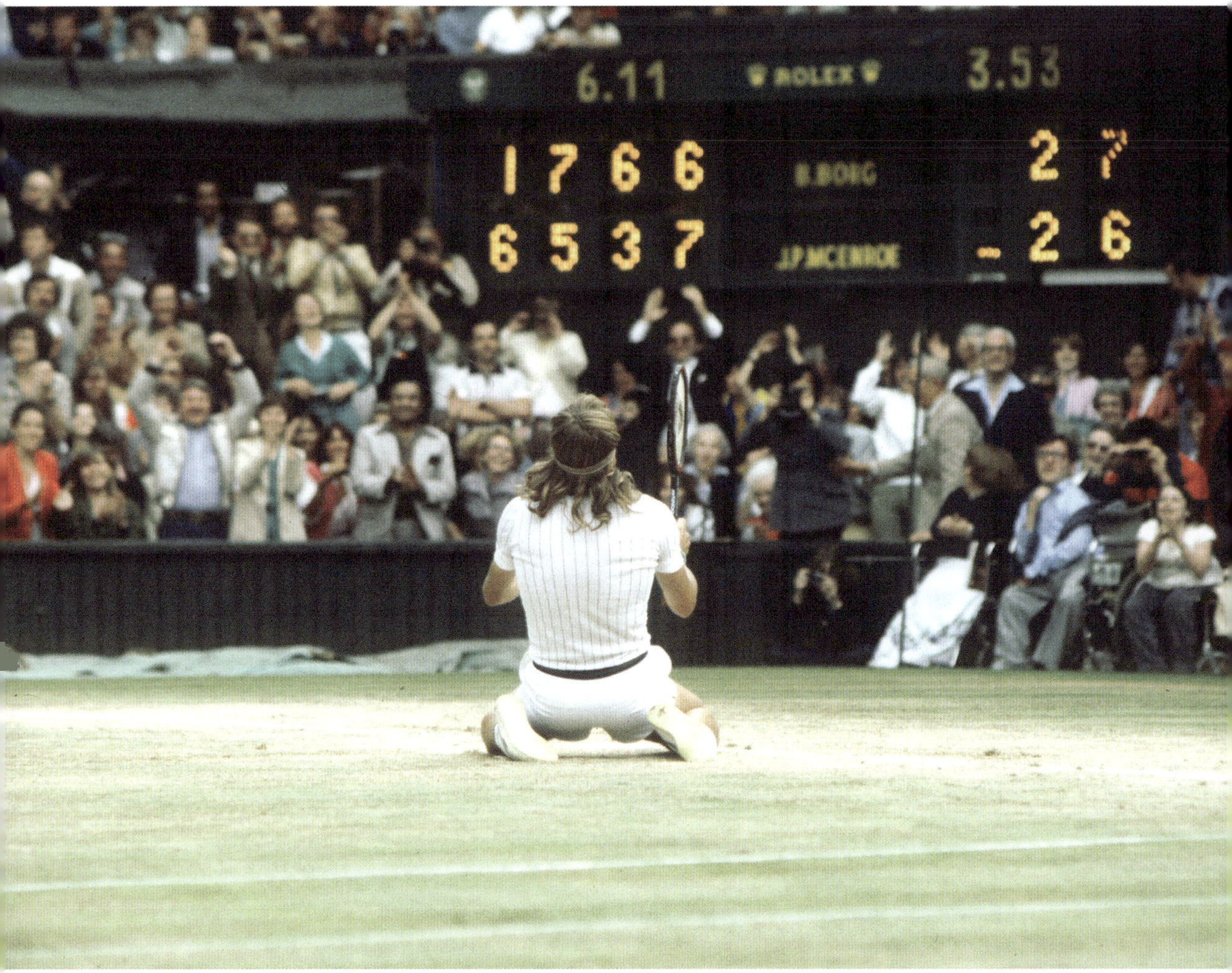

6.11
ROLEX
3.53
1 7 6 6
B.BORG
2 7
6 5 3 7
J.P.MCENROE
- 2 6

17

TIME STAMPING CENTRE COURT

Borg at Wimbledon

MICHAEL L. BUTTERWORTH

Sports media and fans are obsessed with defining athletes and events as the "greatest ever." Communication studies scholar Daniel A. Grano argues that such declarations are invested in the idea of "eternity," which "expresses desires to live during and bear witness to a continuity of advances in human capacity."[1] At the same time, our collective drive to witness greatness *in our own time* conflicts with the pervasive sports nostalgia that compels us to honor the triumphs of *another time*. Scholars of public memory note that sports provide "particularly vivid, compelling, accessible material" for making sense of life in the here and now.[2] Thus, sports observers are forever chasing greatness, whether it is through our remembrances of the past, our celebrations of the present, or even our speculations about the future.

I begin with these observations because they appeal to my sensibilities as an academic and fan. As a rhetorical critic, I have devoted a good amount of my scholarship to the study of "public memory" and its political uses in contemporary sport.[3] As a fan, I am often guilty of romanticizing previous eras in the sports I follow closely, even when I am acutely aware of those eras' considerable flaws. This applies well to one of my favorite sports, tennis, which is often on the periphery of mainstream coverage in the United States.

Although the first two decades of the twenty-first century have showcased some of the most prolific athletes in the history of the sport—Serena and Venus Williams, Roger Federer, Rafael Nadal, and Novak Djokovic, in particular—the high point of tennis' American popularity came two generations earlier, in the 1970s. The advent of the Open Era, the development of color television, the spectacle of the "Battle of the Sexes," and the emergence of marketable (if controversial) personalities launched the sport into the mainstream. Beyond the professional game, popular fitness trends combined with improved racket technology to lead as many as 34 million Americans to play tennis by the mid-1970s.[4]

In professional tennis, the 1970s were dominated by a series of compelling rivalries that showcased competing styles and personalities, often amplified by national identities defined by the Cold War. The Chris Evert–Martina Navratilova rivalry is widely heralded as the greatest tennis has ever seen, but others throughout the decade helped elevate the sport. There is an argument to be made, however, that the definitive tennis conflict came as the decade ended and the 1980s began. Although contained to a shorter time period, the contests between Sweden's Bjorn Borg and the United States' John McEnroe endure as some of the best moments in the sport's history. And, for many tennis observers, their legendary clash at Wimbledon's Centre Court remains the greatest match ever played.[5] The 1980 Championship was the first time the two players faced each other in a Grand Slam tournament, and it would be the last time Borg defeated McEnroe at one of tennis' four biggest events. The final score, 1–6, 7–5, 6–3, 6–7 (16–18), 8–6, was punctuated by the fourth set, won by McEnroe in an epic tiebreaker that remains unmatched in its drama and athletic artistry.

It is nearly impossible to revisit the 1980 men's final without immediately registering its place among the greatest matches in tennis history, thus bringing me back to sport's focus on eternity. This is true of all sporting accomplishments, but I think it is worth lingering over Borg's triumph at Centre Court. There are many images of that match that continue to resonate, perhaps none more so than that of a weary and jubilant Borg dropping to his knees after clinching the match, his fists lightly clenched and head thrust backward in an exuberant yell. There are several photos of that moment, including those showing Borg from the front and side. I am especially drawn to Bob Thomas's photo, taken from behind Borg and revealing a celebratory crowd and the final score. The image captures Borg's familiar features—especially the long blonde hair bound by the ever-present headband—but equally directs viewers to the trappings of the All England Lawn Tennis Club, especially its finely trimmed grass court and the Rolex-sponsored scoreboard. It is, I think, one of the great sports photographs of the twentieth century.

Bob Thomas is among the most recognized sports photographers of the late twentieth century, especially in the United Kingdom. He began his career as a seventeen-year-old in the mid-1970s, and by the time he captured Borg's celebration in 1980, he was leading the Bob Thomas Sports Photography agency and shooting sporting events around the world. His work is familiar to many sports fans, but he has two distinctive claims to uniqueness. First, his photograph of greyhounds racing at a dog track became the cover image for one of the most successful Britpop albums of all time, Blur's 1994 album *Parklife*.[6] Second, and more controversially, Thomas holds the copyright for an image of one of football's most iconic (or infamous, depending on your point of view) moments: Diego Maradona's "hand of God" goal during the 1986 World Cup quarterfinal match against England. Thomas did not take the image himself; rather, he purchased the rights to it from Mexican photographer Alejandro Ojeda Carbajal. To this day, photo credits for the image go to "Bob Thomas Sports Photography via Getty Images," a designation that may be legal but has prompted ethical questions about attribution and monetizing photojournalism.[7] In spite of this controversy, the now-retired Thomas played a central role in documenting global sports over the past half-century, and his photograph of Borg at Centre Court is a definitive image of its time.

Revisiting the Borg-McEnroe match affords us an opportunity to think about sports, rivalry, and time. Each of the photos included in this volume are marked by time, and we can trace their histories to know precisely when they were taken. And, yes, we need to check the record to know that the 1980 Gentleman's Final at Wimbledon took place on July 5. Beyond that, Thomas's photo stamps time in significant ways. Knowledge of tennis tells us when Borg was at his championship peak, and a close inspection of spectators' fashion choices—there are some fine-looking lapels in that crowd—tells us we're in the late 1970s or early 1980s. Significantly, though, the Centre Court scoreboard reveals so much more. The match has concluded at exactly 6:11 P.M. after three hours and fifty-three minutes of play. Below those designations lie the traces of the match's evolution, like acts in an epic play. And there, just beneath the ubiquitous "Rolex," are the legendary names forever linked to Wimbledon's legacy: "B Borg" and "JP McEnroe."

Box scores help tell the story of any given event, regardless of the sport. Tennis is uniquely revealing for at least two reasons. First, each set in tennis functions as a microcosm of the match. More so than an inning in baseball or a quarter in basketball, for example, tennis sets have definitive "winners." Players are rewarded by winning sets, not by accumulating points or games. If, for instance, a player won a match, 6–4, 1–6, 6–4, 1–6, 6–4, a cumulative score would show the winner with just twenty games and the loser with twenty-four. This scenario is not possible in other mainstream sports. As a result, there is heightened drama to each set, especially in championship matches. In addition, a best-of-five match parallels the dramatic structure of a five-act play, thus reflecting the metaphor of drama that has long applied to sport.[8] Second, the spotlight on individual athletes in singles tennis gives more explanatory power to each entry in the overall score. The greatest matches, in particular, are interpretable through the story crafted by the results of each set. In a five-set match, the loser still "wins" twice, meaning that twists in momentum and thin margins of victory are evident in the score. Perhaps the best parallel here is to baseball, where the box score indicates each player's individual results over the course of multiple at-bats. Still, I maintain the final score in tennis animates the mythic quality of a match in ways other sports cannot.

Beyond the epic quality of a five-set match, the scoreboard also makes present what is otherwise absent from the photo—McEnroe. In short, Borg's triumph is amplified by the significance of his rivalry with McEnroe. Even those with minimal knowledge of tennis will have some familiarity with Borg-McEnroe, which, as noted above, is arguably the definitive rivalry in the history of men's tennis. Several accounts have detailed the appeal of this rivalry,[9] but at least a couple features are worth noting here. First, the clash between the two players had been anticipated for a few years. Borg had first arrived at Wimbledon in 1973, where his poise and good looks made him tennis' first "rock star."[10] McEnroe himself credits Borg as the player who sparked the "electricity" of the era's tennis boom.[11] By the time McEnroe debuted in 1977, reaching the semi-finals, Borg had become the game's best player. The anticipation of a championship meeting was heightened by the contrast in the players' personalities and playing styles. If Borg was the rock star, McEnroe was the punk rock counter-statement—at least, this seems to be the common trope applied in retrospect.[12] McEnroe's infamous explosive temper made him impossible to ignore and, for many British observers, equally impossible to like. When the players were announced for the 1980 final, part of the notoriously polite Centre Court crowd greeted McEnroe with boos.

The contrast in temperament between the two men has long defined public memory of the rivalry in general and the 1980 championship in particular. Although that framing works well for books and movies, it also risks distracting from what is arguably the most compelling feature, that they were two of the best players in the sport's history, each playing their best tennis. Sports fans and members of the media often set high expectations for championship contests, only to be disappointed by an anticlimactic outcome. It is rare in sports to see the best athletes or teams face one another and to respond with their highest level of performance. Borg and McEnroe were entirely different yet evenly matched—they played each other fourteen times, with each winning seven matches. The photo of Borg winning the 1980 Wimbledon title cannot capture the entirety of this period, of course. But it reflects one of the reasons the match endures—its greatness is about the quality of play in the moment, but it also gestures toward the promise of what is yet to come. Indeed, Borg and McEnroe would meet in the final match at Wimbledon and the U.S. Open in both 1980 and 1981, further elevating the status of their rivalry.

The image of the exultant Borg kneeling before the crowd and the display of his triumph over McEnroe exemplifies the *agonistic* dimension of sport. I have written elsewhere about the capacity of sport to model agonistic forms of competition,[13] where conflict and difference is managed not through the antagonistic impulse to eliminate one's opponent but through an agonistic respect for someone who shares the same competitive space. Political theorists have turned to agonism to manage conflict and enhance democratic culture. The appeal of a sport-based metaphor lies in the assumption that, regardless of any ill feelings between competitors, the rivalry depends on the relative health and success of both sides. This certainly was the case between Borg and McEnroe, where the disappointment of one match ending was tempered by the promise of another match to come.

Borg's victory and Thomas's photo have taken on added significance over the years, in part because we know now that the rivalry was to be short-lived. Borg won another French Open title in 1981, but he lost to McEnroe at Wimbledon in 1981 and at the U.S. Open in 1980 and 1981. Following the defeat in New York in 1981, Borg infamously left the court before the trophy presentation, effectively retiring from tennis. In retrospect, then, we can view the celebratory image of Borg as a way to capture his final moments at the top of the sport. The crowd reaction is jubilant, in part because of the quality of the match but also because they are awed by seeing someone win a fifth consecutive championship. They may not know it at the time, but they are forever part of a specific chapter in tennis history.

If the photo time-stamps Borg's career and his rivalry with McEnroe, it also does so for the era in tennis. On the one hand, the photo is nearly timeless. After all, Centre Court at Wimbledon still largely looks as it did in 1980, and the color photograph, though slightly faded, could be mistaken for a more recent vintage. Even the very clear markers of the era—Borg's short shorts and wooden racket—are largely obscured by the angle. Nevertheless, the photo is undoubtedly a product of its moment, a snapshot of what is often remembered as the golden age of tennis. This is not to suggest that the level of play in 1980 was better than other eras, including the present one. Clearly, the degree of conditioning and athleticism that characterizes the sport today renders its previous era quaint by comparison. Again, the photo hints at the changes to come. Part of the story of Borg's ascendance was a legendary work ethic and training regimen. This, too, factors into the contrast with McEnroe, a gifted athlete who notoriously favored playing doubles over structured practices and thought little about regulating his nutrition and diet. Borg, meanwhile, worked tirelessly to perfect his strokes and relied on his superior athleticism and conditioning to wear down his opponents. In the photo's background—but in plain sight for Borg—is the match's duration of three hours and fifty-three minutes. Although longer matches had certainly been played, the length of the Wimbledon final revealed the importance of Borg's ability to outlast any other player. As has been characteristic of most athletes in the past four decades, tennis players now prioritize nutrition and off-season conditioning. Especially given the endurance required to play a sport that features so much movement, these practices have revolutionized how it is played. It is fair to suggest this began with Borg.[14]

More than signaling a shift in off-court training practices, the photo also stands as perhaps the most representative snapshot of tennis's first phase of the Open Era.[15] The tennis boom of the 1970s featured a range of memorable personalities and relied on various styles of play. And, as sports psychologist Jim Loehr suggests, average fans could still identify with the technology and technique required to play the sport. This point may explain some of the nostalgia that is prompted by the photo (and the era). Loehr observes,

"Today, people can't play the game they're watching on TV. It's like it's become a sport outside their reach, so they go back to a time when life was slower, the ball was slower, and the rackets were primitive. The players were human and you really felt you knew them."[16] This is an overly romanticized view of the era, yet it does capture a certain quality that can no longer be attributed to tennis.

As much as racket technology has transformed the style of play on the court, the greater change has been the global corporatism that now shapes tournament organization, sports media, and player interaction. Four decades after the Borg-McEnroe clash, tennis facilities worldwide are superior, broadcasts are more plentiful and accessible, and nearly everyone involved in the game makes considerably more money. But it is all a bit homogeneous, as well. The Grand Slam tournaments—the Australian Open, French Open, Wimbledon, and the U.S. Open—retain their unique charms, but the distinctions between them appear to have diminished.[17] And, while players bring a range of personalities to the court, they now share a mutual investment in the synergy between corporate sponsors and branding. Borg's disappearance from the U.S. Open in 1981 was noteworthy because he failed to appear alongside his rival in the trophy presentation. Were the same thing to happen today, the absence would surely be noted as a missed opportunity to thank the sponsors.

The changes in tennis, which have similarly affected other sports, have yielded some wonderful outcomes. Yet for all the athleticism on display and the greatness of more contemporary rivalries such as Pete Sampras-Andre Agassi, Steffi Graf-Monica Seles, Venus Williams-Serena Williams, and Roger Federer-Rafael Nadal, nothing quite recaptures the convergence of circumstances that make Borg's triumph so memorable. Whether or not the 1980 final against McEnroe is still seen in tennis circles as the *best* match ever played is not the point. Rather, its status as the *greatest* match is sustained by Borg's career trajectory, the uniqueness of his rivalry with McEnroe, and the legacy of the golden age of tennis. The photo taken by Bob Thomas allows us to revisit that moment, sweet lapels and all, and appreciate that greatness regardless of our own place in time.

NOTES

1. Daniel A. Grano, *The Eternal Present of Sport: Rethinking Sport and Religion* (Philadelphia: Temple University Press, 2017), 32.

2. Stephen G. Wieting and Judy Polumbaum, "Prologue," in Stephen G. Wieting, ed., *Sport and Memory in North America* (London: Frank Cass, 2001), 4.

3. For examples, see Michael L. Butterworth, "Militarism and Memorializing at the Pro Football Hall of Fame," *Communication and Critical/Cultural Studies* 9 (September 2012): 241–258; Michael L. Butterworth, "Public Memorializing in the Stadium: Mediated Sport, the Tenth Anniversary of 9/11, and the Illusion of Democracy," *Communication & Sport* 2 (September 2014): 203–224; and Michael L. Butterworth, "George W. Bush as 'The Man in the Arena': Baseball, Public Memory, and the Rhetorical Redemption of a President," *Rhetoric & Public Affairs* 22 (2019): 1–31.

4. Randy Walker, "Do Half the Number of Americans Play Tennis Now than the 1970s?" *World Tennis*, August 13, 2015, http://www.worldtennismagazine.com/archives/12152.

5. There is considerable debate about this, of course, and Rafael Nadal's victory over Roger Federer in the 2008 Wimbledon final often ranks ahead of Borg-McEnroe. For more on this, see Jake Curtis, "Ranking the 10 Most Epic Matches in Tennis History," *Bleacher Report*, July 10, 2013, https://bleacherreport.com/articles/1697051-ranking-the-10-most-epic-matches-in-tennis-history.

6. Steve Fairclough, "Greatest Album Photography: Parklife by Blur," *Amateur Photographer*, July 5, 2021, https://www.amateurphotographer.co.uk/latest/photo-news/150319-150319.

7. David Davis, "The Man Who Captured the Hand of God Has Been Erased from History," *Defector*, January 14, 2021, https://defector.com/the-man-who-captured-the-hand-of-god-has-been-erased-from-history/.

8. For example, see John Lahr, "The Theatre of Sports," in *Sport in the Socio-Cultural Process*, ed. M. Marie Hart (Dubuque, IA: Wm. C. Brown, 1972), 105–116.

9. Aside from regular features in sports media, there was a cluster of material produced in 2011 that focused on this rivalry. See Matthew Cronin, *Epic: John McEnroe, Björn Borg, and the Greatest Tennis Season Ever* (Hoboken, NJ: John Wiley & Sons, Inc., 2011); Stephen Tignor, *High Strung: Bjorn Borg, John McEnroe, and the Untold Story of Tennis's Fiercest Rivalry* (New York: Harper, 2011); and *McEnroe/Borg: Fire & Ice*, written by Aaron Cohen (Home Box Office, 2011), 1:05:00.

10. Cronin, *Epic*, 50.

11. John McEnroe with James Kaplan, *You Cannot Be Serious* (New York: G. P. Putnam's Sons, 2002), 6.

12. Both Cronin and Tignor feature this idea in their books. The HBO documentary edits a montage of McEnroe's outbursts to "Anarchy in the UK" by punk rock legends the Sex Pistols.

13. For example, see Michael L. Butterworth, "Sport and the Quest for Unity: How the Logic of Consensus Undermines Democratic Culture," *Communication & Sport* 8 (2020): 452–472.

14. For the record, McEnroe also credits Czech legend Ivan Lendl for advancing the physical elements of the sport in the mid-1980s. Reflecting on Lendl's fitness as well as tennis's shift to graphite racket technology, he writes, "The combination of fitness and racket power had left me out in the cold. The master of the wood racket was heading toward extinction." McEnroe with Kaplan, *You Cannot Be Serious*, 213. McEnroe's professional decline and Borg's ill-fated comeback in 1991 (wood racket included) further demonstrate how fixed in time the 1980 match remains.

15. Prior to 1968, the Grand Slam tournaments in tennis were only for amateurs. Since 1968, they have been "open" to professional players as well.

16. Quoted in Cronin, *Epic*, 213.

17. My thanks to Mackenzie Pike for conversations that have helped shape this insight.

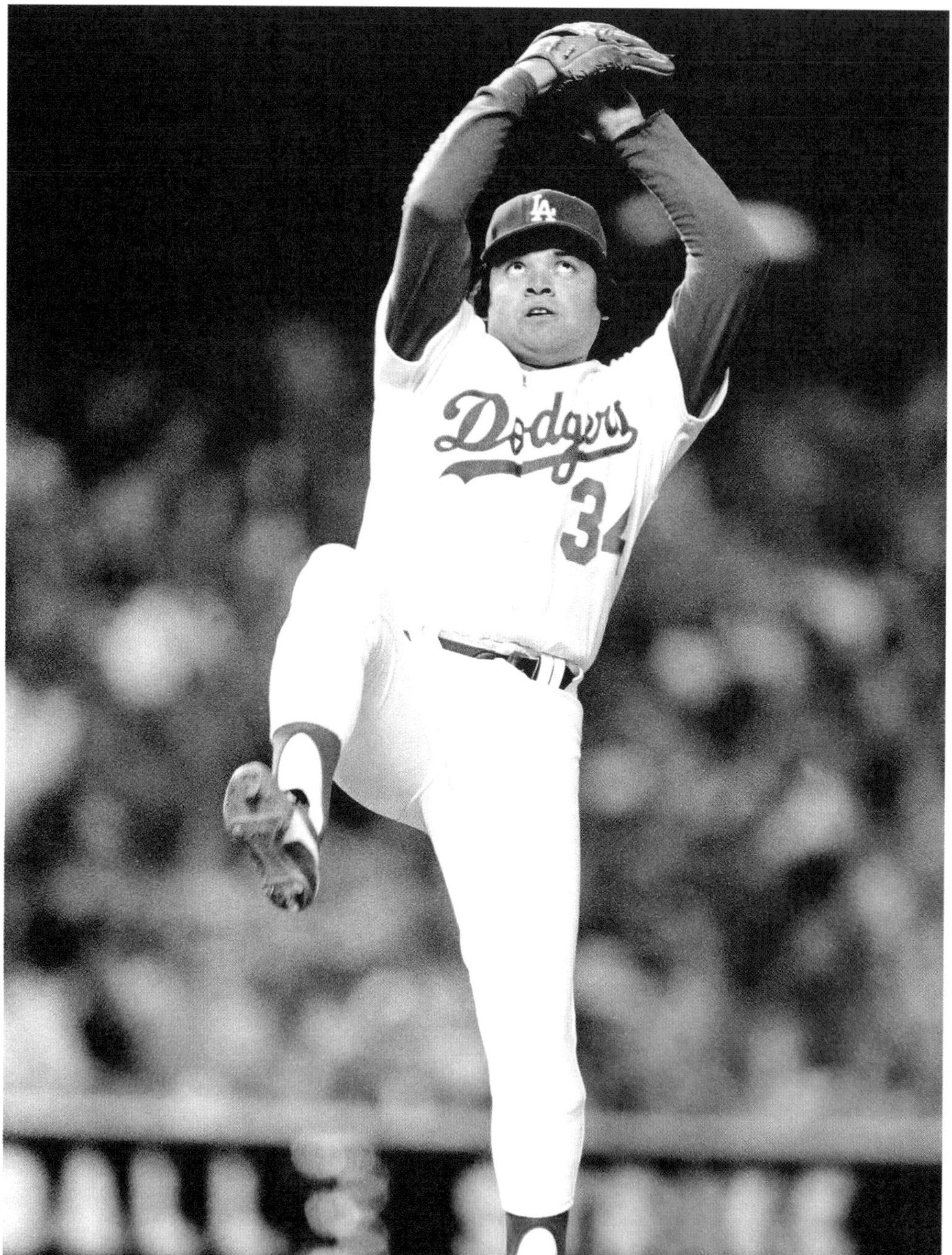
Dodgers
34

18

THE ART OF FERNANDO VALENZUELA

Baseball and Chicanx Culture in California

BERNARDO RAMIREZ RIOS

Fernando Valenzuela stretches his arms high above his head. His baseball mitt creates a slight shadow from the brightness of the stadium lights. The shadow hides his grip on the ball in darkness; the light only exposes the small of his wrist, and everything else is a mystery. The iconic LA Dodgers hat sits atop Fernando's head, and his shaggy hair spills out underneath, covering his ears. The hat's crown reflects like a mirror, creating a slight halo. With Fernando looking up at the heavens, the image might even appear angelic to some. Fernando's gaze is high up in the sky, away from his target. His left eye rolls back so much his eyelid covers it partially. The long sleeves of his blue undershirt and white home jersey drape his upper body as he slightly grimaces and takes a short breath. Fernando contorts his body and wrinkles the Dodgers script across his chest and number. A year after this picture was taken, the whole baseball world would recognize Dodgers number 34. Fernando's body is stocky—in Spanish, we might call him gordito (pudgy). His belt strains to contain his thick torso, and his legs are like tree stumps. Fernando tilts toward the background with his left leg slightly bent. The bottom of his right cleat faces the foreground, and his right leg is nearly waist-high. His left toes wrinkle his cleat as it cements into the pitcher's mound. His body is balanced between his raised mitt and high-kicked leg.

In 1980, Jayne Kamin-Oncea started as a staff photographer for the *Los Angeles Times*, where she worked for twenty-six years. That same year, Fernando Valenzuela made his first appearance for the Los Angeles Dodgers. The rookie photographer captured the rookie pitcher from the first-base side of the field, which is the preferred angle for capturing right-handed batters. Left-handers constitute only about 30 percent of Major League pitchers, so the photo is a unique perspective. The background of the image is a gradient blur from top to bottom. The top is black, with shadows tucked deep underneath the stadium balcony. The blur of the crowd—a spatter of black, white, and gray—suggests what would come to be known as Fernandomania, a phenomenon which would come into focus the following season (1981). The bottom illuminates the faint outline of the pitch count (balls and strikes). The background is blurry and out of focus, but the foreground captures the details of Fernando's windup.

Windup

The photograph captures an essential characteristic of Fernando's pitching style: his windup. The artist Richard Montoya describes his windup as ritualistic, ceremonial, and uniquely representative of Mexican culture.[1] A ritual is a repetitious symbolic practice. From a cultural standpoint, the purpose of any ritual is to provide consistency and order to the individual and group. Fernando elongates his body, stretches his arms and mitt above his head, and kicks his leg high enough that the bottom of his cleat seems to be kissing the sky. His body could be likened to a stretched rubber band. Fernando's high kick wasn't unique—in fact, many pitchers kicked high during their windup—but the fluidity and height of his kick matched his intensity. Fernando's style was spiritual because it spoke to a desire to deliver something special every pitch, and Fernando delivered a remarkable rookie season, one for the record books.[2] The photograph captures Fernando in the moments before the release. He looks away from the target—home plate—and veers into the sky. Some photographs even capture the pitcher with his eyes rolled back as if a divine power overtook his body before he delivered the pitch. Some Latinx households in the Southwest view Fernando's notoriety in the mass media and dominance on the field as divine intervention. It was common to find Latinx youth replicating Fernando's famous windup and his poster adorned many household walls. Watching Fernando play was a religious experience for some people. Sometimes he would grace household religious altars because, for many Latinx people, he was a part of us.[3]

The depth of field in the photo focuses on Fernando in the foreground and blurs the background. The speckles of the crowd in the background seem insignificant, but the unrecognizable spots in the background (Angelenos in the U.S.) ignited a surge of Latinx awareness in the U.S. Fernando came into focus at the same time Latinx culture was beginning to receive mainstream recognition in the U.S. Of course, Fernando was not the first Mexican baseball star. In 1903, another player named "Valenzuela" starred in exhibitions in Mexico.[4] Yet Fernando arrived in the U.S. when identity politics was beginning to take shape, which the Dodgers organization recognized as a marketing opportunity.[5] In the late 1940s, the Dodgers set a precedent by integrating Major League Baseball with Jackie Robinson, Don Newcombe, and Roy Campanella, among others, but the Dodgers lacked a superstar representing the Latinx population in Los Angeles.

The historical significance of the Dodgers organization frames the pathway to Fernando's integration into the larger Latinx community in the Southwest. The team's owner, Walter O'Malley, moved the Dodgers from Brooklyn to Los Angeles in 1957. The team's legacy of integration and inclusion paralleled the liberal culture of California. However, the city of Los Angeles acquired the land for Dodger Stadium via eminent domain. Chavez Ravine was predominantly a Latinx neighborhood. Residents were forced to sell their property and, in some cases, forcefully removed by the LAPD. When the team broke ground on Dodger Stadium in 1959, after a year of struggle with the local Latinx population in Chavez Ravine, many were saddened and confused about the organization's trajectory. For many years, some Angelenos with generational ties to Chavez Ravine maintained their distrust and did not support the Dodgers.[6] But as the years passed, the relationship between the Dodgers and the Latinx community improved. Fernandomania is a story about the presence of Latinx people in the U.S., a process in which generations of Mexican Americans retaught the U.S. and the mainstream media about "play" while contributing to sociopolitical action in race, class, and ethnicity.[7] Before Fernando, many Latinx MLB players brought their unique skills to the Major Leagues. Still, more importantly, they brought a new flavor to baseball, and many fans developed an appetite for it. They played the game with confidence and pizazz. The mainstream media recognized the Latinx consumer's purchasing power, and Fernandomania erupted. On the surface, the mainstream media controlled the

Fernando narrative by portraying it as a shining example of the American dream.[8] Still, the narrative's market value was always in the hands of the generations of Latinx Angelenos.[9] They were active writers, scholars, engineers, artists, doctors, lawyers, and members of every other profession woven into the fabric of American society.

Bull Ring

Amid Fernandomania, Dodgers fans gave Fernando Valenzuela the nickname El Toro (The Bull). Bullfighting fans adore the matadors and throw roses at their feet. In baseball, the matador equivalent is the batter, standing in the box, waiting to react to the bull's charge. The bull in this photograph is wearing number 34. The batter is to the left, out of the frame. From the batter's viewpoint, Fernando is a bull rushing toward him. One could imagine the shaggy hair spilling out from under his baseball cap as a pair of horns, and his feet—one of them digging into the pitcher's mound and the other suspended high in the air—as a pair of hooves. El Toro comes from the countryside, is rough around the edges, and has an unorthodox pitching style. He tightly grips the ball's seams with his hand and secures the leather high above his head. Meanwhile, spectators shift in their seats and the batter clutches the bat. Will it be a fastball, a slider, or a screwball? Like a bull, Fernando kicks his leg high, which sends a message to the batter that something powerful will soon be upon him; his kick is a giant leap forward, setting into motion the first step of a charge. The dirt on his cleats is visible to those in the opposing team's dugout.

Is he standing in La Loma, Palo Verde, or Bishop? The former neighborhoods where Dodger Stadium now stands were home to Mexican American families, and they were sanctuaries of ethnic rigidity.[10] Similar to those in Fernando's hometown in Mexico, the residents of Chavez Ravine had limited resources, but they created a community through culture and fortitude. Resiliency is at the core of Mexican culture, and we see this in Fernando's toes dug deep into the pitcher's mound, his experience with struggles generating his tremendous force. The raw and unpredictable power of El Toro transcends borders, time, and space. He symbolizes hope and prosperity and connects with the hearts of many who, despite their struggles and sacrifices, charged forward for a better life. For the Latinx community in Los Angeles, Dodger Stadium became a bull ring, like Plaza de Toros México (Mexico Bull Stadium).

Screwball

In the photograph, Fernando's glove hides his grip on the ball under the shadow of the stadium lights, so it is impossible to analyze the type of pitch he threw. Most people familiar with the Fernandomania saga would guess the unknown pitch was a screwball. A screwball breaks in the opposite direction of a slider or curveball and is difficult to master. Fernando's execution of the screwball transformed baseball fandom for Latinx fans in the Southwest. This unique pitch, which was seldom used in Major League Baseball, would change Fernando's life and the lives of generations of Dodgers fans. There he was, in Chavez Ravine, a young prospect with potential. Although Fernando played in the Mexican professional league, he was still considered a prospect in the making because he had not been challenged at the Major League level. The Dodgers signed him as a prospect in 1979, and coaches thought he needed time to refine his craft. However, due to a fluke injury to a starting pitcher, Fernando took the mound to compete at the highest level of baseball on opening day in 1981. Unbeknownst to Fernando, his power, skill, and grit epitomized generations of Dodger faithful and soon-to-be fans with Mexican heritage.

In Los Angeles, a Spanish-speaking Dodger was iconic for the Mexicans, Mexican Americans, Chicanos, and recently arrived Central Americans. In *Deportes: The Making of a Sporting Mexican Diaspora* (2020), José M. Alamillo writes, "Even before I learned about César Chávez, Martin Luther King Jr., and other civil rights leaders, I had one Latino role model—Fernando Valenzuela."[11] Although Fernando's background, experience, and identity played a considerable role in developing his narrative, his exceptional play in 1981 solidified his place as one of the best pitchers in the world. His Mexican identity, coupled with his accomplishments on the field, allowed for cultural changes in the treatment, perception, and inclusion of the Latinx population in the U.S.

Fernando arrived at an opportune time, on the heels of the Chicano civil rights movement that was primarily based in California but extended to Latinx farmworker communities across the U.S. César Chávez initiated momentum for the unionization of farm workers in the 1960s. Afterward, Chicano communities around the country created organizations to address the multitude of challenges the Latinx community faced (and in some cases still face). Over the following years, Chicano communities and organizations across the country addressed issues such as equal pay, the Vietnam War, housing policies, educational opportunities, immigration policies, and many other community-led initiatives. Ronald Reagan's first term as president in 1981 coincided with Fernando's debut, and the socioeconomic policies surrounding issues of immigration connected with the previous struggles of the Chicano community. It was not a coincidence that the Reagan administration dismantled much of the social programming that benefitted the Chicano community. Fernando planted himself on the pitcher's mound amid a U.S. recession and feelings of frustration and despair. Fortunately, the Latinx community and the broader public used him as an outlet for inspiration, and Fernandomania was born.

The aura of this photograph is familial and grounded in Latinx heritage. Scholar Jorge E. Moraga explains the intersection between sports and the "browning of America" by illustrating how demographic changes parallel the sociopolitical initiatives of Latinx youth in Los Angeles.[12] For many Latinx families in the U.S. Southwest, whether they were recent arrivals or generations old, this photograph represents *la lucha* (the struggle). The struggle to overcome is a cultural tradition for Latinx families with generational histories of migration. Fernando arrived fresh off the heels of the Chicano Moratorium, a political action that revolutionized the ethnic landscape for Latinx individuals in the U.S. In 1968, Chicano students in East Los Angeles organized a series of protests against the Los Angeles Unified School District high schools for inequality. During the East Los Angeles Walkouts, there were clashes with the LAPD; like many similar situations, some young people suffered severe injuries.[13] The first Chicano studies department was established at CSU Los Angeles the same year. In the following years, labor organizer César Chávez campaigned throughout California to advocate for farmworker rights—most of the farmworkers were of Mexican descent—and to establish the United Farm Workers Union. Shortly after, in the 1970s, organizing initiatives such as breakfast programs sparked leadership in the Latinx communities. In East Los Angeles, a group of Chicano artists started a community center for the arts called Self-Help Graphics, a barrio arts program that embraced Mexican history and integrated it into the Mexican American experience. That history came to life a few years later when Fernando took the mound to make his first Major League appearance.

Jayne Kamin-Oncea's black-and-white photograph symbolizes Fernandomania and the duality of a nation. The eminent scholar W. E. B. Du Bois wrote about the double consciousness, or the duality that Black Americans experience in the United States.[14] Regarding the duality of Latinx Americans, feminist scholar and poet Gloria Anzaldúa expanded the concepts of resistance and oppression to the borderlands and described how language is a political power that affects mobility.[15] Anzaldúa embodies the difficulty of duality, the legacy of colonialism, and how it explains and impacts the daily life of Latinx people in the U.S. In the stark contrast between the light and dark areas of the photo, one can see the duality of Latinx identity formation in the U.S. For example, some may see this photo and use English to describe its visual components. Others may use Spanish to paint a realistic view of the photo while also adding poetic, magical elements. Magical realism is a style of literary fiction and art often associated with Latin-American literature because it's deeply rooted in the ethos of Latinx culture. In the same light, we see the duality in the movement in the photo, the power rising beneath, the legs pushing up from the earth, the torso twisting and coiling to harness kinetic energy, and the pocketed arm tucked inside. At the opposite end, a look up toward the heavens, a slight nod to the gods, a bit of faith because the power beneath is strong and can sometimes be scary. Fernando Valenzuela is a legend for many Latinx people in the U.S. because he exemplifies the beauty within the struggle. What a beautiful picture it is.

NOTES

1. Gustavo Arellano, "Fernandomania @ 40," *Los Angeles Times*, 2021, https://www.latimes.com/sports/fernandomania.

2. Adrian Burgos, "'I Look Up to the Hills, from Where Cometh My Help,'" December 1, 2018, https://www.lavidabaseball.com/el-profe-i-look-up-to-the-hills-from-where-cometh-my-help/.

3. Gustavo Arellano, "The Gospel of Fernandomania: Forty Years Later, Fernando Valenzuela Still a Mexican American Icon," *Los Angeles Times*, April 7, 2021, https://www.latimes.com/sports/dodgers/story/2021-04-07/fernando-valenzuela-fernando mania-religious-experience.

4. William H. Beezley, "The Rise of Baseball in Mexico and the First Valenzuela," *Studies in Latin American Popular Culture* 4 (1985): 3–13.

5. David G. LaFrance, "Labor, the State, and Professional Baseball in Mexico in the 1980s," *Journal of Sport History* 22 (Summer 1995): 111–134.

6. Priscilla Leiva, "The Complicated Relationship between Latinos and the Los Angeles Dodgers," *Smithsonian Magazine*, October 22, 2020, https://www.smithsonianmag.com/smithsonian-institution/complicated-relationship-between-latinos-and-los-angeles-dodgers-180976109/.

7. David Wood and P. Louise Johnson, *Sporting Cultures: Hispanic Perspectives on Sport, Text and the Body* (New York: Routledge, 2008).

8. Jorge E. Moraga, "Reading Fernando Valenzuela and Fernandomania: Broadening Americanness One Pitch at a Time," in *The Circus Is in Town: Sport, Celebrity, and*

Spectacle, edited by Lisa Doris Alexander and Joel Nathan Rosen (Jackson: University Press of Mississippi, 2021), 255–277.

9. Moraga, "Reading Fernando Valenzuela and Fernandomania," 263; David G. LaFrance, "A Mexican Popular Image of the United States through the Baseball Hero, Fernando Valenzuela," *Studies in Latin American Popular Culture* 4, no. 1 (1985): 14–22.

10. Erin Victoria Zamora, "Buried under Dodger Blue: Racial Rhetorical Criticism, Public Memory, and Fernandomania" (PhD diss., Arizona State University, 2020).

11. José M. Alamillo, *Deportes: The Making of a Sporting Mexican Diaspora* (New Brunswick, NJ: Rutgers University Press, 2020), 1.

12. Jorge E. Moraga, "On ESPN Deportes: Latinos, Sport Media, and the Cultural Politics of Visibilities," *Journal of Sport and Social Issues* 42, no. 6 (2018): 470–497.

13. Robert J. Lopez, "The East L.A. Walkouts of 1968," *California State University Los Angeles Magazine*, Winter 2018, https://www.calstatelamagazine.com/university-news/cal-state-la-east-la-walkouts-1968.

14. W. E. B. Du Bois, *The Souls of Black Folk* (Boston: Bedford Books, [1903] 1997).

15. Gloria Anzaldúa, *Borderlands/La Frontera: The New Mestiza*, 2nd edition (San Francisco: Aunt Lute Books, [1987] 1999).

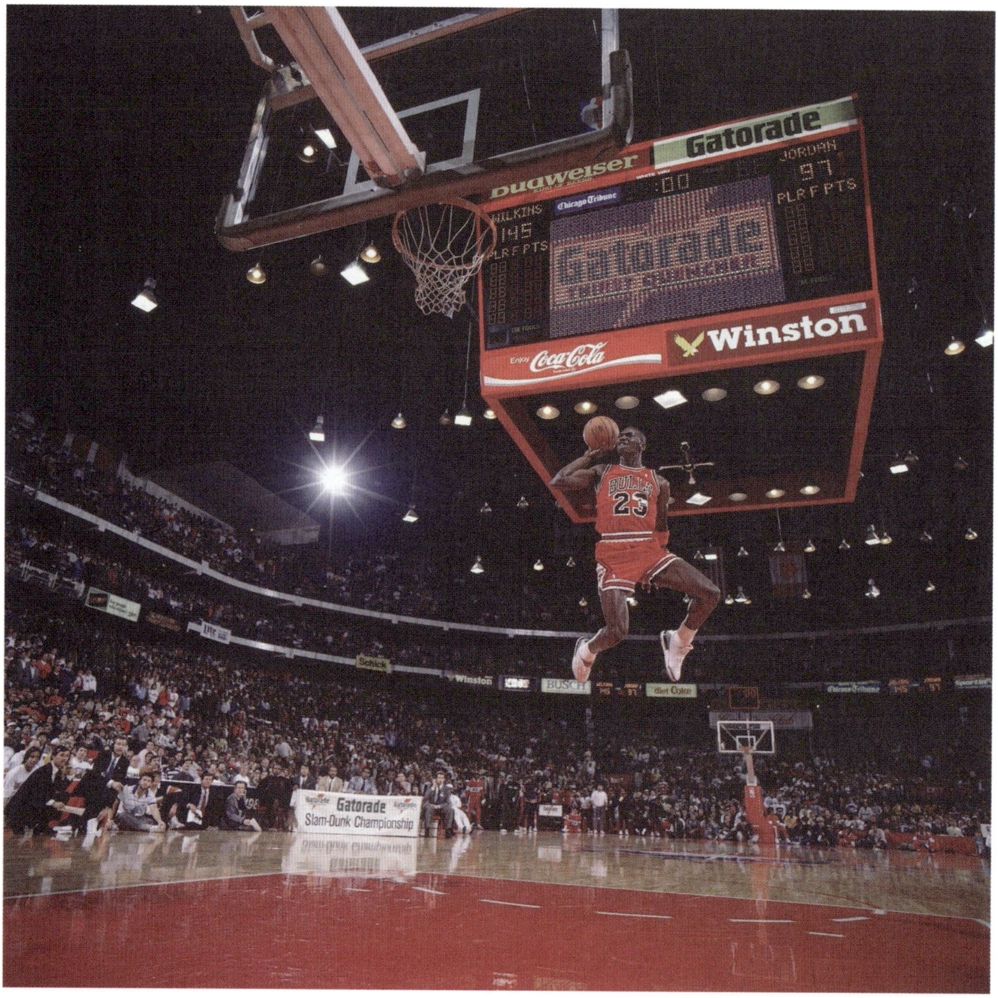
Gatorade
Budweiser
Chicago Tribune
WILKINS
145
PLR F PTS
JORDAN
97
PLR F PTS
Gatorade
Winston
Enjoy Coca-Cola
BULLS
23
Schick
Winston
BUSCH
diet Coke
Gatorade
Slam-Dunk Championship

19

MICHAEL JORDAN AT THE 1988 SLAM DUNK CONTEST

The NBA and Nike Take Flight in the New Gilded Age

SEAN DINCES

Michael Jordan called it "a picture-perfect weekend." The superstar guard for the National Basketball Association's Chicago Bulls had just won the Most Valuable Player award in the league's 1988 All-Star Game. Facing off against a who's who of NBA greats, including Earvin "Magic" Johnson and Hakeem Olajuwon, Jordan netted forty points, tacking on eight rebounds, three assists, four blocks, and four steals for good measure.[1] And "His Airness" did it in front of a fanatical sellout crowd at Chicago Stadium, the Bulls' home arena. Perfect, indeed.

The most iconic image from the All-Star weekend, however, did not come from MJ's performance during the game. It was taken the day before, when *Sports Illustrated*'s Walter Iooss Jr., stationed along one of the baselines, captured Jordan's final attempt in the Slam Dunk Contest. Moments before, Dominique Wilkins, the Atlanta Hawks small forward whose acrobatic dunks had earned him the moniker "Human Highlight Film," had brought his point total in the final round of the contest to 145 with what the *Sacramento Bee* described as a "triumphant two-handed rim-rattler."[2] Jordan needed at least a 49 out of 50 on his last dunk to best Wilkins and defend his contest championship from the previous year. "I was nervous because I knew

I needed something spectacular," the Bulls phenom later admitted.[3] Dribbling from the baseline at the opposite end of the floor from Iooss, Jordan accelerated across half-court, leapt from the free-throw line, and . . . missed. He had one more try. On his final opportunity, Jordan went for the same dunk he had just bricked. He slammed home what Doug Cress of the *Los Angeles Daily News* described as a "flying, one-handed stuff" that "brought the sellout crowd . . . to its feet."[4] The judges scored it a perfect 50. Jordan retained his Dunk Contest title, and Iooss snapped one of the most recognizable photographs in NBA history.

Former NBA executive Brian McIntyre, who remembers giving up his spot on the baseline to Iooss so the photographer could have the perfect angle on Jordan's last dunk, watched the two shots—Jordan's and Iooss's—take shape simultaneously. "I'm watching [Walter] as I'm watching Michael," McIntyre recalls. "After [Walter] got the one famous shot [with the scoreboard in the background], he looked at his camera and kissed it. He knew he had it."[5] Iooss's success owed much to careful planning. He made a point to speak to Jordan before the event. "I explained that it was really important for me to get a good picture—as if he cared—and it would help if I knew which direction he was going, so I could see his face." MJ graciously agreed to indicate which way he planned to go on his dunks by pointing with his forefinger in a particular direction right before. Iooss adds that after being disappointed with sub-par lighting during the 1987 Dunk Contest, he "set up the lights [around the camera in 1988] so that it was a little more theatrical looking. . . . Not the standard lighting that you do in an arena."[6] The result: an image that has graced the walls, in poster form, of countless basketball fans across the world.

In the ensuing days, the spectacle Iooss captured on film was eclipsed, at least partially, by accusations that the contest judges unfairly tipped the scales in favor of Jordan to appease the Chicago crowd. According to David Kahn of the *Oregonian*, "Among the nation's basketball writers, there was little doubt that the five-man panel of judges was swayed by the Chicago Bulls fans." Many believed that the judges jobbed Wilkins on his last dunk. The Atlanta Hawk received perfect scores on his first two jams in the final round against Jordan, but only a 45 out of 50 for his third, which some impartial observers thought was Wilkins's "best dunk of the day."[7]

America's sportswriters could not resist the temptation to use Chicago's infamous history of political corruption as a metaphor. The *Orlando Sentinel*'s Barry Cooper wrote, "In a town famous for hard-fisted machine politics, local hero Michael Jordan . . . won the NBA slam-dunk crown when . . .

Wilkins suddenly sustained misfortune at the ballot box." Wilkins "now knows how Richard Nixon felt when Cook County swung the 1960 presidential election to John Kennedy," quipped Barry Bloom in the *San Diego Union-Tribune*.[8]

Neither Jordan nor Wilkins did much to quell the controversy. The former conceded after the contest that "if it wasn't in Chicago, it might have gone the other way," and that he was "shocked" by the judges' scoring of Wilkins's final dunk. That Wilkins felt jilted by the judges came through loud and clear when he announced a few days later that he would not compete in another Dunk Contest outside of Atlanta.[9] The first drafts of the dunk's history thus became bogged down in discussions of allegedly biased judging. Decades later, the shroud over the affair remains. "To this day, many believe Wilkins was the rightful winner," the Associated Press noted in 2020.[10]

This controversy has arguably obscured the fact that when Iooss photographed Jordan's dunk, he recorded more than an awe-inspiring feat of athleticism. Intentionally or not, he generated a powerful visual metaphor for major historical shifts that Jordan stood at the very center of—namely, the ascent of the NBA from a backwater of American professional sports to a wildly successful global enterprise buoyed by MJ's marketability. Jordan's opponents on the court, however, were not the only casualties of this success story. The NBA's growing profitability depended on the increasing dominance of an economic model that concentrated more resources in the hands of transnational corporations and celebrities, typically at the expense of working people. Placing Iooss's photographic record of Jordan's dunk in a wider historical context reminds us that the business of sport was anything but exceptional within the larger history of capitalism at the end of the twentieth century. The increasingly globalized sporting spectacles produced by leagues, teams, and sponsors reinforced intensifying inequality and exploitation inside and outside of the U.S. In this regard, they encapsulated what some economists have referred to as the "New Gilded Age," during which the concentration of wealth and power at the top has reached extremes reminiscent of the early twentieth century.[11]

The late seventies and early eighties were bad times for the NBA. David Stern, who became the league's general counsel in 1978 and rose to be its commissioner six years later, asserted, "We were looked upon as a league that was too black, too violent, and too drug-involved."[12] On-court fights were common. Stern insists the media exaggerated the drug problem; however, the mere association of a league of mostly Black professional athletes with drug use in the context of the Reagan era—a period in which the war on drugs and racial resentment escalated in tandem—alienated many fans. Television coverage of the league suffered. National broadcasts became increasingly inconsistent. Things got bad enough that some NBA Finals games during the early 1980s appeared on tape delay.[13]

During these dark ages of the NBA, the Bulls' popularity took a hard hit. Local interest in the team waned during several abysmal seasons in the late 1970s and continued to ebb as a resurgence of the Chicago Bears football team distracted fans. Between the 1980–1981 and 1983–1984 seasons, average attendance at Bulls home games fell from more than 9,500 to fewer than 6,400.[14]

However, just as "Bears fever became an epidemic of wonderful lunacy," the Bulls morphed, in the words of the *Chicago Tribune*'s Paul Sullivan, "from Chicago's unloved stepchild to favorite son."[15] The selection of Michael Jordan in the 1984 NBA draft sparked an epic turnaround that culminated in 1998, when he led the Bulls to their sixth NBA title in eight years. Shortly thereafter, *Sun-Times* sportswriter Jay Mariotti waxed poetic about Jordan's importance to the Second City: "He gave Chicago a shot of self-esteem that made our chests swell and our lungs roar every springtime."[16] Jordan's final dunk in the 1988 Slam Dunk Contest and the electric response by the fans in Chicago Stadium were early indications of his power to change the Bulls' fortunes.

MJ's impact transcended Chicago, of course. He revolutionized the NBA's marketing reach, not just because of his athletic skills, but also because of where he came from and how he carried himself. Historian Walter LaFeber explains that the guard "grew up in a close-knit middle-class family" in a part of North Carolina that "missed the worst of the civil-rights violence."[17] This helped shape Jordan's public persona, which foregrounded his dedication to traditional values, hard work, personal responsibility, and an aversion to controversy. He thus stood as a sort of antithesis to Muhammad Ali (perhaps the only American athlete of the twentieth century who garnered as much global fame as Jordan). Whereas Ali made a point to confront and indict the status quo, often at significant personal cost, Jordan was primarily focused on his on-court performance, as well as cultivating what he described as a "positive image."[18] This contrast explains why the 1988 photo, even though it highlighted the physical prowess of a Black man at a moment when NBA executives worried that their league was "too black," held such appeal. Jordan, by comparison to Ali, functioned as a hero around whom people from different ethnic, racial, and economic backgrounds could rally. In 1991, sociologist John Koval explained that Jordan "fills all the needs of white, middle-class Americans. . . . He's a nice guy, he speaks well . . . he doesn't threaten middle-class America."[19]

Jordan's unthreatening yet inspirational image constituted the ideal vehicle for the league's marketing initiatives. The Dunk Contest was a case in point. The rival American Basketball Association first introduced the event during its All-Star Game in 1976, which marked the league's final year before it dissolved and the NBA absorbed four of its franchises. The NBA kept the contest in 1977, but in a different form—one in which select players participated in "a season-long one-on-one [dunk] competition that played out during halftimes of its league's few nationally-televised contests." The league then abandoned the event until 1984 when Rick Welts, then the NBA's director of national promotions, was, in his own words, "try[ing] to find corporations to invest marketing dollars into the NBA." Welts and his colleagues rebooted the contest in the original ABA format—that is, during halftime at the All-Star Game—in hopes of enticing new sponsors, ultimately securing backing from Gatorade and American Airlines.[20] Jordan's mass appeal, along with his highlight-laden performances in the event in 1985, 1987, and 1988, cemented the contest's place as a hallmark of each NBA season. It became a spectacle that captivated fans and sponsors alike.

Iooss's 1988 Dunk Contest photograph encapsulated this emerging symbiosis between the league and corporate America. Arguably, the most noticeable aspect of the image besides the airborne Jordan is the ubiquity of advertisements. The word "Gatorade" dominates the scoreboard above and behind MJ, not to mention the front of the judges' table situated toward the bottom-left of the frame. Regarding the former, the image effectively presents Jordan as lifting or supporting a Gatorade logo that takes up nearly as much space in the picture as he does. Additional ads in the background promote various brands of beer, soft drinks, cigarettes, credit cards, and razors. In-stadium advertising was nothing new. Yet Jordan's popularity dramatically enhanced the appeal of NBA advertising for companies eager to associate their products with excellence, excitement, and respectability.

Jordan also became the lynchpin of the NBA's efforts in the early 1990s to use the Olympic Games to increase the exposure of its stars to a wider audience, especially outside the U.S. His Airness helped lead the 1992 Dream Team, the first U.S. Olympic basketball squad consisting of top NBA talent, to a gold medal in Barcelona. LaFeber notes that the frenzy around Jordan and his Olympic teammates "grew so intense that the Dream Team chose to live in high-security seclusion apart from the other athletes." MJ "was the focal point of the media and public." The awe he inspired throughout much of the world was made obvious when a journalist from Japan covering the 1992 Games asked Jordan, "How does it feel to be God?" MJ had become a high-value global commodity. Thanks in large part to him, by the beginning of the new millennium, fans could watch the NBA All-Star Game in more than two hundred countries and more than forty languages.[21]

For the NBA, the capture of new domestic and international markets in the Jordan era translated into a stratospheric boost in demand for the league's product. Prices, revenues, and profits surged. Between 1984, the year the Bulls drafted MJ, and 1998, the year the Bulls won their sixth NBA championship, the league's annual revenue from national (U.S.) television broadcast rights grew from $25 million to $1.1 billion. A decade later, the figure reached an astronomical $4.6 billion. Between the 1989–90 and 1995–96 seasons, the Chicago Bulls' estimated pre-tax profits jumped from $7.3 million to $33.1 million. By the new millennium, they exceeded $50 million.[22] When Chicago real estate investor Jerry Reinsdorf organized a group to purchase the Bulls in 1985, it paid $9.2 million for the team. *Forbes* estimated the franchise's value in 2022 at $3.7 billion. Reinsdorf is now a member of America's billionaire class thanks in large part to the team's appreciation.[23] Simply put, Jordan helped make those with major stakes in the NBA *a lot* richer.

This improvement in the fortunes of owners like Reinsdorf had consequences for ordinary fans' access to the sports and athletes they loved. Jordan's star power significantly increased interest in the NBA among the wealthy and well known. By the mid-1990s, sitting courtside had become a status symbol for celebrities, politicians, and corporate bigwigs. The increased clamoring for seats by rich people helped drive ticket prices through the roof. During the 1984–85 season, the cost of the most and least expensive ticket to a Bulls games stood at $15 and $4.50, respectively. When the 1997–98 campaign kicked off, the respective prices had soared to $425 and $20. That same season, the average Bulls ticket price (weighted by the number of seats at each pricing level) reached nearly $46. This rapid inflation meant that a single, relatively modest outing to a Bulls game for a family of four in 1994 amounted to the better part of the average *total* annual expenditures on entertainment for most American households. As Rick Telander of the *Sun-Times* wrote in 1997, "there are millions of folks who can't get into the United Center with the wealthy swells to see their heroes."[24] The same story played out in NBA cities across the country.

It was more than escalating ticket prices that made it harder for ordinary fans to see their favorite teams in person. To encourage and exploit demand for live sporting events among the affluent, franchises like the Bulls developed new venues that prioritized "premium seating" such as luxury suites and "club sections" (areas that require annual subscriptions and offer exclusive access to luxury concessions) at the expense of traditional seating. In NBA arenas built since 1987, premium seats have typically made up around 19 percent of total seating capacity, in contrast to about 5 percent in the venues they replaced. When Iooss took the photo of Jordan in the 1988 Dunk Contest, Chicago Stadium had one suite, and there is no luxury seating visible in the image itself. Six years later, 216 suites and club seats dominated the middle tiers of the United Center, the Bulls' new arena. Had Iooss snapped the picture then, luxury seating would have dominated much of the background behind Jordan. Despite containing significantly more square footage than their predecessors, new stadiums like the United Center contained, on average, nearly 1,600 fewer non-premium seats. The reason is clear: owners decided to dedicate a much larger proportion of the new facilities to luxury suites, club seats, and high-end retail and concessions outlets. That the Bulls and other franchises sold more non-premium seats as expensive season-ticket packages meant an even greater reduction in access for working- and middle-class families.[25]

The transformation of NBA venues into playgrounds for the rich was one indication of the massive upward redistribution of wealth that characterized the U.S. economy at the end of the twentieth century. From the mid-seventies to mid-nineties, real incomes for most Americans stagnated or fell due to withering attacks by economic and political elites on organized labor, as well as aggressive outsourcing by American firms. The reduced labor costs that came with moving jobs overseas enabled companies to funnel more cash to shareholders and executives. In 1975, the average CEO of an American company ranked in the top 350 firms by sales earned about 26 times a typical production or nonsupervisory worker. By the end of the millennium, the ratio had soared to more than 365—a jump even more staggering than the one captured in Iooss's 1988 photo.[26]

Nike, producer of the shoes Jordan sports in the Iooss image, profited handsomely from the combination of expanded market reach and effective labor-cost-cutting. Arguably, the firm did more than any other entity to convert the NBA superstar into a high-return investment and global icon. Nike used cable and satellite television, as well as the early internet, to globally disseminate savvy ad campaigns such as the series of commercials featuring film director Spike Lee as Mars Blackmon opposite Jordan. The latter's on-camera charisma and superhuman work ethic made him the perfect purveyor of the shoe company's "Just Do It" slogan. Nike CEO Phil Knight came to understand that Jordan was the most efficient spokesperson possible: "You can't explain much in sixty seconds, but when you show Michael Jordan, you don't have to." The results made it difficult to argue with Knight. Between 1985 and 1995, the firm's global revenues skyrocketed from $946 million to $6.5 billion.[27]

The growth of Nike's profitability simultaneously depended on Knight's unceasing efforts to shift production outside the U.S. As the twentieth century ended, Nike shuttered plants in America and opened new ones in places such as South Korea, taking advantage of cheaper labor costs. When wage pressures grew in South Korea, Nike moved production to Taiwan, Indonesia, and eventually China. During the early 1990s, young Indonesian girls working in Nike factories barely earned $1.60 a day to make shoes that ultimately sold for $70. (The $20 million that Jordan made representing the firm in 1992 exceeded the total payroll for all of its Indonesian factories that year!) Nike's development encapsulated the larger transformation of the U.S. economy away from a model dependent on a sprawling domestic manufacturing base and consumption driven in large part by decent industrial working-class wages. In the "New Economy" of the Jordan era, American firms increasingly focused on the invention and dissemination of spectacle, leaving the task of tangible production to others.[28]

Americans outside of the professional, managerial, and executive classes suffered mightily from this shift. Their predicament was not as precarious as that faced by Indonesian factory workers, but new low-wage service jobs in the U.S. could not fill the void left by the disappearance of unionized factory positions. More Americans entered the ranks of the economically insecure, and Chicago was no exception to this trend. In 1970, the city hosted more than 497,000 manufacturing jobs. Twenty years later, the number had plummeted by more than half to just over 216,000. In the apparel industry, where Nike wielded so much influence, the story proved even more dire. Nearly 20,000 workers toiled in Chicago's apparel factories in 1970. By 1990, the figure had collapsed to less than 7,900.[29]

Too add insult to injury, the corporations that profited off Jordan in this context did everything possible to avoid paying taxes that would fund programs and infrastructure that might help American workers cope with deindustrialization. In the case of Nike, the company has become so adept at exploiting its decentralized structure and an increasingly pro-corporate political climate to depress its tax liabilities that it now regularly pays *nothing* in federal U.S. income taxes. Moreover, it has availed itself of massive public—that is, taxpayer-funded—subsidies, including more than $2 billion from the state of Oregon after the company threatened to relocate some of its operations elsewhere. For their part, the Bulls enjoyed millions of dollars in property tax breaks every year on the United Center and an array of other less lucrative local subsidies. In fact, conservative estimates indicate that Reinsdorf and his partners recouped at least 49 percent of the arena's initial construction costs by virtue of their property tax savings. This meant less money for schools and other essential services for Chicagoans.[30]

With distance from the event itself, and some attention to the broader historical context, something other than Jordan's athleticism and attractiveness comes into focus from looking at the 1988 Dunk Contest photo: MJ was one of the most useful assets in corporate America's effort to expand its profitability and power at the close of the twentieth century. As the economic fortunes of the average American have declined amid historic levels of wealth and income inequality, the NBA and Nike have flourished thanks to their cultivation of the Jordan brand. It is very difficult to imagine such successful inroads into new markets without MJ in the vanguard. But as the experience of workers inside and outside the U.S. attests, Jordan lifted a select few along with him as he elevated above the rim, leaving the rest behind to try their luck in the grueling arena of the New Gilded Age.

NOTES

1. Joel Bierig, "Hot Time for Jordan," *Chicago Sun-Times*, February 8, 1988; "1988 NBA All-Star Game," Basketball Reference, https://www.basketball-reference.com/allstar/NBA_1988.html; Mark Zeigler, "East Triumphs as Jordan Wins MVP Trophy," *San Diego Union-Tribune*, February 8, 1988.

2. "Hometown Politics Rule Dunk Contest," *Sacramento Bee*, February 7, 1988.

3. Quoted in Glenn Nelson, "Jordan Flies Friendly Skies to Victory," *Seattle Times*, February 7, 1988.

4. Doug Cress, "Wins Contest after Following Doctor's Advice," *Los Angeles Daily News*, February 7, 1988.

5. Quoted in "Michael Jordan vs. Dominique Wilkins: An Oral History of the 1988 NBA Slam Dunk Contest," NBC Sports, February 11, 2020, https://www.nbcsports.com/chicago/bulls/michael-jordan-dominique-wilkins-1988-nba-slam-dunk-contest-oral-history.

6. "Walter Iooss Jr. Discusses Classic Michael Jordan Photo," *Sports Illustrated*, February 17, 2015, https://www.si.com/nba/2015/02/17/walter-iooss-jr-michael-jordan-1988-nba-dunk-contest-photo.

7. David Kahn, "Judges Say Jordan Has the Right Stuff," *The Oregonian*, February 7, 1988; "Hometown Politics Rule Dunk Contest."

8. Barry Cooper, "Jordan Dunks Dominique with Perfect Full-Court," *Orlando Sentinel*, February 7, 1988; Barry Bloom, "Stars Tune in to Jordan's Jam Session," *San Diego Union-Tribune*, February 8, 1988.

9. "Bird Is Top Gun, Jordan Walks on Air in Contests," *St. Louis Post-Dispatch*, February 7, 1988; "Wilkins Says Enough to Slam-Dunk Contests," *Houston Chronicle*, February 12, 1988.

10. Associated Press, "Jordan, Wilkins Reflect on Memorable '88 Dunk Contest Battle," February 14, 2020, https://www.foxsports.com/stories/nba/jordan-wilkins-reflect-on-memorable-88-dunk-contest-battle.

11. Larry Bartels, *Unequal Democracy: The Political Economy of the New Gilded Age* (Princeton, NJ: Princeton University Press, 2017).

12. David Stern quoted in John Feinstein, *The Punch: One Night, Two Lives, and the Fight That Changed Basketball Forever* (New York: Little, Brown and Company, 2002), 21.

13. Walter LaFeber, *Michael Jordan and the New Global Capitalism* (New York: W. W. Norton, 2002), 47–58. See also Matthew Schneider-Mayerson, "'Too Black': Race in the 'Dark Ages' of the National Basketball Association," *International Journal of Sport and Society* 1, no. 1 (2010): 223–233.

14. Schneider-Mayerson, "'Too Black': Race in the 'Dark Ages' of the National Basketball Association," 223; Rodney Fort, "NBA Attendance Index," Rodney Fort's Sports Business Data, https://docs.google.com/spreadsheets/d/17GsWSvBhV-_8a3XcS3HCXtQbR_gmp-oQ/edit#gid=32354424.

15. Paul Sullivan, "Bulls: From Unwanted to Beloved in 25 Years," *Chicago Tribune*, February 4, 1991.

16. Jay Mariotti, "It's All Over Now: MJ Walking Away," *Chicago Sun-Times*, June 12, 1999.

17. LaFeber, *Michael Jordan and the New Global Capitalism*, 29.

18. LaFeber, *Michael Jordan and the New Global Capitalism*, 88.

19. Edward Walsh, "Chicago Savors a Rare Title," *Washington Post*, June 14, 1991.

20. Kelly Dwyer, "1977 NBA Slam Dunk Champ Darnell Hillman Is Finally Given a Trophy, 40 Years Late," Yahoo Sports, March 9, 2017, https://sports.yahoo.com/news/1977-nba-slam-dunk-champ-darnell-hillman-is-finally-given-a-trophy-40-years-later-204834425.html; Charles Curtis, "30 Years Later: An Oral History of the NBA's First Slam Dunk Contest," *Bleacher Report*, February 13, 2014, https://bleacherreport.com/articles/1923532-30-years-later-an-oral-history-of-the-nbas-first-slam-dunk-contest.

21. LaFeber, *Michael Jordan and the New Global Capitalism*, 64, 84–85, 169.

22. Rodney Fort, "NBA TV Contracts," Rodney Fort's Sports Business Data, https://docs.google.com/spreadsheets/d/1FB3-Qmz5l-qyKUholF7vbfOvH-fsLkH-/edit?rtpof=true.

23. "Jerry Reinsdorf," *Forbes*, July 9, 2022, https://www.forbes.com/profile/jerry-reinsdorf/?sh=335cad336d28; "Chicago Bulls," *Forbes*, accessed July 9, 2022, https://www.forbes.com/teams/chicago-bulls/?sh=6be87f0f5c11.

24. "Data Files and Updates," Sean Dinces, https://www.seandinces.com/data-files; Sean Dinces, *Bulls Markets: Chicago's Basketball Business and the New Inequality* (Chicago: University of Chicago Press, 2018); Rick Telander, "Bulls Know How to Throw a Party," *Chicago Sun-Times*, June 17, 1997.

25. Dinces, *Bulls Markets*, 60, 63–65, 260; Sean Dinces, "The Attrition of the Common Fan: Class, Spectatorship, and Major League Stadiums in Postwar America," *Social Science History* 40 (Summer 2016): 356.

26. Lawrence Mishel and Jori Kandra, "CEO Pay Has Skyrocketed 1,322% since 1978," Economic Policy Institute, August 10, 2021, https://www.epi.org/publication/ceo-pay-in-2020/.

27. LaFeber, *Michael Jordan and the New Global Capitalism*, 15–18, 54; Phil Knight quoted in LaFeber, *Michael Jordan and the New Global Capitalism*, 63; *Nike, Inc. Annual Report* (Beaverton, OR: Nike, 1995), 1; Form 10-K for Nike, Inc. (Washington, DC: U.S. Securities and Exchange Commission, 1996), https://www.sec.gov/Archives/edgar/data/320187/0000320187-96-000014.txt.

28. LaFeber, *Michael Jordan and the New Global Capitalism*, 104–107; Richard Barnet and John Cavanagh, *Global Dreams: Imperial Corporations and the New World Order* (New York: Touchstone, 1994), 328.

29. *Where Workers Work in the Chicago Standard Metropolitan Statistical Area*, 1970 ed. (Springfield, IL: Illinois Department of Labor, n.d.), 25; *Where Workers Work in the Chicago Standard Metropolitan Statistical Area*, 1990 ed. (Springfield, IL: Illinois Department of Labor, n.d.), 19.

30. Matthew Gardner and Steve Wamhoff, "55 Corporations Paid $0 in Federal Taxes on 2020 Profits," *Institute on Taxation and Economic Politics*, April 2, 2021, https://itep.org/55-profitable-corporations-zero-corporate-tax/; "Subsidy Tracker Parent Company Summary: Nike," *Good Jobs First*, accessed July 10, 2022, https://subsidytracker.goodjobsfirst.org/prog.php?parent=nike&page=1; Dinces, *Bulls Markets*, 193.

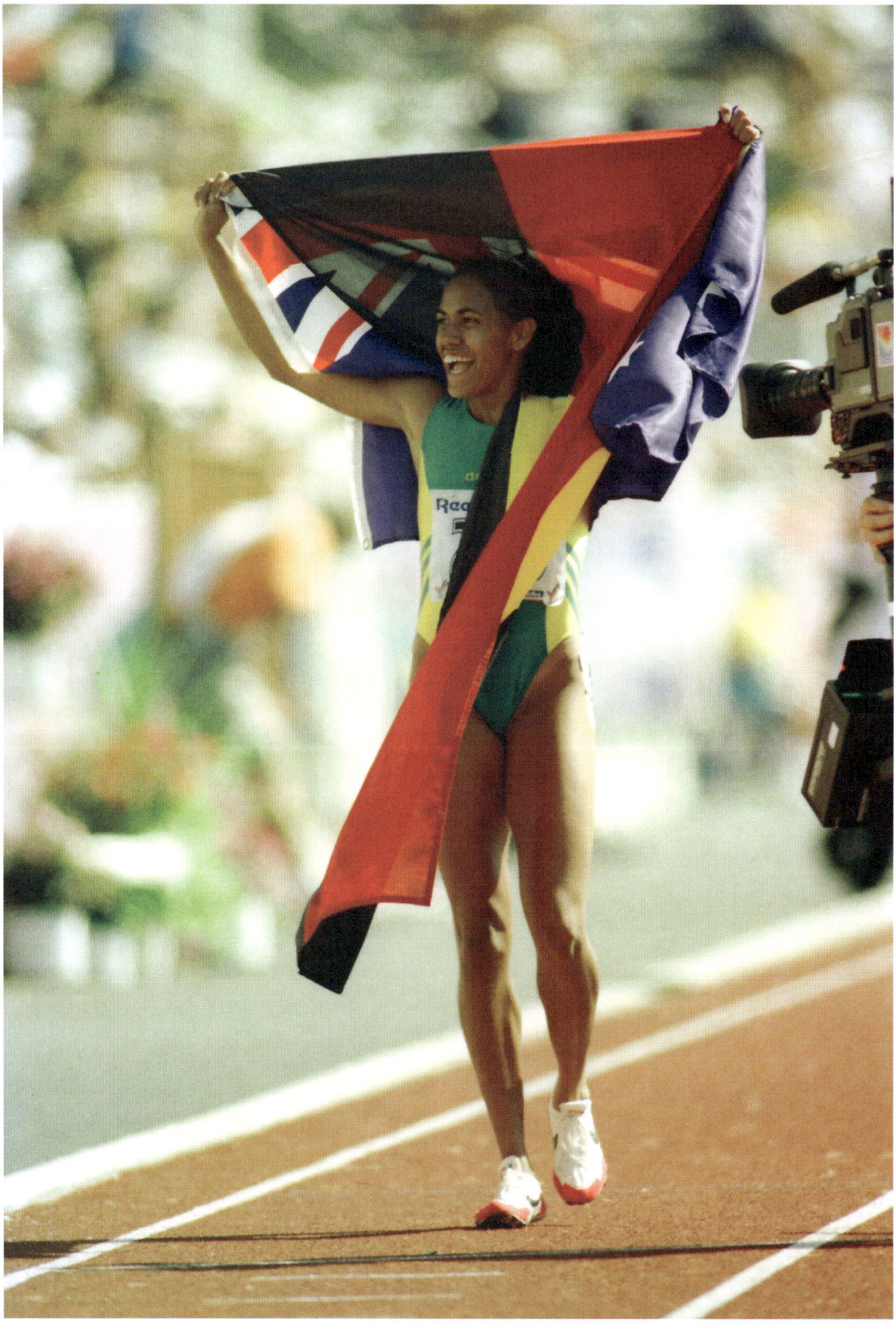

20

SOVEREIGN CELEBRATION

Cathy Freeman, 1994

MATTHEW KLUGMAN AND GARY OSMOND

Brimming with joy, Cathy Freeman grabbed a flag for her victory lap: the red, black, and yellow Aboriginal flag. And then she seized a second, the Australian flag, with its British Union Jack prominent in the upper-left corner. Smiling broadly, both flags draped around her shoulders, she celebrated her triumph while those in the stands applauded.[1] The gathered photographers snapped away. The resultant pictures were immediately compared to the most famous images of sport and race—the Black Power Salute of 1968 and, more locally, the Noongar Australian Rules Footballer Nicky Winmar's 1993 on-field declaration that he was "Black and proud." Soon the photographs of Freeman celebrating with both flags would become some of the most powerful, contentious, and memorable images in Australian history.

Cathy Freeman had just won the 400 meters at the 15th Commonwealth Games in Victoria, Canada, in a games record of 50.38 seconds. A Kuku Yalanji and Birri Gubba woman, Freeman was the first Aboriginal woman from the lands now known as Australia to win an individual event at a Commonwealth Games.[2] Previously a member of Australia's 4 × 100 meters gold medal–winning relay team at the 1990 Commonwealth Games, and subsequently named the 1990 Young Australian of the Year, the twenty-one-year-old runner's international fame was yet to come. Athletically, that recognition would gather momentum with Freeman's victory in the 200 meters just days later, pick up speed in the 1996 Atlanta Olympics, be boosted by World Athletics Championship gold medals in 1997 and 1999, and reach a crescendo in the Sydney 2000 Olympics when she became *the* defining athlete of those games. It was in this moment in 1994, however, that Freeman began shaping the iconography of Australia and created one of the great, iconic, images of sport and race.

Freeman's victory, and her performance, were recorded by several photographers, among them John Feder. One year earlier, Feder had taken one of only two already iconic shots of Nicky Winmar protesting racial abuse from Australian Rules Football spectators.[3] While attuned to sporting drama and protest, and the importance of capturing a moment, Feder recalls that he was nevertheless "absolutely shitting [himself] that [he] didn't miss the picture." Feder says, "Back then it was totally manual focus so I had a 600 mm lens tracking her down the straight to the finish. Thankfully all went well and when she had both flags on I knew I had a strong picture."[4] Australian novelist J. P. Powell has observed, "You really only saw photos when you closed your eyes or looked away."[5] We have chosen to write about this image taken by Feder because it is what we conjure when we close our eyes and recall Freeman in 1994.

The sight of Freeman proudly wearing both flags quickly "became the image of the Games" while also inspiring much debate in Australia.[6] It was also a "big lounge-room moment for Aboriginal people" around Australia.[7] Here we focus on the responses of Aboriginal and settler Australians to the image and its meanings, its resonance, and its power. In so doing, we hope to unsettle what has become a dominant, comfortable narrative of national reconciliation that largely elided Freeman's role, agency, and intentions. Instead, we explore questions of pride, sovereignty, and possession, along with the complicated legacy of this profound image that Freeman (partially) created yet settler Australians sought to make palatable.

Sovereignty vs. Possession

Created in 1971 by Luritja/Wombai man Harold Thomas in discussion with Gumbainggir scholar and activist Gary Foley, the Aboriginal flag became the defining symbol of Australia's burgeoning Black Power movement, flying proudly at the Aboriginal (Tent) Embassy in 1972.[8] It also signified a key difference between the Black Power movements of the United States—which were centered on civil rights—and Australia, where First Nations people came together to work for "land rights and self-determination," to quote Foley and fellow scholar Edwina Howell.[9] The flag colors were thus red ochre for the soil, yellow for the sun, and black for the pride of the Black peoples of the continent.[10]

More broadly, the Aboriginal flag was one of many forms of resistance to the devastating British invasion of Australia in 1788 and the genocidal settler colonialism that followed. The British invasion was characterized by massacres of First Nations people, the spread of deadly diseases, the disavowal of Indigenous relations to land, and the deliberate destruction of hundreds of cultures and languages. In addition to being systematically dispossessed, Aboriginal and Torres Strait Islander people also were denied citizenship for generations, endured racist and discriminatory laws and practices, and suffered socioeconomic disadvantage in health, education, and justice. Just before leaving Australia for the Commonwealth Games, Freeman had curated an extraordinary image of herself running in front of a mural of Aboriginal elders in chains. Taken by Wayne Ludbey, the other photographer who documented Winmar's protest, it was an image that, among other things, asked settler Australians to think more deeply about the history of invasion, and the way it still shaped the present.[11]

The Aboriginal flag was a particularly important statement of sovereignty in the face of this dispossession and associated injustice. Indeed, it unsettled notions of Australian identity. As the Goenpul scholar Aileen Moreton-Robinson has brilliantly detailed, "Australian national identity is built on the disavowal of Indigenous sovereignty because the nation is socially and culturally constructed as a white possession."[12] By 1994, the legal, social, cultural, and political basis for this identity was being publicly debated. In 1992, the Australian High Court had ruled that the Meriam people of the Torres Strait had historic territorial rights.[13] The fiction of *terra nullius*—that First Nations people in Australia were effectively landless when the British arrived in 1788—was finally overturned. Yet when Cathy Freeman packed an Aboriginal flag in her luggage before heading overseas to finalize her preparations for the 1994 Commonwealth Games, the flag was still unrecognized by the Australian Government.

Sport was one arena in which Aboriginal peoples, in particular, had long held national prominence, often in numbers disproportionate to their populations. Although sport remained a significant place of racism and discrimination, it was also a rare site of opportunity to gain a national voice.

Prominent First Nation athletes such as Yorta Yorta man Sir Doug Nicholls and Arrernte and Kalkadoon man Charlie Perkins had used the platform of sport to help bring about much-needed change. Yet sport could also be a space where white Australians attempted to "possess" exotic (non-white) others. The white people who loved Doug Nicholls in the 1930s and Nicky Winmar in the 1990s often regarded these Aboriginal men as "one of ours," while still racially discriminating against those whom they thought of as "other."

Doug Nicholls knew that First Nations people around Australia were following his deeds and felt that he was playing for them.[14] Freeman's immediate explanations for wearing both flags indicated a similar awareness: "I won the gold today and I did what I wanted to do. I carried both the Aboriginal flag and the Australian flag on the victory lap. I know a lot of people would be happy to see me win, Black Australians and white Australians, and that way they could *all* share in what was a great moment for me."[15] Lost in the immediate controversy that followed was the clear indication here that Freeman was aware that many Aboriginal people would feel alienated if she had only carried the Australian flag, which was a symbol of their dispossession. Freeman also stressed the personal importance of the Aboriginal flag—it "motivates me," she explained[16]—and spoke to how her win might inspire many Aboriginal people, many of whom "lack the confidence to do what they want to do."[17]

The first to react was Arthur Tunstall, the powerful and conservative secretary and treasurer of the Australian Commonwealth Games Association, and chef de mission of the Australian team in 1994. Tunstall, who had earlier told a racist joke about Freeman and Gundijtmara boxing world champion Lionel Rose, reprimanded Freeman, threatened to send her home, and forbade her from repeating her action at the Games.[18] Queensland federal parliamentarian Bill Taylor was also highly critical, claiming that Freeman had favored the Aboriginal flag by selecting it first and making it more prominent.[19] For Taylor and many others, Freeman's act was divisive. Mike Gibson, writing in Sydney's (Rupert Murdoch–owned) *Daily Telegraph Mirror*, argued that "the problem is that the Aboriginal flag—which Cathy sees as a symbol of unity—represents entirely the opposite . . . It is a flag they associate with anger. A flag that divides us. A flag of protest."[20] Another columnist claimed that Freeman's victory lap "sends the message that Australia is a divided nation."[21] A caption on Feder's photo reflected this angle: "Serious political dimension: Cathy Freeman carries the Australian and Aboriginal flags after her Games win."[22]

These reactions typified the logic of white possession. Tunstall regarded Freeman as a subject whom he could order around, while for Taylor and Gibson, the mere use of the Aboriginal flag in Freeman's celebration undermined the supposed unity of Australia.

Others, however, praised Freeman and defended her against the criticism she received. While some people framed her gesture as an act of (national) patriotism,[23] most supporters lauded her action as an expression of Aboriginal pride. Chairman of the Northern Land Council and Yolngu man Galarrwuy Yunupingu said, "Cathy was celebrating her Aboriginality as well as her victory for Australia." Federal Aboriginal Affairs Minister Robert Tickner hailed Freeman as a "tremendous role model" for budding Aboriginal athletes. Sports Minister John Faulkner said, "She's proud of her Aboriginal heritage and she demonstrated that."[24] Reflecting overwhelming bipartisan support, both the prime minister, Paul Keating, and the leader of the federal opposition, Alexander Downer, faxed letters of support to Freeman in Canada. Keating was unequivocal: "In the circumstances, your carrying of both flags was an important reminder of your pride in your heritage as an Aboriginal Australian."[25] Despite this support, many Australians responded negatively. A narrow majority of the Murdoch newspaper readers in Melbourne (*Herald Sun*) and Sydney (*Daily Telegraph Mirror*) surveyed immediately afterwards felt it was wrong for Freeman to run with the flag.[26] Nationally, however, one poll reported that 74 percent of Australians supported her actions.[27]

Reconciliation, Agency, and Innocence

A few days later, Cathy Freeman defied Arthur Tunstall by once again draping herself in the Aboriginal and Australian flags after she won the 200 meters. It was a further statement not just of her own individual agency, but of how important it was to her to include the Aboriginal flag in her celebrations. Notably, Tunstall did not have the political power to follow through on his threat to send her home. Instead of fanning the controversy, Freeman's actions after her 200 m victory spurred a counternarrative that saw her as working to reconcile Black and white Australia. "Cathy's uniting double," proclaimed one emblematic headline.[28] Such commentary is echoed in subsequent scholarly analyses that construct Freeman as the "embodiment of reconciliation."[29] But just what did this reconciliation entail?

The narrative of reconciliation was driven in part by several Indigenous Australians. Marcia Langton, a Yiman and Bidjara woman who was then policy officer for the Cape York Land Council and is now a leading scholar on Aboriginal issues, argued that Freeman advocated national reconciliation "in the most natural and thrilling way we could imagine."[30] Lest any reader be unsure of just *what* Freeman was aiming to reconcile, a journalist explained that she had "acknowledged the need for reconciliation between Australia's original inhabitants and the later settlers who took the land away from native peoples."[31] The "powerful symbolism" of Freeman's flag action, argued Terry Garwood, a Yorta, Wemba Wemba, and Wergaia man from Aboriginal Affairs Victoria, advanced the process of reconciliation "in a way in which I believe all Australians should feel proud."[32]

Implicit in this framing of reconciliation was a reading of the Aboriginal flag as a banner of sovereignty. In other words, if the flag was to be a symbol of reconciliation, the reconciliation would need to involve the land rights and self-determination that the flag represented. For that was the meaning of the flag to Freeman and other First Nations people from the lands now known as Australia. Yet instead of emphasizing Freeman's intentions and grappling with the changes required for a true reconciliation, many commentators largely denied Freeman's agency, despite her immediate announcement about the flag's motivating influence. Instead, they portrayed it as an innocent action that brought people together in a feeling of joy—as if reconciliation might simply be an affective moment with no structural consequences. As if settler Australians could feel good while not having to give anything up.

In the contemporary written commentary, few acknowledged Freeman's intent to make a statement to First Nations people in Australia by choosing to run with the flags. One journalist called it "a pre-conceived plan to flaunt her personal statement,"[33] but the overwhelming reading was that hers was a "spontaneous" and "innocent" act.[34] In this innocent-apolitical-spontaneity analysis, comparisons were sometimes drawn to the 1968 Black Power salute protest on the medal dais in Mexico City by Tommie Smith, John Carlos, and Australian Peter Norman, and the iconic photograph of that gesture that was sometimes reprinted with the Freeman story. The comparisons downgraded Freeman's agency: "Her moment of triumph seemed an emotional, spur-of-the-moment thing—not a radical political gesture, like the famous black power salute."[35] Peter Norman himself weighed in to support Freeman against Tunstall's criticisms, but he described her actions as "pure and innocent" and her demonstration as "happy" in stark contrast to the somber 1968 protest pictured alongside his commentary.[36]

In the lead-up to the 1994 Commonwealth Games, the Australian press had already trivialized and infantilized Cathy Freeman.[37] Despite the stories of racism against her and others that Freeman drew attention to, she was rendered as an acceptable "Aborigine" in the words of Eualeyai/Kamillaroi woman and scholar Larissa Behrendt.[38] That is, she was considered to be "non-confronting, amiable, modest and successful in the dominant culture." Now the Australian press clung to a depiction of Freeman as innocent, even though she readily acknowledged intentionally packing the Aboriginal flag to wave if she won a gold medal.[39]

Indeed, the flag was already stored in Freeman's suitcase in photographer Wayne Ludbey's car earlier in 1994 when Freeman curated the mural photograph to awaken settler Australians to the realities of the past and present. In Canada, she gave it to a friend, asking him to wave it as she approached the finish line.[40] Her biographer describes this decision as "extraordinarily premeditated" and as offering "an insight into the Freeman mind" and her wish to make a statement.[41] He described her flag-waving as her "amazing coming out" and as "an act of atonement for all the pent-up hurt within a shy Aboriginal girl who grew up with the word 'shame' attached to her embarrassment about being black in contemporary Australia."[42] He cited Freeman speaking of her motivation to instill pride and self-esteem in Aboriginal people.[43]

The Possession of a Historical First Nations Moment

The 1994 Commonwealth Games were politically freighted for First Nations people, which amplified Freeman's feelings of racial pride. The night before her race, she had watched dancers from the Tjapukai dance theater, an Aboriginal group that included her cousin, perform at the Victoria Harbour Festival.[44] The previous year had been the International Year of Indigenous Peoples, and the Games' opening ceremonies and medal designs celebrated Canadian First Nations people and culture: Freeman's gold medal for the 400 meters was carved with the image of a wolf from the Coast Salish Nation, created by Charles Elliott of the Tsartlip Band.[45] Representatives from the Coast Salish, Nuu-chah-nulth, and Kwagiulth communities on the Games' Native Participation Committee explained the importance of these representations: "We want the world to know there are still aboriginal people here."[46]

Freeman helped assert the presence of First Nations people, as did Sioux woman Angela Chalmers, who carried the flag for Canada at the opening ceremonies and who won gold in the women's 3,000-meter race on the same day that Freeman took the 400 meters.[47] Chalmers promoted First Nations visibility and empowerment, and a Canadian First Nations newspaper commented that Freeman "echoed the sentiments expressed by Chalmers . . . that it's important to be a role model for other Indigenous peoples."[48] Freeman and Chalmers were not alone. Hurdler Kyle Vander-Kuyp, a Worimi and Yuin man from Australia, raced in the semifinal round of the men's 4 × 100-meter relay wearing a singlet sporting a map of Australia with a small Aboriginal flag sewn into the middle. He was photographed wearing this flag, and the Canadian press commented on it in its coverage of Freeman's actions.[49]

However, it was Cathy Freeman draped with the Aboriginal and Australian flags that became the lasting image of the 1994 Commonwealth Games. As the Abenaki (Odanak) scholar Christine O'Bonsawin notes, Freeman's actions arguably brought the (Australian) Aboriginal flag into "global prominence."[50] Nevertheless, Freeman clearly stated repeatedly that her wearing the Aboriginal flag was a gesture of pride and celebration aimed at Aboriginal Australians. In doing so, she positioned the Aboriginal flag as at least equal in importance to the Australian flag. As equally sovereign. Yet despite Freeman's statement of pride and celebration of Aboriginal sovereignty, many settler Australians centered themselves, eliding Freeman's agency and instead reading her action as a feel-good moment of innocent reconciliation that did not require further action on land rights or self-determination for First Nations people. In this reaction, the Aboriginal flag was made more palatable to white Australia. At times, it has been possessed as a symbol of easy reconciliation rather than as unsettling notions of Australian identity. In 1995, the Australian Government recognized the Aboriginal flag as an official flag of Australia. Freeman's action and the photographs were instrumental in this decision.[51] The flag now hangs from local, state, and federal government buildings. Yet no treaty has been signed with any First Nations people in Australia. The lands that were invaded remain possessed and unceded.

NOTES

1. "And then they applauded for six minutes as she paraded around their stadium proudly draped in, firstly, the Aboriginal flag and then, shortly afterwards, teamed with the Australian flag." *Herald Sun* (Melbourne), August 25, 1994, 69.

2. We use the terms "Aboriginal" and "Torres Strait Islanders" to distinguish between the two officially recognized groups of Indigenous, or First Nations, peoples in Australia, and where known we refer to the specific First Nations to which individuals belong.

3. Matthew Klugman and Gary Osmond, *Black and Proud: The Story of an Iconic AFL Photo* (Sydney: NewSouth Publishing, 2013).

4. John Feder, email to authors, March 1, 2022.

5. J. P. Powell, *The Brisbane Line*, Kindle version, 2020. Permission to quote granted by publisher and author, March 10, 2022.

6. *Daily Telegraph Mirror* (Sydney), August 25, 1994, 1.

7. Kyle Vander-Kuyp, in Amanda Smith, "Cathy Freeman and the Flags; Boxing for Nerds," Sporty, ABC Radio National, August 17, 2019, https://www.abc.net.au/radionational/programs/sporty/cathy-freeman-and-the-flags-boxing-for-nerds/11418576.

8. Mathieu Gallois, *The Aboriginal Flag*, PhD dissertation, University of Sydney, 2017.

9. Gary Foley and Edwina Howell, *A History of the Media Strategy of the Aboriginal Land Right, Black Power and Self-Determination Movement*, 4. See http://www.kooriweb.org/foley/essays/pdf_essays/media%20strategy%20of%20black%20power%20movement.pdf.

10. ABC Radio National, "Harold Thomas—Creator of the Aboriginal Flag," Dimensions in Time, March 25, 2002, cited in Mathieu Gallois, "The *Aboriginal Flag* as Art," *Australian Aboriginal Studies* 2 (Fall 2016): 59.

11. Gary Osmond and Matthew Klugman, "A Forgotten Picture: Race, Photographs, and Cathy Freeman at the Northcote Koori Mural," *Journal of Australian Studies* 43, no. 2 (2019): 203–217.

12. Aileen Moreton-Robinson, *The White Possessive: Property, Power, and Indigenous Sovereignty* (Minneapolis: University of Minnesota Press, 2015), xxi.

13. Peter H. Russell, *Recognising Aboriginal Title: The Mabo Case and Indigenous Resistance to English-settler Colonialism* (Sydney: University of New South Wales Press, 2006).

14. Sean Gorman, Barry Judd, Keir Reeves, Gary Osmond, Matthew Klugman, and Gavan McCarthy, "Aboriginal Rules: The Black History of Australian Football," *International Journal of the History of Sport* 32, no. 16 (2015): 1947–1962.

15. *Herald Sun* (Melbourne), August 25, 1994 (City ed.), 2, our emphasis.

16. *Herald Sun* (Melbourne), August 24, 1992 (PM Update ed.), 2; *Herald Sun* (Melbourne), August 25, 1994, 3.

17. *Herald Sun* (Melbourne), August 25, 1994 (City ed.), 1, 69.

18. *Herald Sun* (Melbourne), August 25, 1994 (PM ed.), 1.

19. *Herald Sun* (Melbourne), August 25, 1994, 1, 2. Full quote from Taylor in *Newcastle Herald*, August 25, 1994, 1.

20. Mike Gibson, *Daily Telegraph Mirror* (Sydney), August 26, 1994, 10.

21. Paul Grey, *Herald Sun* (Melbourne), August 26, 1994, 15.

22. *Herald Sun* (Melbourne), August 26, 1994, 15.

23. *Herald Sun* (Melbourne), August 25, 1994, 1.

24. *Newcastle Herald*, August 26, 1994, 1 (Yunupingu); *Herald Sun*, (Melbourne), August 25, 1994, 2 (Tickner); *Herald Sun* (Melbourne), August 26, 1994 (City ed.), 2 (Faulkner).

25. *Herald Sun* (Melbourne), August 28, 1994, 4. Both faxed letters are published in *Daily Telegraph Mirror* (Sydney), August 27, 1994, 144.

26. *Herald Sun* (Melbourne), September 3, 1994, 20; *Daily Telegraph Mirror* (Sydney), August 27, 1994, 144.

27. Adrian McGregor, *Cathy Freeman: A Journey Just Begun* (Sydney: Random House, 2000), 170.

28. *Sun-Herald* (Sydney), August 28, 1994, 1.

29. Toni Bruce and Christopher Hallinan, "Cathy Freeman: The Quest for Australian Identity," in *Sport Stars: The Cultural Politics of Sporting Celebrity*, ed. David L. Andrews and Steven J. Jackson (London: Routledge, 2001), 261.

30. *Daily Telegraph Mirror* (Sydney), August 26, 1994, 11.

31. *Newcastle Herald*, August 26, 1994, 8.

32. *Herald Sun* (Melbourne), August 26, 1994 (PM ed), 14.

33. "Roach on Monday," *Newcastle Herald*, August 29, 1994, Sport section, 4.

34. Commentators have called the flag laps of honor "spontaneous." See George Morgan, "Aboriginal Protest and the Sydney Olympic Games," *OLYMPIKA: The International Journal of Olympic Studies* XII (2003): 33; *Herald Sun* (Melbourne), August 26, 1994 (City ed), 3; Paul Grey, "Freeman's Spontaneous Victory Lap," *Herald Sun* (Melbourne), August 26, 1994, 15; *Sun-Herald* (Sydney), August 28, 1994, 1; *Koori Mail*, September 7, 1994, 20. This interpretation has been repeated by scholars: Morgan, "Aboriginal Protest and the Sydney Olympic Games," 33: regarding "innocence," see Karl Malakunas, *Herald Sun* (Melbourne), August 26, 1994 (City ed), 3; *Herald Sun* (Melbourne), August 25, 1994 (PM ed), 2.

35. Paul Grey, *Herald Sun* (Melbourne), August 26, 1994, 15.

36. *Herald Sun* (Melbourne), August 25, 1994 (PM ed), 2.

37. Osmond and Klugman, "A Forgotten Picture."

38. Larissa Behrendt, "Cathy Freeman and the Politics of Sport," *Journal of Australian Indigenous Issues* 4, no. 1 (2001): 27–29.

39. Caroline Wilson, *Age* (Melbourne), September 11, 1994, Agenda section, 2; see also *Herald Sun* (Melbourne), August 25, 1994 (City edition), 3.

40. McGregor, *Cathy Freeman*, 165.

41. McGregor, *Cathy Freeman*, 165.

42. McGregor, *Cathy Freeman*, 167.

43. McGregor, *Cathy Freeman*, 189.

44. McGregor, *Cathy Freeman*, 165; *Adelaide Advertiser*, August 25, 1994 (2nd edition), 23, 26.

45. Canada's Sports Hall of Fame, "1994 Commonwealth Games—Victoria," http://canadasports150.ca/en/british-empire-games-commonwealth-games/1994-commonwealth-games-victoria/36.

46. Chris Wood, "Dreams of Glory: Athletes from 51 Countries Begin the Quest for Gold in 10 Official Sports," *Maclean's*, August 22, 1994, http://archive.macleans.ca/article/1994/8/22/dreams-of-glory.

47. Canada's Sports Hall of Fame, "1994 Commonwealth Games—Victoria."

48. Steve Newman, "Chalmers Smokes 'Em to Capture Gold," *Regional Windspeaker,* August 29–September 11, 1994, R1, http://data2.archives.ca/e/e448/e011197624.pdf.

49. Steve Newman, "Freeman Unfurls Aboriginal Pride," *Regional Windspeaker,* September 12–25, 1994, R5, http://data2.archives.ca/e/e448/e011197625.pdf.

50. Christine O'Bonsawin, "From Black Power to Indigenous Activism: The Olympic Movement and the Marginalization of Oppressed Peoples (1968–2012)," *Journal of Sport History* 42 (Summer 2015): 205.

51. Dominic Shaw, "A Symbol of Unity: Freeing the Aboriginal Flag," *BYU Law Review* 47 (Winter 2021): 363; Australian Institute of Aboriginal and Torres Strait Islander Studies, "The Aboriginal Flag," https://aiatsis.gov.au/explore/aboriginal-flag.

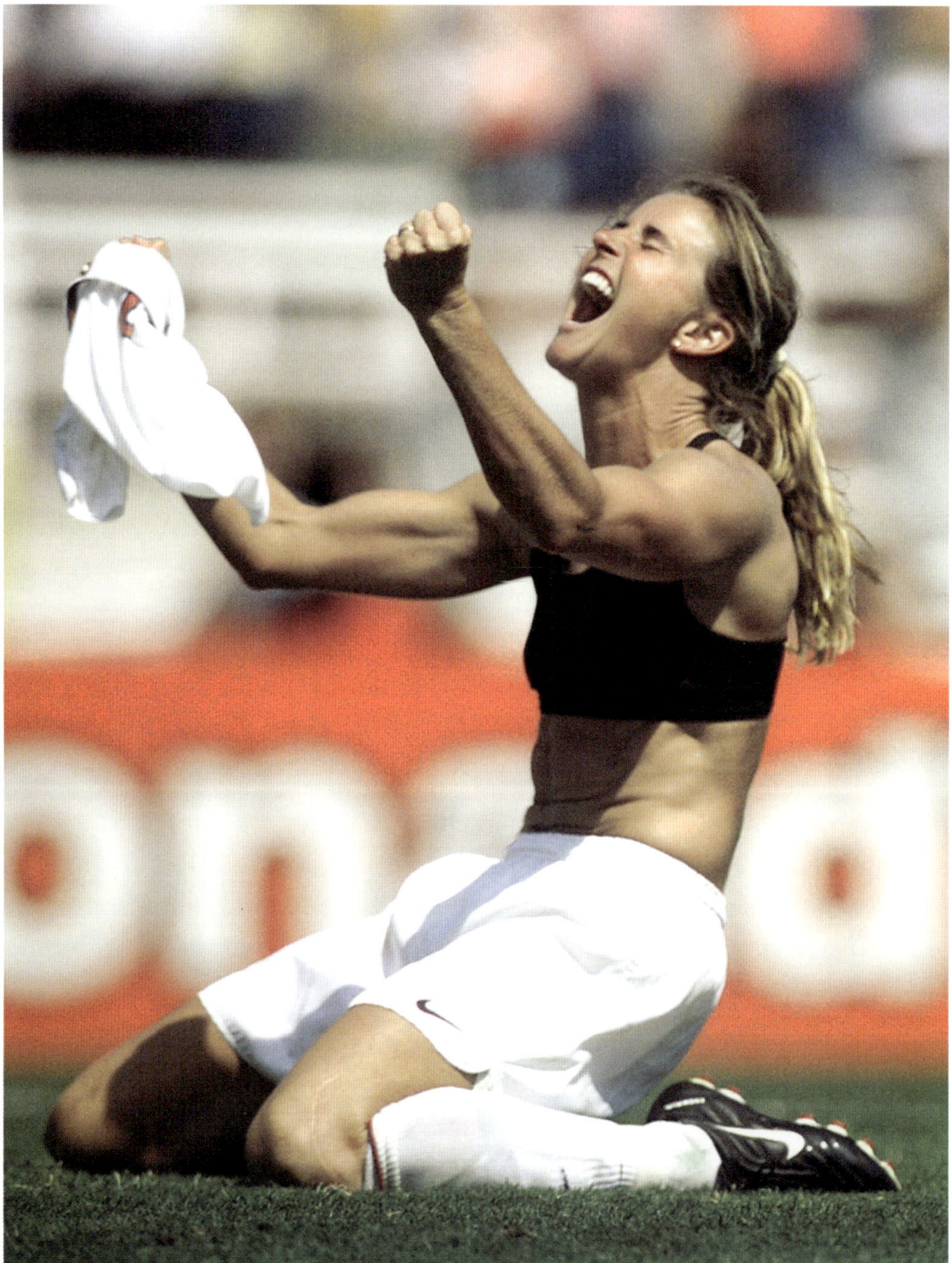

21

MOMENT OF VICTORY

Brandi Chastain and the 1999 World Cup

SARAH K. FIELDS

The moment was represented as the end and the beginning while being in the middle, and it received massive media attention. After scoring the game-winning penalty kick for the United States (U.S.) at the 1999 Women's World Cup, Brandi Chastain ripped off her jersey, dropped briefly to her haunches with her fists clenched and arms raised, roared in emotion, and then stood, turned, and embraced her teammates who had run toward her from the center line. Her celebration marked the end of a triumphal tournament for the U.S. Women's National Team (USWNT) players and for the organizers of the U.S. tour. The U.S. and global press heralded the tournament as the beginning of the world taking women's sport, not just soccer, seriously. In fact, the victory was the second World Cup the USWNT had won; few people noticed the first in 1991. The USWNT would go on to win another two within the next twenty years, tallying four World Cup titles by 2019. The 1999 tournament win was the middle of the USWNT's history. Numerous cameras captured Chastain's celebration, and the image of her shirtless on her knees became the image of the tournament representing both the team's and female athletes' victory. The image was also parsed for its perceived sexuality. The moment, and by association, the photo(s), became iconic and were important in establishing, if not the beginning, at least the next major chapter in women's soccer. Without this moment, today's soccer scene might be different.

The Moment and the Photos

The photograph is defined by its context. Without context, Chastain's position, radiating emotion, could be motivated by either frustration or joy; within the context of victory, the waves of tension Chastain exudes clearly include joy. Chastain has dropped to her knees and is resting her hips back towards her heels. In this picture she is captured more in profile with her left side facing the camera. Her body is tanned but not sunburned as one might expect after a soccer tournament concluding with 120 minutes of game time in the Southern California sun in July. Her head is thrown back, eyes shut, mouth open in a kind of roar, baring her top teeth. Her blonde hair hangs down her back in a slightly messy ponytail. Her right fist clenches her wadded up jersey, her left is balled up. She pumps both fists upward. The pose highlights her toned body, and the indentation between biceps and triceps is striking. The muscles on her forearms and shoulders are striated and flexed as if in a bodybuilding pose. Even her core is tensed; her well-defined abs are below her black sports bra. Her lower body is nearly completely covered in shorts going halfway down her thighs and soccer socks pulled up to just below her knee. The famous Nike swoosh is prominent on her white shorts and black cleats. In the bit of skin showing between shorts and socks, the faint scar from an ACL operation visibly arcs the side of her left knee. The camera doesn't show the matching scar on her right knee. This is the built body of a successful professional athlete. As Chastain put it, "I ran my ass off for this body."[1] The scar(s) attests that she paid for that body in sweat, effort, and pain. This is also the body of a victorious athlete roaring in and enjoying her success, unabashedly releasing all the emotions of a long tournament. In the background is a blurry image of the boards around the field with white lettering on a red field. Above them are the fans in the background, mere blobs of color. This is Roberto Schmidt's photograph.[2]

The image of Chastain's celebration is important and iconic, but there were numerous photos of that brief moment. In the roughly two seconds Chastain was alone in her victory celebration before her teammates swarmed her, multiple photographers captured her from different angles. Sometimes the only way to tell the photos apart is by the advertising on the boards surrounding the field and the position of her hair. Schmidt of Agence France-Presse (AFP) snapped several frames of her in profile, including the subject of this essay. He also photographed Chastain on her knees, either rising up from her haunches or settling into them. Where Schmidt's photos were published at the time is unclear, but others took similar shots that appeared in U.S. papers. Anacleto Rapping of the *Los Angeles Times* and Lacy Atkins of the *San Francisco Examiner* and the Associated Press (AP) shot photos much like Schmidt's from a slightly different angle—the boards behind Chastain are clearly a Coca-Cola ad in Rapping's photo, which ran on the front page of his paper. Atkins's nearly identical, but slightly tighter shot made her a 2000 Pulitzer Prize finalist. The *Newsweek* cover ("Girls Rule") from July 19, 1999, featured a very similar photo by Dan Helms of *NewSport*, with only a differently placed strand of hair differentiating it from Schmidt's photos. Keith Birmingham of the *Pasadena Star-News*/SCNG had a similar photo (Chastain's head is back and in profile with McDonald's on the board in the background), and he seems to have shot the photo while right next to Schmidt. Jed Jacobson also had a similar angle, but the back of an official appears in his frame, distracting viewers from the victorious Chastain. Robert Beck of *Sports Illustrated* shot one photo straight on of Chastain in focus with her teammates blurrily running towards her and the crowd in the background which graced the *SI* cover on July 19, 1999, with the title "Yes!" Hector Mata of the AFP caught a similar shot as Beck's but was tighter on Chastain. Tracking down all the photographs of that moment and where they were published is almost impossible. The key takeaway is the photographers (many of whom were not sport photographers, and few of whom had shot women's soccer matches previously) all recognized the historical and cultural significance of the moment and tried to capture it.

The mere fact that so many photos were taken of these few seconds when Chastain celebrated alone indicates just how many people and members of the media were paying attention to this game. The large international press presence and numerous photographs signify the sudden cultural relevance the 1999 USWNT had achieved. There were no iconic magazine or newspaper cover photos after the USWNT won the first Women's World Cup in 1991 (the event only officially called that in retrospect because FIFA was reluctant to call a women's tournament a World Cup). The image of Chastain on her knees taken by so many talented photographers is proof that the women's game had arrived in 1999.

The Moment's Context

The number of photographs of Chastain's celebration is unsurprising because everything about the final match of the 1999 World Cup was record-setting and thrilling. More than 90,000 spectators filled the Pasadena Rose Bowl, the largest crowd ever to attend a women's sporting event in the United States (and perhaps the world). This was the first women's World Cup to be held in large-capacity stadiums and to have every match televised; an estimated 40 million U.S. viewers watched the final game. Some 2,500 journalists and photographers covered the tournament.[3]

At the finals on July 10, 1999, the capacity crowd, including President Bill Clinton, and a record television audience witnessed the scoreless ninety-minute match and subsequent thirty-minute overtime between China and the U.S. With the game still tied at zero after overtime, by FIFA rules, the teams began taking penalty kicks. The pressure on those playing in this intense match ratcheted even higher during the isolating one-on-one moment. The rules were that whoever had more goals after the first five players on each team shot, won. If the score was still tied, another five players would shoot. Penalty kicks are nerve-wracking for players, coaches, and fans. The scenario favors the shooter, which means the pressure is on the shooter. Even for the best players in the world, penalty kicks can be more about nerves and controlling emotions than skill. On the flipside, if the goalkeeper can stop just one shot, her team has a good chance of winning. Briana Scurry, the U.S. goalkeeper, believed she could stop one shot. And she did. She blocked the kick of the third Chinese shooter. It was the only blocked penalty kick of the day, opening the door to victory—if the remaining U.S. players could score. After the first four U.S. kickers scored, Brandi Chastain had the chance to win the game.

Chastain wasn't the planned fifth U.S. shooter. She had a history of being a reliable penalty kicker, but in the months prior to the World Cup tournament, she had banged one off the cross bar against the Chinese team in a warm-up event and the U.S. had lost the game. Perhaps that missed shot got in her head because she began missing penalty kicks in practice. The U.S., however, needed to adjust its lineup of the first block of five because Michelle Akers, who would have shot first, had left the game with exhaustion and a probable concussion. Only players on the field at the end of overtime can participate in the shootout. The U.S. coaches debated whether to use Chastain. They ultimately decided to give her the shot, but with a twist: Chastain is right-footed, and they asked her to take the kick with her left, non-dominant foot. The coaches felt that she had become predictable with her right foot; a left footed shot would be unexpected and different. Chastain told the coaches she could do it.[4]

The shot was perfect. Although the Chinese goalkeeper Gao Hong correctly guessed which side of the net Chastain would aim for and dove in that direction, Chastain's shot had enough pace and was so well placed the keeper could not stop it. Because of Scurry's save, Chastain became the hero, and her celebratory moment became iconic.

The Link between Scurry's Save and Chastain's Kick

Despite the one-on-one nature of penalty kicks, like the rest of soccer, they are a team event. For the U.S. to win the 1999 World Cup, Briana Scurry had to make one save and all the U.S. shooters had to make their shots. Chastain had the privilege and luck to be the final shooter, so she got the famous moment and photos and much of the glory, but Scurry's save on the third Chinese kicker's shot gave the U.S. the chance to win. Photographers captured Scurry's save from several angles, and these action shots are impressive, as the diving Scurry lays full-out, but they were not the photos chosen for the covers of *Time*, *Newsweek*, or *Sports Illustrated*. Perhaps they were not chosen because it was not the end of the game, perhaps they were not selected because they were action shots and historically most photos of female athletes are taken during non-action moments, if not actually posed. Perhaps they were not chosen because Briana Scurry is African American and was fully clothed.

Perhaps Scurry's photo could not be the iconic image of the 1999 World Cup because she was not one of the team's more iconic figures. Sport studies scholar Eileen Narcotta-Welp persuasively argues that Scurry was always marginalized on this USWNT, despite her centrality as the starting goalkeeper. She was, as Scurry described herself, "the fly in the milk," as the only non-white starter on the team.[5] An African American lesbian, Scurry was not the All-American, white, blonde, girl-next-door athlete. Thus, she received less media coverage than many of her white teammates; ABC even panned the camera away when she received her medal after the win to return to the more popular, white, superstar Mia Hamm.

Further, after the match, when replays of her save had run repeatedly, Scurry's ethics and sportsmanship were called into question because she had left the goal line slightly before the ball was kicked, a violation of FIFA rules.

If Scurry had been penalized, the Chinese player would have retaken the kick, but the official made no such call, and no formal complaints were made at the time.[6] Most goalkeepers leap forward on penalty kicks to cut down the kicker's angle and to increase their odds of making the save—it is commonplace among talented keepers. Regardless, rather than recognizing her heroic role in the win, some condemned Scurry for not keeping her feet planted on the line, thus belittling her contribution to the team's victory. Her moment of success was as important as Chastain's, but it was not to be the tournament's iconic moment.

The Sexualization of the Chastain Photo

Speculation was rampant as to why Chastain removed her jersey after burying her shot. Male athletes, including soccer players, regularly removed their shirts in celebration of good plays and victories in the 1990s. It was so common that in 1996 FIFA banned removing shirts during a match because it wasted time and cut airtime coverage of the jerseys' sponsor logos. Some speculated Chastain and Nike planned it as a marketing stunt to promote Nike's women's gear, particularly its sports bra. However, the bra's logo was much smaller than those on her shorts and shoes, barely visible in the photos taken straight on and not visible in profile photos; that was some poor marketing if that had been the strategy. Chastain herself said afterward that she took the shirt off in a moment of "temporary insanity."[7] Although Chastain's sports bra covered more skin than a bikini top, different commentators perceived her action as everything from a mimicry of the men to a marketing ploy to a striptease. Most pundits fixated on sexualization.

Because of the long history of sexualization of female athletes and of the athletes on this USWNT specifically, some sexualization of the photo(s) of the shirtless Chastain was inevitable. Numerous scholars have articulated the connection between sexualization and the marketing of women's sport, particularly in the 1990s. Communication scholar Helene A. Shugart notes that prior studies established that photographic coverage of female versus male athletes was much more likely to be in nonathletic poses or contexts and that players who fit conventional white femininity and beauty standards were most likely to be photographed.[8] The USWNT fit this profile as did this iconic soccer moment—there were few, if any, published pictures of Chastain shooting the final penalty kick. Sport scholars Nancy E. Spencer and Lisa R. McClung argue "the notion that sex appeal enhances the popularity of women in sport is closely related to the importance of conveying femininity."[9] The overwhelming coverage of Chastain's shirtless celebration promoted this narrative.

Sport sociologists and media studies scholars who analyzed the media representations of the team and the tournament repeatedly note the emphasis on the women's appearance and bodies. One study asserts that part of the popularity of the '99 USWNT was that the U.S. public appreciated the media's representation of the players' conventional attractiveness juxtaposed with their obvious strength, fitness, and competitiveness. The authors add that players, like Scurry, who didn't fit the "girl-next-door" norm of white, heterosexual, middle-class femininity were "rendered invisible."[10] Chastain was conventionally attractive and profoundly fit and strong, and her moment was rendered the most visible of all.

Some players themselves contributed to the attractive narrative by intentionally promoting their image as the sexy girl next door. Julie Foudy, a starting defender, once jokingly referred to some members of the USWNT as "booters with hooters," but the quip became a tagline for many to indicate the team's attractiveness. A few weeks prior to the tournament, Chastain herself furthered this sexualization by appearing in *Gear*, a men's magazine, nude with strategically placed soccer balls. Prior to the tournament, Chastain had appeared on *Late Night with David Letterman* and signed Letterman's copy of her *Gear* photo. He announced that the team was filled with "Soccer Mamas" and called them "Babe City." The team played along and sent him a photo, regularly displayed on his show, in which the players appear to be wearing only *Late Night* T-shirts. It was a trade: Letterman talked the team up before, during, and after the tournament, and they allowed their perceived attractiveness, femininity, and sexualization to be part of that promotion. Given this history, the shirtless Chastain was the inevitable key image from the tournament.

Sport studies scholar Jaime Schultz studied the obsession with Chastain's sports bra and concludes the image's complicated interpretation depended on the viewer's perspectives. In the moment, Chastain lost control of her representation, allowing it to be perceived in many ways. Some viewers saw the shirt removal as a "striptease," as numerous reporters and commentators described it, ignoring the fact, as Schultz writes, that "her gesture bears little resemblance to a seductive act" and left her still fully covered.[11] The sexualization of her body at that moment fit with the historical representation of sexy female athletes who were more important as sex objects than as athletes. Others, Schultz acknowledges, saw Chastain's body as that of a fit athlete who had worked and trained hard to develop a muscular, strong, talented body. This was the narrative of empowered women that was common in the 1990s; however, even that narrative had limits. The July 19, 1999, *Newsweek* magazine cover (complete with its image of a shirtless, almost thirty-one-year-old Chastain) announced "Girls Rule!" rather than Women Rule.

The USWNT's 1999 World Cup victory was a remarkable moment in sport generally and in women's sport particularly. The coverage of the finals was on network television, not on cable, meaning that anyone with an antenna could see the game. I watched the finals in a small cabin in the north woods of rural Michigan with a few friends and family who had gathered for the match. We were ecstatic with the American women's victory. As a young sport studies scholar, I knew the significance historically and culturally for female athletes, but in that moment, I was a fan, one who was thrilled to see the women get their moment in the spotlight. I had been the only girl on my second-grade soccer team some twenty-five years earlier, and in 1999 I was caught up in the moment seeing women my age win a World Cup while the world watched. I recognized the talent, dedication, discipline, and effort of the USWNT's athletes, and indeed of all those who competed in the tournament. Later when I saw the photos of the shirtless Chastain on her knees, I saw it through my own lens, as Schultz suggests. I saw Chastain, powerful in her joy, roaring her emotion, and I knew that her pose could have been the same if she had missed and sunk to her knees in frustration, rage, and disappointment. Because she had won, it was exhilaration, and I, and other viewers, saw in the iconic pose captured by so many cameras the powerful and symbolic moment of so many watching one woman celebrate her team's historic victory.

The Moment That Launched a Future

Chastain's moment on her knees, radiating the kind of strength, power, and emotion which the media had previously limited to male athletes, was broadcast around the world. Simply in being so widely disseminated, even if for the parsing of sexualization, the image of a muscular, formidable athlete roaring in victory changed the image of a female athlete. Years later, Scurry would credit the photo(s) with propelling the popularity of women's soccer forward: "What her image showed is a literal transformation of an opinion of women from one way to another way. That it was cool to have muscles and to be fit and to be strong. So in that regard, for the greater good of the game, her image would go a lot further for a lot longer than mine would have gone."[12] Years after Robert Beck's photo appeared on the cover of *Sports Illustrated*, the photographer introduced himself to Chastain and she shocked him by crediting the cover with showing a new image of female athletes to a global audience, inspiring countless women and girls.[13] Chastain's moment was perhaps the most widely disseminated moment in women's sport history; it was immortalized in her statue outside the Rose Bowl for the twentieth anniversary.[14] The moment of celebration in July 1999 at the end of the game, in the middle of a run of World Cup titles, was the beginning of the USWNT and women's sport moving more powerfully into the future.

NOTES

1. See Rick Reilly, "The Goal Goal Girls," *Sports Illustrated*, July 5, 1999, https://vault.si.com/vault/1999/07/05/the-goal-goal-girls.

2. This image is at https://www.gettyimages.com/detail/news-photo/brandi-chastain-of-the-us-celebrates-after-kicking-the-news-photo/51615545?adppopup=true. I selected this photo out of the many, many options somewhat randomly because it was accessible and the rights were less expensive.

3. "FIFA Women's World Cup USA 1999," Fifa.com, https://www.fifa.com/tournaments/womens/womensworldcup/usa1999.

4. See Jere Longman, *The Girls of Summer: The U.S. Women's Soccer Team and How It Changed the World* (New York: Perennial, 2000) and Caitlin Murray, *The National Team: The Inside Story of the Women Who Changed Soccer* (New York: Abrams, 2019).

5. Eileen Narcotta-Welp, "A Black Fly in White Milk: The 1999 Women's World Cup, Briana Scurry, and the Politics of Inclusion," *Journal of Sport History* 42 (Fall 2015): 383.

6. After decades of debate about the rule, FIFA changed it in 2020 to allow a retry on the penalty kick only if the "goalkeeper's offence clearly impacted on the kicker." See "Law 14: The Penalty Kick," https://www.thefa.com/football-rules-governance/lawsandrules/laws/football-11-11/law-14—-the-penalty-kick.

7. Longman, *The Girls of Summer*, 279.

8. Helene A. Shugart, "She Shoots, She Scores: Mediated Constructions of Contemporary Female Athletes in Coverage of the 1999 US Women's Soccer Team," *Western Journal of Communication* 67, no. 1 (2003): 1–31.

9. Nancy E. Spencer and Lisa R. McClung, "Women and Sport in the 1990s: Reflections on 'Embracing Stars, Ignoring Players,'" *Journal of Sport Management* 15 (October 2001): 320.

10. Neal Christopherson, Michelle Janning, and Eileen Diaz McConnell, "Two Kicks Forward, One Kick Back: A Content Analysis of Media Discourses on the 1999 Women's World Cup Soccer Championship," *Sociology of Sport Journal* 19 (2002): 180.

11. Jaime Schultz, "Discipline and Push-Up: Female Bodies, Femininity, and Sexuality in Popular Representations of Sports Bras," *Sport Sociology Journal* 21 (2004): 191. See also Jaime Schultz, *Qualifying Times: Points of Change in Women's Sport* (Urbana: University of Illinois Press, 2014).

12. Olivia Christian, "Brandi or Briana: A Question of What Might Have Been," *WBUR: Only a Game*, October 5, 2018, https://www.wbur.org/onlyagame/2018/10/05/briana-scurry-brandi-chastain.

13. Heidi Peiper, "The Story behind One of the Most Iconic Sports Photos of All Time," *Starbucks Stories & News*, July 7, 2019, https://stories.starbucks.com/stories/2019/the-story-behind-one-of-the-most-iconic-sports-photos-of-all-time/.

14. Des Bieler, "As USWNT Celebrates, Brandi Chastain Statue Unveiled Outside Rose Bowl, *Washington Post*, July 11, 2019, https://www.washingtonpost.com/sports/2019/07/11/uswnt-celebrates-brandi-chastain-statue-unveiled-outside-rose-bowl/. In August 2022, England's Chloe Kelly ripped her shirt off in celebration of the winning goal in overtime of the European Championship final, but although others compared it to Chastain's moment, Kelly said it was a tribute to her favorite English male player. Travis Yoesting, "England's Brandi Chastain Moment? Not Quite—Chloe Kelly Reveals Alternative Inspiration," *The 18.com*, August 1, 2022, https://the18.com/en/soccer-entertainment/chloe-kelly-celebration-meaning-brandi-chastain.

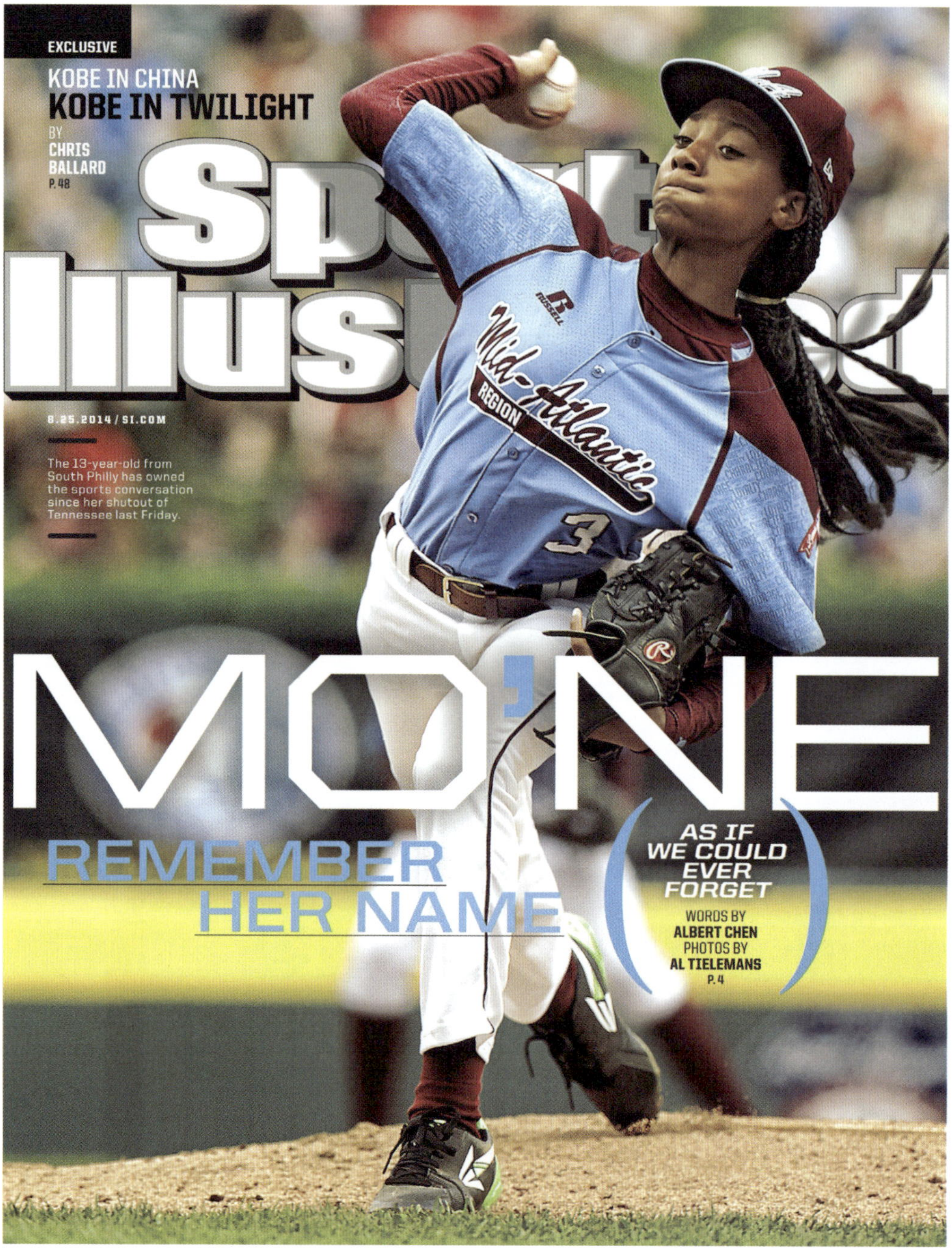
EXCLUSIVE
KOBE IN CHINA
KOBE IN TWILIGHT
BY
CHRIS
BALLARD
P. 48
Sports Illustrated
8.25.2014 / SI.COM
The 13-year-old from South Philly has owned the sports conversation since her shutout of Tennessee last Friday.
MO'NE
REMEMBER HER NAME
AS IF WE COULD EVER FORGET
WORDS BY
ALBERT CHEN
PHOTOS BY
AL TIELEMANS
P. 4
Mid-Atlantic
REGION
3

22

PLAY BALL

Mo'ne Davis and the Visualization of Athletic Girlhood in *Sports Illustrated*

SAMANTHA WHITE

In the late summer heat of August 2014, thirteen-year-old Mo'ne Davis stands on a baseball diamond in Williamsport, Pennsylvania, seemingly unfazed by the weather and the task at hand. Braids splaying from underneath her cap, her focused look expresses her goal as the pitcher for the Taney Dragons of Philadelphia at the Little League World Series: *Strike them out.*[1] As she set her body in motion to throw her next pitch, photographer Al Tielemans captured an image of Davis on the pitcher's mound, her face expressing a sense of determination, confidence, and vulnerability. The photograph of Davis, a teenage Black girl at the Little League World Series, would soon grace the cover of *Sports Illustrated*, elevating her to a national stage where she received accolades from professional athletes, politicians, and celebrities who recognized her historic status as the first girl to pitch a winning game and the first girl to throw a shutout in the Little League World Series. Juxtaposed against the cover image were the words "Remember her name" with the phrase "As if we could ever forget" trailing shortly behind, suggesting Davis's iconic achievements and representations would remain part of a collective American sporting memory.

The *Sports Illustrated* cover of Mo'ne Davis cemented her place in the history of one of sports media's most influential institutions, as well as the history of baseball. Before Davis, a Little League Baseball player had never been featured on the cover of *Sports Illustrated* during its sixty years of circulation. Furthermore, Davis represented not just a shift for *Sports Illustrated,* but the Little League organization. During the summer of 2014, Davis became the eighteenth girl to ever play in the Little League World Series since its creation in 1947. As the only Black girl to ever play in the tournament, Davis's presence symbolized both a historical achievement and an indictment on the lack of opportunities and outreach for other Black girls in baseball.[2] Circulated to readers across the country, the *Sports Illustrated* cover reflected not only individual messages about Mo'ne Davis, but collective stories about the historical and contemporary state of baseball in American society and Black girls' and women's places in these narratives.

The image of Mo'ne Davis on the cover of *Sports Illustrated* demonstrates how sports photographs can challenge and reproduce hegemonic representations of age, race, gender, and athleticism. First, the photograph of Davis builds upon a collective history of Black girls' and women's athleticism in baseball where they have often been rendered invisible in terms of participation and representation. Situating Davis's story into a larger genealogy of Black girls and women in baseball acknowledges the foundation constructed by those people whose contributions to America's pastime were overlooked. Second, the photograph amplifies Davis's body in motion and challenges passive representations of athletic girlhood. The *Sports Illustrated* image of Davis disrupts normative ways of documenting the athletic lives of girls by prioritizing visually active, rather than static, physicality. Finally, the relationship between the photograph and the cover story reveals postfeminist ideologies that uphold liberal forms of gender and racial progress. These narratives focused on Davis's success rather than question why there were not *more* Mo'ne Davises. Examining the multiple meanings layered within the photograph helps us explore the often-contradictory representations of Black girls' athleticism, showing that these photographs often stimulate new, complex questions rather than provide simple and straightforward answers about notions of history and progress in sports, especially for marginalized communities. As historian Mike Huggins notes, sport historians can employ a variety of different methods when thinking about visual culture—and these methodologies encourage new ways of thinking about image, movement, and sport.[3]

Visualizing a Collective Story of Black Girls and Women in Baseball

The *Sports Illustrated* cover of Mo'ne Davis placed her at the center of American sports culture during the summer of 2014. In the process, she ruptured imaginations of Little League Baseball as a space primarily for the nation's young white boys. During the early years of the organization, Little League often intentionally propagated this image. Founded in 1939 by Carl Stolz, Little League Baseball promoted American exceptionalism and espoused democratic ideals by deploying programs and rhetoric that brought local, national, and international youth together through the perceived unifying qualities of sport. And yet in the organization's first decades, Little League Baseball often excluded those "left out of the postwar liberal order: African Americans and women."[4]

Despite this intentional exclusion, the experiences of African Americans, girls, and women remain central to baseball history. Although the National Organization for Women sued Little League Inc. in 1973, resulting in New Jersey's Supreme Court effectively striking down gender discrimination in Little League in the state, the history of girls in baseball begins long before that legal decision.[5] As political scientist Jennifer Ring argues, "women have played for nearly two centuries in the United States yet still are greeted with astonishment and disbelief, as though they are eternally the first girls ever to play baseball."[6] During the early to mid-twentieth century, girls and women played on baseball teams in community organizations, high schools, and colleges, and they participated in professional leagues such as the All-American Girls Baseball League (1943–1954).[7] And yet generalizing the historical experiences of girls and women in baseball risks overlooking the deep racial lines that persisted in sporting organizations, such as the exclusion of Black girls and women from the all-white All-American Girls Baseball League and their participation in the Negro leagues.[8] Unlike their white counterparts, Black female baseball players faced sexism *and* racism in baseball. By viewing the photograph of Davis as part of a lineage of Black girls and women in baseball, rather than a singular snapshot, Davis' achievements emerge as monumental and part of a long history of inclusion and exclusion in sports.

Tracing the genealogy of Black girls and women in baseball extends to not only histories of their participation in the sport, but histories of their representations in the sport media. Through visual images, media institutions circulated a visual culture of Black female baseball players to readers and viewers across the country. During the 1950s, Black newspapers such as the *Pittsburgh Courier* transmitted stories about Toni Stone, Connie Morgan, and Mamie Johnson, three storied professional players on Negro league baseball teams.[9] In fact, Mamie Johnson, a former member of the Indianapolis Clowns in the Negro American League, watched Mo'ne Davis play at the Little League World Series and several years later remarked that Davis was "the reincarnation of me when I was her age."[10] The circulation of sports content about Black girls in baseball extended to television. On July 13, 1954, a Fort Worth, Texas, TV station reported the experiences of eighteen-year-old Glorius Conrad, a Black girl who played shortstop for the semi-pro Green Monarchs, a local team in the Dallas area. The news report noted that Conrad "loves baseball and figures that a girl can do as well as a man if she really wants to."[11] Analyzing the past and contemporary experiences of Black girls and women in baseball requires interrogating "what those historical barriers of discrimination and marginalization mean for girls who are interested in participating in Little League Baseball today."[12] Davis's *Sports Illustrated* cover situates her in a larger history of Black girls and women in representations of baseball. At the same time, the image also asserts her own distinct place in sport media history through constructing discursive visual cultures of Black girl athletes.

Girlhood in Motion

When images of Mo'ne Davis reached mailboxes and newsstands across the country, readers who picked up the *Sports Illustrated* magazine witnessed a different type of cover star: a young, Black female baseball player, a type of athlete who, in its sixty years of circulation, had never been featured on the front of its publication. Girls and women in other sports did not fare much better on the covers of *Sports Illustrated*. Sociologists Jonetta D. Weber and Robert M. Carini found that "from 2000–2011 . . . women appeared on only 4.9 percent of covers."[13] The dearth of girls and women on the covers of *Sports Illustrated* reflected dominant ideologies of sports as a masculinist enterprise. During the early aughts, the *Sports Illustrated* covers that featured teenagers such as Anna Kournikova and Maria Sharapova reflected the ways that media coverage often sexualized young female athletes.[14] Sociologists Cheryl Cooky and Lauren Rauscher recognize the power of sport media representations to "contribute and amplify disparities in girls' sport participation."[15] Acknowledging these disparities, which include a lack of female athletes, the sexualization of female athletes, and a focus on the whiteness of female athletes, reveals the ways that sport media representations perpetuate systemic inequalities. Davis's representation does not eliminate these disparities but operates as a model of representational disruption by providing new ways of imagining Black athletic girlhood in the public sphere.

By emphasizing Davis's body in motion, the *Sports Illustrated* cover locates her athleticism as a focal point of attention. In the photograph taken by Al Tielemans, Davis stands on the pitcher's mound as she grips the baseball in her right hand. With her arm raised and one foot behind the other, the Tielemans image captures her just before she releases the ball. Tielemans, a *Sports Illustrated* photographer, learned of Davis and her team while reading the *Philadelphia Inquirer* and asked an editor if he could travel to Williamsport to cover the tournament. Tielemans wanted "to capture the electrifying thirteen-year-old female pitcher and infielder" which included her "70-mph fastball and a menacing curveball that gave opposing batters fits."[16] His desire to see her athletic skill is reflected in his photographs, which depict Davis as a steely and determined competitor deserving of the attention of a national sports media publication.

Visually documenting Davis as a physical and competitive athlete primarily challenges normative depictions of young female athletes. In publications such as *ESPN Magazine* and *Sports Illustrated*, as analyzed by media studies scholar Cynthia M. Frisby, "women athletes are frequently portrayed on magazine covers in non-athlete roles," while men are shown "active in their sport settings."[17] Photographs in which the subject remains static limits and erases their athleticism. These photographs often emphasize the double standards faced by male and female athletes and can also reveal the "pervasiveness of sexualization and objectification of female athletes found on the covers of popular sports magazines."[18] The marginalization of female athletes is also extended to publications aimed at younger readers. Even in *Sports Illustrated for Kids*, girls are primarily featured in "posed" stances rather than action shots.[19]

Through locating her body in motion, the *Sports Illustrated* cover presents a vision of athletic girlhood that embraces physicality rather than bodily aesthetics. The image of Davis is visual evidence of her sporting ability, as the photograph emphasizes her baseball expertise through her clear demonstration of her pitching skills. By foregrounding the experience and knowledge of a young Black girl, the *Sports Illustrated* cover offered a transgressive model for visualizing the contemporary and future state of America's pastime. In a society in which "dominant cultural constructions marginalize Black women's imagery," Davis's image instead presented Black girls as visionaries in baseball.[20] However, a contentment with this kind of visual progress also lulls consumers into a false sense of belief that barriers in sport for girls, particularly girls of color, have been eliminated. Framing the success of an individual girl such as Mo'ne Davis as evidence of social change advances superficial forms of progress over systemic action.

Postfeminist Narratives of Girls in Sports

On the *Sports Illustrated* cover, a crowd of spectators sits behind Mo'ne Davis as she gears up to throw her next pitch. The image renders the spectators as an unrecognizable mass of shapes, objects, and colors. The focus of the *Sports Illustrated* cover is on Mo'ne Davis. And yet the obscurity of those behind Davis also symbolizes the ways the media framed her as an exceptional and singular figure. By constructing Davis as a sporting anomaly, the sports media—as well as Little League Baseball—could applaud her achievements without a deep reckoning of systemic failures that provided few avenues for other girls. The *Sports Illustrated* cover disrupted normative cultural views about Black girls' place in baseball while simultaneously revealing the limits of representational progress.

Leaving the structure of baseball critically unquestioned—or that of sports writ large—risks reproducing postfeminist ideologies of girls and women and sports. Attention to postfeminist logics should compel scholars to ask larger questions regarding, as sociologist Kim Toffoletti deftly poses, "what is distinctive about how gender is articulated in contemporary sport media" and how these articulations inform representations of the self in the public sphere.[21] Within a postfeminist landscape, girls and women receive messages that assert that the power and responsibility for changing the course of their athletic landscape rest within them, an argument rooted in neoliberal self-determination rather than a critique of inequalities in sporting systems. These postfeminist ideologies identify their participation in sport as indicative of individual choice and their achievements as evidence of the eradication of systemic barriers that restricted the experiences and representations of female athletes in the past. Cultural studies scholar Angela McRobbie asserts that postfeminism erases the "little trace of the battles fought, of the power struggles embarked upon, or of the enduring inequities which still mark out the relations between men and women."[22] Sports organizations and media corporations often amplify the stories of female athletes such as Mo'ne Davis without reflecting upon the historical collective stories of Black girls and women in baseball who came before her or express a commitment to investing in Black girls and women's future in the sport.

Attention to Davis's construction as a postfeminist icon reveals the ideological messages embedded in Al Tielemans's photograph and the cover story written by sportswriter Albert Chen. Media coverage heralded temporary symbolic gains while avoiding systemic examination of the intersection of racism and sexism in baseball. Indeed, as Cheryl Cooky states, "public celebration of girls' and women's sport does not always translate into increased participation, increased opportunities, or broader shifts in the *structural* landscape of sport."[23] The photograph of Mo'ne Davis on the cover of *Sports Illustrated* and its corresponding article reveals how the relationship between text and image constructs narratives about sport as a meritocratic space. In the cover story about Davis, which provides readers with a background of her Philadelphia roots and her love of sports, the text erases the ways race and gender inform her life, an act which advances the idea that much of American society has moved past interrogating how social locations shape people's material lives.

While the cover story discusses Davis's gender on a superficial level, little space is devoted to the significance of this category. There is no mention of historical girls and women in baseball who came before her, an absence that elevates Davis's status as a singular and exceptional girl rather than a piece of a collective story about female athletes playing baseball. Additionally, the article does not address the current participation of girls in Little League Baseball, which could provide an additional examination of gender inequalities within the organization. Instead, the article deploys postfeminist rhetoric that amplifies and individualizes her labor and productivity. The article notes her qualities, such as her status as "an honor student who makes the hour-plus commute from her home in southwest Philadelphia to the school in the Chestnut Hill neighborhood . . . she typically doesn't return home until nearly 7 P.M., sometimes later" and how she is a role model for girls in her community.[24] This critique is not meant to undermine Davis's values and personal work ethic, which are impressive. Instead, according to cultural studies scholar Dawn Heinecken, narratives such as these reveal how "the construction of the liberated girl subject erases the social and structural inequities" embedded in sporting narratives.[25] Chen's article highlights Davis's individual accomplishments rather than question a system in which there are few Mo'ne Davises within baseball.

Attention to intersectionality also reveals how coverage of Davis in *Sports Illustrated* evades a deeper interrogation not just of gender but also of race.[26] On the *Sports Illustrated* cover, as Davis throws a pitch, text positioned next to her connects her body to the city she called home. The cover describes her as "The 13-year-old from South Philly."[27] The evocation of Davis's connection to Philadelphia opens up possibilities to tell vibrant stories about the city's history of fielding and hosting Negro league teams and the diverse communities that currently live across South Philadelphia. Rather than present a rich, complicated, and historical account of the neighborhood, the magazine flattens South Philadelphia into a place "where some of the city's poorest neighborhoods are located." Additionally, the magazine centers narratives that examine "inner-city baseball, the challenges it faces, and how . . . it can still triumph."[28] The phrase "inner-city baseball" avoids explicitly naming not only the ways that race shapes sports, but also the ways that race shapes Philadelphia, Davis's life, and the lives of her teammates.

The relationship between the cover and the text promotes Davis as a symbolic model of exceptionality, hard work, and progress. These beliefs advance postfeminist ideas that suggest gender equality has been achieved due to the visibility of female athletes in the public sphere. The mobilization of Davis's image by *Sports Illustrated* and Little League Baseball allowed these institutions to demonstrate the illusion of progress in sport media representations and sport participation without any real commitment to amplifying the voices and experiences of young Black female baseball players. Treating Davis as an outlier encouraged people to see her as an exception to the rule rather than part of a community of other Black girls who play or are interested in playing baseball. The lack of engagement with the intersection of age, race, and gender remains a failed opportunity for Major League Baseball and Little League Baseball. Instead of prompting greater outreach for girls—especially Black girls—the reception and circulation of Mo'ne Davis's image suggested a successful mission of attracting and retaining female athletes in baseball. There is still time to make room for more Mo'ne Davises.

In the summer of 2021, Mo'ne Davis returned to Williamsport, Pennsylvania, to provide commentary on the Little League Baseball World Series for ESPN. A college softball player at the historically black Hampton

University, she spent some of the summer working as a broadcast analyst for Kidcast, ESPN's telecast for younger viewers. Davis offered insight into hits, pitches, steals, and saves at the same championship she'd played in seven years earlier. Standing on the pitcher's mound once again, Davis threw a ceremonial pitch to Ella Bruning, the only girl to play in the 2021 World Series. The act connected both ballplayers in a long history of girls in baseball.[29]

The image of Davis and Bruning did not end up on a *Sports Illustrated* cover. It did not lead to retrospective articles on girls in baseball. It should have. The afterlife of this photograph leads us to questions we should ponder: How do we amplify the histories of girls and women, particularly Black girls and women, who have shaped baseball? What does girls' current participation in baseball look like? And what kind of future in baseball exists for girls such as Davis and Bruning? The image, like the one of Davis in 2014, reveals the potential for sports photographs to pose more questions, more critical inquiries, and more scholarly possibilities.

NOTES

1. The Taney Dragons, now the Philadelphia Dragons, changed its name in 2020 due to its association with Justice Roger Taney, who supported the Dred Scott case, a decision which legally institutionalized segregation in the United States. Xiemena Conde, "Philly's Taney Dragons to Drop the Controversial Name, a Reminder of the Dred Scott Decision," *WHYY*, June 25, 2020, https://whyy.org/articles/phillys-taney-dragons-to-drop-the-controversial-name-a-reminder-of-the-dred-scott-decision/.

2. "The 20 Girls Who Have Made Little League Baseball World History," https://www.littleleague.org/girls-with-game/girls-who-have-played-in-little-league-baseball-world-series/.

3. Mike Huggins, "The Sporting Gaze: Towards a Visual Turn in Sports History—Documenting Art and Sport," *Journal of Sport History* 35 (Summer 2008): 318–319.

4. Michael H. Carriere, "'A Diamond Is a Boy's Best Friend': The Rise of Little League Baseball, 1939–1964," *Journal of Sport History* 32 (Fall 2005): 373.

5. Jennifer Ring, *Stolen Bases: Why American Girls Don't Play Baseball* (Urbana: University of Illinois Press, 2009), 122.

6. Jennifer Ring, *A Game of Their Own: Voices of Contemporary Women in Baseball* (Lincoln: University of Nebraska Press, 2015), xxiv.

7. Susan Cahn, *Coming on Strong: Gender and Sexuality in Women's Sport* (Urbana: University of Illinois Press, 2015), 140–163. Also see Debra A. Shattuck's *Bloomer Girls: Women Baseball Pioneers* (Urbana: University of Illinois Press, 2017).

8. Amira Rose Davis, "No League of Their Own: Baseball, Black Women, and the Politics of Representation," *Radical History Review* 125 (May 2016): 74–96.

9. Davis, "No League of Their Own," 83.

10. "Mamie Johnson on Mo'ne Davis," MLB Film Room, December 21, 2017, https://www.mlb.com/video/mamie-johnson-on-mo-ne-davis-c1870513483.

11. WBAP-TV, Fort Worth, Texas, July 13, 1954, North Texas Libraries, Special Collections, https://texashistory.unt.edu/ark:/67531/metadc726231/.

12. Alan Brown and Dani Parker Moore, "Lizzie, Mamie, & Mo'ne: Exploring Issues of Racism, Classism, and Sexism in Baseball," *Study and Scrutiny: Research on Young Adult Literature* 4, no. 2 (2020): 70.

13. Jonetta D. Weber and Robert M. Carini, "Where Are the Female Athletes in *Sports Illustrated*? A Content Analysis of Covers (2000–2011)," *International Review for the Sociology of Sport* 48, no. 2 (2013): 199.

14. "SI Women's Covers: The 2000s," *Sports Illustrated*, https://www.si.com/more-sports/2010/02/05/05sis-womens-covers-the-2000s#gid=ci025583e84006251I&pid=anna-kournikova.

15. Cheryl Cooky and Lauren Rauscher, "Girls and the Racialization of Female Bodies in Sport Contexts," in *Child's Play: Sport in Kids' Worlds*, ed. Michael Messner and Michela Musto (New Brunswick, NJ: Rutgers University Press, 2016), 76.

16. Wilton Jackson, "How Mo'Ne Davis's SI Cover Came to Be" *Sports Illustrated*, June 8, 2022, https://www.si.com/mlb/2022/06/08/mone-davis-2014-little-league-world-series-sports-illustrated-cover.

17. Cynthia M. Frisby, "Sacrificing Dignity for Publicity: Content Analysis of Female and Male Athletes on '*Sports Illustrated*' and '*ESPN the Magazine*' covers from 2012–2016," *Advances in Journalism and Communication* 5, no. 2 (2017): 131.

18. Cynthia Frisby, "Sexualization and Objectification of Female Athletes on Sport Magazine Covers: Improvement, Consistency, or Decline," *International Journal of Humanities and Social Science* 7, no. 6 (2017): 29.

19. Jacquelyn Cuneen and M. Joy Sidwell, "Gender Portrayals in *Sports Illustrated for Kids* Advertisements: A Content Analysis of Prominent and Supporting Models," *Journal of Sport Management* 12, no. 1 (1998): 46.

20. Akilah R. Carter-Francique and F. Michelle Richardson, "Controlling Media, Controlling Access: The Role of Sport Media on Black Women's Sport Participation," *Race, Gender & Class* 23, no. 1–2 (2016): 13.

21. Kim Toffoletti, "Analyzing Media Representations of Sportswomen—Expanding the Conceptual Boundaries Using a Postfeminist Sensibility," *Sociology of Sport Journal* 33, no. 3 (2016): 205.

22. Angela McRobbie, "Post-feminism and Popular Culture," *Feminist Media Studies* 4, no. 3 (2004): 260. Also see Jess Butler, "For White Girls Only? Postfeminism and the Politics of Inclusion," *Feminist Formations* 25 (Spring 2013): 35–58.

23. Cheryl Cooky, "Understanding Popular Culture Images of 'Girl Power!' and Sport," in *Learning Culture through Sports: Perspectives on Society and Organized Sports* ed. Sandra Spickard Prettyman and Bryan Lampman (New York: Rowman and Littlefield Publishers, 2010): 211.

24. Albert Chen, "Mo'ne Davis, Taney Take Center Stage at Little League World Series," *Sports Illustrated*, August 20, 2014, https://www.si.com/more-sports/2014/08/20/mone-davis-taney-little-league-world-series.

25. Dawn Heinecken, "Empowering Girls through Sport? Sports Advice Books for Young Female Readers," *Children's Literature in Education* 47, no. 4 (2016): 339. See also:

Dawn Heinecken, "Gender and Jockography: Post-feminism and Resistance in Female Sports Autobiographies," *Feminist Media Studies* 16, no. 2 (2016): 325–343.

26. Chen, "Mo'ne Davis."

27. Chen, "Mo'ne Davis."

28. Chen, "Mo'ne Davis."

29. David Adler, "Mo'ne Davis, Ella Bruning Connect on 1st Pitch," MLB, August 24, 2021, https://www.mlb.com/news/mo-ne-davis-throws-first-pitch-to-ella-bruning.

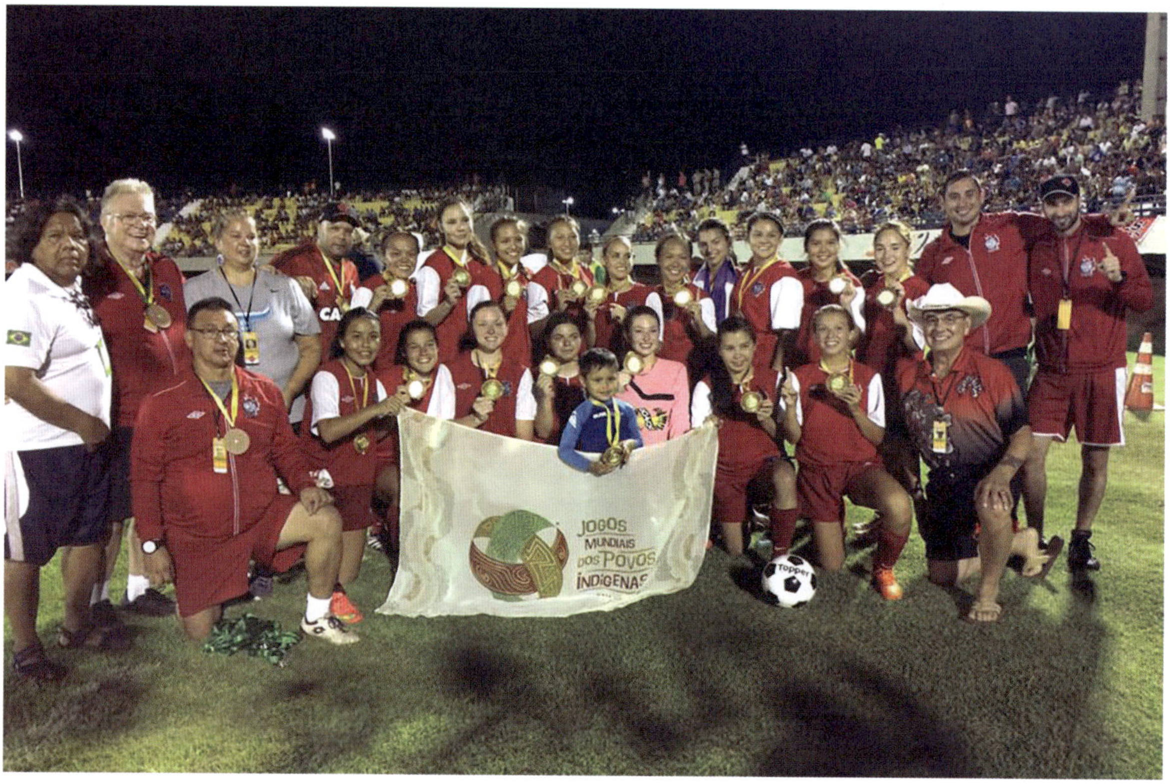
JOGOS
MUNDIAIS
DOS POVOS
INDÍGENAS

23

TO DREAM AGAIN

The Founding of NIFA and the First World Indigenous Women's Soccer Champions

CHRISTINE O'BONSAWIN

For most championship teams, posing for a team photo has become commonplace. Yet the images captured and widely circulated in such photographs are often remarkable, and deeper analysis usually uncovers extraordinary histories and stories of individual perseverance and collective triumph. The post-match image of the Native Indian Football Association (NIFA) Women's Indigenous Team following its gold medal victory at the first World Indigenous Games in 2015 is no different than other iconic photographs of championship teams in that it represents a story of success and imparts the joy and pride of those in the photo.[1] Nonetheless, a closer inspection of this photograph reveals a perhaps more complex history. This photo includes teammates, coaches, and staff, typical of most championship team photographs, but also family members—mothers, fathers, daughters, siblings, and cousins—as well as revered cultural, spiritual, and political leaders, including Elders and Chiefs.[2] This photograph, shot in the typical post-victory style, is representative of more than team success, joy, and pride. This photo can be read as a story about relationships, resiliency, and survivance.

It was in October 2015 when the NIFA women's national team was triumphant at the first World Indigenous Games, held in Palmas, Brazil, on the territories of the Akwẽ-Xerénte people. These finals took place in front of approximately 10,000 boisterous and partisan spectators at Palmas Stadium in a championship final involving the NIFA and the local Xerénte women's teams. The NIFA team consisted of seventeen players and six staff members from nine First Nations communities across Canada, including Sḵwx̱wú7mesh, Tla'amin, Quatsino, Dzawada̱'enux̱w, 'Na̱mgis, Cowichan, Kanesatà:ke, Kahnawà:ke, and Akwesasne. With the home team reaching the finals, the mood in the stadium was electric, and the two teams played a hard-fought battle, ending in nil-nil at the end of regulation. The NIFA women were ultimately victorious in shootouts, thus cementing their place in history.[3]

The history of this Indigenous women's soccer team and their victory at these inaugural games cannot be neatly positioned within a standard historical account; it is entangled with and juxtaposed against a complex history of settler colonialism.[4] And yet this history is distinctly independent of such narratives and may properly be understood to exist within multifaceted and dynamic cultural processes that precede, prelude, and elude colonial boundaries. It is connected to the mental, physical, emotional, and spiritual aspects that guide the lives of Indigenous peoples and reaffirm the past, present, and future status of Indigenous nations as autonomous and self-determining. Indigenous women have always played a central role in the mental, physical, emotional, and spiritual life of Indigenous nations. The success of this NIFA women's team at the inaugural World Indigenous Games demonstrates this reality. These Indigenous women were not only respected world soccer champions but also, importantly, revered cultural catalysts, political leaders, physical contributors, mentors, and role models within their respective families, communities, and nations.

Soccer History on Coast Salish and Kwakwa̱ka̱'wakw Territories

I first became aware of this vibrant all-Indigenous soccer community after moving to Coast Salish territory, specifically the lands of the lək̓ʷəŋən and W̱SÁNEĆ peoples, in 2007. Shortly after arriving in the Pacific Northwest, I was invited to play with the Kingcome Wolverines, a women's team from the remote Kwakwa̱ka̱'wakw community of Kingcome Inlet, located in the lands of the Musgamakw Dzawada'enuxw. Moving to the West Coast meant that as an Abenaki person, or Easterner, I had relocated to a place far from my own family, community, and home territory. The invitation to play on this team allowed me to continue participating in the sport I love, make meaningful friendships, and build relationships with individuals and families throughout Coast Salish and Kwakwa̲ka̲'wakw territories. Although I do not come from these territories, the invitation to participate in these all-Indigenous soccer spaces has meant that I have been surrounded by teammates, friends, and community. It has also meant that I have had the opportunity to learn about the rich cultural and political histories of these Indigenous nations, as well as the long and storied history of all-Indigenous soccer in the Pacific Northwest.

The vision and eventual underpinnings for this elite all-Indigenous national soccer program are properly located in the Pacific Northwest, specifically on the territories of the Coast Salish and Kwakwa̲ka̲'wakw peoples. For over a century, soccer has enjoyed a place of central importance to numerous Indigenous communities throughout these West Coast Indigenous territories. Although Coast Salish and Kwakwa̲ka̲'wakw peoples have long participated in various forms of foot and ball games, soccer, in its modern form, was brought to these territories in the mid- to late nineteenth century. Dano Thorne (bottom row, far left of the photo), a member of Cowichan Tribes and founder of NIFA, explains, "It's all about soccer in our community and in my family. It's been going for over a hundred years. We have English ancestry dating back to my great-grandfather, Billy Thorne. He was one of the pioneers to bring the game to Vancouver Island in the late 1880s."[5] Regrettably, Indigenous soccer experiences throughout these territories have since become entangled with the calamitous history of Indian residential schools, which operated in various forms across Canada for over a hundred and fifty years.[6] In these neglectful, harmful, and often violent places, many Indigenous children, boys and girls, learned to play the game. For many of these children, however, soccer spaces became sites of refuge, where they could turn to escape harm and abuse, albeit temporarily. In these violent spaces, many of the children—now survivors of these horrific institutions—developed a love for the game, which they have since handed down to their children, grandchildren, and great-grandchildren.

For over sixty years, Indigenous-organized soccer has thrived throughout Coast Salish and Kwakwa̲ka̲'wakw territories, primarily owing to the efforts of families and communities who have worked industriously to bring players and families together in celebration of culture and nationhood. Since

1958, for example, 'Na̱mg̱is First Nation has organized a community-wide event in 'Yalis (commonly known as Alert Bay, British Columbia) during Father's Day weekend. Although there are many events associated with June Sports celebrations, including a salmon pageant, parade, opening and closing ceremonies, and foot races, it is the soccer tournament, consisting of youth, women's, and men's divisions, that continues to attract upwards of a thousand participants and spectators to this small island community, which has fewer than a thousand permanent residents. Other celebrations and competitions similar to June Sports have sprung up throughout Coast Salish and Kwakwa̱ka̱'wakw territories over the last six decades. Notably, the Totem Tournament, which has been hosted regularly on Easter weekend since 1962 on lək̓ʷəŋən territory (commonly known as Victoria, British Columbia), has become the largest all-Indigenous soccer event on the West Coast. The late John Rice Sr. of Songhees Nation founded the annual tournament sixty years ago. Over the years, it evolved into a family responsibility and has affectionately become known to most as simply the Rice family tournament. Other notable family and community-organized Indigenous tournaments on Coast Salish and Kwakwa̱ka̱'wakw territories include the Buckskin Tournament, held annually on Mother's Day weekend since 1968 in Cowichan territory (commonly known as Duncan, British Columbia), and the Golden Wings Tournament, held annually on the July long weekend since 1972 on the territories of the We Wai Kai and Wei Wai Kum First Nations (commonly known as Campbell River, British Columbia). These are just a few examples of the many celebrations throughout the Pacific Northwest where families and communities come together to celebrate culture and nationhood and simply participate in the sport they love.

The history of Indigenous soccer throughout these territories exists mainly within the oral records of community members who have long shared stories of some of the greatest players and teams to have represented their communities and nations on local, provincial, national, and international levels. One of the greatest players of all time was Xulsi'malt (Harry Manson), a Snuneymuxw man who competed between 1898 and 1912, captaining the all-Snuneymuxw Indian Wanderers that captured the Nanaimo city championship in 1904. Xulsi'malt also played with the predominantly white Nanaimo Thistles that regularly qualified for the provincial championships and ultimately won the provincial title in 1907.[7] Only in recent years has mainstream Canada learned of and thus recognized the achievements of this outstanding Snuneymuxw athlete who, at long last, was inducted into the Canada Soccer Hall of Fame in 2014, Canada's Sports Hall of Fame and the

Nanaimo Museum Sports Hall of Fame in 2015, and the BC Sports Hall of Fame in 2016. Xulsi'malt is one of many gifted Indigenous soccer players from these territories, and the story of his talents and successes has only seeped into mainstream view and accounts in recent years. Nonetheless, there are countless more stories of individuals like Xulsi'malt, as well as teams that have achieved similar success locally, nationally, and internationally. The story of the first world Indigenous women's soccer champions, the 2015 NIFA women's national team, is but another.

The Emergence of the Native Indian Football Association (NIFA)

The success of the NIFA Indigenous Women's Team in Palmas, Brazil, is mainly due to the long and rich history of all-Indigenous soccer on the west coast, particularly throughout Coast Salish and Kwakwa̲ka̲'wakw territories. From within these geographic, cultural, political, spiritual, and athletic spaces, the vision for an all-Indigenous elite national soccer program flourished. In 1990, NIFA was founded by Dano Thorne, a Cowichan Tribes member and current head coach of the program. Graham Cope, former all-Indigenous tournament referee, born in Stoke-on-Trent, England, helped organize the first NIFA tour. Although significant Indigenous soccer talent existed throughout Coast Salish and Kwakwa̲ka̲'wakw territories at this time, limited competitive opportunities existed for these players, some of whom were believed to be as skilled and talented (if not more so) than national and professional players. As Thorne explains, "NIFA was created because we [Indigenous people] fell through the cracks. There was no select team program, no all-star teams, no opportunities to help our people dream again. To dream about making it into the higher level of soccer in our country."[8]

Following its founding in 1990, the first NIFA team was formed—a men's team comprised of elite Coast Salish and Kwakwa̲ka̲'wakw players. At its creation, NIFA founders envisioned a program built around soccer excellence; however, they also recognized that culture and holistic well-being were central to the success of NIFA and its players. NIFA continues to be guided by its founding mission, which is "To promote a holistic approach addressing mental, physical, emotional and spiritual well-being of players as they strive for their potential."[9] In preparation for the first NIFA tour, organizers and selected players attended training camps and participated in fundraisers to cover travel expenses for their May 1991 trip to the United Kingdom. Appropriately, the composition of NIFA from the outset incorporated knowledgeable soccer *and* cultural leaders. On this first NIFA tour, the men's team competed against established teams from cities and townships across the United Kingdom, including teams from Stoke-on-Trent and Eccleshall, concluding their tour with a 2-1-2 record.[10] Following the team's on and off-field successes in this inaugural tour, owing mainly to the perseverance of team leaders, the support of family in their home communities, and, of course, player skill, NIFA founders set their sights on future opportunities. The creation of an elite women's team was next on the horizon.

In 1992, the first NIFA women's national team was formed, and soon thereafter players and staff embarked on a five-country European tour in its first competitive tour. Over the next thirty years, the NIFA women's national team has traveled worldwide, and with much success, to places such as Germany, Austria, Spain, Portugal, Holland, Italy, Australia, Hawai'i, Cuba, Argentina, and Brazil, to name a few.[11] The geographical reach of NIFA not only expanded in an international competitive sense but also in terms of team composition. Whereas NIFA began in the early 1990s as an elite soccer program on the West Coast, comprised predominantly of Coast Salish and Kwakwa̱ka̱'wakw players, with a mainly regional and provincial focus, in recent years NIFA has expanded to include players from other regions of the country. I had the honor of playing on the NIFA women's team that traveled to Cuba in 2009 and was one of few Indigenous players not from Coast Salish and Kwakwa̱ka̱'wakw territories. Throughout the last decade, strong relationships have been established between NIFA leadership and other Indigenous nations, including Kanien'kehá:ka (Mohawk) communities in Quebec and Ontario. Further, NIFA has prioritized youth programs, recognizing the importance of grassroots development and the potential of Indigenous youth—the future leaders of our communities and nations. At present, NIFA works with over three hundred players from various age groups as well as Indigenous communities across the country.[12]

Importantly, over the last two decades, NIFA has garnered the support and recognition of prominent sporting and political bodies. For example, in June 2011, the provincial Union of British Columbia Indian Chiefs, by resolution, offered its full support to NIFA and called on the mainstream soccer community, specifically the British Columbia Soccer Association and Canada Soccer Association, to support NIFA in its efforts to develop and provide opportunities for Indigenous players at the grassroots and international levels.[13] In July 2016, the federal Assembly of First Nations offered its full support, recognizing NIFA's over twenty-five-year history of soccer excellence, and called on regional and national soccer organizations to support NIFA, specifically through fiscal commitments, in the development of Indigenous soccer across Canada.[14] Although Indigenous political leaders summoned a call for greater financial support and resources, NIFA's success is due largely to the perseverance of its committed leaders, such as Thorne and William Wasden Sr. (top row, second from left of the photo), an Elder, advisor, and NIFA coach, and to the players who have made significant personal, professional, and financial sacrifices, and in doing so have brought much pride to their families, communities, and nations. While NIFA has included men's and youth teams over the years, the women's national squad has emerged as its flagship program. As such, the NIFA women's national team was well positioned for great success in 2015 and to start, in Thorne's words, "the greatest two-week run in the history of Indigenous football in the world."[15]

Indigenous Sisterhood, Mentorship, and Gold in Palmas

As Anishinaabekwe scholar Tricia McGuire-Adams explains, all too frequently "settler colonialism tells a story about Indigenous women in a multitude of negative tones: That Indigenous women are not high achievers; that we have too many babies, with too many fathers; that we are too promiscuous and do drugs and alcohol, which leads us to be murdered and/or missing; that we are not healthy and well; and that we are not physically strong."[16] The story of this NIFA women's team, and the NIFA women's program generally, offers a welcome corrective to settler colonialism's faulty narrative about Indigenous women, our bodies, and our behaviors. A closer inspection of team members (including those in the photograph), and all those who played before them, suggests that these women are high achievers; that they are loving mothers, aunties, sisters, daughters, granddaughters, friends, and teammates; that they are healthy and well; and that they are physically strong. And although their love for the sport does not fully guard them against threats of violence—a burden all Indigenous women carry—their love of soccer helps ensure their safety because of the long hours they spend on the pitch, where they are physically safe, and because they are nurtured within an ethos of responsibilities between Indigenous women, an Indigenous sisterhood where there is the giving and receiving of teachings.[17]

According to Cree-Métis scholar Tracey Lindberg, "In the context of indigenous knowledge, the political language of sisterhood and the cultural linguistics of relations intersect, resulting in definitions of roles, responsibilities, and obligations of indigenous relations that are complex and gendered."[18] Yet Indigenous sisterhood is not determined by virtue of gender alone. Gender itself does not speak to spiritual and cultural obligations, nor does it account for shared knowledge, experiences, and unspoken secrets between Indigenous women. Indigenous sisterhood is premised upon unspoken understandings, knowledges, and responsibilities shared between Indigenous women—even women without kinship relations. In Lindberg's words, Indigenous sisterhood helps to "ensure that the effects of colonization do not wound me too deeply. [My Indigenous sisters] take care of my physical, emotional, and spiritual needs. For these reasons, they are my family."[19] The success of this NIFA team, and the women's program more generally, is premised on an Indigenous sisterhood. The women who participated on this particular NIFA women's national team, and those who came before them, understand such responsibilities and are mindful of the giving and receiving of such teachings. I have experienced and witnessed this firsthand. In sports contexts, this might be understood as a form of mentorship. Relationships between the players on this team, and their responsibilities to one another, were crucial elements to this NIFA team's success.

The history of the World Indigenous Games can be traced to 1977 and the efforts of Wilton "Willie" Littlechild, a Cree Chief, national Indigenous political leader, residential school survivor, and advocate for Indigenous sport from Ermineskin Cree Nation at Maskwacîs in Treaty 6 territory (in what is commonly known as central Alberta). At this time, Littlechild put forward a motion at the World Council of Indigenous Peoples' meeting in Kiruna, Sweden, inviting its support for a World Olympic Games for Indigenous peoples.[20] It would take over four decades to come to fruition, largely owing to the work of dedicated individuals and organizations, such as Littlechild and the Inter Tribal Council (an Indigenous peoples organization in Brazil), before the first World Indigenous Games were held in 2015, involving over two thousand athletes from numerous Indigenous nations globally.[21] Similar to NIFA's founding, the concept of a World Indigenous Games arose because Indigenous leaders recognized systemic discrimination in mainstream sport systems and that alternative routes and steppingstones for Indigenous athletes needed to be established.[22] Considering its long history and proven success in international competition, the NIFA women's national team was well positioned to compete and contend at these inaugural World Indigenous Games.

Twenty-three women were initially selected for this NIFA team, including players from First Nations communities in British Columbia, Quebec, Ontario, and Saskatchewan. Despite the verbal endorsement from important political bodies such as the Union of British Columbia Indian Chiefs and the Assembly of First Nations, some players were unable to join the team due to a lack of funds and resources. Specifically, there was a lack of government and sponsorship support, making it exceedingly difficult for team organizers and players to cover training and travel expenses. In the end, seventeen players representing nine First Nations communities in British Columbia, Quebec, Ontario, and Saskatchewan, traveled to Akwẽ-Xerénte territory to compete in the games. The team consisted of sisters, cousins, friends, and even those who had not previously met, strangers who became not only teammates but friends in a few short weeks.

Like most successful teams, this NIFA squad was a balance of experienced players and young talent. In selecting the team, the coaching staff made a conscious decision to include a couple of players who were not only seasoned veterans but also good mothers, positive role models, and promising leaders in their communities. These veteran players and leaders performed important roles on and off the pitch. They were tasked with the responsibility of building up their teammates in a safe and supportive space and serving as healthy role models for not only their younger teammates but also for the children and the youth of their nations, some of whom traveled to Brazil to cheer on their mothers, aunties, cousins, and family members. Traveling to the World Indigenous Games with Margaret (top row, eighth from right of the photo), a mother of two at the time, was her young daughter. It was Margaret's hope that her daughter's experiences at these international games would open "her eyes up to the bigger world and the bigger picture out there of athletes." Lacey (top row, seventh from right of the photo) was selected team captain not only because she was the oldest and could keep up with the youngsters, but more so because, in the words of Thorne, "her leadership was endless." Lacey had an exceedingly important responsibility on the team given that two of the youngest players, aged sixteen and seventeen, also came from her community. For these players, Lacey has always been an inspiration.[23]

The NIFA women's road to victory at these World Indigenous Games was certainly not easy. In a thirty-two-team field, the women had to battle not only exceptional teams in round-robin play but also harsh elements, with temperatures reaching greater than 40°C some days, to make it to the semi-finals, where they faced the favored team from Peru. Following a hard-fought match, the NIFA women emerged victorious and were set to meet the local Xerénte women's team in the championship final. Thorne described the NIFA women's victory in shootouts at these inaugural World Indigenous Games as one of

> the most sacred of victories. . . . The 2015 team, and the teams which came before, is truly a remarkable story of leadership and passion by the seventeen young ladies and the excellent coaching staff. They took the gold medals and won the hearts of their families and communities, and created standards for everyone to follow—a tribute to the players and coaches, support families and NIFA, and to honor First Nations and Indigenous women in our traditional lands in BC and Canada.[24]

As such, this photograph is representative of much more than team success, joy, and pride. It tells a story about family, spirituality, leadership, and survivance. Most fittingly, Grand Chief and World Indigenous Games founder Willie Littlechild was in attendance for this gold medal women's soccer match and there to celebrate this historic victory, sticking around long enough to be included in this iconic photograph (bottom row, far right of the photo).

Since 2015, the NIFA women's national team has achieved further success. In 2017, the team defended its championship title at the second World Indigenous Games, hosted by Enoch Cree Nation in Treaty 6 territory in Alberta, Canada. Unfortunately, the pandemic forced World Indigenous Games organizers to postpone the third iteration of the games, scheduled for October 2021 in Rio de Janeiro, Brazil, delaying the NIFA women's chance for a three-peat. In the interim, the successes of this 2015 championship team have been recognized elsewhere. In 2021, the NIFA women's national team was inducted into the BC Soccer Hall of Fame and the North American Indigenous Athletics Hall of Fame in 2022. Sharing this history and celebrating the success of this team is undoubtedly warranted, not only because of the incredible feats of these women, but perhaps more importantly because their achievements in Brazil and beyond have instilled hope for Indigenous girls and young women who may also aspire to be cultural catalysts, political leaders, mentors, and role models within their respective families, communities, and nations. And yes, to dream of becoming world champions, too.

NOTES

1. This photograph of the post-match NIFA women's national team is different from other iconic photos of championship teams, including many represented in this collection, in that this picture was not captured by a professional photographer but rather by a family member who traveled to Akwẽ-Xerénte territory with the team to support their loved ones and the NIFA team. Consequently, the quality of this photo is lower than that of other photographs included in this collection, as this picture was taken by a relative who rushed to the field and captured the moment with a cell phone.

2. Front Row (L-R): Dano Thorne (Cowichan, Head Coach and NIFA Lead), Brittany Harry (Tla'amin), Lylee Horn (Kahnawà:ke), Rachel Leborgne (Kahnawà:ke), Wynonna Cross (Kanesatà:ke), Lason Taylor ('Namgis and Skwxwú7mesh, son), Melody Horn (Kahnawà:ke), Jasmine Hunt (Quatsino), Tiorahkose Jacobs (Kahnawà:ke), Grand Chief Willie Littlechild (Ermineskin, Grand Chief and World Indigenous Games Founder). Back Row (L-R): Carlos Terena (Xané, World Indigenous Games Founder and Coordinator), William Wasden Sr. ('Namgis Elder and NIFA Coach and Advisor), Anna Thompson (Akwesasne, Trainer/Medical), Harry Rice (Kahnawà:ke, Assistant Coach), Brandi Francis (Tla'amin), Justine Laughren (Skwxwú7mesh), Danielle Dawson (Dzawada'enuxw), Lokokweienstha Porter (Akwesasne), Lacey Baker (Skwxwú7mesh), Taylor Francis (Akwesasne), Jenna Thompson (Akwesasne), Kiera Peterson ('Namgis), Crystal Laughren (Skwxwú7mesh), Jason Taylor ('Namgis, Assistant Coach), Lucas Cooper (Kahnawà:ke, Equipment Manager).

3. Justin Beddall, "Squamish Nation Soccer Players Score Gold at Brazil's World Indigenous Games," *North Shore News*, November 15, 2015.

4. C. L. R. James, *Beyond a Boundary* (New York: Pantheon Books, 1963); Michael A. Robidoux, *Stickhandling through the Margins: First Nations Hockey in Canada* (Toronto: University of Toronto Press, 2021), 4.

5. Quoted in *Nutsamat Shqwaluun*, produced by Dano Thorne (Anthem Jackson Productions, 2019), documentary, 5:10.

6. Truth and Reconciliation Commission of Canada, *Honouring the Truth, Reconciling for the Future: Summary of the Final Report of the Truth and Reconciliation Commission of Canada* (2015).

7. Duncan McCure, "Aboriginal Star Hailed as 'Pioneer' by Soccer Hall of Fame," *CBC News*, November 7, 2014, https://www.cbc.ca/news/indigenous/aboriginal-star-hailed-as-pioneer-by-soccer-hall-of-fame-1.2822153.

8. *Nutsamat Shqwaluun*, 2:58.

9. Native Indian Football Association, NIFA Constitution (December 1, 2010), 10. See http://www.nifasoccer.net/docs-and-films.html.

10. The NIFA record in this United Kingdom tour included two wins, one draw, and two losses. Graham Cope, "Native Indian Football Association," March 5, 1992.

11. NIFA Soccer Program, Native Indian Football Association (November 26, 2010).

12. Peter Mothe, "All-Native Soccer Team Gets Ready to Represent Canada at the World's First Indigenous Games," *The Georgia Straight*, May 19, 2015.

13. Chiefs Council, Union of British Columbia Indian Chiefs, *Support for the Native Indian Football Association of BC (NIFA) Soccer Programs, resolution no. 2011-28* (June 2, 2011).

14. Assembly of First Nations, *Support for the National* [sic] *Indian Football Association Canada, resolution no.23/2016* (July 13, 2016).

15. "Introducing NIFA Indigenous Women's Team Canada 2015: Soccer Hall of Fame BC Member," BC Soccer Hall of Fame & Heritage Archive, accessed May 23, 2022.

16. Tricia McGuire-Adams, *Indigenous Feminist Gikendaasowin (Knowledge): Decolonization through Physical Activity* (Cham, Switzerland: Palgrave Macmillan, 2020), 1.

17. Tracey Lindberg, "Not My Sister: What Feminists Can Learn about Sisterhood from Indigenous Women," *Canadian Journal of Women and the Law* 16, no. 2 (2004): 342–352.

18. Lindberg, "Not My Sister," 342.

19. Lindberg, "Not My Sister," 348.

20. Janice Forsyth and Kevin B. Wamsley, "'Native to Native. . . . We'll Recapture Our Spirits: The World Indigenous Nations Games and the North American Indigenous Games as Cultural Resistance," *International Journal of the History of Sport* 23 (March 2006): 303.

21. Alexis White-Mobley, "A Gathering of Nations: First-Ever World Indigenous Games Held in Brazil," *Cultural Survival Quarterly Magazine* 39 (December 2015): https://www.culturalsurvival.org/publications/cultural-survival-quarterly/gathering-nations-first-ever-world-indigenous-games-held.

22. Forsyth and Wamsley, "Native to Native," 303.

23. Mothe, "All-Native Soccer Team Gets Ready."

24. "Introducing NIFA Indigenous Women's Team Canada," BC Soccer Hall of Fame & Heritage Archive.

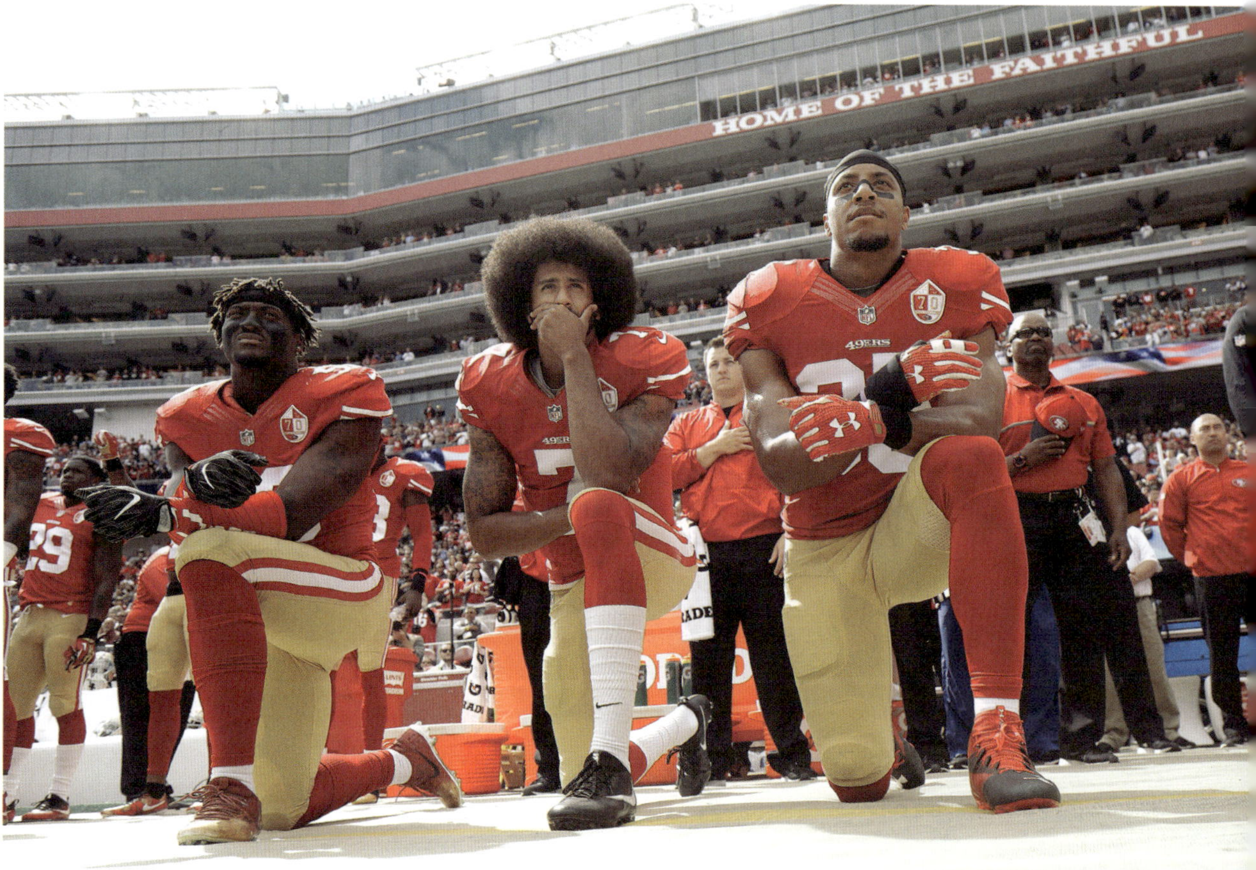
HOME OF THE FAITHFUL
49ERS

24

KAEPERNICK'S CLICHÉ

TIMOTHY B. SPEARS

The decisive moment has a special meaning in sports photography. With cameras trained on the flow of movements—the headed ball, the knockout punch, or the ski carving a mogul—photojournalists seek to capture the spirit of competition in single images borne of split seconds. But the time-stamped aesthetic that French photographer Henri Cartier-Bresson famously described—a "precise organization of forms" that gives the moment "its proper expression"—assumes a different power when the photograph circulates online, shared and liked across social media platforms. Then it can become a cliché, not necessarily worn-out and trite, although that is possible, but part of an assemblage of images and text that recalls a form of visual culture that emerged in nineteenth-century France when the creation of glass plates, known as *cliché verre*, enabled the mass production of photographs. In this definition of cliché, a photograph's meaning evolves as it resonates with other images, other decisive moments, that are already circulating in the world. Today, a cliché might be called a meme, though in the earlier usage it referred more to a history that is revealed through photographs than an image or idea that is replicated on the internet.[1]

I begin with these two notions of photographic meaning to help explain why the image of Colin Kaepernick commanded the public's attention during the 2016 National Football League season and beyond. A Black quarterback on the San Francisco 49ers, Kaepernick decided to kneel during the playing of the national anthem to protest racial injustice, especially the killing of Black Americans by police. Kaepernick knelt—and other athletes followed his lead—as part of the Black Lives Matter movement that took hold after the Black teenager Michael Brown was shot to death by police in Ferguson, Missouri, on August 10, 2014. When photographs of the kneeling quarterback went viral, he became the movement's most visible activist, somehow understanding that to wield power he had to become a cliché.

In the summer and fall of 2016, many photos of a kneeling Kaepernick appeared in the media, though the best-known shot is probably the picture that AP photographer Marcio Jose Sanchez took at the October 2, 2016, game between the 49ers and the Dallas Cowboys, held at Levi's Stadium in Santa Clara, California. In this photograph, Kaepernick anchors the middle of the frame, flanked by safety Eric Reid to his left and linebacker Eli Harold on the right. The three men are kneeling in front of the 49ers bench, each with their right knee on the ground and left leg in a tripod position. The symmetry of their pose extends above the waist: Kaepernick's left hand covers his mouth—like man thinking—while Reid and Harold's arms are crossed above their left knees, their gloved hands displaying Nike and Under Armour logos. Behind the men, other 49ers (all Black) are standing for "The Star-Spangled Banner," some with their fists in the air. On the other side of the frame, two San Francisco staff members (one white, the other Black) have their hand or hat over their hearts, while a third (Asian American perhaps) stands with his hands behind him. The scene is dominated by people of color. In the far background, fans are on their feet for the anthem and ready for the start of the game, their role as spectators clarified by the press box and loges above them and the banner near the top of the photo that reads "Home of the Faithful." The phrase announces that Levi's Stadium belongs to the fans—it is their house—but here the words also echo the patriotic ideals that the kneeling men seek to emphasize and the brave space they create through their protest.

Certainly, this was a decisive moment, but it is not an action shot. Like the photograph of runners Tommie Smith and John Carlos with their black gloved fists thrust upward at the 1968 Olympics, it showcases a drama that took place apart from the competition. But in contrast to that protest, which happened after Smith won a gold medal and Carlos a bronze, this one was staged beforehand and one of its effects, played out in multiple protests, was to keep Kaepernick off the field and prohibit him from playing in future NFL games. And "staged" is the right term, since Kaepernick orchestrated this protest as if he were sitting for a formal portrait that Sanchez might have taken with a large format camera—for instance, a 4 × 5 view camera with a tripod and drop cloth—instead of the hand-held DSLR with mechanized firing capacity that photojournalists typically bring to sporting events. By taking a knee, Kaepernick, Reid, and Harold implicitly invited Sanchez to make a team picture whose power resides in its collective purpose. Together the athletes and photographer joined forces to bring other people into the frame, galvanizing the movement with each new decision to kneel and every additional picture taken of that pose.

This was not the first time that Kaepernick and Reid had taken a knee. At the start of three games in the 2016 pre-season, beginning on August 14, Kaepernick sat on the bench during the national anthem. As he told one reporter, when asked about his decision to sit, "I am not going to stand up to show pride in a flag for a country that oppresses Black people and people of color. To me, this is bigger than football, and it would be selfish on my part to look the other way. There are bodies in the street and people getting paid leave and getting away with murder."[2] Then on September 1, before the 49ers' final pre-season game against the San Diego Chargers at Qualcomm Stadium in San Diego, Kaepernick knelt. So did Eric Reid. The picture that AP photographer Chris Carlson filed after the game shows them in front of their bench, behind a screen of staff members and military personnel, who are standing between the players and the field.

Kaepernick is visible in this photo, but Reid is not, at least not fully. Reid did not dress for the game because he already had a starting position, whereas Kaepernick was battling for his job and had to play to prove himself, but Reid's black shirt and hand peek out from behind the legs of a 49ers staffer. The choice to kneel was Kaepernick's, prompted by a conversation he had with Nate Boyer, a former Green Beret and one-time long-snapper, who had been following Kaepernick's decision to sit and told him that it was a tradition in the Army for soldiers to kneel in recognition of fallen comrades. This gesture, Boyer suggested, would carry more symbolic weight than sitting on the bench. The Chargers game was also "Salute to the Military" night at Qualcomm, a moment when San Diego, home to a several Navy and Marine bases, honored American military personnel and their families.[3]

That Kaepernick chose to kneel at the intersection of football and military culture was hardly an accident. As a sport aimed at "toughening" young men, football served the needs of the military as early as World War I, when recruits played the game at training camps in the United States, a practice that continued during World War II. During the Vietnam War, the NFL promoted its patriotic credentials by arranging militaristic halftime pageants and sending players on goodwill trips to Southeast Asia, though the players' willingness to go on these excursions did not necessarily mean that they supported the war. Following the attacks on September 11, 2001, the NFL worked to burnish its reputation as America's game by sponsoring "Salute to Service" nights and raising money for military causes.[4] Kaepernick's protest tested the meaning of the NFL's nationalistic stance. Would the playing of the national anthem and salute to the flag give him space to exercise his rights to free speech? Would his identity as a Black man in a league dominated by Black players but managed and owned by white men and supported by a mostly white fan base impede his activism?

Not surprisingly, the action taken by Kaepernick and his teammates ignited a volatile public debate over the symbolic meaning of their kneeling. Current and former players, some of them activists themselves, debated the merits of their protests. Presidential candidate Donald Trump claimed on August 29, 2016, that the protest was a "terrible thing" and that Kaepernick should consider moving to a country "that works better for him."[5] Days later—on September 7—NFL Commissioner Roger Goodell distanced the league from Kaepernick's actions. He acknowledged that Kaepernick had a "right" to protest but, he said, "I don't necessarily agree with what he is doing." American society was "imperfect," yet players should be "respectful" of the nation's shared values and seek to unite the people rather than divide them. Goodell explained, "I think it's important to have respect for our country, for our flag, for the people who make our country better; for law enforcement, and for our military who are out fighting for our freedoms and our ideals."[6] The mainstream press mostly sided with the activists, citing both First Amendment rights and the significance of their cause, while on social media feedback also seemed to skew toward Kaepernick.[7]

Following the San Diego game, the players sharpened the iconography of their protest by setting up closer to the field. So when Kaepernick and Reid knelt before the season opener against the Los Angeles Rams on September 12—held at home on Monday night in front of a national television audience—Marcio Sanchez had an unobstructed view, and his photograph seems to place the two men in the spotlight. At the same time, on the other side of the field, several Rams raised their fists in solidarity with Kaepernick and Reid. Three days earlier, in Denver, Broncos player Brandon Marshall also took a knee. Meanwhile, on September 4, soccer star Megan Rapinoe had knelt before her game with the Seattle Reign, explaining that she wanted to support Kaepernick and that as a gay woman she understood "what it means to look at the flag and not have it protect all your liberties."[8] By mid-September, college and high school football players across the nation were taking a knee and creating what journalist Dave Zirin calls "the Kaepernick effect."[9]

What does it mean to kneel? On football fields, players routinely take a knee when joining a meeting, often clustering around a coach. In formal spaces, most often in church, kneeling is a position of supplication and humility that acknowledges the presence of a higher authority. In African American history and culture, taking a knee has a powerful and contradictory significance. The contradictions are manifest in photos of Rev. Martin Luther King Jr. and his colleagues kneeling and praying for the Lord's guidance in the battle for civil rights. Their body language speaks to transcendent powers. But the images also recall the subjugation of Black people, the brutal history of which is captured by representations of the prostrate slave, about to be whipped by a white master. In postbellum representations of Abraham Lincoln, especially statues, artists refigured this image to show a grateful slave bowed down before the Great Emancipator and a benevolent God.[10]

In Sanchez's October 2 photograph, Kaepernick, Reid, and Harold might resemble statues, but their muscled, athletic presence, as coiled as it is prayerful, does not suggest memorial acceptance, but rather purposeful resolve, a pause before whatever action might ensue from the reflection signaled by Kaepernick's sampling of Auguste Rodin's 1904 sculpture, *The Thinker*. Together, the group constitutes an updated version of what historian Derrick White calls the "sporting congregation," his term for the interconnected communities that historically Black colleges and universities fostered through the development of successful football teams in the early to mid-twentieth century. Under the leadership of coaches such as Jake Gaither (Florida A&M) and Eddie Robinson (Grambling), football was "both familiar and different"—familiar because the game was the same and aimed at molding the character of young men, but different from the programs at prominently white institutions because the sport was inseparable from the Black colleges' larger effort to promote independence in a segregated, racist culture.[11]

By kneeling, Kaepernick and other Black players no doubt exercised their power as celebrity athletes in twenty-first-century America. But as critic Gerald Early points out, even though elite athletics "is perhaps the most theatrical and emotional form of ritualized honor that we have left in the world," the Black men and women that compete in this space do not necessarily enjoy the same privileges as white athletes. Early asserts, given "the stigma that African Americans bear as socially inferior people, the ghost of slavery frequently haunts virtually any physical labor they may choose to perform."[12] Arguably, Kaepernick felt the effects of this legacy when the NFL appeared to blackball him for his protests. But he did not become a ghost. Instead, he took ownership of his image and sought to direct the future of his decisive moment.

What seems clear from this still-evolving history is that soon after Kaepernick decided to take a knee he was thinking strategically about how he could use his image to advance the cause of Black Lives Matter. Significantly, in the months following his August 2016 statements to the press, he rarely spoke in public about his protests. When he became a free agent after the 2016 season and was unemployed, at least by the NFL, he preferred to communicate on social media, especially Twitter, where, by the fall of 2018, he had posted more than 11,000 times. And increasingly, his posts were retweets—words, images, or videos that others circulated which he then shared under his name. Thus Kaepernick spoke "without speaking," as the *New York Times* put it, supported by allies who made sure that he would not be silenced. In April 2018, Amnesty International honored him as an Ambassador of Conscience and, at the ceremony in Amsterdam, he talked briefly about his commitment to social justice.[13] By then he had already built his brand, an achievement that Nike formalized in commercial terms when the sporting goods manufacturer signed him to a marketing deal in the fall of 2018. The first advertisement of the Kaepernick "#JustDoIt" campaign was a tightly framed black-and-white photograph of his face, which he launched from his personal Twitter account. Nike also pasted a caption on the image, emphasizing one lesson that could be drawn from the quarterback's activism: "Believe in something. Even if it means sacrificing everything."[14]

Combining images and text is a common strategy on social media, and here the call to belief was imbedded in a network of real-life tableaus and photographs of protests that had been expanding for more than two years. Unsurprisingly, the reaction to the Nike campaign mirrored the response to the kneeling campaign, as outraged fans (or consumers) countered with their own online posts, for instance, photos of Nike socks with the Swoosh cut from the tops and promises to boycott the company.[15] Fifty years earlier, it would have been unthinkable for a corporation to support Tommie Smith and John Carlos's or Muhammad Ali's protests. Now, with a diverse, international customer base, Nike's objectives were not so different from Kaepernick's. The company understood it was good business—responsible corporate citizenship—to market the quarterback's willingness to "take a stand," as Nike founder Phil Knight might say. Indeed, one year after endorsing Kaepernick's campaign, Nike claimed a $6 billion increase in "brand value" and a sizeable upswing in sales.[16]

Although the photographs that Marcio Jose Sanchez took in the fall of 2016 documented Colin Kaepernick's civil rights campaign, they also advanced it. Their significance, like the protests themselves, evolved over time. This last point became painfully clear on May 25, 2020, when George Floyd, a Black man in Minneapolis, was killed by a white policeman, Derek Chauvin, who knelt on his neck for nine minutes and twenty-nine seconds. As news and images of the murder spread, the act of kneeling took on new meaning. Floyd's death ignited street protests and supercharged the movement, prompting many more Americans to support the credo "Black Lives Matter." Then on June 5, Roger Goodell announced on Twitter: "We, the NFL, condemn racism and the systematic oppression of Black People. We, the NFL, admit we were wrong for not listening to NFL players and encourage all to speak out and peacefully protest."[17] The quarterback was unsigned, but the vision of Colin Kaepernick had become a cliché to move the nation.

NOTES

1. Henri Cartier Bresson, "Foreword," in *The Decisive Moment* (New York: Simon & Schuster, 1952), n.p.; Catherine E. Clark, *Paris and the Cliché of History: The City and Photographs, 1860–1970* (New York: Oxford University Press, 2018), 8–9; Alex Beneviste, "The Meaning and History of Memes," *New York Times*, January 26, 2022, https://www.nytimes.com/2022/01/26/crosswords/what-is-a-meme.html.

2. Cindy Boren, "A Timeline of Colin Kaepernick's Protests against Police Brutality, Four Years after They Began," *Washington Post*, August 26, 2020, https://www.washingtonpost.com/sports/2020/06/01/colin-kaepernick-kneeling-history/; quoted in Steve Wyche, "Colin Kaepernick Explains Why He Sat during National Anthem," NFL.com, August 27, 2016, https://www.nfl.com/news/colin-kaepernick-explains-why-he-sat-during-national-anthem-0ap3000000691077.

3. Cam Inman, "Colin Kaepernick Takes Knee during Anthem, Joined by Eric Reid," *East Bay Times*, September 1, 2015, https://www.eastbaytimes.com/2016/09/01/colin-kaepernick-takes-knee-during-anthem-joined-by-eric-reid/.

4. Elliott J. Gorn and Warren Goldstein, *A Brief History of American Sports* (New York: Hill and Wang, 1993), 177–181; John Sayle Watterson, *College Football: History, Spectacle, Controversy* (Baltimore: Johns Hopkins University Press, 2000), 202–203; Jesse Berrett, *Pigskin Nation: How the NFL Remade American Politics* (Urbana: University of Illinois Press, 2018), 66–75; Adam Kilgore, "For Decades, the NFL Wrapped Itself in the Flag. Now, That's Made Business Uneasy," *Washington Post*, September 6, 2018, https://www.washingtonpost.com/sports/for-decades-the-nfl-wrapped-itself-in-the-flag-now-thats-made-business-uneasy/2018/09/06/bc9aab64-b05d-11e8-9a6a-565d92a3585d_story.html.

5. Eric Branch, "Sit and Cause Uproar: White House, Trump, Harbaugh Weigh in on Kaepernick," *SFGATE*, August 29, 2016, https://www.sfgate.com/49ers/article/Sit-and-cause-uproar-White-House-Trump-9191817.php.

6. Quoted in "Roger Goodell: I Don't Necessarily Agree with Colin Kaepernick's Protest," *Sports Illustrated*, September 7, 2016, https://www.si.com/nfl/2016/09/07/roger-goodell-colin-kaepernick-national-anthem-protest-comments.

7. Jules Boykoff and Ben Carrington, "Sporting Dissent: Colin Kaepernick, NFL Activism, and Media Framing Contests," *International Review for the Sociology of Sport* 55 (November 2020): 832–835, 844–845.

8. Quoted in John D. Halloran, "Megan Rapinoe Kneels for Anthem at NWSL Match," American Soccer Now, September 4, 2016, http://americansoccernow.com/articles/megan-rapinoe-kneels-for-anthem-at-nwsl-match.

9. "Colin Kaepernick Kneels for Anthem; 2 Rams Raise Fists in Protest," *Chicago Tribune*, September 12, 2016, https://www.chicagotribune.com/sports/ct-nfl-niners-rams-spt-20160912-story.html; Dave Zirin, *The Kaepernick Effect: Taking a Knee, Changing the World* (New York: the New Press, 2021).

10. "Group of Civil Rights Prays," AP Images, accessed March 30, 2022, http://www.apimages.com/metadata/Index/Watchf-AP-S-AL-USA-APHS237659-Group-of-Civil-Ri-/f70831865cd34aa9866c07e7d060b232/1/0; Kirk Savage, *Standing Soldiers, Kneeling Slaves: Race, War, and Monument in Nineteenth-Century America* (Princeton, NJ: Princeton University Press, 1997).

11. Derrick E. White, *Blood, Sweat, & Tears: Jake Gaither, Florida A&M, and the History of Black College Football* (Chapel Hill: University of North Carolina Press, 2019), 22–23. See also Samuel Freedman, *Breaking the Line: The Season in Black College Football That Transformed the Sport and Changed the Course of Civil Rights* (New York: Simon & Schuster, 2013).

12. Gerald L. Early, *A Level Playing Field: African American Athletes and the Republic of Sports* (Cambridge: Harvard University Press, 2011), 3, 6.

13. Benjamin Hoffman and Talya Minsberg, "The Deafening Silence of Colin Kaepernick," *New York Times*, September 4, 2018, https://www.nytimes.com/2018/09/04/sports/colin-kaepernick-nfl-anthem-kneeling.html; "Colin Kaepernick: Ambassador of Conscience," Amnesty International, https://www.amnesty.org/en/latest/news/2018/04/colin-kaepernick-ambassador-of-conscience/; "Colin Kaepernick Will Not Be Silenced," *GQ*, November 13, 2107, https://www.gq.com/story/colin-kaepernick-will-not-be-silenced.

14. Kevin Draper and Ken Belson, "Colin Kaepernick's Nike Campaign Keeps NFL Anthem Kneeling in Spolight," *New York Times*, September 3, 2018, https://www.nytimes.com/2018/09/03/sports/kaepernick-nike.html.

15. Draper and Belson, "Colin Kaepernick's Nike Campaign."

16. Jeff Beer, "One Year Later, What Did We Learn from Nike's Blockbuster Colin Kaepernick Ad," *Fast Company*, September 5, 2019, https://www.fastcompany.com/90399316/one-year-later-what-did-we-learn-from-nikes-blockbuster-colin-kaepernick-ad.

17. Ken Belson, "As Trump Rekindles N.F.L. Fight, Goodell Sides with Players," *New York Times*, June 5, 2020, https://www.nytimes.com/2020/06/05/sports/football/trump-anthem-kneeling-kaepernick.html.

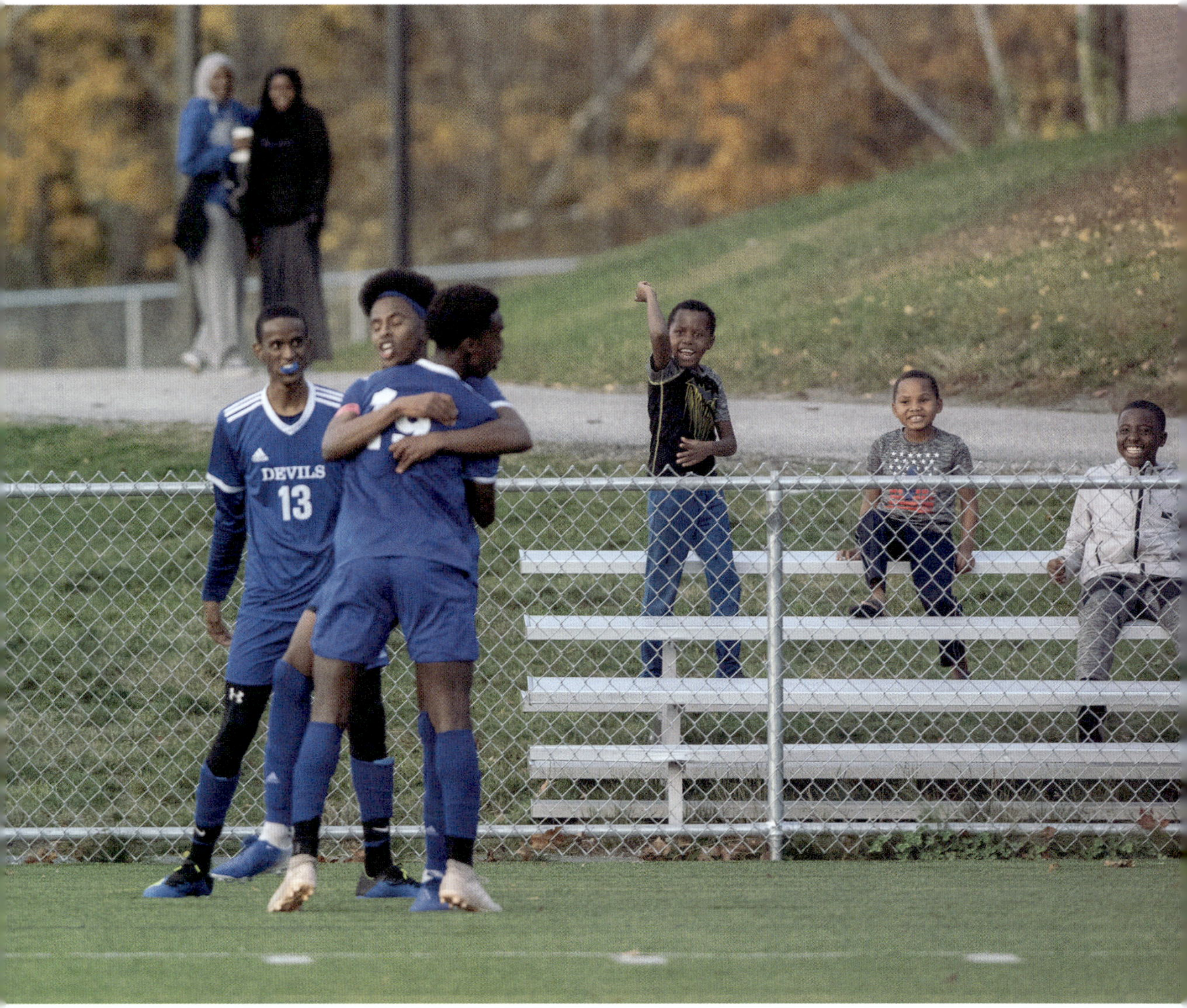
DEVILS
13

25

THE HUG

Finding a Community's Future on the Pitch

AMY BASS

On first glance, I thought the photograph of what I now call *The Hug* was a classic celebration image, a joyful instant in small-town sports caused by a successful penalty kick or the sound of the buzzer signifying the game was won. Our trained eyes digest such images within the tried and true "rule of thirds," a composition structure that divides an image uniformly into three parts, vertically and horizontally, with the focus positioned at the crossroads of the dividing lines.

With this photo, my eyes fixed on how Lewiston High School's standout soccer star, Bilal Hersi, hair pushed back by a blue headband, embraced teammate Suhaib Nur while Ayub Hassan looked on, blue mouthguard dangling from his lips. On the other side of the field's fence, three grinning boys dressed in sweats cheered from the bleachers—one standing with his fist clenched overhead—for what had just transpired. Up the hill, just out of focus, stood two smiling teen girls dressed in a cultural cacophony of hijab and hoodies, long skirts and sneakers.

While I appreciated the photo's composition, I first marveled at how much Ayub looked like his older brother Dek, who stood in the same space just a few years ago. Dek is a main character in my book *One Goal* (2018), which uses the 2015 Lewiston Blue Devils boys' soccer championship season, featuring a starting lineup composed almost entirely of refugees, as a window into the recent and rapid migration of thousands of Somalis into this French-Canadian city in Maine, profiling the hatred they faced as well as the success stories they delivered.

Primarily, the photograph, taken by *Lewiston Sun Journal* photographer Russell Dillingham, tells a sport story. Dillingham took the photo on October 30, 2019, after Hersi scored in the first half during the Maine Boys Class A North quarterfinal match against Hampden Academy, a home game, as indicated by their blue uniforms. Hersi, inarguably the greatest soccer player in Lewiston High School's history, finished that game, a 5–1 Blue Devils' victory, with three goals and two assists despite being double-marked. *Sun Journal* sportswriter Wil Kramlich's story about the game featured several of Dillingham's action shots, such as Lewiston's Abdilahi Abdi fighting for a loose ball against Hampden's Morgan Tash and then driving the ball down the pitch.

Such photos rely on our knowledge of the game, giving sports photographers an advantage in making meaning. The game's rules offer insight as to where good shots might be, what scholar Markus Stauff calls "identifying elements"—team colors, a player's number, and instant results on the scoreboard.[1] Because of this foundational knowledge, we know how to read two players hugging, as well as fans cheering in the stands. Thus, Dillingham's image did not need a caption to convey that something good had just happened.

However, when we take in the characters more deeply—the players on the field, the boys in the stands, and the young women in the background—we see that something more significant is going on beyond a goal in a playoff game on a beautiful fall afternoon in Maine, orange and yellow leaves filling the background while the grass beyond the turf of Lewiston's Don Roux Field holds onto its green. With this photo, Dillingham had shot the visual counterpart of a sequel to my book on race, community, and soccer, somewhat answering a question I often get from readers: What's going on in Lewiston today?

Sport beyond the Age of Mechanical Reproduction

Dissecting photos, argues sport historian Mike Huggins, requires us to "explore their context, content and meaning, and the play of intention, myth, silence, and power . . . When we explore a picture, we need to follow its performative trajectories, map its social biographies, and acknowledge the primary content for grappling with the mutability of its meaning."[2] Establishing context, of course, is critical; it creates a narrative map for us to understand what we are looking at and helps establish our gaze. *How* we look at a photograph is as important as *what* we are looking at, with multiple ways of seeing within whatever time and space we occupy, as well as the time and space of the photo. In this way, Huggins continues, "gaze is a crucial feature of public sporting experience."[3]

Sports photos are usually relegated to the sports section of a publication, creating an "everyday nature" that scholar Lynda Nead contends is why they are often overlooked.[4] However, changes in the news industry have expanded the medium from a daily print edition to the wealth of representations afforded by videos, galleries, and slideshows, making it harder to spotlight where shots with a more sophisticated editorial sensibility can surface while allowing a broader range of photographs to see the light of day.

Dillingham understands how technology has changed what he can accomplish with his camera, but still thinks that one photo should be enough to get the job done. "It's more than just snapping photos and moving on—I want to grab my readers and be able to tell a story," he says. "Telling an entire story with one photo back in print—now we have more opportunity to package things with video, and so on, but back in the day, you had to capture everything. The reader shouldn't have to read the caption if the photo is good enough."[5]

The *Sun Journal*'s support of local photography is not the norm today. As sports media scholars Richard Haynes et al. point out, "sports photojournalists must grapple with a range of challenges that collectively threaten the very sustainability and future of their art, ironically at a moment when the image has never been as ubiquitous or as important . . . for demonstrating athletic prowess."[6] The newspaper published *The Hug* in an online gallery; it was the eighth of ten photos. "Fans and teammates celebrate a goal by Lewiston's Bilal Hersi, headband, left," read the caption, "during the first half of Wednesday's playoff game against Hampden Academy."

I first encountered the photo on Dillingham's Facebook page. "I am always in awe at the skills of high school athletes these days, soccer in particular," he posted alongside the photographs. "If you have not been to a Lewiston soccer game in a while, treat yourself to the next one as they advanced in the state tournament with a victory over Hampden Academy today. I had some good action shots but I think my favorites today were more candid moments."[7]

"I cannot describe to you how many emotions I feel when I take this photo in!" commented a longtime Lewiston teacher about *The Hug*, while a *Sun Journal* colleague succinctly stated, "This one is a gem."

"The comments were so gushing," Dillingham remembers. "It made me feel good, and it reflected how the community felt."

That I discovered this image on Facebook is an example of how the growth of social media has altered our visual landscape. In this case, a professional photojournalist used Facebook to create greater circulation for an image he felt needed more attention, encouraging multiple readings of it—what scholar Mike O'Mahony calls a "plurality of interpretative possibilities."[8] Social media, of course, is only one of the ways that sport has broadened its spectatorship, moving beyond the stands, beyond radio and television, and into hourly check-ins with various online platforms that provide additional ways for people to experience sports, whether via livestream or after the fact.

Yet even amidst the chaos of Facebook, the photo stood out as visually stunning and perfectly composed: the players standing in unspoken conversation with the three cheering boys; the two girls looking on from afar. Its aesthetic ensures that while sports photos are generally about people, the landscape plays an important role alongside the spectators and athletes, lending to the photo's powerful ability to not only disseminate information about the game but also to provoke questions. Did the young women pause and take a look because they heard the cheering, becoming stakeholders in this game alongside the ardent fans with front-row seats? Did the boys know the importance of a game in late fall, that it was likely do-or-die to take the next step toward a championship berth?

As most people with even the faintest understanding of Maine and Mainers should appreciate, the chief takeaway from this image goes beyond what the players or fans might be thinking or how it fulfills technical standards of good photography. This is in part because, as Rafael Marfil-Carmona et al. posit, "the commitment to expressiveness goes beyond the exercise of faithful reproduction of formal characteristics or, at least, the selection of reality is precisely the one that offers the greatest degree of visual poetics in photographs that have nuances of great importance in the final message and in their perception."[9]

The story of Lewiston soccer, as I write in *One Goal*, is inspiring and edifying. It can be thought of as a quintessentially American story, impossibly local and yet with global concerns regarding who belongs and where. It provides a window into how an economically stressed former mill town in one of the whitest states in the country came to be a model of African refugee resettlement, with soccer a significant bridge between longtime Mainers and predominantly Somali newcomers. Amidst a wealth of cultural differences, coaches and players created a critical center in figuring out how the city could move forward with its new residents, as the shared passion for soccer forged a pathway to healing fractures that the arrival of thousands of newcomers did not necessarily create, but exposed.

Thus, while the comradery expressed by Hersi and his teammates makes for a happy photo, it is the game's spectators who take the image's meaning to the next level, offering a snapshot of Somali achievements in the city and a glimpse of what lies ahead. The exaltation of the boys on the bleachers, their razor-sharp focus on the game clear, positions them as the future of what else may take place on that field someday. The young women who remain in the background, a bit blurry but still belonging, represent the confidence of Somali girls at school, emerging as leaders in academics and clubs, but (with a few exceptions) not yet on center stage in Lewiston sports.

A Photographer's Community

Dillingham takes seriously the photographer's fundamental role in Lewiston's growing refugee community. Because of what he describes as a "hard beginning" with the newcomers, he knew that building trust was essential to capturing Lewiston's transformation on camera. "They themselves were very reserved, shy, and afraid, and we saw it walking down the street," he remembers of the early days of the Somalis settling into the city. "They wouldn't look at you and God forbid if you pulled out a camera."

Dillingham worked hard to establish relationships within the new community, even leading a camera club at Longley Elementary School, which included kids from the poorest neighborhoods in Lewiston. Twice a week after school, Dillingham brought cameras and snacks to Longley and talked to the kids, many of whom were Somali, about photography. "It was more of a social thing," he recalls. "I was embedded in the community—they grew up with me, and it helped a lot. Over and over and over again, they would see me taking photos and that comfort level developed."

Dillingham also thinks that publishing stories and photos that highlighted the good of the community helped a lot. "They came to understand what our jobs were and they knew we didn't have an agenda."

"Now," he continues, "they are all 'TAKE MY PICTURE!' Even the older ones, including the parents—they understand what I am there to do and that I am not trying to get them. It's part of being in the community."

So is soccer. While World Press Photo (WPP) claims soccer is the most photographed sport in the world, high-profile soccer shots are a relatively recent phenomenon for the *Sun Journal*. Lewiston was, is, and likely forever will be a hockey town, with twenty-five boys state championship titles and a girls' program that has produced four state titles in its relatively short history. Dillingham played hockey and a little soccer as a kid, and finds hockey, which according to WPP is the least photographed sport worldwide, to be the hardest to shoot.[10]

"Soccer," he says, "is like shooting fish in a barrel—if you have ten minutes to shoot any sport to have something really good, soccer would be that sport. There's so much going on—the facial expressions, the closeness, the action, the relationships—everything is right there. You have so many opportunities."

Sport photography, again, has predictability to it because of the rules of each game: when it starts, pauses, and ends, and when moments of celebration will befall the victor and flashes of despair will envelope the vanquished. "Sport's focus on performance, competition, and quantifiable results," Stauff observes, "has consequences for the way images are taken, how they circulate, and how they get entangled with other media."[11]

But photojournalism does more than just record what happened. It informs, tells a story. And Dillingham's image of Hersi, his teammates, and their fans covers far more of Lewiston's story than the merriment on the field. Is the photo really about Bilal celebrating yet another goal? Or is it about the cheering boys in the bleachers who might hope to someday wear those uniforms? The photograph allows for this deeper reading, giving *Sun Journal* readers the chance, as Huggins puts it, "to see familiar things differently," capitalizing on the "symbolic language systems" encompassed in visual objects.[12]

Lewiston is not known as a sport mecca. And yet its most famous sport moment, the heavyweight championship bout between Muhammad Ali and Sonny Liston, rescheduled to Lewiston's Colisée because of an odd twist of circumstances, produced one of America's most famous sport photographs: Neil Leifer's iconic image of a towering Ali standing over a felled Liston, a first-round knockout from a so-called phantom punch during their 1965 title fight, which Carlo Rotella expertly unpacks in this volume. Leifer has explained what many consider to be the best sports photo of the century as having had a bit of luck. "Luck in sports photography is everything and what separates the top sports photographer from the ordinary is that when he or she gets lucky, they don't miss," he's said of his famous photo. "That is the key. But you have to be lucky."[13]

Dillingham does not entirely agree. "It's still all about the moment," he says, thinking about how he prepares for a shot. "We wait for the moment, we anticipate, we set ourselves in the position to get it and we cannot be afraid to fail—things don't always turn out, you wait and wait, but sometimes the moment doesn't happen."

To understand the significance of *The Hug*, to set up the photo so that the spectators are as important as the players on the field, Dillingham had to appreciate the community and its history, particularly the ebb and flow of its racial tensions around the refugee migrations. That understanding took work, and Dillingham recognizes how his worldview evolved in terms of Lewiston's radical demographic transformations, particularly as Somali players began to dominate soccer.

The New Lewiston

Bilal Hersi, the son of Abdullahi Abdi and Nadifo Isaak, epitomizes that change. He has been the center of many *Sun Journal* soccer photos, whether from his days in a Blue Devils uniform, his later career playing Division I soccer for Siena College, or as a member of the Somali National Team. He was the third of his brothers to play for Lewiston. In 2014, his older brother, Abdijabar, became the first Somali coach in Lewiston schools, and his father—Coach A to most players—runs recreational leagues and tournaments and serves as the unofficial righthand confidant to the Blue Devils coaching staff.

As a two-year captain and the all-time leading scorer of the storied Blue Devils, Bilal was used to being photographed. He personifies how "great players," as Roland Barthes observed, "are not stars, they are heroes," validated by the boys watching him from the bleachers.[14] He led two state championship high school teams, was a two-time Gatorade Player of the Year and a three-time All-American, and was named the Global Premier Soccer National Team Player of the Year. Everyone at the *Sun Journal* knew him well. But Dillingham knew that the moment of the hug was special—and he was prepared:

> I have shot photos like this forever—action is great, the guy scoring the winning goal. But to tell more, and give the reader something that they don't normally see. The symmetry, the background, it just really sang. I've shot so many of Bilal scoring goals, shooting—game action. But I saw those kids sitting in the bleachers, I'd seen them before, and I was ready for it. They were cheering. I could've focused on the celebration of the players but that element in the background was too cool. I was thinking these kids who are celebrating on the field were once in the same position as the kids on the bleachers. I won't be surprised if they are on the field in a few years.

Born and raised in Lewiston, the grandson of the founder of the *Sun Journal,* Dillingham returned to his hometown after graduating from Assumption College, setting aside his dreams of becoming a psychologist in a big city because he could not shake the summers he spent working in the newspaper's press room. He picked up a camera thinking that his own background with sports, combined with a good eye, would enable him to anticipate good shots.

"I began to fill in on vacations, cranking, and began to outshoot some of the staff photographers," he remembers. "As nepotism has it, that's how I got my start. I fell in love with everything about it."

Dillingham's personal attachment to Lewiston's transformation over the last two decades helps explain why *The Hug* exists. It is a clear example of how photography is never an unbiased medium, not just because of the ability to edit—especially in the digital age—and crop, brighten, and saturate, but also because, as scholar Margaret Carlisle Duncan observes, "photographers constantly impose their own aesthetic, professional, and cultural standards on photographs . . . determining what should be the subject of the photograph and how that subject should look before the shot is ever taken."[15]

"I can't reinforce the fact enough that it is so much more than taking the sports photos," says Dillingham. "As good as those photos are, it is something like this that is more impactful, that has more emotion. It isn't just Bilal scoring. Someone who isn't a sports fan would stop and look at this photo."

Yet it is also important to recognize the counternarratives that can make a photograph "a slippery customer," in the words of Stuart Hall, with "competing" and "contested" interpretations always in play.[16] Dan Gish, who was longtime head coach Mike McGraw's assistant for many years before taking the team's reins after McGraw retired, remembers a moment just a few days before the 2015 championship game when a friend said to him, "You know, I'm from Lewiston, and I know what Lewiston pride is all about and that's not it."[17] Gish walked away, dismayed at his friend's not-so-subtle sentiment about a varsity team composed largely of African refugees. The episode demonstrates how some might digest the photo from a different point of view. While Dillingham wanted to illustrate how a community comes together, as well as what the future might look like, the Somali migration stirred a range of reactions, including racist and Islamophobic vitriol.

But perhaps the palpable enthusiasm of the boys on the bleachers on a stunning fall day watching a high school soccer game, their dreams something we can only assume, erases, even combats, some of the hatred, offering us a front-row seat to a very American story. In an era in which fandom is no longer defined by fans' physical presence at a game but rather their dedication to their TV, phone, or computer, preventing them from grabbing an autograph or even a high five, this photograph, with almost old-fashioned logic, provides a vision for this team, this city, and—maybe—this world. It is the boys, along with the young women behind them, readying themselves to walk through the door to their future, who represent what is to come, not just in terms of the team but the community writ large. These spectators make clear how, as Huggins argues, images are "powerful historical agents in their own right," perhaps especially when they highlight the "power relations and social interactions" within the context of when and where they were taken, and by whom.[18] In this way, these high school soccer fans take on important roles as signifiers of the hope the newcomers brought to Lewiston. The city's bench is deep, literally and figuratively.

NOTES

1. Markus Stauff, "The Assertive Image: Referentiality and Reflexivity in Sports Photography," *Historical Social Research* 43, no. 2 (2018): 57.

2. Mike Huggins, "The Sporting Gaze: Towards a Visual Turn in Sports History—Documenting Art and Sport," *Journal of Sport History* 35 (Summer 2008): 318.

3. Huggins, "The Sporting Gaze," 320.

4. Lynda Nead, "Stilling the Punch: Boxing, Violence and the Photographic Image," *Journal of Visual Culture* 10 (December 2011): 309.

5. Russell Dillingham, phone interview with the author, January 24, 2022. All subsequent quotes from Dillingham are from this conversation and follow-up emails.

6. Richard Haynes, Adrian Hadland, and Paul Lambert, "The State of Sport Photojournalism: Concepts, Practice and Challenges," *Digital Journalism* 5, no. 5 (2017): 637.

7. Russell Dillingham's personal Facebook page, accessed October 31, 2019.

8. Mike O'Mahony, "Through a Glass Darkly: Reflections on Photography and the Visual Representation of Sport," *Historical Social Research* 43 (2018): 32.

9. Rafael Marfil-Carmona, Pilar Puertas-Molero, Félix Zurita-Ortega, Gabriel González-Valero, "Photography and Sport: Study of the Didactic Value of Reference Images in Photojournalism, Analysis of the Winning Photos of the World Press Photo in 2017," *Journal of Human Sport and Exercise* 13, no. 2 (2018): 546.

10. Haynes, Hadland, and Lambert, "The State of Sport Photojournalism," 643.

11. Stauff, "The Assertive Image," 68.

12. Huggins, "The Sporting Gaze," 312.

13. Dave Mondy, "How Things Break," *Iowa Review* 44 (Winter 2014/15). Neil Leifer quoted in David Katz, "Neil Leifer on Being Good, Being Lucky," *The Post Game*, December 23, 2011, http://www.thepostgame.com/interviews/201112/neil-leifer-sports-photographer-interview-sports-illustrated-ali-liston-giants-col.

14. Quoted in Marfil-Carmona et al., "Photography and Sport," 542.

15. Margaret Carlisle Duncan, "Sports Photographs and Sexual Difference: Images of Women and Men in the 1984 and 1988 Olympics," *Sociology of Sport Journal* 7 (1990): 23.

16. Stuart Hall, *Representation: Cultural Representations and Signifying Practice* (London: Sage, 1997), 9.

17. Quoted in Bass, *One Goal*, 244.

18. Mike Huggins, "The Visual in Sport History: Approaches, Methodologies and Sources," *International Journal of the History of Sport* 32 (2015): 1816.

ACKNOWLEDGMENTS

As one would expect, this book has been truly collaborative at every turn, and it is our pleasure to acknowledge many of the people and institutions that contributed to making *Sports through the Lens*.

First and most obviously, we are grateful to our talented contributors. Their willingness to share their time, energy, knowledge, and insight made this book happen. Their generosity, professionalism, and patience are deeply appreciated.

Some of this work was initially presented at the annual meeting of the North American Society for Sport History (NASSH), an organization that has nurtured our work and careers and has been one of our most important intellectual and professional homes. Many NASSHers—too many to list here—made valuable comments on this work that improved it. Thank you.

Maureen writes: When I was ten, I received a subscription to *Sports Illustrated*. Every week, I was transported by the images and stories in it, largely conveyed by their amazing photographs. I relied on those photographers to transport me to the sidelines and rarely thought about their artistry and skill. Now I know better.

My deepest appreciation for Dan Nathan and Sarah Fields. Doing a project like this with friends is a privilege. Their wit, wisdom, and intellect bring me joy on a regular basis and I'm looking forward to the next collaboration. Their friendship over the decades continues to be a genuine treasure.

A hearty thanks to my walk and talk buddies, Timi Poeppelman and Cindy Long Nicholson.

I'm grateful for the support of the College of Health and Human Services at Sacramento State University.

As with all things in my life, this experience was made even sweeter by sharing it with my family, Mary and Quinn Maguire. Mary, your generosity of spirit and devotion are unparalleled—simply put, I'm just a better me with you by my side. Quinn, you are my favorite athlete to photograph, but more importantly, an amazing kid who fills my life with laughter and love.

While we were working on this book, my grandmother, Florence Tully, died; she was 101. She came of age during the Great Depression and World War II, and her interest and participation in sport paled in comparison to my own. As she aged into her nineties, we began to talk more about her early life, aided by old photos. One day, I happened upon a black-and-white image of her on skis. You can imagine my surprise, both upon finding the image and the narrative she told connected to it. Those storytelling sessions were central to my own thinking about how a seemingly simple image is a critical piece of evidence in our own sporting narratives. I miss her terribly and am so thankful for those images and her stories.

Dan writes: I am deeply grateful to Mo, who had the idea that became this book, and to Sarah for her indefatigable work securing the rights and permissions for the images in these pages—and for our rich intellectual conversations, good cheer, and years of friendship.

For many years, my Skidmore College colleagues Erica Bastress-Dukehart, Beau Breslin, John Brueggemann, Matt Hockenos, Beck Krefting, María Lander, Andrew Lindner, Susan Matrazzo, Pat Oles, Tammy Owens, Aaron Pedinotti, Greg Pfitzer, and Jeff Segrave have been supportive of my work, generous, stimulating, and, well, lots of fun.

Additionally, Skidmore College's Faculty Development Committee and Associate Dean of the Faculty Janet Casey's support of this book was invaluable and is appreciated.

Susan Taylor, Ben and Zoë Nathan, Jerrilyn Matthews, Irvin Nathan, and Judy Walter are the most important people in, and the foundation of, my life. My debt to them is incalculable; my gratitude is deep.

Sarah writes: We greatly appreciate the financial support that the University of Colorado Denver provided to obtain the rights to the images in this book. We specifically thank the Office of Research Services, the College of Liberal Arts and Sciences, and the Department of Communication for funding. Thanks as well to Michelle A. Médal of the COMM Department who worked tirelessly to help manage and distribute the funds.

I would also like to thank my colleagues at CU Denver who always offer sage advice and support: Michelle Comstock, Boram Jeong, Amy Hasinoff, Sarah Hagelin, Lisa Keränen, Gillian Silverman, and Sarah Tyson. Further, without Dawn Comstock, I would be nowhere: thank you. I also thank Mo and Dan for including me in this project and modeling great editorial skills. They are and have been great colleagues and friends.

At the University of Texas Press, Robert Devens, Casey Kittrell, Sarah McGavick, Mia Uribe Kozlovsky, Lynne Ferguson, and Aaron Teel all contributed to and championed this project and made it better. We are grateful for their support and to have this book in the Terry and Jan Todd Series on Physical Culture and Sports.

This book is dedicated to Susan Birrell and Tina Parratt—teachers, mentors, colleagues, and friends. Their fingerprints are all over our work. With love and gratitude.

CONTRIBUTORS

AMY BASS is a professor of sport studies and chair of the Division of Social Science & Communication at Manhattanville College. She is the author of several books, including *Not the Triumph but the Struggle: The 1968 Olympic Games and the Making of the Black Athlete* (2002) and *One Goal: A Coach, a Team, and the Game That Brought a Divided Town Together* (2018), which was named a best book of 2018 by *Library Journal* and the *Boston Globe*. She is a frequent contributor to CNN, as well as other mainstream media outlets, and has worked across eight Olympic Games for NBC Sports, winning an Emmy Award for Live Event Turnaround in 2012.

ASHLEY BROWN is the Allan H. Selig Chair in Sport and Society in U.S. History at the University of Wisconsin-Madison. She is the author of *Serving Herself: The Life and Times of Althea Gibson* (2023). Among her other works are "Swinging for the State Department: American Women Tennis Players in Diplomatic Goodwill Tours, 1941–1959," published by the *Journal of Sport History*, and "'Uncomplimentary Things': Tennis Player Althea Gibson, Sexism, Homophobia, and Anti-Queerness in the Black Media," which appeared in the *Journal of African American History*.

MICHAEL L. BUTTERWORTH is a professor in the Department of Communication Studies, Governor Ann W. Richards Chair for the Texas Program in Sports and Media, and director of the Center for Sports Communication & Media in the Moody College of Communication at The University of Texas at Austin. His research explores the connections among rhetoric, democracy, and sport, with particular interests in national identity, militarism, and public memory. His books include *Baseball and Rhetorics of Purity* (2010), *Sport and Militarism: Contemporary Global Perspectives* (2017), *Sport, Rhetoric, and Political Struggle* (2019), and the *Handbook of Communication and Sport* (2021).

Following twenty-three years of practicing law, with an emphasis on military matters (e.g., defense counsel in the courts-martial cases "The Presidio 27" and "The Pendleton 14"), **HOWARD J. DE NIKE** earned a PhD in cultural anthropology from the University of New Mexico. De Nike has taught at San Francisco State University, University of New Mexico, and the Fromm Institute. His interests in retirement include ornithology and sports (see "The Phoebe, Me, and the

Giants," in *NINE: A Journal of Baseball History and Culture*).

SEAN DINCES is an associate professor in the Department of History, Political Science & Ethnic Studies at Long Beach City College (CA). He is the author of *Bulls Markets: Chicago's Basketball Business and the New Inequality* (2022). For more on his teaching, research, and writing, see www.seandinces.com.

CHRIS ELZEY is a faculty member in the History and Art History Department at George Mason University. He teaches various courses on sport history, as well as global history. He also oversees the Sport and American Culture minor at George Mason. Among the topics he has written on are sport and the Cold War, and basketball history. He is the co-editor of *DC Sports: The Nation's Capital at Play* (2015).

RUSSELL FIELD is an associate professor in the Faculty of Kinesiology and Recreation Management at the University of Manitoba. His research explores sport and social justice. He is the author of *A Night at the Gardens: Class, Gender, and Respectability in 1930s Toronto* (2023); coauthor of *The History and Politics of Sport-for-Development: Activists, Ideologues and Reformers* (2019); and editor of the forthcoming *Winters of Discontent: The Winter Olympics and Half a Century of Protest and Resistance in/through Sport*. He also has a research interest in visual representations of sport and is the founder and executive director of the Canadian Sport Film Festival.

SARAH K. FIELDS is a professor of communication at the University of Colorado Denver. She is the author of *Game Faces: Sport Celebrity and the Laws of Reputation* (2016) and *Female Gladiators: Gender, Law, and Contact Sport in America* (2005), as well as the co-editor of *Sport and the Law: Historical and Cultural Intersections* (2014). She has authored or coauthored over eighty book chapters and articles in scholarly journals such as *Journal of Sport History*, *Journal of Sport Management*, *American Journal of Sports Medicine*, *Journal of Athletic Training*, and *JAMA: Pediatrics*.

JONATHAN FINN is a professor of communication studies at Wilfrid Laurier University. He is the author of *Capturing the Criminal Image: From Mug Shot to Surveillance Society* (2009) and *Beyond the Finish Line: Images, Evidence and the History of the Photo-Finish* (2020) and editor of *Visual Communication and Culture: Images in Action* (2012). His current research examines the use of self-tracking technologies in sport and fitness and is funded by the Social Sciences and Humanities Research Council of Canada. In 2023, he received the Award for Teaching Excellence in the category of Innovation from Wilfrid Laurier University.

GEORGE GMELCH is an emeriti professor of anthropology at the University of San Francisco and Union College. Before becoming an anthropologist, he played baseball in the Detroit Tigers organization. His earliest research was in Ireland among nomadic

Irish Travelers. Subsequent research was on return migration (Ireland, Newfoundland, and Barbados), fishing communities (Alaska and Newfoundland), nomadic Gypsies (England), tourism work (Barbados and the Napa Valley), mobile work and community (Newfoundland), and the culture of professional baseball. He is the author and editor of fifteen books dealing with these subjects. He is married to anthropologist Sharon Gmelch.

ELLIOTT J. GORN teaches history at Loyola University Chicago. He is author of *The Manly Art: Bare-Knuckle Prize Fighting in America* (1986), *Mother Jones: The Most Dangerous Woman in America* (2022), *Dillinger's Wild Ride: The Year That Made America's Public Enemy Number One* (2009), and *Let the People See: The Story of Emmett Till* (2019). He is coauthor, with Warren Goldstein, of *A Brief History of American Sports* (1993).

ALLEN GUTTMANN taught American and European cultural history at Amherst College, as well as several German and Japanese universities, from 1959 until 2013. Of his eleven sport history books, the most theoretically important is *From Ritual to Record: The Nature of Modern Sports* (1978), which has been translated into French, German, Italian, Portuguese, Chinese, Japanese, and Korean. His most readable book is *Sports: The First Five Millennia* (2004). His most recent book, illustrated with over one hundred images, is *Sports and American Art from Benjamin West to Andy Warhol* (2011).

MATTHEW KLUGMAN is an associate professor at Victoria University who studies the intersecting histories of images, race, emotions, sports, gender, sexuality, medicine, science, migration, and bodies. Klugman is a senior research fellow at the Institute for Health and Sport, a member of the Community, Identity and Displacement Research Network, and the co-convenor of the VU Olympic and Paralympic Research Centre.

NEAL MCCABE is the coauthor, with Constance McCabe, of *Baseball's Golden Age: The Photographs of Charles M. Conlon* (1993) and *The Big Show: Charles M. Conlon's Golden Age Baseball Photographs* (2011). He is also the co-producer, with Henry W. Thomas, of the audio version of Lawrence S. Ritter's *The Glory of Their Times: The Story of the Early Days of Baseball Told by the Men Who Played It* (1998).

DANIEL A. NATHAN is a professor of American studies at Skidmore College. He holds the Douglas Family Chair in American Culture, History, and Literary and Interdisciplinary Studies. The author of the award-winning *Saying It's So: A Cultural History of the Black Sox Scandal* (2003), Nathan has also published in *Aethlon*, *American Quarterly*, *Journal of American Studies*, *Journal of Sport History*, among other periodicals. He is the editor of *Rooting for the Home Team: Sport, Community and Identity* (2013) and *Baltimore Sports: Stories from Charm City* (2016), and the co-editor (with George Gmelch) of *Baseball Beyond*

Our Borders: An International Pastime (2017).

CHRISTINE O'BONSAWIN (Abenaki) is an associate professor of history and Indigenous studies at the University of Victoria. Her scholarship in sport history and Indigenous studies take up questions regarding the appropriation and subjugation of Indigenous peoples, identities, and cultures in Olympic history, as well as the legal and political rights of Indigenous peoples in settler colonial Canada, particularly in hosting the Olympic Games and other mega-sporting events on unsurrendered Indigenous territories.

GARY OSMOND is an associate professor of sport history in the School of Human Movement and Nutrition Sciences at the University of Queensland. His research focuses on the experiences of Aboriginal and Torres Strait Islander peoples in Australia during the twentieth century and on new approaches to investigating and reframing those pasts.

BERNARDO RAMIREZ RIOS is an associate professor of anthropology at Skidmore College, specializing in sports, migration, and identity studies. His scholarship contributes to understanding the relationship between sporting culture and the migrant experience, especially regarding youth. His book *Transnational Sport in the American West: Oaxaca California Basketball* (2019) provides an in-depth look at basketball in Oaxaca, Mexico, and its cultural impact on migrant communities in California. His work focuses on the anthropology of sports and the intersection of race, ethnicity, and basketball culture.

CARLO ROTELLA is the author of books about cities, literature, boxing, blues, and other subjects, the most recent of which is *The World Is Always Coming to an End: Pulling Together and Apart in a Chicago Neighborhood* (2022). He contributes regularly to the *New York Times Magazine*, and his work has also appeared in the *New Yorker*, *Harper's*, and *The Best American Essays*. He has received a Guggenheim fellowship and the Whiting Writers Award, and he is a professor of English, American studies, and journalism at Boston College.

TERRY ANNE SCOTT is an award-winning historian, author, and speaker. She is a former professor of American history and the current director of the Institute for Common Power. Scott is the author of several books, including the Ottis Lock Endowment Best Book Award-winning *Lynching and Leisure: Race and the Transformation of Mob Violence in Texas* (2022) and the forthcoming *From Bed-Stuy to the Hall of Fame: The Unexpected Life of Lenny Wilkens*. She is also the editor of *Seattle Sports: Play, Identity, and Pursuit in the Emerald City* (2020). Scott appears in several critically acclaimed documentaries and serves as an associate editor of the *Journal of Sports History*.

JONATHAN SILVERMAN is a professor of English at UMass Lowell and the editor of *Astros and Asterisks: The*

Houston Sign-Stealing Scandal Explained (2023). He is the coauthor with Michael Hinds of *Johnny Cash International: How and Why the World Loves the Man in Black* (2020), winner of the Peggy O'Brien Book Award; author of *Nine Choices: Johnny Cash and American Culture* (2010); the coauthor with Dean Rader of *The World Is a Text: Writing, Reading, and Thinking about Culture and Its Contexts* (2003); and the co-editor with Meghan Sweeney of *Remaking the American College Campus* (2016). He has served as a Fulbright scholar in Norway.

MAUREEN M. SMITH is a professor in the Department of Kinesiology at Sacramento State University, where she is also the faculty athletic representative. She is the author of *Wilma Rudolph: A Biography* (2006), and coauthor of *(Re)Presenting Wilma Rudolph* (2015), winner of NASSH Book Award. She is the co-editor of *San Francisco Bay Area Sports: Golden Gate Athletics, Recreation, and Community* (2017), winner of NASSH Anthology Award, and author of *More than Cricket and Football: International Sport and the Challenge of Celebrity* (2016). She is the editor of the *Journal of Sport History*.

TIMOTHY B. SPEARS is a college professor emeritus at Middlebury College. He is the author of *100 Years on the Road: The Traveling Salesman in American Culture* (1995), *Chicago Dreaming: Midwesterners and the City, 1871 to 1919* (2005), and *Spirals: A Family's Education in Football* (2018). He is working on a photographic study of the American national cemetery system.

TRAVIS VOGAN is a professor in the School of Journalism and Mass Communication and the Department of American Studies at the University of Iowa. He is the author of *The Boxing Film: A Cultural and Transmedia History* (2020), *ABC Sports: The Rise and Fall of Network Sports Television* (2018), *ESPN: The Making of a Sports Media Empire* (2015), and *Keepers of the Flame: NFL Films and the Rise of Sports Media* (2014).

SUSAN WARE is the author and editor of numerous books on twentieth-century U.S. history, women's history, and biography, including *Game, Set, Match: Billie Jean King and the Revolution in Women's Sports* (2011), *Title IX: A Brief History with Documents* (2007), and *Why They Marched: Untold Stories of the Women Who Fought for the Right to Vote* (2019). From 2012 to 2022 she was the general editor of the biographical reference work *American National Biography*, and from 2016 to 2022 she served as the Honorary Women's Suffrage Centennial Historian at the Schlesinger Library of the Harvard Radcliffe Institute.

EDMUND F. WEHRLE is a professor of history at Eastern Illinois University, where he has taught since 2000. He is author of *"Between a River and a Mountain": The AFL-CIO and the Vietnam War* (2005), and coauthor of *America in the World: Ideas, Trade and Warfare* (2011). His most recent book is *Breaking Babe Ruth: Baseball's Two Decade Campaign against Its Greatest Star* (2018). He is preparing a manuscript profiling rebellious sports figures of the 1960s and 1970s, tentatively titled *Jock Liberation.*

SAMANTHA WHITE is an assistant professor of sport studies at Manhattanville College. Her research examines historical and contemporary representations of Black girls in sports. Her research also explores Black outdoor recreation. Her work can be found in *Girlhood Studies: An Interdisciplinary Journal*, the *Journal for Sport History*, and *Aethlon: Journal of Sport Literature*.

PHOTO CREDITS

8 Salvator v. Tenny, June 25, 1890, at Sheepshead Bay Race Track, Sheepshead Bay, New York, by John C. Hemment, photo courtesy of Keeneland Library Hemment Collection.

18 Ty Cobb of the Detroit Tigers sliding into third base in 1909, Hilltop Park, New York, photo by Charles M. Conlon.

28 Jack Dempsey knocks down heavyweight champion Gene Tunney, Soldier Field in Chicago, September 22, 1927, photo from *New York Daily News* Archive/*New York Daily News* Collection via Getty Images.

36 A portrait of Babe Ruth by Nickolas Muray, taken in 1927, courtesy of the George Eastman Museum.

46 German fencer Helene Mayer on the medal podium at the 1936 Olympics in Berlin, photo from Bettmann Collection via Getty Images.

54 Althea Gibson and Alice Marble, West Side Tennis Club in Forest Hills, New York, August 28, 1950, photo by Curt Gunther/Bettmann Collection via Getty Images.

64 Willie Mays's catch of Vic Wertz's deep fly ball in the 1954 World Series, New York Giants versus Cleveland Indians, Polo Grounds, New York, photo by Frank Hurley/*New York Daily News* Archive Collection via Getty Images.

74 Jackie Robinson of the Brooklyn Dodgers steals home in Game One of the 1955 World Series versus the New York Yankees, September 28, 1955, photo by Mark Kauffman/*Sports Illustrated* via Getty Images.

84 Alan Ameche of the Baltimore Colts scoring the game-winning touchdown in "sudden death" overtime against the New York Giants, Yankee Stadium, December 28, 1958, photo by Neil Leifer/*Sports Illustrated* via Getty Images.

94 Heavyweight champion Muhammad Ali standing over Sonny Liston in their rematch, Lewiston, Maine, May 25, 1965, photo by Neil Leifer/*Sports Illustrated* via Getty Images.

104 Kathrine Switzer in the Boston Marathon, April 19, 1967, photo by Harry Trask/*Boston Traveler* via *Boston Herald*, courtesy of 261 Fearless.

114 American sprinters Tommie Smith and John Carlos at the 1968 Olympics giving the Black Power Salute in Mexico City, October 16, 1968, photo by John Dominis/Bettmann Collection via Getty Images.

126 New York Jets quarterback Joe Namath sunning by the pool days before Super Bowl III vs. the Baltimore Colts, Fort Lauderdale, Florida, January 9, 1969, photo by Walter Iooss Jr./*Sports Illustrated* via Getty Images.

136 Secretariat wins the Belmont Stakes, June 9, 1973, Belmont Park, Elmont, New York; photo by Bob Coglianese.

148 Paul Henderson of Canada scoring the tie-breaking and series-clinching goal versus the Soviet national team, September 28, 1972, Moscow, photo by Frank Lennon/*Toronto Star* via Getty Images.

162 The U.S. men's Olympic team celebrating "The Miracle on Ice" against the Soviet national team, February 22, 1980, Lake Placid, New York, photo by Heinz Kluetmeier/*Sports Illustrated* via Getty Images.

174 Bjorn Borg winning the Wimbledon Championships Men's Singles final against John McEnroe, July 5, 1990, Wimbledon, England, photo by Bob Thomas Sports Photography via Getty Images.

184 Fernando Valenzuela of the Los Angeles Dodgers pitching at Dodger Stadium, 1980, Los Angeles, California, photo by Jayne Kamin-Oncea via Getty Images.

194 Michael Jordan of the Chicago Bulls at the 1988 Slam Dunk contest, Chicago, Illinois, photo by Walter Iooss Jr./*Sports Illustrated* via Getty Images.

206 Aboriginal Australian runner Cathy Freeman at the 1994 Commonwealth Games in Victoria, Canada, photo by John Feder/Newspix.

218 American soccer player Brandi Chastain after scoring the game-winning penalty kick against China to win the 1999 World Cup in the Rose Bowl, Pasadena, California, photo by Roberto Schmidt/AFP via Getty Images.

230 Little League pitcher Mo'ne Davis, August 2014, Williamsport, Pennsylvania, photo by Al Tielemans/*Sports Illustrated* via Getty Images.

242 The Native Indian Football Association women's national team after winning the first World Indigenous Games in 2015, photo courtesy of Dano Thorne.

256 Quarterback Colin Kaepernick of the San Francisco 49ers kneeling before playing the Dallas Cowboys on October 2, 2016, at Levi's Stadium in Santa Clara, California, photo by Marcio Jose Sanchez/AP Photos.

266 Lewiston High School soccer players celebrate, October 30, 2019, Lewiston, Maine, photo by and courtesy of Russ Dillingham/*Sun Journal* (Lewiston, Maine).

INDEX

NOTE: Italicized page numbers indicate material in photographs or illustrations.